DECLINE AND RENEWAL

DECLINE AND RENEWAL:

EUROPE ANCIENT AND MODERN

R.C. Mowat

New Cherwell Press · Oxford

First published in Great Britain 1991
by New Cherwell Press
7 Mount Street, Oxford OX2 6DH
Copyright © 1991 R.C.Mowat

British Library Cataloguing in Publication Data
Mowat, R.C.
Decline and renewal : Europe ancient and modern
1. Europe - History - 450 BC to 1990 AD
I. Title
940

ISBN 0-9517695-0-2 (hbk)
ISBN 0-9517695-1-0 (pbk)

Cover design by Jacques Welter

Printed in Malta by Interprint

FOREWORD

My thanks go to my wife and a number of friends and relatives who have had a part in making this book. Particularly I am indebted to the late John Griffith of Jesus College, Oxford, former Public Orator of the University, who twice read the ancient history chapters and whose comments were invaluable, to Dr. Oswyn Murray of Balliol College, Oxford, for his note on the hetairai, to Dr. David Burr for help with the quotation from Joachim da Fiore, and to Paul Newman for the quotation from his paper "The Context and Practice of Soviet Banking Reform", published by St. Antony's College, Oxford (1990); also to Michael Hutchinson and to my brother John, who gave valuable advice on pruning. Others who read part or all of the typescript at various stages, giving information and encouragement, and making helpful suggestions, were Lord Blanch, David and Sheila Price, William Conner, Harry Addison, Garth Lean, Desmond Sullivan, Allan Griffith, Dr. Charis Waddy, Mary Melville, Geoffrey Gain, Kenneth Rundell, Rex Dilly, Henry Macnicol, Peter Hannon, Ian Sciortino, Professor Günter Schmidt, Dr. Rosemary Hollis and Dr. Paul Joyce. I am indebted to André Chouraqui for reading the typescript and permitting extensive quotations from his writings. Also to Julie Windsor for word-processing the book, and to my son David for setting additional material and for the arduous work of processing corrections and emendations, and generally preparing the book for publication. I have also valued the advice of Terence Goldsmith and John Faber concerning the production.

I apologise to others whose names have been inadvertently omitted, and for cases of non-acceptance of advice. I take full responsibility for all blemishes. Any opinions, ideas or interpretations of events are purely personal, and are not presented as those of any party, association or organisation.

R.C.M.

ACKNOWLEDGEMENTS

Grateful acknowledgement is made to the following publishers to quote from copyright material: Faber and Faber Ltd., *Selected Letters of St. Francis de Sales*, edited by E. Stopp; Hamish Hamilton Ltd., *The Sixth Continent* by Mark Frankland; HarperCollins Publishers Ltd., *Jean Monnet: Memoirs*, and *Dietrich Bonhoeffer* by Eberhard Bethge; Hodder and Stoughton Ltd., *The KGB* by John Barron; Michael Joseph Ltd., *The Waking Giant* by Martin Walker; Methuen and Co. Ltd., *The Reconstruction of Western Europe 1945-51* by A. Milward; Oxford University Press, *The Letters of Pliny*, translated by A.N. Sherwin-White (1966), and *The Ancient Concept of Progress* by E.R. Dodds (1973); Penguin Books, *Pagans and Christians* by Robin Lane Fox (London 1986), and *The Sixteen Satires* by Juvenal, translated by Peter Green (Harmondsworth 1974); Random Century Group, *Children of the Arbat* by Anatoli Rybakov, translated by H. Shukman (Hutchinson), *Mr. Norris Changes Trains* by C. Isherwood (Hogarth Press), *Germans against Hitler* by T. Prittie (Hutchinson), and *Cancer Ward* by Alexander Solzhenitsyn (The Bodley Head); Sheed and Ward Ltd., *The Confessions of St. Augustine*, and *Religion and the Rise of Western Culture* by Christopher Dawson; Grosvenor Books, *Japan's Decisive Decade* by Basil Entwistle; Weidenfeld and Nicolson Ltd., *A History of the Modern World* by Paul Johnson, and *The Family, Sex and Marriage in England 1500-1800* by Lawrence Stone; SCM Press Ltd., *The Cost of Discipleship* by Dietrich Bonhoeffer; Harvard University Press and the Loeb Classical Library, *Letters and Panegyricus* by Pliny (trans. 1969), and other works.

PLAN OF THE BOOK

The Introduction and first two chapters discuss the meaning of "decline" or "decadence", and whether our Western Civilisation can properly be regarded as in decline since the advances in science, technology and medicine are continuing; secondly, whether comparisons are valid with an earlier civilisation since technology has made ours different in so many ways, and has also spread world-wide. It follows that, whereas the outcome of the Greco-Roman period of decline was the coming of two new civilisations, Byzantium and the West, the change taking place in civilisation today may be more like the turning of a page of history such as happened some seven thousand years ago, when primitive tribalism began to give place to settled agriculture and civilisation "as we know it".

Indeed an epochal change of this kind is needed since the hazards to the survival of humanity in our present condition are so menacing. Again, as in ancient times, the apocalypse looms and millenarian movements arise. (See also Chapter 7 (2).)

Since family life and the relations of the sexes, particularly in marriage, are basic in society, a study follows of the new ideal of married partnership as it evolved during a period when the older norms and standards of manners and morals became less regarded. A contrasting development, in Roman times, is comparable with "the sexual revolution" of the 1960's. (Ch. 3)

In Antiquity a profound change took place in society due to the spiritual upsurge, as shown in religion and philosophy, by way of Stoicism and religions from the Orient. Christianity excelled its rivals in bringing salvation and new moral guide-lines, with resultant changes in personal living and all aspects of culture. (Ch. 4) At the same time remarkable personalities appeared who exemplified these trends, on both the political and spiritual levels. The influence of Christianity was all-important even when escapism played a part in withdrawal from the world by way of monasticism. (Ch. 5 (1), (2)) Its strong moral challenge, together with the courage of the martyrs and its charitable work, brought it so far to the fore by the 4th century that Constantine made it the official religion of the Roman Empire. (Ch. 4 (3); ch. 5 (3)) During the following period other remarkable personalities, inspired by their Christian faith, pioneered the new civilisations. (Ch. 6)

After a brief period around 1000 AD when the new civilisations were in a state of equilibrium, political, social and religious

developments brought in the modern "Hellenistic Age". (Ch. 7 (1))
The spiritual upsurge was particularly marked in the West in the
Pietist type of Christian faith, with Protestant, Catholic, and eventually
Anglo-American evangelism forming "streams", (Ch. 7 (3)) whose
convergence (Ch. 10) contributed to the launching of the European
Community, with the kind of political and economic structures needed
in the future civilisation. (Ch. 13) But as in the ancient world, the
spiritual upsurge which brought about this development was diverted
into rival faiths or ideologies, such as nationalism, Marxism or Nazism,
providing the mystique for states which oppressed or martyred their
dissidents. (Chs. 8, 11, 12)

In Eastern Europe the civilisation of Russia - successor of
Byzantium - was set back by the Mongol occupation, with a time-lag
of three centuries compared with the West. Catching up with the
West was achieved, on certain levels, in the 18th and 19th centuries,
but the militarism and dictatorial methods of Peter the Great and some
of his successors sapped enterprise and spontaneity. These qualities
were already weak in Russia due to the subservience of the Church to
the State, which became more marked under the Tsars. (Ch. 9 (1), (2))
Eventually Lenin and his successors attempted to replace the
ecclesiastical monopoly of Orthodoxy with that of Marxism, canalising
but also repressing the spiritual upsurge already apparent in the 19th
and early 20th centuries. (Ch. 9 (3)) This attempt had the contrary
effect of stimulating the moral and spiritual factor among dissidents,
which (exemplified in remarkable personalities) may set new cultural
trends in motion to renew the civilisation whose decline seems more
catastrophic than in the West. (Ch. 12 (2))

If there is to be a renewal of civilisation, whether in East or West
(or together), and if parallels with Antiquity are valid, it can only
come through renewal at the moral and spiritual base of society, as
expressed particularly in married partnership and the family. (Ch. 14
(1)) "The nibbling and hacking away of absolute standards" and other
factors of decline have to be reversed. Signs of this are evident in
Russia as in the West. The way to new life has been demonstrated
down the ages by those who have turned God-ward and sought His
direction, leading not merely to personal change but strategies which
have brought new life to communities and nations. Beyond such
strategies there is one transcending the human scale, in which
members of the the world's great faiths increasingly are participating.
But in the war of good against evil, evil does not give up easily: the
crisis now coming over the world demands decision and dedication by
a creative minority, to lead the nations away from the abyss towards
a new kind of civilisation. (Ch. 15)

At the end of each section the reader's attention is drawn to any comment (apart from brief biographical details) appearing in "Notes and Commentary", which follows the text. Bibliographies for each section are at the end of the book: quotations are indicated by page numbers at the end of individual references, in the same sequence as in the text.

CONTENTS

1. **Definitions and comparisons:** *a "falling away" from a "great age": (a) Periclean Athens, republican Rome, (b) 19th century Western Europe; Russia: decadence or under-development? Value judgements and historical theories: Thomas Arnold, Vico. Arnold's pessimism.*

2. **The 19th century: progress or decadence?** *preventing decadence: Christianity (A.P. Stanley), inventions (Lecky). Theories of progress: Hegel, Marx. The 1860's: progress in industry, medicine, public health, armaments. Evolutionary theories: Darwin, Marx/Engels. Cultural exuberance. Matthew Arnold:* Culture and Anarchy: *Hellenism and Hebraism. Faith in education: T.H. Green.*

3. **Fin-de-siècle anxiety:** *a "dark age" coming (Bosanquet); civilisation like a doomed liner (Kierkegaard); Christianity and democracy as causes of corruption (Nietzsche); drifting through wars towards "a sort of Roman Empire" (Burckhardt); degeneracy, hysteria, eroticism, drugs, pornography (Nordau).*

1. **The Classical world and the modern West:** *warring states, colonies, resistance to superpowers (Persia, Turkey); Pax Romana cf. Pax Americana; decline of Roman Empire cf. decline of American imperium. De-moralisation and insecurity.*

2. **Political and spiritual salvation in the ancient world:** *saviours ancient and modern. Rise of science; decline of faith in the Olympians; decline of city-state and rise of empires led to new philosophy, and*

3. **The Gorbachev Revolution**: *Andropov and Gorbachev recognise need for moral revolution; stagnant economy, corruption - comparisons with time of Alexander II; social and political problems; religious and class motivations; falling standards;* glasnost *and proliferation of ideas and discussion groups; prospects for constitutional change; need for economic breakthrough, but difficulties in changing the system; need for change in mental climate and end of one-party state; agriculture; unrest of nationalities and ethnic minorities; Gorbachev's vision of world change; his call for truth, but difficult to accept truth in Soviet history; a precondition for* perestroika.

1. **Resolving conflicts: reintegration with nature**: *ancient and modern superpowers; wars and ideological conflict; rich/poor classes and nations; Robert Carmichael: closing the gap between the developed and developing countries.   Social dynamic: co-operation and conflict. Growing points of the new society, ancient and modern: Japan and the Japanese factory.   Global civilisation: the world as "our neighbour". Man takes over from nature; reintegrating; the triumph of science.*

2. **The democratic alternative to Marxism-Leninism**:   *Soviet options; 1989 and 1848.   Leninist atheism and the suppression of spontaneity.   The alternative - democracy based on moral and spiritual values; the approach to conflict-resolution. Gorbachev's move in freeing religion. The restoration of moral absolutes. Starting with oneself: "an inner change of character".*

3. **The strategy of world change**: *the Christian leaven in Antiquity and today; the challenge of the prophets; transforming humanity. The world's creative minority: strategy; the role of silence; humanity's zero hour; moral guidelines. The spiritual upsurge in Russia and Central Europe. The lessons of history.*

INTRODUCTION

"We can assert with some confidence that ours is a period of decline", wrote T.S. Eliot in 1948, "that the standards of culture are lower than they were fifty years ago; and that the evidences of this decline are visible in every department of human activity." In saying this Eliot is taking us back to the nineties of the last century, when voices were being raised - not for the first time - that decadence in Europe had begun. He maintains that "we can distinguish between the higher and lower cultures; we can distinguish between advance and retrogression."

Inherent in any judgement about "advance or retrogression" are the values which we cherish. Our evaluation - the very word implies values - is subjective. We cannot pretend to objectivity; we believe that some things are good, others bad. Moral philosophers discuss these terms, and this can be enlightening, especially when absolute standards are under review. Paul Johnson in his *History of the Modern World* pinpoints the acceptance of Relativity not only as a way of understanding the cosmos, but as an excuse for abandoning absolute standards in morals and manners, and hence as the major cause of decline during this century. "At the beginning of the 1920's" he writes, "the belief began to circulate for the first time at a popular level "that there were no longer any absolutes ... The public response to relativity formed a knife ... to help cut society adrift from its traditional moorings in the faith and morals of Judaeo-Christian culture."

Similarly J.M. Roberts in *The Triumph of the West* speaks of the time when "artists, philosophers and scientists were nibbling and hacking away at the absolute standards of the old confident West".

If a period is characterised by a falling away from standards and achievements in *all* areas of life there would be no difficulty in describing it as decadent. But if the falling away takes place only in some areas, while there are new, creative developments in others, we cannot be entitled to blanket the whole epoch as decadent. In this case judgement tends to be arbitrary. We may be looking at the glass half empty, whereas others will see it as half full.

In any case, whatever the area of life under review, decadence is meaningful in terms which we try to define, of falling away from previously accepted norms and standards. From another angle it denotes one aspect of transition - because new developments are always taking place, which may blossom into another "great age" of the particular society, or into one or more new civilisations.

Decline and renewal, in fact, are constant characteristics of human society. But the decadence in which we are finding ourselves now may herald something more than the birth of a new civilisation, assuming we do not blow ourselves up or totally degrade our habitat before that could happen. It may be more like turning a page of history such as occurred when the first civilisations appeared.

As the second millennium of our era draws to a close mankind faces a crisis of the gravest import. The word "crisis" means "decision", and what has to be decided is whether we destroy ourselves (either by nuclear annihilation or environmental degradation) or begin living together in sufficient concord for war to be eliminated and for the creation to be cherished.

Much can be learnt from surveying previous periods of transition, of decadence and renaissance. But the new factors of industrial and technological development, making possible as never before an age of either abundance or destruction, together with the "one world" of speedy travel and instant communication, suggest a change more profound than the rebirth of an old, or the birth of a new civilisation. Because if such a new civilisation were to appear after the travail of the present epoch, it would have to be in many ways unlike all those that have gone before. More than a renaissance, it would be a revolution in human living, comparable to that which came about some 7,000 years ago, when homo sapiens began to plant seeds and settle down, abandoning his hitherto largely nomadic life of hunting, food-gathering and fishing.

Once people began to make permanent settlements, some of these grew into cities, and a new type of society came into being - civilisation, at first in a few scattered patches - the Nile and Indus valleys, the Fertile Crescent, the Yellow River - while the mass of mankind (though not numerous by present standards) remained at the stage which we patronisingly call savagery. After several millennia the situation has been reversed: civilisation has become the norm, with Stone Age people appearing as survivors from a forgotten past.

But while civilisation is now global in extent, involving close and sensitive relationships among a large variety of races and ethnic groups world-wide, human nature has not obviously changed. There are still the aggressive, self-regarding instincts inherited from our remote ancestors, as well as the gregarious, caring and co-operative impulses. To expect human nature to change in the face of the threat to human existence may be visionary, but without change in the motivations and character of the leading groups in every country and at all levels of society, the future is gloomy indeed.

Compared with the many millennia since recognisable humans evolved from their hominid forebears, the mere six or seven during which there has been civilisation is only a brief time-span within which to make any but superficial adjustments in life-style. The original conditions of proto-civilisation, self-sufficient and limited in extent, may well have demanded little change from the attitudes of tribalism, though further adjustments were needed as civilisations met and trade grew over wider areas. Before long empires were forming, to be overthrown in some cases by hordes of migrating nomads, and rebuilt under new regimes.

Civilisations, empires, migrations - the rise of cultures and nations, and their decline - dark ages and renewals: this chapter of history is also one of spiritual crisis. Men were searching for the meaning of existence, exploring the spiritual realm, and analysing human relationships, while teaching and legislating for their improvement. For several hundred years, from China to Greece, from Iran to Arabia, prophets, sages, and the founders of the world's great faiths appeared. A new era in human consciousness dawned, the first sign, it may be hoped, of that deeper change in human nature - or at least in the characters of a sizeable element of the human race - to initiate an age of abundance for all as the alternative to decadence and destruction. A tiny minority pioneered the first civilisations - a drastic change in life-style, habits and ideas. Another minority today are demonstrating the same pioneering potential. The world *can* be saved from disaster, but the cost will be a revolutionary change in mankind's way of living at least equivalent to that which saw the birth of the earliest civilisations.

Though our present age is unique in many respects, it is not so unique that we cannot learn from the Neolithic Revolution which initiated agriculture and eventually civilisation, from the "axial" period of empire building and spiritual crisis, and from the turning-point in the Greco-Roman "world" when the Hellenistic civilisation declined and two new ones appeared in its place: Byzantium, with Russia as its successor, and Latin Christendom, parent of our modern "West".

Our present decline points to a similar development, despite the differences between our industrial, technological civilisation and that of Greece and Rome. And as in the last period of Antiquity when new life was springing up amidst the decay, so today the new is coming to birth amidst the old. Large populations in Asia and Africa are now practically derelict. The hunger and squalor of those camping in the slums and shanty-towns is more than equalled by the miseries of the unnumbered refugees from tyranny and misrule. The colossal injustice of all this wretchedness in contrast to the easy living of the West and the prosperous classes elsewhere cries aloud to heaven. This and the threat of total disaster for all of us presses upon the collective conscience of humanity - alongside the hope, and even the promise, of a new kind of world society, where people and nations genuinely care for one another, and resources and work are equitably shared. The sense of injustice, the threat of disaster, and the hope of a new and better world in a situation where the old certainties and guide-lines have crumbled, combine to produce the spiritual crisis of the modern world and the upheavals which are its expression.

Recent events - notably in connection with the Gulf War - may make revision of some judgements necessary. We have been seeing the emergence of one superpower instead of two; the USA has shown itself again in its full hegemonial role. It has not, or not yet, created something like the Roman Empire in decline, as forecast by the Swiss historian Burckhardt, but utilising successfully the American-created United Nations and its Security Council, it has shown under George Bush its potential to build an "order" (though not necessarily a world-order). The Pax Americana, which appeared to be coming into existence over large parts of the planet in the immediate postwar years, may - with the waning of the cold war - again become a reality in areas such as South-East Asia where (as in Vietnam) it failed.

The clash of cultures and related political forms is as striking now as the ancient clash of Hellenism, in its post-Alexander or Roman phase, with those represented by Persia and the Syriac culture. The enormous energy - spiritual, moral, political and military - liberated by Mohammed among the Arabs led to Islam taking over the Persian-Syriac-Egyptian region. Spreading far beyond these bounds, it became culturally and politically a world-leader for several centuries.

Then came the long Turkish occupation, with a similar arresting effect on the Arabs to that of the Mongols on the nascent civilisation of Russia. There was also the destructive effect of Christian bigotry and aggression on Islam's brilliant culture in Spain.

Various parts of the world have been going through the trauma resulting from Marxism-Leninism, even in its decline. Its grip on Russia was in part due to Russia's urge to catch up with the West. A similar urge, with resulting rivalry and psychological malaise, is producing another chapter of upheavals and traumata, as Islam struggles with the West's will to dominate and against its cultural penetration. The problems are aggravated by the West's ignorance - its apparent incapacity to understand or appreciate much that lies outside its familiar purview - ignorance and a sense of superiority. This has been vividly illustrated by incomprehension of Muslim outrage over The Satanic Verses, and the build-up of Saddam Hussein, for which the West must bear full responsibility, as also for the war which has followed, with its ghastly human and physical destruction.

My approach to this subject came as a result of going through some family papers. Among them I found a printed lecture by Bernard Bosanquet entitled Some Thoughts on the Transition from Paganism to Christianity. Bosanquet was one of a group of undergraduates at Balliol College, Oxford, in the 1870's; another being my grandfather C.S. Loch - they became life-long friends.

These undergraduates, who were to achieve distinction in various fields, owed much to Thomas Hill Green as a fellow of the College; he later became Professor of Moral Philosophy at the University. Bosanquet also became a philosopher, eventually to be acclaimed as "the most representative English philosopher of his generation".

In his lecture Bosanquet presented the Greco-Roman world in decay, yet producing new philosophies and religions, and new forms of art, architecture and literature. Eventually these ideas and cultural forms blosssomed in the civilisations of Byzantium and the Medieval West. Now, he opined (writing at the turn of the century), we are at a stage when similar processes are at work. He developed this theme in another lecture printed in 1901, *Reflections on the Idea of Decadence*.

Attempts by Hegel, Marx, Spengler and others to deal with such questions have led to the formulation of laws like those in physics or biology. These formulations, though attractive (especially to politicians) are controversial, and generally suspect to professional historians. Nevertheless the studies of philosophers of history and universal historians like Arnold Toynbee have contributed to our thinking by their global scope, with their comparisons of data from a vast number of disparate sources. My approach is more limited, dealing with civilisations which are European (though the term has to be stretched beyond purely geographic Europe). Within this relatively restricted field, and without any attempt to formulate laws, a study of situations in the past, which suggest analogies with some of those today, may be both enlightening and challenging.

Comment: Fritjof Capra on the change in civilisation. (p.263)

CHAPTER ONE

ANCIENT AND MODERN DECADENCE

1. Definitions and comparisons: *a "falling away" from a "great age": (a) Periclean Athens, republican Rome, (b) 19th century Western Europe; Russia: decadence or under-development? Value judgements and historical theories: Thomas Arnold, Vico. Arnold's pessimism.*

As Bosanquet puts it, decadence is relative to a prime. It follows a period of "a very great achievement, whether in art, science, or government, of such a kind as causes and implies a high tension of life on the part of a whole community, or some large section of it. Owing to one or more various causes, whether external or internal, this great achievement is no longer sustained." Its tradition may remain, along with some of its elements, whether in thought, art, or manners and morals, but "this tradition and these fragments, though held in reverence, cease to be understood as the thing itself was understood when it existed in all its grandeur."

A survey of our period of decline may help us to identify its characteristics. When did it begin? There were different views about this as far back as the middle of the last century. If we pursue this line of inquiry we come up against similar difficulties as in the case of Greece and Rome - the decline of the two culture areas did not take place simultaneously. The Greek decline is usually said to begin with, or just after, the Periclean Age of Athens; the Roman decline at the end of the Carthaginian wars. In our case we have also two different (but related) culture areas, which correspond roughly with the ancient Greek-speaking and the Latin-speaking West. We may perhaps agree with Nietzsche, Burckhardt and others that our Western decline was beginning by the middle of last century - but at that point Russia was a developing country undertaking important reforms, and enjoying a brilliant era in literature and art.

What has happened since the mid-19th century? One answer is that our Western decline has continued - pretty steadily, while the Eastern progress was thwarted and diverted into an impasse by the Bolshevik Revolution. After 70 years it is questionable whether Russia's creative springs can be restored to the point where it can begin progressing again, for all the efforts a would-be reformer like Gorbachev may make - or whether it too has been caught up in a syndrome of decadence like the West.

Until the Bolshevik Revolution there was a growing closeness and assimilation of the two culture areas, expressed particularly in literature and art. If Russia is now beginning to return to its pre-1917 line of development, it may be that it will enter a new creative phase which will also be one of approximation to and assimilation with the West - but this could also mean an intensifying of those elements of decadence (drugs, drink, divorce, etc.) which are also evident in the West.

With this approach we can view the situation of our twin culture areas as a unity, and try to distinguish the common factors which may promise development into a new type of civilisation including both East and West - and because both culture areas extend far beyond the geographical boundaries of Europe this possible evolution will have to be viewed also in a global context.

There are difficulties in deciding whether or to what extent a civilisation is decadent, because even at a period which may be regarded as a peak various flaws can be perceived. The great age of Greece is taken to be the 5th century BC, when the Persians were defeated and Athens vied with Sparta for supremacy. At the time the city-state flourished, the citizens governing themselves according to democratic forms (the word itself was theirs), producing sculpture, architecture, painted vases, plays and other literary works of a perfection never surpassed, as well as philosophical and scientific treatises of genius. But looked at from another point of view, these states oppressed their empires, which they built up with frequent wars, not without treachery towards allies and opponents and treason within their own ranks. The brilliant culture, the democratic freedom, were the privilege of a few, in states where slaves may have outnumbered citizens, and where (at least in Athens) women were equated with slaves. The lowly status of women - their exclusion from public life and from the enjoyments of their menfolk in theatre and sport (let alone participating in acting or athletics) were part of a restricted relationship of men with women, complemented - for the men - by paederasty, a close relationship of men with youths.

Much the same could be said of Rome during the great age of the Republic and its victory over Carthage, though its decline is alternatively dated as beginning after the Antonine period some three centuries later. The abundance of slaves, the luxury and materialism of the upper classes, the in-fighting of the generals, produced a situation which Romans themselves regarded as decadent. But was this for the most part merely an upper-class phenomenon, limited to Rome and some other cities? And in the midst of this decadence were there not significant developments in governing vast areas containing many people of different races and traditions, and in making possible a better life for women, slaves and the underprivileged in general?

By using the phrase "a better life" it is evident that values are involved, and this brings a subjective element into any discussion of decadence. It was the business of philosophers like Green and Bosanquet to discuss what was meant by goodness or happiness. Without defining these terms, Thomas Arnold, a historian of the previous generation, could simply assert that in the midst of Rome's decadence Christianity was "a power of good" bringing virtue and happiness to those who otherwise were "in a condition of hopeless suffering". He contested Gibbon's thesis that Christianity was a major contributor to Rome's decline and fall, which was much more due, he thought, to the lack of participation by the people in managing the affairs of the nation, as well as a failure to develop industry and commerce - "the people had in themselves no principle of activity, but were taught on every occasion to look for aid or permission to the government". But while observing the happiness that Christianity brought to individual lives, Arnold did not attribute to it the power to remould society and regenerate civilisation.

He was influenced by the Italian Giovanni Battista Vico (1668-1744), the forerunner of Hegel, Marx, Spengler and others whose approach involved schematic periodisations of history. Vico naturally drew his examples from the Classical world, where the earliest communities recognisable as states passed (in his view) through aristocratic or monarchic government, until the plebs made their challenge and gained some of the power (this phase, in the case of the Romans, bringing them to their zenith as "the master people in the world") - but then corruption sets in marked by civil wars, tyranny and anarchy. Providence may supply a remedy "if one like Augustus" springs up - otherwise the state is reduced to the province of a nation better than itself, or sinks into "the ultimate civil malady", its people living "hideous lives in the deepest solitude of spirit and will", until there is eventually a reaction to "original simplicity". Providence then restores "piety, faith and trust", and state-building begins again.

Although accepting this pattern, Arnold was ambiguous in his thinking. He believed in "the tendency of society to become more and more liberal". Materialism and warfare might arrest this. Seeing parallels in Greek and Roman history, he specified "the critical period" for any people to be the time "when wealth begins to possess the ascendancy formerly enjoyed by the nobility; and the contending parties in the state assume the forms of rich and poor". But, he wrote, "the great enemy of society in its present state is war", producing disorder which "terminates in despotism ... if this calamity be avoided the progress of improvement is sure".

But with Arnold pessimism predominates. He doubted that

European civilisation would escape the evils that materialism and war would engender. In the Ancient World regeneration had come through the Germanic invaders who transformed the "elements comprising the legacy of Antiquity" into "something new". The Europe of his own day, he believed, had reached the stage of Antonine Rome, and he did not see any nation or any "continent peopled by youthful races" who could be "the destined restorers of our worn-out generations."

"Modern history appears to be not only *a* step in advance of ancient history, but *the* last step; it appears to bear marks of the fullness of time, as if there would be no future history beyond it ... If ... we are living in the latest period of the world's history, that no other races remain behind to perform what we have neglected or to restore what we have ruined, then indeed the interest of modern history does become intense, and the importance of not wasting the time still left to us may be incalculable".

The only possible exception among the world's races, he noted, which might have a regenerative role, was the "Sclavonic" - "and when we consider that the Sclavonic race wields the mighty empire of Russia, we may believe that its future influence on the condition of Europe and the world may be far greater than that it exercises now."

Besides being a leading historian of his day, Arnold was well-known as the reforming headmaster of Rugby, whose influence continued after his time on Rugbeians like Green and his own son Matthew.

Comment: The Victorian comparisons between people and situations of Ancient Greece and those of the 19th century. Meaning of "decadence". (p. 263)

2. **The 19th century: progress or decadence?** *Preventing decadence: Christianity (A.P. Stanley), inventions (Lecky). Theories of progress: Hegel, Marx. The 1860's: progress in industry, medicine, public health, armaments. Evolutionary theories: Darwin, Marx/Engels. Cultural exuberance. Matthew Arnold:* Culture and Anarchy: *Hellenism and Hebraism. Faith in education: T.H. Green.*

A Rugbeian who came directly under the influence of Arnold before he resigned his headmastership to become Professor of Modern History at Oxford in 1840 was A.P. Stanley, the "Arthur" of *Tom Brown's Schooldays*, and later a celebrity as Dean of Westminster. Stanley accepted Arnold's view that, on the analogy of "the heathen world", the "later stages of European civilisation ... would have been ages of cheerless decline", but he challenged his assumption that decay was almost inevitable, on the grounds that Christianity possessed "the peculiar privilege of restoring the lost and raising the dead", not only in the case of individuals but also of nations.

"Instead of the sickly literature of the last ages of Greece and Rome, we have a school of poetry, concerned indeed with the same subjects, but imparting a deeper and more vigorous tone to the national mind than any of its predecessors; instead of a tame submission to the downward stream, we have a universal attempt throughout Europe, to counteract it by national education; instead of being driven by the scepticism of the 18th century into utter unbelief and sensuality, we seem to be gradually attaining a further footing than ever on truth and reality. Above all, we live in an age of hope, certainly not in an age of general despondency."

These conclusions were echoed a generation later by W.E.H. Lecky in his *History of European Morals from Augustus to Charlemagne* (1869).

"The causes which most disturbed or accelerated the normal progress of society in antiquity were the appearance of great men, in modern times they have been the appearance of great inventions. Printing has secured the intellectual achievements of the past, and furnished a sure guarantee of future progress. Gunpowder and military machinery have rendered the triumph of barbarians impossible. Steam has united nations in closest bonds ... There can be no question that the intellectual tendencies of modern times are far superior to those of antiquity, both in respect to the material prosperity they effect, and to the uninterrupted progress they secure."

Even war was a necessary element in progress: "war is, no doubt, a fearful evil, but it is the seed-plot of magnanimous virtues, which in a pacific age must wither and decay."

There was much in the 19th century to support the view that European civilisation was not only hale and hearty, but enjoying a thoroughly creative phase. To take the decade of the 1860's, it saw enormous leaps in productivity and trade, particularly in Britain, where Lancashire with its cotton was "the hub of the industrialised world". Pasteur's discoveries about germs, with subsequent medical applications, particularly by Lister in surgery, were revolutionary. Another outcome was the drive for pure water and a clean environment, with resultant gains in public health and the mastering of diseases such as cholera and typhus. In other areas Germany was coming into the lead, with her scientists vying with men like Clerk Maxwell in Britain, shortly to make electricity available for a vast range of applications. Production of iron and steel, speeded by the

Bessemer and other processes, leapt ahead, for these were necessities in the age of steam. Every year more factories were belching smoke, and railways were proliferating in all directions.

A more sinister aspect of progress, alongside these developments, was the increase and perfecting of the instruments of destruction. The American Civil War provided the opportunity for testing the Gatling gun, and the products of Krupp gave superior fire-power to the Prussians in the war against France.

Darwin's work, a landmark in the biological sciences, also shattered biblical concepts about the origins and development of the planet by bringing evolutionary theories into vogue. These before long affected historical writing. But the theory of history which was to exert overwhelming influence for the next hundred years was that of Marx. This had already been launched - enhanced by the journalistic flair of Engels - in *The Communist Manifesto*, and was now set forth in *Das Kapital* (vol.1,1867).

In culture, narrowly defined, the sixties were exuberant: *War and Peace, The Brothers Karamazov, Les Misérables, Great Expectations, Brandt* and *Peer Gynt, The Idylls of the King, Abt Vogler* and *Rabbi ben Ezra*. In music Wagner reigned supreme with the *Meistersingers of Nuremberg*. Fine art saw the ascendancy of France: Courbet, Daumier and Manet.

Prosperity was trickling down - cheap cotton goods enabled underclothes to be changed more often. But the horrors of the Irish famine a few years before had shown up the prevalence of poverty and the constant liability to destitution among the masses. Employed workers might be better off, but unemployment in the periodic depressions was a catastrophe in millions of homes at a time when welfare services in all European countries were of the sketchiest. Riots and demonstrations alarmed the upper classes, even if no more harm was done than demolishing Hyde Park's railings.

The Hyde Park demonstration of 1866 was for increasing the number of electors under the 1832 Reform Act by giving the vote to rate-paying householders. This was but one of many upheavals which had continued spasmodically in Europe since the French Revolution of 1789. The surge towards parliamentary democracy and universal suffrage could also be accounted progress.

For the optimists, hope lay in the spread of education, with other measures of reform. This was the conclusion of Matthew Arnold, better known as a poet than as an Inspector of Education, and celebrated as the author of *Culture and Anarchy*. Like all thoughtful Victorians, he was conscious of the squalid conditions and sheer misery in which many of his fellow-countrymen were living. It was not a question merely of warding off the anarchy which might result if these conditions were not improved. Arnold's call is for compassion, together with the spread of knowledge, to give the children "in these festering masses, without health, without home, without hope", a fair chance for their "moral life and growth".

But beyond these social evils was the spiritual and cultural barrenness of those who could and should be responsible. The general attitude in an age dominated by the machine was to live a mechanical routine-ridden existence, with money-making as the main incentive. Much more than that of Greece and Rome, modern civilisation had become "mechanical and external, and tends constantly to become more so".

For Matthew Arnold it was not only Christianity but also "Hellenism" which showed the way to change. Together these currents from Athens and Jerusalem could transform ordinary people, Barbarians, Philistines, or the Populace, "according to the law of perfection" - for perfection must be the aim, so that our best self can emerge "at the expense of our old untransformed self." And early Christianity showed how this could be done: "the importation of Hellenism" had renewed Hebraism, by criticising those elements which had become mechanical, and so gave men "a new motive-power" by which to live.

This was the hope cherished by such as Arnold as the middle decades of the century ended. He had been struck when travelling in Germany by the public system of education there - "almost the only great civilising agency directly at work" on the common people. With enough education in England, he concluded in *Culture and Anarchy*, the penetration of sweetness and light could counter "that mechanical character" which in Britain "is shown in the most eminent degree" - though culture would have "a rough task" and its preachers "likely to have a hard time of it" coping with our "strong individualism", our "maxim of 'every man for himself', our want of flexibility, with our inaptitude for seeing more than one side of a thing".

To many besides Matthew Arnold, education was the way forward, along with schemes of social betterment. The second half of the 19th century saw immense progress in providing primary education for the children of most European countries, partly under Church auspices as in the past, partly under the State. In secondary education, whether of the technical or grammar variety, the State took an increasing share, while old universities were reformed and new ones founded.

In England the tutorial system at Oxford and Cambridge distinguished these universities from those of Scotland and the Continent. The pioneering at Oxford was mainly the work of Benjamin Jowett and his colleagues at Balliol, who were ready to give an hour, or more if required, each week to helping their pupils

individually with their work.   They also arranged parties at farm-
houses in the vacations, besides breakfasts and other social occasions
during term.   One of their pupils was T.H. Green.   Brought up on the
classics and influenced by the vogue for German philosophy, he was
an independent-minded thinker and a searching critic in matters
educational and social.   For him the dominating political event of the
sixties was the American Civil War - "the most important struggle that
the world has seen since the French Revolution" - and his relief was
proportionate when victory went to the North over the "slave-holding,
slave-breeding and slave-burning oligarchy, on whom the curse of God
and humanity rests".   Like Arnold, though only temporarily, he took
on work as an assistant school-inspector, and produced a weighty and
influential report (1868) for the Commission inquiring into middle-
range education.   He was comitted to the temperance movement for
countering the evils arising from cheap alcohol, and gave a lead by
opening a coffee-shop in the Oxford suburb of St. Clements.

Besides supporting legislation in such matters, he undertook civic
work, the first college tutor to be elected a Councillor for Oxford City.
One of his great objects while on the Council, and one which was duly
achieved, was to set up a grammar school for the city.   He contributed
substantial sums for the building and scholarships.

Corruption in elections had to be curbed if there was to be "a
parliament which has the interest of the struggling classes of society
at heart".   The "degradation and hopeless waste" due to drunkenness,
which could be seen "at every turn, even in Oxford," was linked with
"the disgraceful traffic in votes" for "a parliament which is in fact a
sort of club of rich men", unfitted to deal with the "immense
commercial interest ... fattening upon the evil, and of course doing all
it can to disguise it."   As part of this fight he supported the petition by
which the newly-elected MP for Oxford was unseated for bribery in
1882.

Green was not only a reformer who was prepared to commit his
time and money generously for the causes he believed important.   He
was a professional philosopher whose main concern was "the moral
training of a generation of potential national leaders".

Comment: T.H. Green's Christian beliefs and philosophy. (p. 264)

3. **Fin-de-siècle anxiety**: *a "dark age" coming (Bosanquet); civilisation like a doomed liner (Kierkegaard); Christianity and democracy as causes of corruption (Nietzsche); drifting through wars towards "a sort of Roman Empire" (Burckhardt); degeneracy, hysteria, eroticism, drugs, pornography (Nordau).*

Bosanquet, following Green, placed particular value on the advance of democracy - the legacy of Athens and of the English and French Revolutions - which had endowed the ordinary man with "the power and right to have an articulate opinion." But now (he was writing in 1892) everything worthy of the name of culture was in danger of being submerged and corrupted by the torrents of trivia, trash and sheer poison which the printing presses were pouring out. The machinery of communication had become more important than "the substance" to be communicated. "Never before in the history of the human race have the facilities of thought and expression been so distributed as to render possible so wild and immeasurable an ocean of error. For positive error ... has now taken the place of ignorance. Far from having reached its climax, the movement towards a modern Dark Age has probably but just begun."

This grim prognosis was qualified by Bosanquet in his definition of a "Dark Age". He applied the phrase to states of mind rather than to historical periods. The overlaying of "the substance" of culture constituted darkness as the 19th century ended.

"There is *nothing* which large sections of the educated populace (in all ranks of society) will not believe. There is no absurdity so gross as not to find its able journalistic supporters. There is no opinion which is not maintained, by persons equipped with full powers of articulate expression, with a granite obstinacy and indifference to reason and experience. There is nothing so bad in art and literature that it will not be welcomed with exultation by an enthusiastic crowd, quite capable of maintaining their conceptions in language, to all appearance, not unworthy of the Republic of letters."

Eventually there could be a "reanimation of the form of culture by its substance", defined as "a body of science, art, and literature, parallel to that which was laid on the advocates of Christianity in the Middle Ages, but at a higher level." Meanwhile the absence of authority or consensus in matters of culture "constitutes our peculiar modern form of the Dark Ages."

Bosanquet was more hopeful than others who spoke with prophetic voices. A generation earlier the Danish philosopher, Kierkegaard, had castigated the press even more trenchantly as an evil in society, "simply because of the power of diffusion, which is a quite disproportionate means of communication for small matters ... a kind of madness, which tends to turn the whole community into a madhouse ... If I were a father and had a daughter who was seduced, I should by no means give her up; but if I had a son who became a journalist I should regard him as lost."

Kierkegaard's pessimism about civilisation went to the extreme limit. He had no faith that Christianity could be a dynamic force to rejuvenate society - from the earliest times, in his view, it had been watered down to become merely an anodyne to keep people comfortable in their worldly lives. "The history of Christendom is the history of the subtle discarding of Christianity." The only hope was in "the single man" who could make the leap of enthusiasm by deciding to follow closely "the Model", Jesus, ready "to stand alone, forsaken, scorned and ridiculed." He could then "serve in suffering and help indirectly", but even so would have little effect on an evil and sinful world which had fallen away from God.

"I understood perfectly well", he wrote, "that I could not possibly succeed in taking the comfortable and secure *via media* in which most people pass their lives. I had either to throw myself into perdition and sensuality, or to choose the religious way absolutely as the only thing." He broke off his engagement to his fiancée, and as a single man, in both senses, he followed his prophetic calling. But he knew that his message would be ignored, and catastrophe would result.

> "Imagine a very great ship, greater, if you will, than the biggest ships we have at present; suppose it has room for 1,000 passengers, and of course it is equipped on the greatest possible scale with conveniences, comforts, luxuries, etc. It is towards night. In the cabin they are having a merry time, everything illuminated in the most resplendent way, everything glitters; in short all is merriment and good cheer ... and the merriest of all is the captain.

> "The white speck is there in the horizon; it will be a dreadful night. But no one sees the white speck or divines what it means. But there is one that sees it and knows what it means - but he is a passenger. He has no command on the ship and is unable to do anything decisive. However, to do the only thing in his power, he sends a message to the captain to come on deck for an instant. There is considerable delay; finally he comes out but will listen to nothing, and with a jest he hastens down to the noise and reckless joy of the society in the cabin, where the captain's health is drunk and he responds complacently. In his anguish the poor passenger ventures once more to disturb the captain; but now the captain has even become discourteous to

him. Nevertheless the speck in the horizon remains unchanged - 'it will be a dreadful night.'"

Even though, for Kierkegaard, human society had always been the same, given over to the power of evil, he recognised a certain falling off from the creative energy and passion of the previous age which had culminated in the French Revolution. "A revolutionary age is an age of action; ours is the age of advertisement and publicity." Nietzsche a few years later had no doubts that decadence had already overtaken Europe. Neither Christianity nor democracy gave hope. Christianity, in his view, was "one of the chief instruments for the advancement of decadence," while democracy was part of the general corruption. Culture was being "uprooted in the increasing rush of life, and the decay of all reflection and simplicity ... The nations are drawing away in enmity again and long to tear each other to pieces."

Hope lay in that most basic of man's urges, the will to power. Responding to this, a new type of man would arise, the superman. Among Nietzsche's vivid but none too coherent images, the role of the superman was partly iconoclastic, casting down the idols of a dead or dying past, partly "a living lighthouse of unconquerable life," and partly proclaimer of a new day - "the transformation, the sword of judgement, the great noontide", while waiting and "learning long luminous silence" under the winter sky.

Nietzsche was lecturing at Basel (Basle) in Switzerland at the same time as Jakob Burckhardt, who made his name with another classic of the 1860's, *The Civilisation of the Renaissance in Italy.*

For the illusions of "progress ... the merciless optimism which is springing up everywhere," Burckhardt cast the principal blame on Rousseau as one of the chief inspirers of the French Revolution, "with his doctrine of the goodness of human nature." By the 1870's "the idea of the natural goodness of man had turned, among the intelligent strata of Europe, into the idea of progress, i.e. undisturbed money-making and modern comforts, with philanthropy as a sop to conscience ... The only conceivable salvation would be for this insane optimism, in great and small, to disappear from people's brains."

He warned against "the centaur" of the philosophy of history: the whole conception of such a philosophy was a contradiction in terms, even though the centaur "on the fringe of historical study ... has hewn out some vast vistas through the forest and lent spice to history." His prognosis differed greatly from the vistas of the idealists. In the aftermath of the revolutionary upheavals of 1848 he predicted that "democrats and proletarians, even though they make the most furious efforts, will have to yield to an increasingly violent despotism, for our charming century is made for anything rather than genuine democracy." By the eighties he was speaking of "the coming age of barbarism."

> "Only people do not like to imagine a world whose rulers utterly ignore law ... and who would rule with utter brutality. But these are the people into whose hands the world is being driven by the competition among all parties for the participation of the masses on any and every question."

The most he could hope for was "a few half-hearted decades, a sort of Roman Empire," assailed by the kind of pessimism which became "a generally recognised attitude in the third and fourth centuries." He saw the Franco-Prussian War of 1870-1 as initiating an era of wars, to be ended perhaps by "a great war, with the resulting lasting peace. But what a horrible price to pay!... The final end might well be an Imperium Romanum (only when we are dead, to be sure)." He foresaw the military state which will have to turn "industrialist, with its mounds of men in the yards and factories", for whom "a planned degree of poverty" would be necessary, "with promotions and uniforms." Germany would only survive if "something great, new and liberating" could arise - "it will have to have its martyrs". As for Russia, it would be "reduced to confusion by acts of violence ... sheer, unlimited violence."

Max Nordau could claim a wider European view than others whose lives had been largely passed in their countries. He was a Hungarian Jew, strongly influenced in his student days by his Italian professor. He spent many years in Paris, was deeply familiar with English literature, and wrote in German. His book *Degeneration* appeared in 1892-3. He opens with comments on the fin-de-siècle atmosphere of the time.

> "The prevalent feeling is that of imminent perdition and extinction ... In our days there have arisen in more highly developed minds vague qualms of a Dusk of the Nations, in which all suns and all stars are gradually waning, and mankind with its institutions and creations is perishing in the midst of a dying world."

He defines decadence as "a practical emancipation from traditional discipline ... the trampling underfoot of all barriers which enclose brutal greed of lucre and lust of pleasure ... the shameless ascendancy of base impulses and motives, which were, if not virtuously suppressed, at least hypocritically hidden ... the vanishing of ideals in art, and no more power in its accepted forms to arouse emotion ... The end of an established order, which for thousands of years has satisfied logic, fettered depravity, and in every art matured something of beauty."

He qualifies these remarks: "The great majority of the middle and lower classes is naturally not fin-de-siècle. It is only a very small minority who honestly find pleasure in the new tendencies. All snobs affect to have the same taste as the select and exclusive minority."

Nordau assumes a close relation between degeneracy and decadence. Nearly all degenerates lack the sense of morality, of right and wrong. It can be called "moral insanity." His words about "highly gifted degenerates" calls to mind the youthful Hitler, at that time a boy in Linz. Hitler also had the characteristic traits of "the hysterical person", who could infect thousands or millions with mass hysteria and illusions.

Nordau comments on the "enormous increase of hysteria in our days ... Steam and electricity have turned the customs of life of every member of the civilised nations upside down. People are run-down, fatigued, because of the constant efforts, adversely affecting the nervous system", all of which is aggravated - and this is before the age of radio and television - by exposure to "the thousand events" as they take place "in all parts of the globe ... Humanity has no time to adapt itself to its changed conditions of life", and hysteria, once acquired, can be passed on. Hence the "constant increase in the consumption of narcotics and stimulants." Degeneracy can be the consequence of poisoning by alcohol and tobacco, and is encouraged by the atmosphere of the larger towns. The growing incidence of heart disease is another symptom of the social malaise.

Further down the road of decadence are the "ego-maniacs and filthy psuedo-realists", who are enemies of society of the direct kind.

> "Society must unconditionally defend itself against them ... There is no place among us for the lusting beast of prey ... And still more determined must be the resistance to the filth-loving herd of swine, the professional pornographists ... They have freely chosen their vile trade ... The systematic incitement of lasciviousness causes the gravest injury to the bodily and mental health of individuals, and a society composed of individuals sexually over-stimulated, knowing no longer any self-control, any discipline, any shame, marches to its certain ruin, because it is too worn out and flaccid to perform great tasks.

> "The pornographist poisons the springs whence flows the life of future generations. No task of civilisation has been so painfully laborious as the subjugation of lasciviousness. The

pornographist would take from us the fruit of this, the hardest struggle of humanity. To him we must show no mercy."

CHAPTER 2

PARALLELS

1. The Classical world and the modern West: *Warring states, colonies, resistance to superpowers (Persia, Turkey); Pax Romana cf. Pax Americana; decline of Roman Empire cf. decline of American imperium. De-moralisation and insecurity.*

In many ways our present civilisation has proceeded along lines remarkably similar to those of the Classical "world". This included only part of geographical Europe, but also much territory around the Mediterranean in Western Asia and North Africa. In this respect too Europe is today part of a wider whole, due to one of the two developments whereby modern technology has differentiated our epoch from that of ancient times: the "one world" of rapid transport and instant communication. The other is the tapping of vast sources of energy, with the means of using them equally for construction or destruction.

The parallels between the European states fighting among themselves and the endemic wars among the states of ancient Greece are fairly close. Like the later European states, the Greek cities occupied and colonised surrounding lands and struggled for supremacy among themselves - with occasional concerted action. One such action was in resisting Xerxes and all the might of Persia at Marathon, Salamis and Plataea. These events are part of the great age of Greece (as it is generally regarded), but though Europe's later resistance to the Turks seems to offer a parallel, the victory of Lepanto, the defence of Malta, and the raising of the siege of Vienna, cannot be thrust into quite the same historical pigeon-hole. In modern Europe there were other periods of greatness and grandeur enjoyed by nations after vindicating their freedom: when the Spaniards, after defeating the Arabs, expanded overseas; when the French threw out the English; when the English and Dutch defeated the Spaniards; and when the Russians, having thrown off the Mongol yoke, continued similar exploits against Swedes and Turks, and against the French under Napoleon.

After their victories the Greeks resumed their internecine struggles, with Athens and Sparta building their empires, only to clash in the Peloponnesian War. Comparisons have been drawn, Britain playing a similar role to Athens, Germany to Sparta. But if comparisons are to be made and Britain is cast in the role of Athens, her rival "Sparta" would not be Germany, but France, whose lengthy wars culminated in those of the French Revolution and Napoleon. During their rivalry another state was raising itelf to pre-eminence, Prussia, soon to proclaim its empire over Germany, and to make its bid to dominate Europe and become a world power. Prussia under Bismarck was playing a similar role to Macedon under Philip and Alexander, who raised their country to be the dominant power in the Greek world.

If it is accepted that Britain may be compared with Athens and her sea-empire, the story has a different ending. Whereas Athens lost against Sparta in Sicily, Britain won against France in India and America - hence British imperialism dominated the succeeding century. If Prussia and her creation, the German Empire, are taken to be analogous with Macedon, the story again is different. Whereas Alexander was able to continue Philip's strategy in making Macedon a world-power, Bismarck's achievements could not be emulated by his sucessors, Wilhelm II and Hitler. Philip unified Greece under Macedon's hegemony, enabling Alexander to overthrow Persia and so spread Hellenism throughout "the known world" of his day.

The Hellenistic Age continued during the period when Rome took over the largest part of what had been Alexander's empire, except for Parthia (that part of Persia which regained its independence under the Arsacids). The nearest analogue to Rome is Russia, while our West is the equivalent of the ancient Greek-speaking east (geographically, "modern" is back-to-front with "ancient"). But though Stalin aroused fears in the west of Soviet expansion westwards beyond East Germany and Czechoslovakia, Russia has not attempted to recreate a Roman-style empire over Europe as a whole. Instead the evolution of post-war Europe has gone along quite other lines: one of the differences from Antiquity which suggests that the page of history which again is turning may present not merely a re-run of civilisation as we have known it, but a new type of civilisation whose novel forms may embrace the planet as a whole.

Alexander's empire did not last, and the resulting situation is closely analogous to that confronting the West today in its relations with the rest of the world. Greece proper, like Western Europe, had ceased to dominate international affairs, though it still remained an area of conflict. The former Great Powers of Greece - Athens, Sparta and Thebes - weakened by their long-drawn struggles, had shrunk into a secondary position, being dwarfed by the sucessor states of Alexander's empire. Egypt was restored under Ptolemy, one of Alexander's generals, while what was left of Alexander's conquests in Asia came under Seleucus and his successors. This "Hellenistic World"

Ancient and modern periods compared

5th century BC
Persian pressure on Greece and defeat 490-479 BC: Marathon, Salamis, Plataea.

15th - 17th centuries AD
Turkish pressure on Europe and defeat 1566, 1572, 1683 AD: Malta, Lepanto, Vienna.

5th century BC
Greek imperialism, especially Athens, Sparta.

18th century AD
European imperialism especially Britain, France.

431 - 404 BC
Peloponnesian War: Athens vs. Sparta.

1792 - 1815 AD
French Revolutionary/Napoleonic Wars.

4th century BC
Philip and Alexander: Rise of Macedon.

19th century AD
Bismarck: rise of Prussia/Germany.

3rd and 2nd centuries BC
Rise of Rome. Hellenistic Era (wars).

19th - 20th centuries AD
Rise of USA. Europe's culture worldwide ("world wars").

BC/AD
Augustus restores order: Roman Empire.

1945 AD
USA restores order: American imperium.

End 3rd century AD onwards
Rome declines. Cold/hot conflict Rome/Persia.

1947 AD onwards
Cold wars USA/USSR. Vietnam: decline of American imperium.

400 - 650 AD
Transition to new civilisations: Byzantium and the West.

21st century AD
Transition to new civilisations ? ? ?

included also those regions where Greek colonies had been planted
and trade was active - the area around the Black Sea, and territories
as far west as Sicily and Marseilles.

So today those areas colonised from Europe, notably the
Americas and the older British dominions and South Africa, form part
of our westernised world, alongside Japan and other countries of Asia,
the Mediterranean and the Pacific, which have come strongly under
Western influence. The differences as well as the likenesses are of
course plain - notably that whereas China under the Han Dynasty had
little contact with the Hellenistic world - was in fact a "world" on its
own - today it cannot avoid becoming part of the one world of rapid
communications and interdependence, while still striving to maintain
its separate evolution.

Rome brought not only Greece and the Eastern Mediterranean
under her rule, but North Africa and much of Western Europe as well.
Then her generals began fighting among themselves, until Augustus
gained control and restored order. This period of some 70 years may
be taken as the equivalent of the three and a half decades on our
modern time-scale, from the outbreak of the first World War to
America's restoration of order after the second. The achievement of
Augustus in making possible two centuries of relative peace is similar
to that of Truman and the American leadership in restoring Western
Europe and initiating a period of prosperity which benefited a large
part of the world.

America's hegemony since 1945 created a zone of influence
where economic and military might gave her considerable control.
This American "imperium" replaced its European predecessor of the
19th and 20th centuries, when Britain claimed to emulate the Roman
Peace by imposing the Pax Britannica.

As the war ended it seemed as if a Pax Americana might indeed
become a reality, with American power deployed through the United
Nations and particularly the Security Council where the USA, Russia,
Britain and China could function according to Roosevelt's prescription
as the world's "Four Policemen". But this depended on Stalin being
an amenable partner, and China under Chiang Kai-shek continuing as
America's ally.   Neither condition was fulfilled, and in any case
America was hesitant in undertaking a hegemonial role, let alone a
fully imperial one. The United States had been created by refugees
and emigrants from Europe, who had no wish to become unduly
involved in its affairs, and this was the attitude of their descendants,
as long as American interests and security were not threatened.

Western Europe is only one province under American hegemony.
The crisis of Europe is only part of a much wider crisis, embracing not
only America but the whole world. Since Russia has not taken on the

role of Rome in extending her empire throughout the whole of Europe, and since America's aims have been limited to a kind of hegemony, we do not find ourselves in the last "few half-hearted decades, a sort of Roman Empire" as predicted by Burckhardt. In any case, while the Russian Empire is showing manifold strains, the American hegemony is already becoming precarious, though another hegemony, the Chinese, is operative in Asia.

The weakening of America's power is shown in the failure of her containment policy in Vietnam and Ethiopia, in her humiliation in Iran and her exclusion from that country, and in her impotence to restore order in Lebanon or impose her will on Israel. No Pax Americana sufficed to guard the suffering people in those areas where the rival hegemonies have clashed, nor can America, even when working with Britain and other post-imperial powers, maintain good and honest government in territories where her writ or that of Europe's colonial powers once ran. However, there may be changes in this respect, now that the cold war of the superpowers is over.

This weakness is evident in the economic sphere. The European imperium of the 19th century provided a reasonably stable commercial and monetary system, based on sterling and the gold-standard under the direction of London. After World War II America took over this role, helping world recovery, and particularly that of Europe, by massive and generous aid, and by a system which ensured for 25 years a period of unexampled prosperity. But then the cost of the Vietnam war together with increasingly heavy expenditure on welfare provision in building "the Great Society" brought to an end the monetary arrangements based on the Bretton Woods Conference of 1944. With America's departure from the gold-standard, the dollar joined other floating currencies, and ceased to be a brake on the tendency to inflation which, for various reasons, was afflicting most countries of the world.

Among other evils which it propagates, currency inflation on any scale instills fear and the desire to grab whatever may give security, while greed promotes gambling and profiteering. Corruption assumes dimensions which undercut not merely efficiency and justice but the authority and even the foundations of the State.

De-moralisation means a slide in morals, the more marked when the beliefs and sanctions of previously accepted religions lose their hold. In the free-for-all of a permisssive period the inner barbarities of society are no longer held in check. Violence and brutality become common, as pornography and perversion reach out into every social activity, leaving behind their trail of broken homes, disturbed children and a tendency to aggression which surfaces in cruel sports and spectacles, in the vandalism of hooligans and the rioting of fans.

Drink, drugs, abortion, wife- and child-battering, all take an increasing toll.

In reaction to these evils a strong desire grows in the hearts of many for salvation - for personal salvation and the salvation of society, for peace and security. At a time when wars and internal conflicts are chronic, and mugging and banditry rife, and especially when the view gains ground that the end of all things may be near - at such moments men and women long for saviours who will heal hearts, restore confidence, and offer vision and hope for sane living and perhaps for life in the hereafter.

Comment: Comparisons between Greek and Roman history and modern Western Europe; Rome's war with Persia; America's hegemony (or "imperium") and its decline. (p. 265)

2. **Political and spiritual salvation in the ancient world**: *Saviours ancient and modern. Rise of science; decline of faith in the Olympians; decline of city-state and rise of empires led to new philosophy, and religions of the Orient; escapist philosophies and club life; completeness of revelations; the moral order. Stoics: Seneca and God; Demonax; Musonius Rufus.*

The longing for saviours began when the armies of Alexander and his sucessors, ravaging across the Near and Middle East, broke down the old self-sufficiency and sovereignty of city-states and kingdoms, and took away freedom along with the people they enslaved. For many the satisfactions and security they had found in the city disappeared. Wars and civil wars continued to erupt until Augustus effectively took on the role of political saviour, restoring order over the vast area from Euphrates to Atlantic, from Rhine and Danube to the Sahara. The frontiers were guarded, roads were built, the seas were policed, trade flourished, and the leisured life of a small minority made possible another creative epoch in literature, art and architecture.

Cities, though no longer fully independent, continued as centres of vigorous life. And with political salvation there came spiritual salvation as well. It was during the reign of Augustus that the man was born whom millions in the ancient world and subsequently were to revere as their spiritual saviour, Jesus.

The system of empire devised by Augustus was strong enough to continue throughout the reigns of egomaniacal rulers, Caligula and Nero, and survived Nero's three sucessors, who all died violent deaths in the months which followed his own suicide (68 AD). After some further upheavals the Empire had its longest period of unbroken internal peace, when the sucession was assured by a series of adoptions. Nerva in 98 AD set the fashion with Trajan, followed by Hadrian, Antoninus Pius and Marcus Aurelius, all competent rulers. Unfortunately Marcus Aurelius had a son Commodus, who - though a talented athlete who loved to perform in public - was ill-fitted for supreme authority. With his murder a few years later military pronunciamentos became chronic, setting up rulers or those who aspired to the purple, most dying or being murdered after reigning only briefly, some before even reaching the throne. Revolts and civil wars are the background to impoverishment, civic breakdown and disorder, until the rot was partially stopped by Diocletian and Constantine (284 and 306 AD).

The internal wars which racked the Empire in the third century and continued off and on for a hundred years were not the only cause of the decline. These wars were merely symptoms of a deeper malaise. While the frontiers were still being defended against the German and other tribes, the society which the legions and their local auxiliaries protected was rotting from the roots. But sterility in culture accompanied by depopulation, disorder and currency inflation, was patchy both in time and place. Long before the lowest point was reached the vigorous new growth had begun.

In our times men have arisen claiming to be the saviours of their countries and initiators of new orders - Lenin, Hitler, Mussolini and others, just as many rulers of ancient days claimed and were awarded the title of *soter* or saviour. With modern "saviours" a religious or pseudo-religious ideological element has swayed millions to welcome their despotic regimes - a poor substitute for genuinely spiritual salvation such as was offered in the ancient world by Jews and Christians.

Our "Age of Anxiety" is not unlike that of the ancients. For many of them, when the last century BC drew to a close, the Apocalypse loomed as imminent and inescapable, just as today minds are obsessed by the possibility of nuclear annihilation.

Certainly human-kind moves on a narrow path, where an abyss yawns threateningly and a false step might mean disaster. Is there a way ahead to peace and security, both for souls and society, as there was in ancient times, when the longing for salvation stirred the hearts of multitudes in the Greco-Roman world?

With the rise of science and philosophy in Greece the old religion had lost its appeal for many. A new moral sense developed and an idea of the unity of the divine which the old Olympian polytheism could not satisfy: the deities had been laughed at by cultivated men ever since Homer. Yet the Olympians, allied with the earthier cults of the early inhabitants of Greece, had become the presiding deities of the city-states; their worship had been the theme of the city festivals and of the numerous sacrifices in which all the citizens participated. The city was more than a political unit: it was Church and University as well. It made possible, in theory, the whole of life, the good life. Hence its passionate defence by Plato, Aristotle and Demosthenes, even after it was manifestly obsolescent and unable to survive in its pristine self-sufficiency. Economic and social necessity dictated that there should be larger political units, federations or super-states of some kind. But though the need was seen, men could not find the conviction wherewith to build them. Unity, they saw, was needed - for defence against the Parthian, the barbarian and the Roman, and unity on the economic plane was equally badly needed, especially for Greece where the industries which she had pioneered were being developed elsewhere, so that she was losing her export markets (much as Britain and Europe in general have lost some of their markets today). These difficulties were immensely aggravated by wars and currency barriers.

But those who came nearest to having a belief in the unity of the world, as "the home of gods and men", for the most part shrank from action calculated to bring it into being. Following the teachings of Epicurus or Zeno they aimed primarily at finding inner peace, in detachment from the world around - at its highest a noble philosophy, capable of bracing great statesmen to heroic feats of duty and discipline, but usually accepted as a philosophy of escape, with a vague cosmopolitanism which left the social order to be made or marred by soldiers and businessmen.

At its best this also overrode barriers of class and race. St. Paul was only echoing this view when he spoke in terms of the unity of Jew and gentile, Greek and Scythian, slave and free. But whereas with Paul it was a dynamic faith, capable of remoulding the social order, in other circles and before his day it was for the most part a vague and sentimental aspiration. Individuals might live beyond class, mix with all men and free their slaves, but class was not transformed and the classes were not reconciled. The class war became increasingly bitter as time went on, but there was no ideology of social change, no socialism or communism, to appeal to the discontented or desperate proletariat. They could only rise in bloody revolts, with demands for the cancellation of their debts, distribution of land, and the raising of the dole - with no co-ordination and no wider purpose than immediate advantage. Nor was there a power outside to support them, as Russia has supported such movements today. Rome had only supported them occasionally during her rise to power, when she wished to frighten the bourgeoisie, but it better suited her ruling group, growing rich with trade and loot, to support the haves against the have-nots.

Zeno, the founder of Stoicism, was a Phoenician; philosphers and religious innovators were increasingly to be found among Asians or Egyptians, hellenised perhaps, but not Greeks by origin. In the larger states attempts were made by the rulers to deify their ancestors and even themselves, and to found a cult along these lines as the ideological cement for the community. They took over the local religions, as the Ptolemies took over the ancient cults in which the Pharaoh was divine, both God and ruler of Egypt. They propagated a synthetic religion, that of Serapis, as a means of extending their influence throughout the Hellenistic world.

These religions, local to the Orient, had a vigour and a tradition which gave them an immense appeal. Like the mystery-religions of Greece, themselves of eastern, possibly Indian origin, they often lent themselves to gatherings of small congregations for worship or for initiation. These groups, especially those which were permanent, built new social units transcending the old racial and class barriers - for in them all men were brothers, whatever their background. They met that insistent need for fellowship in an immense and atomised world, where but rarely the friendly all-sufficient environment of the city-state continued or could be recreated. They raised to a higher plane the tendency towards club life in which men were increasingly taking refuge, whether in the market-places and gymnasia where gathered the "gentlemen" of the town, still clinging to leisure and certain material standards on a basis of slave and sweated labour - or in the guilds and *collegia* of the working-men (little more than associations for eating and drinking together, and for friendly-society benefits).

Without being raised to a higher plane this club life was simply a palliative and as such had no answer to a crumbling society, and even encouraged deterioration. It formed another mode of escape, through the short-lived satisfactions of drink and good fellowship, or through becoming the end rather than just a part of life - so that it emphasised the prevailing materialism. In face of the manifold needs of the age some new faith was required which could bring a new morale and sound morals to the individual, develop family life, and turn clubableness into a deeper fellowship of men and women. No self-sufficient fellowship either: what was needed was a common dedication to a spiritual ideal and to a new way of life together. In many respects the groups or congregations of the early Church, even when forced to meet literally underground in the Catacombs, began to meet this need.

Christianity spread through the Hellenistic world as one legacy of the world-wide spiritual travail of the ancient epoch, both in East and West, which includes Confucianism, Buddhism, Hinduism, Islam, the religion of Zoroaster and others. These have made and are making still their essential contribution. The world has become a place where, despite all man-made barriers, ideas circulate and mingle. The streams from all the past have long been flowing together, heightening man's awareness of Reality as it has been revealed to different people in ancient days.

Each revelation once made is in a sense complete. That which came to the Jews was and is still for them complete. For the Christian, besides the Hebrew revelation, there is the Cross, valid for all times and places,

"The point of intersection of the timeless with time".

With the revelation comes the experience and the challenge, to lose the self-directed life in order to find a higher life, and so move in accordance with the moral order - that unseen environment, the framework within which we have our being, and on which the physical and material environment depends. To move in harmony with the moral law is right living in personal life; it is justice, peace, the *maat* of the Egyptians, the *dharma* of the Aryans and Buddhists, the *diké* of the Greeks. The moral law or laws are more potent than man-made laws laid down by the self-directed will; even though death and persecution intervene, they override the human laws and penalties.

"Nor did I think your edict had such force
that you, a mere mortal, could override the gods,
the great unwritten, unshakable traditions.
They are alive, not just today or yesterday:
they live forever, from the first of time,
and no one knows when they first saw the light."
(Antigone to Creon)

By the time of the Roman Empire, virtue as the aim in life and how to achieve it had become the chief concern of the philosophers. Seneca, one of the wealthiest landowners of the Empire, who held a position similar to Prime Minister in the early years of Nero, was a leading exponent of Stoicism at a time when this philosophy had become a religion. Originally from Cordoba in Spain, his father had risen through the legal profession, acquiring estates in Italy and a palace in Rome. Seneca himself had been tutor to Nero, but this and his subsequent service under the Emperor did not save him from being forced to suicide before the reign ended.

For Seneca God is Father, benevolent spirit, guardian, guide, source of moral sense and wisdom, and his maxims for living - freely shared in his role of adviser to others - flow from this belief. This is clear, even when, following the old usage, "God" is used in the plural.

"Consider what great blessings our Father has bestowed upon us ... so many virtues ... so many arts ... the human mind, to which nothing is inaccessible the moment it makes the effort ... the products of the field, all the store of wealth, and all the other blessings that are piled one upon the other ... The fact is, the immortal gods have held - still hold - us most dear, and in giving us a place next to themselves have bestowed upon us the greatest honour that was possible.

"God is training us like a father, and we have our part in the work which his 'manly love' is trying to perfect in us. God does not make a spoiled pet of a good man; he tests him, hardens him, and fits him for his own service ... When shall I be allowed to crush all the stirrings of my lower self, bring them under my control and cry 'Victory!' 'Victory? Over what?' you ask. Not Persia, not Media ... No, not these, but avarice and snobbery and fear of death, before which the conquerors of nations have fallen."

Seneca was certainly put to the test. When he committed suicide his wife tried to kill herself too, but survived.

Seneca was an aristocrat, with several great houses to live in. Another side of this moral and spiritual revolution - though as yet non-Christian - was to be seen in the saintly Demonax (50-149 AD). Originating from Cyprus, this member of the ascetic Cynic movement challenged people with pointed home truths and rugged rebukes. But - in this different from many of his fraternity - he tempered his harsh reproving of sin with gentleness towards the sinner.

"Though he assailed sins, he forgave sinners, thinking that one should pattern after doctors, who heal sickness but feel no anger at the sick. He considered that it is human to err, divine or all but divine to set the fallen on their feet ... He made it his business also to reconcile brothers at variance and to make terms of peace between wives and husbands."

For him there was no question of detachment from ordinary life, even politics. He took a full part in the affairs of Athens, where he settled, speaking out for what he believed to be right, even at the cost of bitter opposition from the public. On one occasion he ended strife among rival factions by going to the Assembly, and "just by showing himself reduced them to silence: then seeing that they had already repented, he went away without saying a word."

This action, so much like that of St. Francis many centuries later healing the quarrel between the majores and minores in Assisi, was in keeping with other characteristics of the *poverelli*; he gave up money, living on the gifts of bread and fruit which the market women and others gladly gave him.

Demonax was 18 when Nero died in 68 AD. In striking contrast with the evils of that reign a number of teachers like him appeared, who showed forth real goodness not only with their lips but in their lives. Some suffered in consequence. As is the way of despotic regimes, Nero had another philosopher, Musonius Rufus, imprisoned and eventually exiled, simply "for the crime of being a sage."

Musonius defined philosophy as "training in nobility of character" and as "the care of the soul", by study which should be started in infancy by both boys and girls and continued throughout life. "To accept injury not in a spirit of savage resentment ... but rather to be a source of good hope to those who wrong us, is God-like", he said. We are made in God's image and should live accordingly.

A life of self-control should begin by discipline in eating and drinking. He was a vegetarian - "people who eat the cheapest food live longest", he said. He esteemed work like farming and shepherding, "living in accord with nature". Students could learn while they worked, and it was ideal for a teacher to have them with him in the country.

Comment: Changes in Greek religion as connected with the decline of the city-state; Seneca. (p. 270)

CHAPTER 3

MORALS AND MARRIED PARTNERSHIP

1. Marriage contracts and romantic love: *Woman's low status; arranged marriages, lack of intimacy; changes during "decadence" towards married partnership: hetairai and romantic love; the New Comedy; country life and The Idylls. Improvement in girls' education and position of women, but eroticism, paederasty, slaves.*

In Greece the city-state fostered the primitive type of democracy, incomplete as it was, not much more than a town-meeting of the male citizens - themselves a privileged group since their life-style was only made possible by an equal or larger number of slaves. But this working model of a self-governing society in which every member took part, holding office as well as voting, set a pattern which no subsequent tyranny or dictatorship could erase.

An epoch of grandeur was that of Greece at her prime. There was then, in Bosanquet's words, "a certain crushing and overwhelming influence exercised by the imperious excitement of that tremendous age." "The true Poetical Drama" flourished, and the creative impulse was shared by a large section of the public, "making them able and willing to sympathise in the constructive effort of the poet and to live up to the tension of his mind."

The period that followed was one of decadence, in the sense of falling away from standards and norms, particularly in art and literature. But at the same time new life sprang up, and new norms and standards were set. Starting with that most basic element in society, the family, new ideals in marriage appeared, and with them came greater value placed on the home and family life. In consequence there were new themes in plays, poetry and romances. The peace and simple joys of the countryside came to be more deeply appreciated, expressed in the *Idylls* of Theocritus and by other writers.

One of the indicators of the decadence or otherwise of a society is its standards of manners and morals, particularly in the relations of the sexes. In this respect Greece, and particularly Athens in its great age, appears already in a condition of decadence - a definite falling away from the norms of married partnership and the position of women described by Homer several centuries before. At that time women were freer and less secluded, and husbands and wives could apparently enjoy conjugal happiness on a fairly equal basis. The return of Ulysses to Penelope is of the highest drama - equally dramatic is his shipwreck on his way home at Scherie, and his reception by Nausicaa, daughter of King Alcinous and his wife Arete (another happily married couple). With her maids Nausicaa has come to do her washing near the beach. In asking for clothes and help the sea-battered Ulysses calls on the Gods to fulfill her heart's desire: "May they give you a husband and a home, and the harmony that is so much to be desired, since there is nothing nobler or more admirable than when two people who see eye to eye keep house as man and wife, confounding their enemies and delighting their friends, as they themselves know better than anyone."

The absorbing interests of public life in 5th century Athens and the full share which the citizen had in it meant that private life had been thrust into the background. Romantic love and the intimacies of home life took a secondary place, and were not much the concern of literature. Literature itself was public, a matter of hearing and seeing plays in the theatre, speakers in the assembly, teachers in the schools and pleaders in the courts. Only when the great age passes has the ordinary citizen both the time and interest for more private affairs.

The citizen in those days was a man - a man who had been born into a free family. No slave could be a citizen, not even a freed slave, nor could resident aliens or women. Not only did public life in the great age leave little time to the citizen for romantic love with his wife, it was practically excluded by the system of matchmaking and the circumstances of married life.

Girls had very little say in choosing their partners, and it was much the same with boys - this was the business of parents or guardians. A match was arranged by the latter with reference to the advantages it might bring them and the ancestral line, by the way of enhanced social connections or dowry. Marriage was not an alliance between a man and a woman, but a contract between two men, the fathers (or guardians) of the girl and of the prospective husband. The object was to ensure male heirs to continue the lineage and the cults connected with it. "At the extreme limit the woman is a reproducing animal who brings a dowry."

Education for girls went scarcely beyond the domestic necessities. Women's place was in the home, and with few exceptions they played no part in public life. With the obligation of virginity before marriage, girls were confined or kept under strict surveillance, which could continue after marriage to ensure the exclusive rights of their husbands.

Not that monogamy was everywhere the rule. In Northern Greece the Macedonian court practiced polygamy, with resulting chronic disputes as the various consorts strove against each other, sometimes with violence or poison, to ensure the succession for their respective sons. But elsewhere monogamous marriages alone could be legally recognised.

It was normal for a girl to be married at 14 to a man of about 30. A wife, whatever her age, continued in law to be regarded as a child. With such discrepancy in age there was little chance for deep affection and intimacy to develop. Even if there was love in the marriage - and this was certainly sometimes the case - the marriage itself might not last long since the expectation of life for a man was only around 45 years, despite some well-attested exceptions, and for women, forced to live an unhealthy indoor life, perhaps less.

The exception here was Sparta, unlike other states in nourishing girls properly and giving them physical training, so that they could bear strong soldiers - though with a strange way of marrying them off. In the rest of Greece, being married young, women tended to outlive their husbands, who anyway could easily divorce them. If they moved on to subsequent marriages the chances of an affectionate partnership were not much greater than before. Although as widows or divorcees they did not lose their dowries, which were taken back for re-use by their fathers or guardians (for at that stage women were still officially wards), they had legally no control over their property and little over any financial transactions - even the shopping was done by their husbands. The physical divisions in the house reinforced the barriers between husband and wife arising from the discrepancy in education. The wife was kept in the women's quarters along with the female slaves (who were isolated to prevent unauthorised pregnancies). In consequence bonds of affection often developed between mistresses and their slave-women which could be stronger than between themselves and their husbands.

In general women's work was equated with that of the slaves, though it seems likely that, as in traditional Mediterranean society today, there were occasions which took them out of the house, enabling them to meet other women. Wives at any rate were expected to be silent and submissive, not meddling with the pleasures of their menfolk. For the latter there was no stigma in using the state-owned brothels or male prostitutes, nor having their slaves as concubines. The disadvantage of these extra-marital relations was that children of such liaisons could not be recognised as citizens in Athens, at least after a law of 451 BC - only as slaves who were their father's property. Hence the need for official marriages to produce legitimate heirs for the *oikos* - the ancestral family line - but since descent was reckoned through the male line and resources were often meagre, families were kept small by various methods including the exposure of infants, especially girls. These, if left in the temples, might be taken for eventual use by the brothel-keepers.

The worst trauma for the Athenians during the war with Sparta was not the battle casualties, nor watching their fields and orchards being ravaged by their enemies' annual incursions. The greatest upheaval was caused by the plague which decimated the inhabitants, penned into the relatively small space between the "long walls", the number being increased by the peasants who had been obliged to seek shelter there. "The catastrophe was so overwhelming," wrote Thucydides, "that men, not knowing what would happen next to them, became indifferent to every rule of religion or of law ... Athens owed to the plague a state of unprecedented lawlessness."

The consequent changes in traditional morality were however not all adverse for woman. The possibility of new relationships between husbands and wives at Athens was shown by the hetairai (companions), mostly from Naucratis and Ionia. Some of these, from being flute-playing call-girls moved on to stable relationships. In this case a girl had to "buy a man, with her fascinations", whereas a wife - relatively secure since her husband would lose her dowry by a divorce - might treat him "with proud contempt." The "companion" would greet him with kisses and "pleasant flattery", giving him a chair, and if he was depressed would "speak consoling words and make him cheerful again". Some were able to improve their charms by "going in for culture and apportioning their time to learned studies". Of this kind was Aspasia, the mistress of Pericles who headed the government of Athens at the height of its power and prosperity (463-431 BC). He had divorced his wife, and found in Aspasia someone intellectually on his level (and even on that of Socrates, who brought his pupils to visit her). Whether or not she was a hetaira in the strict sense, as a kept mistress she started a tradition: Pericles loved her dearly, it was later recounted - "he would kiss her warmly when he left for the Agora and when he returned each day." Such affection was noteworthy because unusual, signalling a trend towards more intimate married partnerships.

Although the possibility of a political career for women, other than royalty, was non-existent, their situation was changing. After the fifth century BC, Menander makes romantic love a major theme in his social comedy, with a sensitive treatment of his women characters and happy endings when young couples are married or reconciled.

In his *Epitrepontes* Pamphile refuses to consider divorce from her unfaithful husband, to which her father is trying to persuade her and so get her dowry back. "I'm here to share his life," she says. "Mishaps occur. I mustn't run away." And when one of her causes of contention is found to be baseless and reconciliation follows, the husband's joy is overwhelming. Another play, *Dyskolos* (The

Cantankerous Man) is set in the countryside, where the Athenian obsession with dowries and promoting socially desirable matches may not have been important, but the fact that the suitor Sostratos is of a wealthy family suggests the change in outlook. It is a case of love at first sight, and for Sostratos this is sufficient reason for seeking the girl's hand, though the old misanthrope of a father has to be squared first.

> "Here I saw a girl.
> I love her. If you call that "crime" then I must be
> A criminal. What else can one say? Only that
> I'm coming here not for *her*, it's her father
> I'd like to see. I'm free-born, I've enough
> Money, and I'm prepared to marry her
> Without a dowry, and I'll swear an oath
> Always to cherish her."

A fortunate accident enables the suitor's friend to be appointed guardian of the girl, while he shows his devotion by proving to her curmudgeonly peasant father that he can labour for hours in the field. Parental attitudes have certainly changed when *his* father tells him -

> "I *want* you to get married to
> The girl you love, I say you must! .....
> I realise that when you're young, it adds
> Stability to marriage if it's love
> That prompts the bridegroom."

The joys and intimacies of the home, as well as the simplicity and peace of life in the country, came to be valued more as other satisfactions diminished, especially those afforded formerly by the full and varied public life of the city. For all the looseness of living, married love and a happy home were an ideal, which for many was realised in fact.

As in Menander's *Dyskolos*, the countryside is the setting for the *Idylls* of Theocritus. Whatever the turmoil going on in the world there is a simpler life among shepherds and goatherds, with their rustic competitions in poetry and song, and their amours - even if these often end in frustration (not to mention the hint of decadence in the ambivalence of their passions). Methods of wooing may be rough and ready, but they can end in success, as when Daphnis wins his girl, and marriage when it comes is celebrated with a hymn of prayer to the Gods for mutual love as well as for fair offspring and prosperity. But for educated people as well as peasants, falling in love is a condition which may be painful. Theocritus advises his doctor friend Nicias that there is no remedy for it, neither unguent nor salve, only the Muses - a remedy without side-effects "but hard to find". In the event Nicias succumbed and married, whereon the poet sent an ivory distaff as a present to his wife. In her new home she will "reign, hailed by her peers 'Queen of the Beautiful Distaff', bearing in mind giver and gift, singer and melody."

In the Hellenistic Age which followed the Athenian-Spartan War, women's chances of education improved along with their legal status. At Pergamon their studies were administered by "Superintendents of the Morals of Virgins". Like boys they competed in recitations, music and reading. Elsewhere there were beauty competitions, and prizes for moral stability and household management. Gymnastics became part of the curriculum, though Sparta had a head-start in this. Their ladies' horses were soon winning prizes at Olympia. In business too women were active, owning two-fifths of the land in Sparta. Some other states gave opportunity for women in business, and a few women acquired political rights and were even chosen as magistrates. Some gained distinction as poetesses.

By contrast Athens went backwards, at least for a time. In a reaction (317-307 BC) a board - all-male of course - was set up, "regulators of women", to censor their conduct and control the lavishness of their entertaining. This was something of an issue at a time when hetairai were appearing with their men at dinner-parties, while - according to the old convention - wives did not eat with their husbands, even privately. But where the hetairai led, fashion followed, and eventually it became acceptable for married couples to dine and dine out together.

Comment: Hetairai; *The Idylls* of Theocritus. (p. 271)

2. **Rome: morals and marriage**: *education for girls; from "contractual" to "consensual" marriage; concubines and girl-friends. Augustus curbs sexual anarchy. Ideals of married partnership: Musonius, Plutarch, Pliny, Ausonius.*

While the position of women in Greece was improving, at least in some respects, during the Hellenistic period, a change in the manners and morals of the ruling class of Rome was on the way. The situation is reminiscent of the impact of the "new morality" in the 1960's and '70's - the culminating phase of the process observed by Kierkegaard in the mid-19th century, and described, as it was getting under way, by writers like Nordau and Bosanquet as the century ended.

In both ancient and modern Europe wars played their part in dissolving old values with consequent cultural anarchy. In the case of Rome, wars of conquest produced booty, slaves and corruption on an ever increasing scale, and the social fabric was shaken by the civil wars and assassinations - the struggles for power of generals like Pompey and Caesar. The enrichment and unbelievable luxury of the most successful survivors was a symptom of the prevailing materialism. The availability of female slaves was a constant incitement to concubinage, which became generally accepted among the upper classes. The notorious womanising of Julius Caesar and other public figures did nothing to keep the old norms of behaviour respected. Many well-ordered homes which had produced Rome's fighting families crumbled, and the famous *gravitas* which had characterised their men and matrons gave way to licentiousness and indulgence. Paederasty and other homosexual practices were imported from Greece.

The changes which made possible sexual licence on the grand scale, at least for those who could afford it, had been accumulating over a long period. As in Greece, upper-class Romans were not merely expected to marry, they were practically obliged to do so (as for slaves, their cohabiting received some legal recognition only at a late stage in the Empire). Women had little say in their choice of partner, but they did not suffer seclusion and lack of education like their Greek counterparts. Girls were sometimes educated as well as, or better than their husbands. Cornelia, Pompey's wife, was "widely read, played the lyre, was good at mathematics", and capable of taking part in a philosophical discussion. Sempronia, wife of one of the Consuls in the late Republic, was well read in Greek and wrote verses. Julia, daughter of Augustus, was a lover of literature, and Plotina, the consort of Trajan, was interested in philosophy.

For free Romans the married state was regarded as highly honourable. The wife played a full part not only in domestic but social life, entertaining at home and dining out with her husband - a very different position from that in Athens. The wedding ceremony was an impressive, even awesome occasion, emphasising the sanctity and durability of marriage, and its object in the raising of families to maintain the ancestral line. But this solemn contract, regarded as binding both partners life-long, increasingly fell into disfavour with young couples as the "liberal" attitudes became fashionable. Women rebelled against a system which tied them irrevocably to their husbands and placed them completely under their authority. They also rebelled against laws laying down restrictions in dress and personal ornaments, coming out in street demonstrations and blockading two of the leading members of the Government in their houses.

"Consensual" marriage took the place of "contractual", the partners deciding to live together only so long as both agreed to do so, though marriages continued to be arranged by parents or guardians. Even in the "free" marriage the wife's father continued to have authority over her, as did the husband's father over his son.   But concubinage, as well as being an adjunct to marriage, came to be an increasingly popular alternative to it, and the euphemism "amica" (girl-friend) came into use in place of "pellex" (kept mistress). As religious sanctions weakened and luxury increased, there arose "a growing unwillingness to incur the responsibility of matrimony."

Close relationships between partners were not unusual. Remarriage was as popular as divorce, and romance was possible the second time round when choice was more open. Stable unions with two or three children were regarded as normal.

Augustus tightened up the marriage laws, with a view to increasing the birthrate and providing soldiers for Rome, but in reinforcing marriage Stoic teaching was more important than legislation. Musonius Rufus was a strong proponent of marriage. A man has to act in the interest of his neighbours, not of himself alone. He should "take thought for his own city, and make of his home a rampart for protection. But the first step towards making his home a rampart is marriage."

> "One could find no other association more necessary nor more pleasant than that of men and women. For what man is so devoted to his friends as a loving wife is to her husband? ... All men consider the love of man and wife to be the highest form of love."

At the same time he extolled a high level of discipline within marriage. He maintained that sexual intercourse was justified only when it occurs in marriage for the purpose of begetting children.

> "Of all sexual relations those involving adultery are most unlawful, and no more tolerable than those of men with men, because it is a monstrous thing and contrary to nature ... In this category belongs the man who has relations with his own slave-maid, a thing which some people consider quite without blame, but if it seems neither shameful nor out of place for a master to have relations with his own slave, particularly if she happens to be unmarried, let him consider how he would like it if his wife

had relations with a male slave."

People were hungry for encouragement and hope. Plutarch, a contemporary of Musonius, lived in the Greek province of Boeotia, far distant from the hectic life of the capital and so not subject to exile. But, though in a cultural backwater, his teaching reached far and wide - teaching which was in large part straight advice on how to live, pleasantly written and illustrated by stories: how to have a happy marriage, how to bring up children and educate one's sons (daughters omitted! though he dearly loved and grieved for his own daughter when she died young), how to read poetry ... For to him and his many readers literature and history could be powerful moulding influences for good.

In his home, surrounded by relatives as well as his wife and children, Plutarch held "a kind of unofficial academy of letters, unorganised, informal" (though only the men participated). He would start the discussion with a talk - sometimes more like a sermon. At the end he would invite those with moral difficulties to remain and be open about their faults and spiritual troubles. This great healer of souls, who also served as a priest at Delphi, had found a faith in the one God, supreme eternal Being and benevolent Providence. Unusually for those days, his kindness and affection extended also to animals.

His philosophy of marriage was that physical union is "the beginning of friendship ... like a joint participation in some great ceremony: pleasure is short but respect, kindness, mutual affection and loyalty" daily spring from it. "In marriage, to love is a greater boon than to be loved: it rescues us from many errors - or rather from all errors that wreck or impair wedlock", notably "the petty, continual, daily clashes between man and wife." When each spouse enters into the concerns of the other and they work together, the partnership which results has the strength of a rope whose strands are intertwined.

His advice was practical. On the old-fashioned system of eating separately, he said: "Men who do not like to see their wives eat in their company are thus teaching them to stuff themselves when alone."

When girls were educated, correspondence between spouses became possible. During his absences on government business, the younger Pliny felt keenly his separation from Calpurnia.

"Indeed I should worry when you are away even if you are well, for there are always anxious moments without news of anyone one loves dearly ... So do please think of my anxiety and write to me once or twice a day ...

"I like to think that you miss me, and find relief in this sort of consolation. I too am always reading your letters, and returning to them again and again as if they were new to me - but this only fans the fire of my longing for you."

Pliny's caring and affection extended into a wider circle of family and friends. To Corella Hispulla about the education of her son, he writes:

> "We must look for a tutor in Latin rhetoric whose school shall combine a strict training along with good manners and, above all, moral standards; for, as our boy happens to be endowed with striking physical beauty among his natural gifts, at this dangerous time of life he needs more than a teacher."

He also brought together a number of parents in his town (Como) to form an association for setting up and running their own school. This was the more altruistic on his part, since he and Calpurnia, to their regret, were childless.

The coming of Christianity strengthened the marriage bond and the concept of partnership of husband and wife as a caring relationship - even if not a completely equal one. But whether or not influenced by Christianity, Ausonius, a poet of the Late Empire, shows genuine warmth in celebrating his wife Sabina whom he lost early in married life - she was only 27, and he never married again. "Through these six and thirty years, unwedded I have mourned and mourn you still ... Cheerful, modest, staid, famed for high birth as famed for beauty ... Age has crept over me, but yet I cannot lull my pain that my house is still silent and that my bed is cold, and that I share not my ills with anyone, my good with anyone. These things feed my wound."

With the collapse of the Western Empire education for girls (other than in household matters) became rare, as it did also for the great majority of boys. The Western world had to wait until the Renaissance for the educated woman to take her place as a fully intimate and co-operative partner with her equally - or more probably more - educated husband. The reappearance of this ideal of married partnership marks a new step forward in the civilisation of the West.

Comment: The family and marriage in Ancient Rome; the women's demonstration against the lex Oppia; compulsive viewing of the games; the lex Clodia, "bread and circuses", and the element of popular democracy; Aristophanes and decadence. Stoic views on "togetherness" in marriage; Pliny the Younger, Calpurnia and women's letters; Ausonius. (p. 272)

CHAPTER FOUR

THE IMPACT OF THE SPIRITUAL UPSURGE

1. **Roman decadence**: *permissiveness and cruelty; dole and "games"; carnage and mass sadism; gladiators and chariot races. Juvenal's* Satires *on decadence.*

Legislation to improve morality is of limited value without strong public support, and this was lacking in the early Empire. Permissiveness and an addiction to cruelty combined to plunge Rome in two or three generations into such a cultural morass that the foundations of State and society were threatened. The "games" which became compulsive viewing for many in vast arenas like the Colosseum had originated as funerary celebrations, having something of the idea of sacrifices in honour of the deceased. But the shows became inflated as ambitious politicians saw in them a way of buying popularity. In the high summer of the Republic in 216 BC, three sons had honoured their father (a Consul) by financing games with 22 pairs of gladiators. A century and a half later Julius Caesar put up 320 pairs (though his father had been dead for twenty years).

The constituency which politicians like Caesar were wooing was in large part composed of the unemployed or semi-employed. Besides "circuses" there was bread - a free provision of bread, pork and oil for every male inhabitant of Rome with the status of citizen, according to the lex Clodia of 58 BC. But whereas these rations were for only part of the population, and were not on a scale to meet the full needs of the recipient families, circuses could be increased *ad lib*. When Titus opened the Colosseum, he inaugurated 11 days of fighting with gladiators and animals, and to celebrate Trajan's conquest of Dacia there were 117 days, when 11,000 animals were killed and 10,000 gladiators fought.

Prisoners of war, criminals, persecuted individuals of both sexes were sent to horrible deaths mauled by fierce animals kept hungry for the purpose. Fights between gladiators were often to the death. Sea-battles were simulated. Mass executions took place. Animals of all kinds were set to fight each other or were butchered in vast numbers.

The carnage was terrifying - deliberately so. The one-time religious element was parodied by dressing those about to be killed as priests and priestesses, and parading them on stage - then stripping them naked for slaughter. What is striking is the way in which these gruesome and demoralising spectacles became accepted at all levels of the population. It needed an unusually thoughtful and sensitive man like Seneca to revolt against the system, and it took many decades even after the Christian Empire was established to abolish the worst of these spectacles.

This mass voyeurism of cruelty arose from the fact that cruelty on a great scale had long been accepted as a necessary social discipline. "Decimation" meant that if a military unit was thought not to have done its best in battle, one out of every ten men was selected to be clubbed to death by his comrades - a drastic way "pour encourager les autres". Crucifixion may have been taken over from the Persians - anyway it became the usual way of dealing with those rebels or criminals who were not tortured to death in prisons or exterminated in the arena. When the slave revolt under Spartacus was crushed 6000 slaves were crucified all along the Appian Way from Capua to Rome, and the Jewish revolt in the next century (67-70 AD) was marked by thousands of crosses on the hills around Jerusalem.

Rome's might was originally due to the battle-quality and discipline of her peasant-soldiers. By imperial times Romans, and even other Italians, seldom saw military service, unless they were upper-class professionals. The shows in the arenas were therefore substitutes for the real thing. Fights staged between bands of gladiators, with carnage as of the battlefields, took the place of the old realities - matched by the fierce partisanship of the equally popular, but less savage, chariot-races. In our modern age football matches play a similar role to the latter, with the same accretions of violence and materialistic motives. For some thoughtful Romans living in the later Republic and under the Empire, it was undoubtedly a time of decadence, a falling away from the virtues and sound morals of the old republican days. "We have now reached a point where our degeneracy is intolerable," wrote Livy in the preface to his *History*. Since the foundation of the Empire it had been a story of "decline in discipline and moral standards, the collapse and disintegration of morality." And Juvenal demands "who could endure this monstrous city, however callous at heart, and swallow his wrath?"

Juvenal's tirade against married women looks back to those times when - with poetic licence - he paints them as having lived exemplary lives. But now

> " ... we are suffering
> the evils of a too-long peace. Luxury, deadlier
> than any armed invader, lies like an incubus
> upon us still, avenging the world we brought to heel.

" ... Filthy
lucre it was that first brought these loose foreign
morals amongst us, enervating wealth that
destroyed us, over the years, through shameless self-indulgence.

" ... Though our armies have advanced
to Ireland, though the Orkneys are ours, and northern Britain
with its short clear nights, these conquered tribes abhor
the vices that flourish in their conquerors' capital."

In denouncing these evils with such force Juvenal followed
earlier writers who had developed this powerful and distinctive type
of literature.   The satiric spirit had pervaded Aristophanes and the
New Comedy, and had flowered in the maxims of the Cynic
philosopher Menippus of Gadara.   The Roman writer Marcus
Terentius Varro (1st century BC) naturalised the art in his mostly lost
diatribes against social evils such as effeminacy and paederasty.
     It is noticeable in the Satires that the men are usually weak, but
the women are strong personalities - unfortunately for doing evil
rather than good - though Juvenal certainly does not spare the men.

"What's all your blue blood worth
if you slip out by night, wrapped in a hooded cloak,
to commit adultery?"

He is also disillusioned about marriage, so often marred by
adultery and ended by divorce - though some of the alternatives he
suggests to his friends are less than morally acceptable.   The point
about Juvenal's tirades is that he felt strongly, explosively about the
evils which were rotting society.

" ... Corruption comes by degrees.
After a while you will find yourself taken up
by a very queer fraternity ... O Father of our City,
what brought your simple shepherd people to such a pitch
of blasphemous perversion?"

Satire was one reaction to the evils of the time, pointing the
contrasts between the high civilisation that people were enjoying and
the sordid realities of their living.   As Juvenal saw it -

"Today the whole world
has its Graeco-Roman culture. Smart Gaulish professors
are training the lawyers of Britain: even in Iceland

there's talk of setting up a Rhetorical Faculty."

Eumolpus, a character in the *Satyricon* by Petronius, though far from a model of virtue himself, says

> "...we are so besotted with drink, so
> steeped in debauchery, that we lack the strength even to study
> the great achievements of the past ...
> Why, even prayers for health and soundness of mind are
> out of fashion nowadays. Money is our only prayer."

Another reaction however *was* through prayer and reflection to search for the sources of spiritual strength and rediscover a firm moral foundation for living. There was a wistful hope on the part of some that the antique virtues could be restored, that some authority would arise - a God-inspired person perhaps who would bring people together and restore vigorous life and sound morality to the declining cities. But the great days of the city were over. It could no longer provide the satisfaction and certainties of the past. Juvenal comments on those living on the dole, with entertainments provided by the State or the rich as their main occupation.

> "Nowadays, with no vote to sell, their motto
> is "couldn't care less". Time was when their plebiscite elected
> Generals, Heads of State, commanders of legions: but now
> they've pulled in their horns, there's only two things that
> concern them: bread and the Games."

For the more thoughtful there could still be hope, and Juvenal has a word for them.

> "If you want my advice,
> let the Gods determine what's most appropriate
> for mankind, and what best suits our various circumstances.
> They'll give us the things we need, not those we want: a man
> is dearer to them than he is to himself ...
> What I've shown you, you could find by yourself: there's one
> path, and one only, to a life of peace - through virtue."

During the later Empire well-intentioned legislation supported private benevolence to curb evils and humanise life. Laws were passed to alleviate the lot of the slave, to endow schools and scholarships, to establish charities. But Government became too corrupt to do the good it wished to do, and therefore inevitably lost authority to enforce its decrees. After the crisis of the late second and third centuries AD, the reforms of Diocletian brought back stability. But these reforms were made at the cost of state-enforced rigidity, tying people to status, class, professions and land in a thoroughgoing totalitarian mould. The free guilds or collegia were taken over by the authorities and turned into fixed groupings of men in their various trades or occupations - shipowners, merchants, builders - all articulated into a corporate state organised and directed from above.

"It is wealth, not God, that compels our deepest reverence," Juvenal had written. The love of lucre proved too strong for the officials whose pay may often have been irregular, sometimes in debased coin or in foodstuffs exacted by a bankrupt state in lieu of money-taxes. Officials sent as inspectors - *curiosi* or others - themselves proved too corrupt to continue in their jobs, and in yet another "reform" would be swept away to be replaced by other officials who in due course went the same way.

The Senate became a rubber-stamp, elections in local government ceased, the Emperor became a despot like the ruler of Persia, living in similar style. While the rich became flagrantly richer, the poor, harassed by tax-gatherers and task-masters, were reduced to the depths of misery. Evading the laws that tied them to land, job or profession, people escaped in droves from "a cruel servitude and the chaos of administration." Brigands moved in gangs up to the gates of Rome itself. Parents exposed children or sold them into slavery. Public buildings were vandalised (sometimes literally by Vandals) and fell into decay. The imperial posting service and other services on the roads became disorganised. The troops long settled on the frontiers melted away as the barbarians pressed inexorably through. Cities, no longer safe, became deserted, and plague speeded the process of depopulation.

Comment: lex Clodia; Menippus; Petronius. (p. 274)

2. The Christian leaven: *religions from the east; conversion and new life; The Golden Ass; Isis, the Great Goddess, Mithras. Pliny and Christians; Christians and Jews: beginning of antisemitism; Christian and Jewish martyrs; the Church's appeal; persecutions; Constantine and the Church's triumph; staying-power of paganism; the old order doomed.*

Through all the upheavals and invasions that marked the later Roman Empire, the groundswell of heightening spirituality continued, with many thousands turning to the religions of the east for comfort and moral guide-lines. Emperors might come and go - many briefly elected by provincial legions before meeting untimely ends - the barbarians might press on the frontiers, pirates might obstruct the sea-lanes and brigands disrupt transport, but the seekers after wisdom and new life continued to grow in numbers and in strength.

Conversion and a new life - the idea was in the air. This is expressed in the novel by Lucius Apuleius, *The Golden Ass*. The hero, transformed by magic which goes wrong into an ass, has every kind of adventure which traditional story-telling and exuberant fantasy could suggest: but then comes a new note in the dénouement. Lucius is duly changed back into a man through the intervention of Isis and her priests, with a thorough conversion as the result, consummated by the initiation experience. The High Priest tells him:

> "Lucius, rescued from a dreadful fate,... to secure today's gains you must enrol yourself in this holy Order ... voluntarily undertaking the duties to which your oath binds you: for her service is perfect freedom."

So Lucius became "a loyal devotee of the great Goddess", and prepared himself by abstinence and chastity as one chosen to be "born again and restored to new and healthy life."

Apuleius is one of those for whom the old deities have become figures of fun with their all too human rivalries and jealousies (as in the story of Cupid and Psyche which he inserts into *The Golden Ass*). They might be equated with the newcomers from the east, who impressed with their dramatic rituals, their priesthoods and processions, their initiations, baptisms and confessions. Traders and seamen brought the Isis religion with them from Egypt and the Great Goddess from Syria. The soldiers brought Mithras and the Sun-God whose original home was Persia - a religion with a high moral challenge set against the background of cosmic war between the powers of good and evil. With Mithras came also the ritual of drenching the neophyte in blood from a slaughtered bull - a ritual which was shared with believers in the Great Mother, Cybele.

Since these cults had similarities with the Christian love-feast, they were regarded by the Fathers of the Church as demoniac parodies. Until the Church triumphed under Constantine it was not clear which body of believers was likely to predominate during this period of intense ideological conflict.

When the younger Pliny was sent as a special commissioner to the Black Sea province of Bithynia at the end of the first century, he was uncertain how to handle the Christians whom he found there, and wrote for guidance to the Emperor Trajan. While awaiting instructions from Rome he had no hesitation in sending to their death those who asserted their faith, unless they were Roman citizens, when they were to be sent for trial to Rome. He asks "whether it is the mere name of Christian which is punishable, even if innocent of crime, or rather the crimes associated with the name."

In fact there were no crimes, as far as he could see, which they had been committing. Some, whose names were given to him by an informer, said they had ceased to be Christians, and demonstrated it by doing reverence to the Emperor's statue and the images of the gods, and by reviling the name of Christ.

"They also declared that the sum total of their guilt and error amounted to no more than this: they had met regularly before dawn on a fixed day to chant verses alternately among themselves in honour of Christ as if to a god, and also to bind themselves by oath, not for any criminal purpose, but to abstain from theft, robbery and adultery, to commit no breach of trust and not deny a deposit when called upon to restore it. After this ceremony it had been their custom to disperse and reassemble later to take food of an ordinary, harmless kind; but they had given up this practice since my edict, issued on your instructions, which banned all political societies. This made me decide it was all the more necessary to extract the truth by torture from two slave-women, whom they call deaconesses. I found nothing but a degenerate sort of cult carried to extravagant lengths."

He concludes that he thinks the question worthy of the Emperor's consideration, since "not only the towns, but the villages and rural districts too are infected through contact with this wretched cult. I think though that it is still possible for it to be checked and directed to better ends, for there is no doubt that people have begun to throng the temples which had been almost entirely deserted for a long time ... It is easy to infer from this that a great many people could be reformed if they were given an opportunity to repent."

The service described by the witnesses followed the pattern of Jewish morning services, the agape or communion taking place later in the day. Since the first Christians had been Jews the liturgy grew out of Jewish forms of worship. Peter, Paul and other early evangelists gave their message to both Jews and non-Jewish "God-fearers" who formed a substantial fringe around the synagogues - the God-fearers finding the message particularly acceptable, since it contained the essence of Judaism in its teaching about God and its moral challenge, together with the Gospel, while not entailing circumcision and other requirements of that faith. But this was the reason why stricter Jews opposed Paul. The quarrel, described in Galatians and Acts, coloured the Gospel story (written after the events in Galatians) and had a part in Christian antisemitism.

Before the time arrived when the Christians were in a position to inflict atrocities on Jews, they suffered, along with Jews, at the hands of the Roman authorities or mobs. Both Christians and Jews stood uncompromisingly by their faith - many of them under the severest persecution - rejecting worship of idols and reverence to images, even that of the Emperor, which might have been regarded as merely a political gesture. Christians, like Jews, believed themselves to be the people of God, distinct from the unregenerate mass of humanity; in the public view they were a peculiar people, not only in their beliefs but in a way of life which set them apart from their fellow-men. Insidious and violent propaganda could easily stir up mob violence. Racialism could be an aggravating factor, since in Rome and the western Empire Christians, like Jews, were often immigrants from the east. Both were in a similar position to Jews in Germany 1900 years later - convenient scapegoats for the ills of State and society, blameable for anything which went wrong. Nero blamed on the Christians the fire which destroyed part of Rome in 64 AD, and Paul was probably among those who perished in the persecution.

Besides large-scale persecutions ordered by the government from time to time, veritable pogroms took place with the connivance of the authorities, but the steadfastness of Christians in the face of death or under torture was one of the strongest recommendations for the faith and won multitudes of new believers. At Lyons in 177 AD popular fury broke out against the Christians, who were mostly recent immigrants from the east. The fearful sufferings of the martyrs, described by a survivor in a letter to the mother-Church in Asia Minor, can still arouse strong feelings of pity and astonishment in a generation inured to the stories of torture and brutality which have become almost commonplace in the 20th century. Men, women and boys were hunted out, imprisoned in the vilest conditions, tortured many times over, resuscitated, put to the beasts in the amphitheatre, and finally - if they still lived - despatched by fire in the "iron chair". Encouraging one another, these won the martyr's crown by their steadfastness in the name of Christ.

The teaching of the Sermon on the Mount and the "splendid and stringent moral code" which each candidate for baptism had to accept, when "every sin was tracked to its lurking-place within", went far beyond the challenge of its rivals, and for this reason had for many the greatest possible attraction. Although the work of the apostles and travelling teachers was an essential part of spreading the Gospel, it was the way of life as lived by most ordinary Christians during the early period of the Church which was impressive. "For over a century and a half it ranked everything almost secondary to the supreme task of maintaining its morality" - its mission "might be described as a moral enterprise, as the awakening and strengthening of the moral sense." It demonstrated on a hitherto undreamed of scale the way in which men and women could care for each other, in maintaining their commitment and fulfilling their duties, with a thorough-going service of help for the sick and for those otherwise in need. The fact that Christians also included pagans in their relief work during times of famine or plague further enhanced their appeal.

The writers and historians of the time show clearly that it was not only the citizens of Rome and Corinth who needed the thunderous challenge of St. Paul for their easy tolerance of immorality, perversion and over-indulgence in food and drink. "Make no mistake: no fornicator or idolater, none who are guilty either of adultery or of homosexual perversion, no thieves or grabbers or drunkards or slanderers or swindlers, will possess the kingdom of God."

By the end of the first century AD, not only were people reaching out to the new spirituality which they found in the religions from the east, particularly Christianity, but the old religion was having a revival. In fact paganism was to fight a stubborn rearguard action before it was vanquished, and it took another three centuries for that to happen. Even then the victory of the Church was sometimes of appearance rather than reality, when old deities continued to be worshipped under new names and "lamps burning before the image of the Virgin took the place of those before the family gods." When pagan festivals, like the chief festival of Mithras, 25th December, were appropriated for Christian purposes, pagan elements were sometimes willy-nilly included.

The Church triumphed in the end because of those who took their stand even unto death when faced by pressure and persecution. Many compromised or abandoned the faith when under attack, but the conviction of those who stood firm, especially of the martyrs, was decisive. Jesus who had been crucified by a Roman Governor and who had risen again, was a real person - not just historical because still present, and so exerted a more powerful appeal and evoked a deeper adoration than any god or goddess of legend. There was also the hope which Christianity gave - more than any other religion, Judaism apart, it looked forward to a great event. The Second Coming should usher in a new heaven and a new earth, in contrast with older religions which located the Golden Age firmly in the past. And without having to wait for the new dispensation, it was always open to the Christian, if he or she lived the life or gained the martyr's crown, to have a place in heaven.

But paganism was strongly rooted. The repeated decrees against it, after Christianity had been made the official religion, show that it was as difficult to eradicate as corruption - against which decrees flowed from the Government, with perhaps even less effect. The temples were shorn of much of their glory when in 410 AD Alaric's Germans occupied Rome, and gold, silver and jewellery were taken in order to make up the ransom. Only after that were the temples closed, and some converted to churches. It took time for the Christian leaven to have its effect. The horrible gladiatorial shows continued for some decades after the dramatic intervention and martyrdom of St. Almachius (Telemachus) in the arena (392 AD).

Comment: Roman novels: *The Golden Ass* and *The Aethiopica*; Trajan's reply to Pliny about the Christians; Roman repression of Jewish revolts; variations in policy towards Jews; martyrs as "the seed of the Church" and other ways in which Christianity appealed to pagans; training and discipline; Philo; Romans and Jews. (p. 276)

3. **Constantine and Byzantium**: *The change from old to new; immigrants. The epoch of empires; bureaucracy and the divinised autocrat as the pattern. Economic strength of the East. The new capital. Reforms. The end of Hellenism. Conflicts of ideas. Waning of rationalism. Byzantium's great age.*

For long the old coexisted with the new. Fortunately for the adherents of the rival rites, the Church did not immediately persecute - it had its own internal problems to solve, particularly in formulating its doctrines. Though disagreeing in matters of faith, and involved in public controversy over the question of restoring the Altar of Victory to the Senate House, the senate leader Quintus Aurelius Symmachus and his kinsman St. Ambrose, Bishop of Milan, continued on friendly terms.

At that point, the end of the 4th century, not only the old religion but the old order as a whole was doomed. The spiritual upsurge which had brought Christianity to power changed peoples' outlook and attitude, eventually even the great establishment families with their vested interests in the status quo.

In another way change was effected by the influx of war-bands and immigrants, Germans, Scandinavians and Slavs. Some of these were accepted as allies for frontier duties, while others forced a passage by arms, as did raiders like the Huns. The legions for long kept multitudes of would-be immigrants out, but a dramatic failure of this policy came about through the Roman defeat at Adrianople in 378 AD.

The pressure on the frontiers was increasing as Gothic tribes tried to escape from the Huns swarming out of central Asia. A large number of Visigoths were given permission to cross the Danube and settle in the relatively empty areas of northern Greece - it was expected that as "federates" they would prove an excellent strengthening of the Roman army. But the Visigoths were not properly looked after, and in some cases were badly treated by the Roman commanders, two in particular, Lupicinus and Maximus.

"Their treacherous greed was the source of all our evils. I say nothing of the crimes which these two men, or at least others with their permission, with the worst of motives, committed against the foreign newcomers, who were as yet blameless; but one melancholy and unheard-of act shall be mentioned ... When the barbarians after their crossing were harassed by lack of food, those most hateful generals devised a disgraceful traffic; they exchanged every dog that their insatiability could gather from far and wide for one slave each, and among these were carried off also sons of the chieftains." (Report by the contemporary historian Ammianus Marcellinus).

As if providing only dogs as food, and in this inexcusable way, was not enough to antagonise the Goths, Lupicinus then murdered the attendants of two chiefs while they were dining with him. The chiefs got away, and the whole tribe then gathered for revenge. After defeating the Romans at Marcianopolis, the Visigoths were joined by Ostrogoths who had crossed the now undefended Danube, as well as by Huns and warriors of the other tribes.

The decisive battle took place near Adrianople in 378 AD, when a whirlwind charge by Gothic horsemen dispersed the Roman cavalry, leaving the legionaries to be squeezed together and trampled down - only a few escaped. The Emperor Valens was killed. Ravaging and massacres followed. Fortunately for the Romans an allied force of Saracen cavalry stiffened the remains of their army in defeating a joint attack by Goths, Alans and Huns, and Constantinople was saved by its walls. Eventually the Government had to do the best it could in settling these immigrants on the land, incorporating some into the army, which it might have done in the first place. But it did not return to this sensible policy without one more Katyn-like slaughtering of a large number who had already been accepted as soldiers.

The Empire was at its worst and only created more problems by acts of treachery and not keeping its word - a fault of which some modern governments have also been blameworthy. In fact it was remarkable for its ability to absorb ethnic groups. In the West it had successfully transformed Spaniards, Gauls and Britons into good citizens. But the Western Government after the division of the Empire became permanent (end of the fourth century) was unable either to keep out or absorb the mass immigration of Visi- and Ostrogoths, Vandals and others who flooded in after the frontiers were breached in 406-7.

The Eastern Government, having learnt the lesson of Adrianople, relied on diplomacy rather than force in dealing with would-be immigrants. Increasing numbers were steadily settled in the Balkans, and when - though not until murderous wars had been fought - a Bulgarian kingdom was established there, the Government of Constantinople was able to win on the cultural level what it had lost on the political and military. The spearhead of its advance, in a great process of cultural radiation, were the missionaries. Acceptance of Christianity meant that the Orthodox Church, with its buildings and liturgy, its monasteries and manuscripts, its icons and embroideries - the whole paraphernalia of Byzantine culture - became part of Bulgaria, and eventually of Russia and other East European countries. It was axiomatic that acceptance of the faith meant accepting in some degree the supremacy of the Emperor. Even before the Bulgars had settled in the land to which they gave their name, their ruler Orhan had been baptised at Constantinople with the Emperor Heraclius as his godfather. Two other Emperors married princesses of the Khazars (though this tribe eventually embraced Judaism). Titles were bestowed on tribal chieftains, who acknowledged "the ideal sovereignty" of the Emperor. In this way was established a community of states to which the term "the Byzantine Commonwealth" has been applied.

Besides those who were trying to get in, many had been forcibly brought in, as slaves captured in war, or bought through dealers. Though many people besides slaves were under restrictions, tied to their land, cities or jobs, there was still scope for movement within the Empire, so that by the third century there was already a considerable mix of population notably in Italy.

At the same time there were parts of the Empire where it was not so much a question of people trying to get in, but rather of trying to get out, or at least establish their cultural and spiritual autonomy (for the two always go together). The situation parallels that of the British Empire - Irish flooding into England in the nineteenth century, while other Irish fought for their country's independence; Indians and Pakistanis gaining independence, while a flood of would-be immigrants press against the restrictions and the well-defended points of entry to Britain. The same could also be said of parts of the former French Empire: the embarrassment caused to the French Government by the existing immigrant communities, especially from North Africa, with a resulting policy of blocking further immigration. "Guest-workers" elsewhere cause similar problems.

Rome, which had ceased for many years to be the effective capital, was sacked by Alaric and his Goths, while the panic-stricken populace vainly sought protection for themselves and their possessions. The Empire itself was torn asunder. In the east, with a strong base in the capital, Constantinople, the old order survived longer but was imperceptibly transformed. As in the west, amidst decadence and disaster, the stirrings of new life appeared. New forms of culture, changes in society and institutions, even in the art of war - all these led to a renewal of the eastern part of the Empire and the birth of Byzantine civilisation, while in the west a Latin-based civilisation took shape.

From 300 BC onwards empires dominated the civilised areas from Europe to the Far East: the empires of Alexander and his successors; Rome and Parthia; the Mauryan and Gupta Empires in India; and the Han Empire in China. Important religions flourished, which helped to preserve or reconstitute the empires: Christianity in Byzantium, Zoroastrianism in Sassanid Iran, Buddhism and Hinduism in India, and eventually Islam in the empire of the Ommayad and Abbasid Caliphs. Of these reconstituted empires, the eastern part of the Roman Empire, Byzantium, was left after the West had relapsed into barbarism.

One institution in particular distinguished the empires of those days - the bureaucracy. A civil service could be dispensed with in a city-state like Athens, where the various administrative functions were carried out by those elected in turn for this work. But empires like the Roman, Byzantine and Sassanian could only function with reasonable efficiency by virtue of office-holders with long-term or permanent tenure - salaried officials concerned with particular sectors like finance, organised as departments of state under a chief minister acting for the Emperor. The Church - Christian, Zoroastrian or whatever - was managed as a department of state.

The pattern for empires had been set at their first appearing, when the whole society was rooted in religion, with no distinction between religion and politics. Pharaoh was "a god by whose dealings one lives, the father and mother of all men." He owned the whole land, every one worked for him; on him depended the order of the universe, the changing of the seasons, the life-giving flooding of the Nile. All subsequent empires were in the same mould, or tended to reproduce it, with a divinised ruler on whom everyone and everything depended, and whose lives he ordered with the aid of the bureaucracy. So it was in Byzantium - by contrast with the West, where Church and State evolved along different lines, eventually to form secular, democratic states. Russia, as Byzantium's heir claiming to be the "Third Rome", took "Caesar" (Czar or Tsar) as its emperor's title, with semi-divine and autocratic attributes. And though Peter the Great laid no claim to divinity, he made the Church more than ever a department of state, strengthening the autocracy which persisted even after the downfall of tsardom. Stalin's cult of personality came near to being a secularised version of the divine ruler, with Marxism taking the place of Orthodox Christianity as the faith of the citizens.

Italy, and with it Rome, had flourished as long as its economic base was strong, both as the market to which goods flowed from every quarter by land and sea, and as a hub of industry exporting pottery and products of all kinds for household use, as well as gold and silver ware and other objects of luxury. But before long industries grew up in the provinces, in Gaul, Spain and elsewhere, rivalling or eclipsing Italy - as in our day first America and now Japan, Singapore and Hongkong have overtaken and in many cases surpassed the industries of Europe. Wars and invaders speeded the process. For all his heroic efforts Marcus Aurelius had not been able to prevent the ravaging of North Italy by the Marcomanni. Craftsmen and businesses had emigrated eastwards, and though the East too suffered invasion, it remained an area of high production and taxable capacity.

If it had not been for a sound economic base and strong defences with well-trained forces, the Eastern Roman Empire would never have survived as the chrysalis for Byzantine civilisation. Much of its territory was richer than most western parts, especially the towns as trading-centres. The tax system, though it bore harshly on many of the population, was able to produce the resources for buying off invaders and sustaining the costly administration and defence. These advantages however would not have availed without some extremely capable rulers backed by generals and administrators of distinction, with the Church playing an essential role in supplying the mystique and spiritual leadership. Of the rulers Constantine I was the most outstanding, changing the course of history by his four major acts of statesmanship: reorganising the Empire, restoring the currency, making Christianity the official religion, and founding Constantinople.

The site of the new capital was an inspired choice, both because its highly defensible situation, strengthened by massive walls, made it almost impregnable, and because of its strategic position between Asia and Europe. The choice of Byzantion (its original name) was sound at a time when the Empire's centre of gravity was moving eastwards, while its situation between the Black Sea and the Mediterranean, with one of the finest natural harbours in the world, ensured its predominance in commerce. It is as if Churchill or some other statesman of vision, presiding over a great empire in decline, could have moved the capital to Singapore, building defences across the Johore Peninsula as strong as those which for a millennium held off all aggressors coming down from Thrace. The city was still vulnerable if a hostile navy pierced the Dardanelles or Bosphorus. When the Arabs succeeded in this exploit they might indeed have gained the city but for the Byzantine secret weapon of Greek fire. The Byzantine victories in the sieges of 668-75 and 716-8 ensured the survival of the new civilisation.

The site was carefully utilised to incorporate features of old Rome. The imperial palace with its grounds stretching down to the sea was next to the hippodrome; there were forums, arenas, triumphal arches and processional ways but instead of temples there were churches. Also, as in Rome, there had to be a *plebs*: a proletariat free from taxation and dependent on a dole of rations, with amusements provided - chariot races and gladiatorial "games" (which divided them into sometimes frenzied factions). There Constantine took up his residence, and thither he attracted some wealthy provincial families, and tried to cajole senatorial families from Rome, for his new Rome had to have a Senate too. He also brought in a sizeable bureaucracy.

Not all the ineptitude of the bureaucracy, the corruption of officials, the conspicuous waste of rulers and their lavish building programmes, not even the endless and costly wars could undermine the capacity of the East Roman populace to pay. The burden fell heaviest on the peasants, and though families were forced to sell out to the landowners or flee for protection elsewhere, the money could still be extracted in areas under government control. When the Germans poured in after the battle of Adrianople, taxation became hypothetical on the lands where they were settled. But other territories, such as North Africa, though lost, were sometimes reconquered and then continued to pay their dues. A reforming emperor like Anastasius could make the system more efficient. His "vindices" brought in the money sufficient to finance the running of the Empire and leave a hefty balance in the treasury when he died.

In large part the success of the economy was the consequence of Constantine's currency reform. The solidus, fixed at 4·48 grammes of gold, remained with that value for a thousand years (until devalued in the latter days of Byzantium) as the major international currency of Western Asia and Europe, and the standard whereby in the Empire all salaries and perquisites were reckoned.

However inefficient by modern standards, the Byzantine bureaucracy threw up some first class administrators and not a few reformers. All except the most senior posts were up for sale, but the fact that these were appointments on merit - in this differing from practice in the West - was undoubtedly one reason for the survival of the State.

The burden of military expenditure and the needs of a numerous bureaucracy meant high taxes had to be wrung from people "diminished by plague and impoverished by constant wars ... What was required in governors and procurators was ruthless efficiency rather than scrupulous probity." Some honest governors were to be found, though "it showed exceptional merit even to be honest." At the same time important reforms were made, particularly by emperors of genuine faith. Constantine instituted the sabbath rest on Sunday, and improved the position of women by reforms in the divorce laws, with severe measures against adultery and rape, while giving legal sanction to Church regulations regarding deaconesses, virgins and widows. He legislated against gladiatorial games - they took time to die out before Anastasius formally abolished them. Anastasius also tried to abolish obscene mime shows, but since this was impossible, subsequent regulations were made to prevent students attending them. For the poorer people even more important were Anastasius' tax reforms, which made the highly regressive taxes bear less harshly on them, and relieved them in times of want. High officials of the court became in some cases renowned for their charitable giving. The condition of slaves was improved. Geriatric homes, hospitals and orphanages were established. An outstanding case of a high official taking responsibility for curbing an evil was that of Florentius, whose keenness to have the law against prostitution at Constantinople implemented led him to donate an estate of his own to the Government, so that the rent would compensate for the tax on brothel-keepers which it stood to lose if they went out of business.

During the decades following Constantine the hold of paganism weakened. "Newly built churches became alternative centres of urban life, offering legal asylum to fugitives, becoming places where slaves too, could be legally freed, where big crowds could meet inside buildings for worship and where people could even expect to find a suitable girlfriend."

The great families of the old order in Rome and other cities were dying out; their successors, if not yet Christians, were not swayed as before by motives making for ostentatious largesse, and their support for the pagan cults dwindled. "The old forms of civic education no longer survived to support them. After 325 we hear no more of the training of a city's youth ... linked with naked exercise, paganism and consenting homosexuality." The civic gymnasia and their officials gradually disappeared, a change which more than any other, it has been said, ended the epoch of Hellenism and brought in the Middle Ages.

The cultural renaissance did not lead to movements for political independence in the Byzantine Empire. But the movements for cultural and spiritual autonomy took the form of embracing doctrines at variance with those of the Emperor and Patriarch at Constantinople, since challenging the official ideology of the State was an important way of expressing dissidence.

The conflicts of ideas then and now have parallels, though the form is different. In those days they concerned the relation of the human and divine natures of Christ. Today the divisions are over various analyses of the social/economic situation, "capitalist" on the one hand, Marxist on the other. The establishment of objective truth, either on the theological or the sociological level, is difficult if not impossible. Ideas are used as the battle-cries of one power-group confronting another.

Despite humanitarianism, almsgiving and welfare work generally - which in scale went far beyond anything witnessed previously - the in-fighting of Christians about doctrine was passionate and obsessive, for similar motives to those which activate the proponents of left and right-wing views today. On the one hand there were the power-preoccupations of the clergy, notably of Alexandria, determined to maintain the pre-eminence of their ancient see against the upstart patriarchate of Constantinople; on another tack were the Egyptian people, reacting against the Greek-dominated Church and culture, and expressing their heritage of three thousand years through the liturgy in their own Coptic language and their devotion to the Monophysite doctrine (the single nature of Christ). A further element which aroused passion in the controversies was the devotion of the Egyptians to the Mother of God as an adaptation of their Isis faith.

Every switch in the line was debated in Church councils, and these were a refuge for the democratic principle originally pioneered by Athens, but now lifeless there and in the other cities where democracy, albeit limited, had once been practised. A strong emperor might impose a compromise, like Constantine at Nicaea, but the

Government did not necessarily succeed in having its own doctrine accepted - a fiery Alexandrian prelate like Athanasius was quite capable of overturning its plan. And if an emperor, like Anastasius, took the Monophysite line, thereby making the Egyptians and Syrians happy, the storm of opposition which arose at Constantinople could scarcely be contained, especially since the two main circus factions, Blues and Greens, took opposite sides in the controversy, with horrifying consequences for law and order. Doctrines about the ineffable could serve a similar purpose as blood-and-soil or class-war ideologies in channelling violence from the terraces to overtly political objectives.

The seventh century was the crisis of the civilisation of the East, starting with the reign of terror instigated by Phocas, who was projected on to the throne by a mutiny in the Balkans. This disgruntled officer, like many others before and since, had the capacity only to make a difficult situation worse, in fact to bring Byzantium to a dark age nadir. While chaos ruled at the capital it was attacked by Avars and Slavs, while the Persians overran Egypt and Syria/Palestine. The situation was only saved when Heraclius, the Governor's son from recently reconquered North Africa, killed the usurper, re-formed the demoralised army, and threw the Persians back. In a rare moment of unity the Patriarch Sergius gave the lead in an outburst of patriotic and religious enthusiasm. But no sooner was this heroic task accomplished than Egypt and the eastern provinces were again overwhelmed by another attack, unexpected and still more powerful, from the Arabs, inspired by their new Islamic faith.

The Muslim invasions cast a shadow over the last years of Heraclius, but they could not stifle the spirit which had inspired the citizens fighting for their city when almost all seemed lost, and then going on to recover their ravaged lands. With the Patriarch Sergius heading the chanting processions, the people had demonstrated their commitment to a life-and-death struggle for faith as well as for country. And when the counter-attack was launched it was in the spirit of a Crusade - several centuries before the West embarked on its holy wars.

The reign of Heraclius marks the watershed between the Byzantium of Justinian redolent of the "Late Antique", where Latin was still the language of the Court, and the Byzantium which was Greek, though not the Greek of Hellas, for all the backward looks to the Classic glories of the past. The Byzantines "never found their way back" to the great age of Greece, never penetrated beyond the rhetoricians and commentators of late Hellenistic times - just as in their work on the Bible they never (since St. Jerome's translation into Latin) got back to the Hebrew. The waning of the rational approach, pioneered by the Greeks of the Classical Age, had left a void in works of criticism and research which limited the literary value of monastic writing, though the debt is enormous to the monkish scribes who copied and preserved so much of the Classical legacy. The antiquarianism of the Late Antique persisted, centered now on sites and relics of Christ's passion, the Holy Family and saints, their lives embellished by hagiographies full of myths and legends.

The heartland of the Empire that remained intact, though more of a unity than before, still failed to gain ideological peace for many years. The image-breaking ("Iconoclast") movement was encouraged by emperors in the 8th century in order to maintain the allegiance of the Isaurians, a puritanical frontier people, whose commitment to the Empire's defence was a political and military necessity, but this roused the opposition of the powerful monasteries and their supporters. This fierce controversy raged, not without violence, for over a hundred years.

At its ending "the great age" of Byzantium began with the Macedonian Dynasty (867-1057), and reached its climax as the second millennium opened. This marked a moment of equilibrium between the three civilisations which now held the stage formerly occupied by Rome and Persia: the civilisations of Byzantium, the West, and Islam. It was during this period that the Caliph al-Hakam II sent an embassy to the Emperor Nicephoros, asking for artists to decorate the *mihrab* (the recess indicating the direction of Mecca) in the vast and magnificent Mezquita mosque of Cordoba. Nicephoros responded by sending not only a mosaic specialist, but also sixteen tons of stone and glass tesserae with which the still existing and resplendent feature was adorned.

For all its internal troubles and the constantly renewed attacks from powerful enemies, Byzantium survived to enjoy splendid periods of prosperity and imperial magnificence. Through its dependencies it irradiated east and west with its culture. The Dome of the Rock at Jerusalem and Monreale Cathedral in Sicily are largely Byzantine creations. Throughout the Dark and Middle Ages Byzantium was the exemplar of civilised and sophisticated society where - at least among the upper classes - forks, to the astonishment of westerners, were used as well as knives at table.

At the same time there was much that was barbaric, in common with the rest of Europe. Though Constantine stopped crucifixion, punishments remained unbelievably cruel. Blinding was freely resorted to, and was inflicted on war prisoners and claimants to the throne. Dissidents were also harshly treated, like Theodore, the reforming Abbot of the great Studios Monastery. He not only spoke out against image-breaking, but affirmed that religious affairs were matters for the Church and that the Emperor's sphere was only state administration. His followers were imprisoned and tortured, and himself almost killed by a hundred lashes. Poorer people suffered as they had suffered for centuries, from tax-gatherers, landlords and invaders. For them there was little justice, and if they tried for it in the courts it was expensive in bribes and fees.

But along with the evils there was much good. At least some of the sick were looked after in hospitals, and some of the aged in old peoples' homes. If medical knowledge did not advance, most of the gains of earlier times were maintained. By comparison with ancient Greece the position of women had improved. Though girls still had little opportunity for formal schooling, they were often taught their letters at home. Many women were readers of the scriptures and religious books, and taught their children to be readers too. Some distinguished themselves as the wives of rulers or as empresses in their own right, some as saints and at least one as a historian of note, Anna Comnena, a princess of the imperial house.

Comment: *Foederati* and their treatment by the Romans; Ammianus Marcellinus; what was Constantine converted to? Anastasius I; girlfriend in church; St. Athanasius; faction-fighting: Blues and Greens at Constantinople; monks and street-demonstrations at Alexandria; Iconoclasm; the revival of scholarship during Byzantium's "great age". (p. 278)

4. **Art and Architecture**: *New life, new forms. Christian influence: Ravenna mosaics; Hagia Sophia.*

The cultural changes in the empire were part of a renaissance in the Near and Middle East, stemming from the reaction of non-Greek peoples to the Hellenism which had become the dominant culture. Not that the reaction was a total rejection. It led to "new versions of the great civilisations of the past, developed in their respective areas under the ... stimulating influence of the Greek Hellenistic civilisation ... the spectacular Gupta renaissance in India, and the Sasanian renaissance of the Parthian and Sakian Greco-Iranian civilisations; and the brilliant growth of a peculiar civilisation and art in Mesopotamia and Syria."

This last area, between the Euphrates and Tigris, was the principal seed ground of the new and revived cultures that sprang up - a renaissance which owed little or nothing to political changes, but was inspired by the coming of Christianity as it fused with the Greek spirit surviving in various modified forms. Such were the origins of the distinctive culture of the Christian Near East, "which had so deep an influence on the Byzantine civilisation and through it on that of Western Europe."

By the end of the second century the dominance of Classical Greek culture was waning. In the fourth century Augustine found it hard to learn the language and knew little of it. As with language so with art and architecture. For long the temples, forums, palaces - the entire layout of cities - had been Hellenist. Public buildings anywhere from Britain to Beirut had similar facades, with characteristic columns and pediments, architraves and decorative motifs. These were based on principles of harmony and proportion which were found in the human form, the central theme of sculpture. Philosophy too stressed these principles, which were enshrined in precepts like the golden mean. But with the "Age of Anxiety", which came on as the second century ended - an age of deep spiritual and social crisis, political upheavals, wars and pronunciamentos - this kind of philosophy no longer satisfied.

In sculpture chaotically mingled figures, sometimes suggesting agonised writhing, express the uncertainty, violence and insecurity of the times, as well as the mental anguish. Representational art had reached a climax in the portrait busts of emperors, senators and their wives. But in the troubled third century disquiet and uncertainty replace the old serenity with an impressionistic capturing of mood and expression by techniques relying on optical illusion, along with the often brutal vigour and urge to power which become stylised in busts of Constantine and his sucessors. The rigid order imposed on society by "God-like" emperors was reflected in a new style of art.

Individuality and feeling are sacrificed to this expression of power and authority. Forms are simplified and standardised. The hair on the colossal head of Constantine at Rome is arranged as if the locks are keyed into an arch. Planes are built up on a geometrically regular pattern. The eyes, "supernaturally large and wide open, express the transcendence of the ruler's personality". This type of art was soon to be taken over by the Church to express the majesty and transcendence of Christ. The ruler, being God-like, was also priestly: his royal robes were also vestments. Eventually the artists and craftsmen who executed such work had to be priests themselves. They created "beauty saturated with spirituality." National styles and popular motifs, many from Persia and Egypt - the equivalent of "pop" or folk art in our day - replace the outworn Classical stereotypes.

The most striking changes came through the spiritual upsurge as it moved in the third century towards belief in the One God, transcendent in majesty but immanent, in a personal sense, in humanity - the Saviour God promising eternal life: a movement throughout the Roman world, predating the triumph of Christianity. When with Constantine church-building was blessed and sometimes financed by the Government, it became possible to provide an appropriate setting in which the liturgy as a sacred drama, or re-enactment of Christ's life and passion, could be performed. Churches began to replace the despoiled and emptying temples, or to take them over. Whereas the temples had usually been designed to impress by their outward form, with perfect proportions as of the human body, neglecting the interior, it was the interior of churches that were now carefully designed to lead the eye along the pillared arcades of the nave, representing the earth, to the sanctuary representing heaven and salvation. So also they were adorned with mosaics. Originally used for floors, these were now designed for walls and vaulted ceilings - another pre-Christian development - with tesserae of brightly coloured stones of glass, shining with gold leaf, and angled to catch the light. Before the Western Empire fell this radiant art could already be seen to perfection in Galla Placidia's mausoleum at Ravenna, with a range of symbolism such as the shepherd (Christ) with his sheep - some of which has links with Classical themes (where for instance the Good Shepherd bearing the sheep which had been lost is the successor of Hermes the Ram-Carrier).

The first phase of Christian art was the bringing of new inspiration to the late Classical forms and techniques, with another range of symbols and modes of expression. Rivers, trees and pastures, and a profusion of birds, beasts and flowers provide the background for saints and prophets, and for Christ - a beardless and youthful philosopher, so different from the stern judge and ruler who looks down from the eastern apses of the later churches. As time went on Christ the Pantocrator, Ruler of all, is still depicted as supreme, but his Mother now appears along with him, and holds him as a child in a style which soon became fixed down to the last detail. So too with the portraits of saints, which made up the icons, great and small, the characteristic products of Byzantine art during the period when monastic influence was at its height.

Symbolism and the expression of spirituality and inwardness vie with, and tend to replace simple but descriptive mosaic statements of Gospel stories, as in Theodoric's San Apollinare Nuovo at Ravenna: veneration and a sense of devotion become the aim, rather than the didactic approach. While in sculpture the perfectly proportioned nude male figure of Classical Greece disappears along with the nude female figure of late Classical and Hellenistic times, in the mosaics and icons the human form disappears altogether under robes and vestments. At

San Vitale (Ravenna) only the ordered majesty and magnificence of Emperor and Empress are to be seen, with their attendants and courtiers - a scene almost equalling that of Christ and attendant saints and angels as they appear in other mosaics. In the same manner the patron saint, Apollinaris, is portrayed in his church at Classe (the old port and naval base at Ravenna), where he stands as the central figure with arms raised in prayer, while the ordered sheep of his flock look up towards him.

Free-standing sculpture goes out, except for occasional statuettes. Bas-reliefs continue, especially in small-scale work in ivory, and in the exuberant imagery of flora and fauna or abstract designs on the capitals of columns in churches, which replace the Ionic or Corinthian styles, as well as on pulpits and other furnishings. In church interiors the many-hued marble panels vie with the mosaics to make them glow with unearthly splendour.

The artist's aim is to present what his inner eye perceives, penetrating the outer forms. Solidity and plasticity have little interest for him, and he ignores perspective, one of the great discoveries of the Classical artists. In the second phase of this artistic revolution backgrounds disappear: the picture is part of the architecture and opens on to the church or palace - one does not look into it as through a window. Rows of martyrs or saints in dignified stance leave no room for a setting other than the architecture around them - they may even replace earlier work, as in San Apollinare Nuovo, where the naturalism of the earlier mosaics that were spared is striking in the lively bounding of the three kings towards the Christ-child, and in the representation of Theodoric's palace. In the portraits of Justinian and Theodora with their attendants, in San Vitale, the immobility of the stylised figures is accentuated by one touch of the old realism in the servant who draws back a curtain.

By Justinian's time architecture too had passed its nadir. Degeneration of Classical forms had ended with blank walls and openings adorned, if at all, by lifeless stereotypes. But within these dull buildings a new spaciousness develops, often aided by a dome, which in the Pantheon at Rome or churches in Northern Syria, foreshadows the glories of Byzantine architecture and its triumphant climax in Justinian's Hagia Sophia. There the architects, with consummate daring and vision, cut off the top of the dome, converting it to a base supported on four great arches joined by spherical pendentives: on this base they placed the lantern with its forty lights to illuminate the vast space 180 feet below - and only on top of that the dome itself with its ribs radiating upwards from their forty piers.

This was the crowning splendour of the New Rome created by Constantine two centuries before. The West had to wait another millennium for the old Rome, which had become the Rome of the popes, to have St. Peter's rebuilt in the style which Byzantium had pioneered, and with a magnificence which was its rival.

Comment: Galla Placidia. (p. 281)

CHAPTER FIVE

CHRISTIAN AMBIGUITIES

1. **Sex, marriage and the family**: *Divergent tendencies: responsibility in the world or withdrawal from it; married life and celibacy. Virginity and celibacy regarded as superior to marriage: St. Paul and St. Augustine. Prenuptial chastity for men not regarded as essential. Augustine's rejection of his mistresses. Comparison of attitudes today with those of Late Antiquity. Eastern religious views, especially Manicheism. Marriage as impeding the love of God.*

As part of the spiritual upsurge during the later Hellenistic Era, Christianity made a determining contribution to the new life in every area of culture and society. But there were two tendencies among its adherents which moved them in different directions. One was to be involved, even reluctantly, in the world as a responsible citizen, the other, more prominent trend, was to withdraw from the world and seek communion with God, alone or in a community. This ambivalence was matched in matters of sex: there were those who married, and those who practised celibacy as a way of coming closest to God. In the first centuries of Christianity withdrawal from the world and celibate chastity went together, though eventually celibates who had entered monastic life, like St. Gregory, found themselves taking leadership in society and the State as well as in the Church.

During the transition from the old civilisation to the new, the Church did not assist actively in the reforming process. For too long the State had been regarded as hostile, or at best indifferent to the Christian faith, and although the Founder's injunction was to render to Caesar what was Caesar's, this principle was applied only grudgingly, and rarely, if at all, in matters of service to the State. Even after Constantine's incorporation of the Church in the Empire, making Christian doctrine the imperial ideology, ecclesiastics might be awed and dazzled by the role surprisingly thrust upon them, but they still felt no concern to "moralise the old Roman machine".

Far from seeking service in public administration, Christians who were decurions, obliged to carry out such duties as tax-collecting, did their best to escape their burdens by ordination. As for state-office, they abandoned or avoided it - were sometimes, like Ambrose, called from it by mass acclaim - and instead undertook duties in the Church or retired, like Paulinus, to country estates and monasteries. Service of the State was often hard for men of conscience - they might jib at the amount of bakhsheesh and tips before any business could be effected, even when these were consolidated into officially recognised fees - though others might be ready to work the system, like the Patriarch Cyril of Alexandria, when by a series of well-placed bribes, he expected to gain the support of the Palace. Purchasing office might not appeal to Christians of conscience, especially since this kind of racket appeared before long also in the Church, and reformers strove hard to curb it - a difficult matter when Church salaries were comparatively much higher than those of the State.

The appeal of celibate chastity reinforced traditional attitudes of male superiority, which affected ideas of marriage and the rights of women. Apocalyptic ideas strengthened such beliefs. Believing the end of the world to be imminent, St. Paul began by regarding marriage as an unnecessary complication (later he wrote positively about it with good advice to couples). Augustine quotes the earlier views of the Apostle approvingly, but in his day the perspective had changed, and there was no longer a general belief that the world was about to end. He put forward another reason for celibacy: there was no need for the begetting of children. Harking back to Old Testament times he explains the injunction of the Lord to the Israelites to be fruitful and multiply as due to the necessity of creating the race. But that work had been completed, and the increase of the Christian community could now be effected by conversion. As an example he suggests that an unmarried woman who had the means could buy a number of slaves and make Christians of them.

Though following St. Paul in placing virginity, if it was a deliberate choice, on a higher level than marriage, he presents marriage as a "good", if entered into and carried out chastely. "Marriage and continence are two goods, whereof the second is better" - just as, comparing knowledge and charity (caring love), both are goods, but charity is better because it "shall never fail". "While his defence of married life was conscientious," says his biographer, "his treatise on virginity was quite lyrical". The contrast is with a Stoic like Musonius in a previous generation, who broke through prevalent attitudes to an understanding of woman's needs, and a vision of partnership in marriage of a wife and a husband, on whom there should be an equal obligation of pre-nuptial chastity as well as continuing fidelity.

Centuries had to elapse before Christianity made pre-nuptial chastity the norm - or at least the standard to be aimed at by men, even if seldom fully accepted or observed (virginity had always been exacted for girls). According to the Roman ethos it was normal and perfectly respectable to have a concubine before marriage, and this was no bar to being accepted into a church congregation - it was only if a man wished to take the further step of baptism that celibacy was enjoined. Such was this hurdle that in the early centuries of the Church men who wished to become Christians would defer baptism until they were on their death-beds. The decision of Augustine to break with his concubine was a necessary preliminary to baptism. Eventual marriage to the heiress whom his mother had lined up for him would still have been possible - the concubine was only a stopgap while waiting for his fiancée to come of age. But other aspects of his decision were to abandon his career as a professor and the social climbing which marriage with the heiress offered. So he broke his engagement, having previously, on his mother's insistence, rejected the woman with whom he had been living for thirteen years and who had borne him his son, and for whom the concubine had been a substitute.

Augustine's experience indicates how limited the idea of marriage was in his day, since this woman, though not formally married to him, had been in all other respects his wife: "I had but that one woman, and I was faithful to her" - and that he was deeply in love with her is shown by his pain at his forced rejection of her. "My heart which had held her very dear was broken and wounded and shed blood - for there was first burning and bitter grief, and after that it festered, and as the pain grew duller it only grew more hopeless." That she also loved him is clear from her decision that on leaving him and returning to Africa "she would never know another man". In modern times it would be strange if a man in a similar situation to St. Augustine would not have thought it his duty, after a Christian conversion, to resume relations with the woman who in all but name had been his wife. If the man, as in Augustine's case, had become the guardian of their son, the incentive for joining together as a family would be that much stronger.

In viewing a life like Augustine's from our modern standpoint it is not a question of passing judgement. He was living in a different world, "ruled by demonic powers", on the other side of "the vast gulf that separates a modern man from the culture and religion of the later Empire". Similarly Augustine was separated, if not by a gulf, at least by a veil, from the Jesus of the Gospels, who treated women on a basis of equality, conversing with them, and helping them even if they were prostitutes. The world-view of the time, coming from other eastern religions, was that suffering and desire were intimately connected, and that salvation was to be achieved by winning freedom from desire. Desire, especially sexual, arose from the flesh, which was accounted evil, and was to be vanquished by spirit, which was good. Hence the value placed on continence and celibacy, along with asceticism of every kind - a different approach to life from the Jesus who turned water into wine at Cana and who "came eating and drinking" - and so was accused of being "gluttonous and a winebibber".

Manicheism, of which Augustine had been a follower in his early years, was a powerful expression of the ascetic outlook. It has been compared with Communism of the nineteen-thirties West European variety, with its core of dedicated activists and its fringe of fellow-travellers. Like Communism too it was a faith or ideology associated with the opposing superpower, in this case Rome's rival, Persia. The difference here is that its Persian founder, Mani, had been rejected in his own country, and had in fact been crucified.

The life of Mani was in some other respects reminiscent of Jesus - the Manichees claimed their faith to be a superior form of Christianity. But unlike Jesus, Mani had deliberately invented his religion, an amalgam of Zoroastrianism, Buddhism and Christianity, designed as a faith to conquer the world. Its basis was the conflict between good and evil, matter, including the body, being in the realm of evil, with sparks of light or goodness imprisoned in it. To enable these sparks to become free, and be absorbed in the Kingdom of Light, was the object of the asceticism, including celibacy, of the elect (*perfecti*). Set over the universe there was a divine Trinity, the Father of Greatness, the Mother of the Living, and the Primal Man. Under the Father's direction the universe was working itself, by a process as mechanical or "scientific" as dialectical materialism, towards an inevitable goal - the ultimate transformation whereby all the imprisoned sparks of light would be reabsorbed in the Kingdom, though the process was hampered by innumerable demons harassing any movement of the soul towards the light.

In later life Augustine came out against men having mistresses before marriage, but he still saw marriage as a second-best, available for those who could not achieve continence - a safety-valve for instincts which it would be much better so to control that they practically ceased to exist. He speculated as to why God, when providing a companion for Adam, did not give him another man: "If it was company and good conversation that Adam needed it would have been much better arranged to have two men together, as friends, not a man and woman."

The ambiguity is there: marriage is a "good", though qualified because by nature it impedes the direct apprehension of God which is open to virgins and celibates. If a man marries he will "care for the things that are of the world, how he may please his wife", St. Paul had said, whereas "he that is unmarried cares for the things of the Lord, how he may please the Lord" - and conversely with the unmarried and married woman. Apprehending God, loving and pleasing Him was the all-embracing aim. As with all true mystics of whatever creed or faith, the First Commandment is everything: "It is with no doubtful knowledge, Lord, but with utter certainty that I love you, " wrote Augustine. "You have stricken my head with your word and I have loved you." In a paean of prose which is also poetry, he calls to mind from "the fields and vast palaces of memory ... the innumerable images brought to it by the senses."

> "But what is that I love when I love you? Not the beauty of any bodily thing, nor the order of the seasons, not the brightness of light that rejoices the eye, nor the sweet melodies of all songs, nor the sweet fragrance of flowers and ointments and spices: not manna nor honey, not the limbs that carnal love embraces. None of these things do I love in loving my God. Yet in a sense I do love light and melody and fragrance and food and embrace when I love my God - the light and the voice and the fragrance and the food and embrace in the soul, when that light shines upon my soul which no place can contain, that voice sounds which no time can take from me, I breathe that fragrance which no wind scatters, I eat the food which is not lessened by eating, and I lie in the embrace which satiety never comes to sunder. This it is that I love, when I love my God."

When he asked (he goes on) "all the things that throng about the gateways of the senses: 'tell me of my God, since you are not He' ... they cried out in a great voice: 'He made us'. My question was my gazing upon them, and their answer was their beauty."

The beauty of married love and the praise and love of God which can come through a married partnership were not on Augustine's list, nor the creation of a microcosm of God's kingdom which is possible in a family. After rejecting his mistress and the woman who could have been called his wife, Augustine did his best to create a family around himself, when he moved from Milan to rural retirement for prayer and philosophical discussion with his mother, his brother and his son, as well as several friends. Later, when Bishop of Hippo, he lived with his close-knit group of like-minded celibates, who called themselves servants or slaves of God (*servi Dei*). He also regarded his flock as his *familia*.

Centuries had to elapse before uninhibited Christian expression of God's love in and through married partnership and the family appears in Europe, pioneered in the thought of St. Thomas Aquinas, and maturing with the freeing of mind and spirit at the Renaissance and Reformation.

Comment: St. Augustine and St. Thomas Aquinas on marriage. (p.281)

2. **Monasteries**: *escapism and new life: the flight from decadence; growing-points of the new society: celibacy; desert hermits; Antony, Pachomius. Influence on moral reform, art, music.*

Analogies have been drawn between the behaviour of cells in the body and the functioning of human society, where the most basic cell is the family. Besides the family there are many other groupings which, when they function well, maintain and build up society. But if they lose the sense of the part they should be playing, their disoriented activity produces cancers in the body social and politic.

The Rome of the Caesars is reproduced, in post-1918 Berlin, in "swinging" London, or any other megalopolis at a similar stage of decadence. Sleazy slums coexist with the fasionable residential areas where "terror and burglary has reduced people to a state of siege." Muggers and political thugs are at work in the streets while prostitutes ply their trade in droves. Homosexuals and perverts take over cafes and nightclubs, sometimes almost entire districts.

One response, during the Greco-Roman decadence, was to flee from a world in the grip, as men saw it, of evil forces. Eager for the salvation of their souls, they felt thay had to escape from the city, with its materialism, its conflicts and its temptations. It was also an escape from the State and its tax-gatherers and regulations. In the country, and more particularly in the desert, a man could be alone with God. Subduing his nature by austerities and prayer, he could attain to an inner knowledge and mystical vision of his Maker. Some of these men, or their followers, formed communities - monasteries, which became "live cells" and growing-points for the civilisations of the future.

Ascetics and celibates were not unknown among the Jews in the later centuries BC, the Essenes being one example of those who reckoned celibacy superior to the married state. In community living they had been pioneers in their Dead Sea retreat. In the Christian period of the Empire, the movement began in Eygpt, with individual hermits whose aims, though spiritual, were entirely personal, and were not concerned with rebuilding society to which the live cells of homes could contribute. Abandoning the world meant negating their sexuality, avoiding or abandoning family resposibilities, and hardening the heart against all natural affection. This could be carried to bizarre lengths by some of those seeking salvation, whether as hermits or in monasteries. To one dedicated man, after fifteen years away from home, a packet of letters was brought from his parents and friends, but he threw it into the fire unopened, exclaiming "what thoughts will the reading of these suggest to me? ... For how many days will they draw off the attention of my heart from the contemplation I have set before me, by the recollection of those who wrote them? Away, ye thoughts of my home, be ye burnt up!" Another man fled from his wife, who refused to be separated from him, but he said "it is better to be divorced from a human being than from God."

When quite large numbers had retreated to the desert, or at least to oases or areas where climatic conditions - perhaps more favourable than those of today - made subsistence possible, rudimentary organisations or "lauras" developed. In the Wadi Natrun it was said that there were fifty lauras making up a kind of republican community 5,000 strong. When these renunciants, having done violence to their humanity and natural affections, returned to the city, as occasionally happened, to take part in the demonstrations and sectional feuding which were endemic in Alexandria, they could take to action of a fanatical and violent kind. One of the worst incidents was the murder of Hypatia, daughter of a well-known mathematician and astronomer, herself a popular lecturer in these subjects and leader of the Neoplatonic/Aristotelian school of philosophy - an extraordinary achievement for a woman in those days. But her "liberated" attitudes and friendship with the Prefect (Governor) of Alexandria (also a pagan) incensed the demonstrators, incited by the contentious Patriarch Cyril (415 AD).

Quite a different picture of saintliness was presented by the book about St. Antony, written by his friend, St. Athanasius, who was an earlier Patriarch of Alexandria (died 373 AD). The book was a best-seller and inspired thousands to follow Antony's example. Among those who were challenged and helped to change by this new type of biography was Augustine, who then pioneered the new type of autobiography with *The Confessions*.

As the son of a prosperous peasant, Antony lacked nothing, when as a young man he inherited the family farm, but hearing in church Christ's injunction to his disciples to sell all and follow him, he acted literally on the behest and gave the proceeds to the poor. He kept a small sum for maintaining his much younger sister, and eventually put her in the care of a group of virgins (for already convents were coming into existence, over one of which the girl later became the Mother). He went himself to live alone in the desert, not to be idle, for he always worked, growing his breadgrain and vegetables, and weaving mats or suchlike. It was during this period that his temptations, vividly described in his biography and by generations of artists in paint, took place.

Victorious in these personal encounters with the Devil and his accomplices, Antony soon gained a reputation for holiness. The

nearby villagers called him "God's friend". For many years he lived
in a tomb, then in an old fort, from which he emerged only after many
years, looking remarkably fit, when friends had broken down the door.
Though intent on solitary communication with the Lord, he was not
anti-social: he was in fact not allowed to be so, since many others
came out to the desert and with them he had "ceaseless conferences",
firing their zeal and becoming their "father and guide". There may be
something authentic in his saying (he spoke only Coptic):

> "Greeks go abroad and cross the sea to study letters, but we have
> no need to go abroad for the Kingdom nor to cross the sea to
> obtain virtue. The Lord has told us in advance 'The kingdom of
> Heaven is within you'. Virtue therefore has need only of our
> will, since it is within us and springs from us. Virtue exists
> when the soul keeps in its natural state."

At one point he left the desert to minister to the victims of
Maximin Daja's persecutions (311 AD), visiting them in the mines and
prisons, encouraging them when on trial and accompanying them to
martyrdom. Back in the desert he was besieged by people wanting
help, who camped outside his cell. He withdrew still further to the
mountain known as Deir Mar Antonios, and continued to grow his
food so as to discourage others from bringing it (he had to request the
wild animals not to damage his garden). If gifts were brought, he
gave in return the baskets which he made. He also visited "the
brethren." "Let us each note", he said, "and write down our actions
and impulses of the soul as though we were to report them to each
other; and you may rest assured that from utter shame of becoming
known we shall stop sinning and entertaining sinful thoughts
altogether."

Judges begged him to come and help settle cases, and sent
defendants out to him for his verdict. A rare visit to Alexandria was
to help Athanasius in his conflict with the Arians. Seeing him there
many pagans wanted to touch him, "and indeed as many became
Christians in those few days as one would have seen in a year." His
biographer concludes: "It was not his stature or figure that made him
stand out from the rest, but his settled character and the purity of his
soul ... The joy in his soul expressed itself in the cheerfulness of his
face."

Life in community was a further development for those who fled
the world. Pachomius, as a soldier, had been helped by Christian
prisoners, and after his military service (around 300 AD) sought
solitude in a ruined temple of Isis, but did not cut himself off from the
world. Subsisting on his vegetable plot, he helped travellers and the

nearby villagers in need. Only then he received baptism and went to live with a hermit, from whom he learned much about the spiritual life, deciding eventually that the best way to salvation was through living in community. He gathered together in a monastery those anchorities of the Thebaid who responded to his call - so many that soon the communities grew to nine. Nor did he cut himself off fully from women or his family, since his sister Mary had organised several convents. Aided by his military experience he issued rules for the communities, arranged visitations and ensured self-sufficiency by imposing the duty of labour in fields and gardens, or in such work as spinning and mat-making. Each community was highly organised, a hive of industry, on a system of three-weekly rotation of the members between the three *tagmata* or military-style divisions charged with the various responsibilities: cooking, the infirmary, sales and purchases, hospitality and arrangements for corporate prayer. "One works on the land as a labourer, another in the garden, another at the forge, another in the bakery, another in the carpenter's shop, another in the fuller's shop, another in weaving big baskets, another in the tannery." Others were working in the shoemaker's workshop, the scriptorium, or weaving young reeds. "And all learn the scripture by heart." Meals were in successive sittings.

Not all hermits or monks were rejecting family ties. As one visitor, Palladius, who resided for some time among them, wrote: "it is quite possible for a man without neglecting his own soul to be influenced by a godly consideration and give assistance to his kinsfolk if they are in want." One of the monks trebled his work for a whole year in order to pay off a debt with which his mother was burdened when she was left a widow - but he would not look on her face. And there were those in the lauras who did not want a fully eremitical life. One retired merchant took on as his commitment caring for the sick in the Wadi, going round to them with fruit, eggs and bread.

The closely regulated monastery was the one which left its mark on the burgeoning civilisations of the day. These were first established, outside Egypt, in Cappadocia, the heartland of Asia Minor. Far from being a flight from family concerns this was something of a family affair, starting with Macrina who founded a community for women on her ancestral property. There followed a monastery founded by her brother Basil. Though of a Christian family, Basil's life-work only began when a conversion experience prompted him to investigate monastic communities in Egypt, Palestine, Syria and Mesopotamia. The life of the monks impressed him greatly. "I admired their continence in living and their endurance in toil; I was amazed at their persistence in prayer, and their triumphing over sleep; subdued by no natural necessity, ever keeping their soul's purpose high and free in hunger, in cold, in nakedness, they never yielded to the body; they were never willing to waste attention on it ... All this moved my admiration."

There was no rejection of the family by Basil and Macrina: they formed a "live cell" of remarkable dynamism which included two other brothers of theirs, both of whom became bishops, Gregory of Nyssa and Peter of Sebaste. Gregory, with his vision and imaginative pen, was an inspirer of the movement, and along with his namesake of Nazianzen - who had been a fellow-student with Basil at Athens - became one of the most distinguished theologians among the Fathers of the Church. Like Augustine at about the same time, Basil gave up an academic career to further his spiritual aim. The combination of good education and family spirit in this group may explain the moderate and sensible arrangements for his communities laid down by Basil in his Rule, including adequate food and a bath three times a year (more often in the case of illness).

Basil was the moral and spiritual leader of his land, carrying on a vast correspondence with fellow-ecclesiastics, academics, governors and civil servants, friends and followers, with tough letters to monks and virgins who had fallen from the disciplined life. Acting on his conviction that bishops were meant to be "physicians of the diseases of the churches", he accepted the Emperor's mandate to establish religious peace in Armenia, and tirelessly travelled, when the rigorous climate of Cappadocia allowed it, in furthering such work, despite continual ill-health (he died aged only 49, in 386 AD). He stood up to the Emperor Valens who tried to browbeat him into accepting Arianism - the Prefect sent by Valens said that no one had ever spoken to him in such a way, and Valens himself was overawed to the point of confusion when he came in person to Basil in his church.

Basil's enterprise of charity took the form of a huge complex outside Cappadocian Caesaraea, containing two hospitals (one for contagious diseases), staffed by doctors and nurses; a home for the poor, a hospice for travellers and strangers, and workshops - all centered on the church, around which were the bishop's residence and clergy houses. Basil put all his money into this "second city" (which eventually replaced the original Caesarea), and into hospices and poor houses in other towns of his diocese, as did the monks who undertook the administration of these places.

Monasteries soon became a power in the Empire, both East and West, centres of a reforming movement which challenged the laxities of the established Church, particularly the sale of benefits and the imposition of fees for ordination. It also challenged the worldliness of clerics, such as bishops appointed for political reasons, or as civil servants due for a reward. It was thought unseemly that ecclesiastics should go to the theatre or race-course, attend gladiatorial shows or indulge in gambling. This puritan drive prescribed celibacy for clergy except those like cantors in minor orders.

Such action was needed, in fact is always needed, since all bodies even with the most spiritual aims have to administer themselves. How to prevent the administrators from becoming bureaucrats, organised in a more or less elaborate hierarchy? When the Church became virtually part of the State it became increasingly assimilated to it. Like the State it was in business, and to a very high degree. Different churches had been granted state monopolies and had invested in tax-free industries. Hagia Sophia had the monopoly for funerals in the capital - sufficiently lucrative to support its considerable establishment of clergy, cantors and doorkeepers. Inevitably there were compromises with "the world", which the monastic movement set itself to challenge.

Monasticism came on at a moment when the new civilisations were settling down, and their organisation and culture were being moulded in forms which would last them a millennium. It attracted powerful personalities who directed the movement towards reshaping the ideas and doctrines, as well as church liturgies, and music. A dominant part was played by Justinian, who (though having an actress wife) was almost as much monk as Emperor, and in the West by the monk Gregory the Great, who in all but name was ruler of Rome.

There was another aspect of monasticism less conducive to cultural progress. Justinian had shared the attitude of those who saw the Academy of Athens as the last redoubt of pagan learning. His closure of the Academy showed how narrow Church-dominated learning was becoming. The salaries of the staff were cut off. Left unprovided and unpensioned, the professors' only hope was emigration, or rather defection to Persia, where they were welcomed at the imperial court. During the period of monastic ascendancy the universities were reduced to the level of theological seminaries or institutes for professional training.

At this time, too, interest in science and mathematics stopped at practical application of discoveries long since made. But practical applications sometimes were of great ingenuity and effectiveness, as with the invention of Greek Fire; or like the feats of calculation and engineering which made Hagia Sofia possible.

The monks contributed much at the formative stage of the young civilisation when, inspired by its new faith, and faced by the appalling threat to its existence, Byzantium threw the invaders back, as the ancient Greeks had thrown back the Persians at Salamis and Marathon. At such moments the new confidence and sense of freedom combine in a phase of creativeness, curtailed in this case by the conflict over images, in which the monks came under prolonged attack and sometimes brutal persecution. The limitations of monastic culture did indeed need to be transcended, though iconoclasm, involving the destruction of so many beautiful and historic works of art, was not the best way of achieving this.

3. **The State: doctrinal rectitude and dissent**: *Constantine imposes orthodoxy; Christianity not monolithic: spiritual experience, belief and heresy. Augustine: Donatists and Pelagius.*

Rome had a record of toleration in matters of religion: exceptions were the persecutions of Jews and Christians under the Empire. When Constantine took steps to make Christianity the official religion he expected unity in the faith. It was inconvenient that the views of Arius, a priest of Alexandria, on the relationship of God the Father and the Son, were at variance with those of some leading clerics, causing much rancorous dissension. At first he was ready to ignore a controversy on a question which was subtle and seemed irrelevant. But when he realised (in the words of Gibbon) that a metaphysical argument can become "the cause or pretence of political contests", he brought together, with considerable effort, some 300 clergy at Nicaea in his palace to thrash out their differences. Then - present but not officially presiding - he virtually imposed a theological formula which was accepted by all but two of the delegates (for the latter exile was the consequence). The rest were invited to a gala dinner, celebrating the Emperor's twentieth anniversary, with a gift at parting.

The State was giving carrot to the orthodox who were now supporting it, and stick to the dissenters. The power of the State was henceforward to reinforce the limits within which "the almost invisible and tremulous ball of orthodoxy was allowed securely to vibrate." Orthodox doctrine was to be an important element in the ideological adhesive of the State.

The leaders of the Church in the Christian Empire were bishops representing for the most part urban congregations. Some of them, like Ambrose, were members of the governing class. Augustine, though coming from an obscure country town in North Africa, was included in this group through taking academic work at Milan (at that time the effective capital of the Western Empire), and entering the circle of Ambrose. Another ecclesiastic of the same period, St. Jerome, moved in the highest circles before migrating to Bethlehem, whither he attracted upper-class Roman ladies as his disciples and assistants while carrying out his great work of translating the Bible into Latin.

Such men all too often found themselves at loggerheads with other Christian leaders whose doctrines or practices did not square with those which they favoured, especially when the matter under dispute touched on what they regarded as a vital issue. A believer, whose conversion experience was in line with one of the central doctrines of the faith, would never let that doctrine be compromised by alternatives. For Augustine, the inflowing of the Holy Spirit, the grace which enabled him to make his crucial decision to abandon his concubine and adopt a life of celibate chastity, was just such an experience. Until he had this experience, or rather was overwhelmed by it, in the famous scene in the garden at Milan, he had not believed that he could live without physically assuaging his lusts. Divine grace became central in his life. His weakness and worthlessness (in his view) necessitated his continued dependence on this source.

In this he was following St. Paul: it was the fact of opening the Testament at Romans xiii, 13, which brought with it the lightning-flash which is at once the revelation of sin, the sense of forgiveness, and a profound spiritual change. "For in that instant, with the very ending of the sentence, it was as though a light of utter confidence shone in all my heart, and all the darkness of uncertainty vanished away." The experience of Augustine was the experience of Paul, just as it was and is the experience of countless Christians past and present. It had to be a central element in the teaching or "doctrine" - and no wonder that Augustine found himself at loggerheads with a Christian like Pelagius, who put little or no emphasis upon it.

The experience of change and the teaching which went with it had been the most potent magnet drawing men and women to the Church when the conflict was joined with old paganism or the vigorous rivals from the east. Christians with this experience were the ones who stood rock-firm under persecution, even unto death, and they had a quality of life and personality, a certainty and a sense of direction, which were enviable and highly attractive to many outside the fold.

Yet to erect any spiritual experience, even the highest and most essential, into a dogma to be imposed as a *sine qua non* on everyone calling themselves Christians, had its dangers. While the infant Church was making its way in the world it had to take its stand - members had to affirm their faith. But once it had won a privileged or supreme position in the State, Christians who maintained the accepted orthodoxy could use other than purely spiritual weapons to impose their views on people who thought differently.

Especially did this danger loom when hierarchy was replacing the democracy of the original *ecclesiae*, when bishops were often recruited from families of the upper urban strata in the Empire.

Aristocratic groupings in East and West, vying for support of Emperor or Pope, provided through their rivalries the heat which sometimes turned theological arguments into blazing conflicts in which no mercy was shown to the vanquished. There were also revolts by those who felt themselves outside these exclusive establishment groups - revolts which took the form of heretical or break-away (schismatical) movements.

This was the more liable to happen since the Church had never been a monolithic institution. Growing up in different centres - the principal ones being Antioch, Alexandria and Rome - the local Churches had developed in different ways. At Antioch, where the Church had grown directly from the Jews and God-fearers of the city, the links between many Christians and Jews remained close. Christians would resort to synagogues on the occasions of Jewish festivals, and tended to maintain or adopt Jewish practices. This explains the abuse which John Chrysostom, the third-century Bishop of Antioch, hurled at the Jews and Judaism, with accusations of devil-inspired practice and worship - he feared lest this powerful competitor might lead his own flock astray, and that the basis of their faith would be undercut.

When Augustine eventually returned to North Africa as Bishop of Hippo (now 'Annaba in Algeria), he was faced by the challenge of several dissident groups. The Donatists represented the country-folk of the olive-growing uplands, who had renounced paganism for Christianity a century before. Speaking Libyan (modern Berber) and regarding as foreign the Latin-speaking Rome-organised cities - fiercely hostile not only to tax-gatherers and officials but to Roman society in general - these people had followed their bishops in setting up their own Church. For them, as for other dissidents, their Church was more "a brotherhood of militant believers than ... an institution for salvation."

Constantine had pronounced against the Donatists, closing their churches and banning their bishops. But neither this action nor the persecution by his sucessor Constans had ended the schism. Augustine had disagreements with them over doctrine, but it was mainly a question of discipline, of including them in the Rome-based Church order. He attempted first by declamation, even writing a "pop" type of song, to bring them round. But when this failed he had recourse to State power for destroying their Church.

In accepting State-violence against the Donatists Augustine was bowing to the spirit of the age. Against Pelagius it was a combat of words, culminating in the latter's rejection as a heretic.

Pelagius was a Briton (his real name may have been Morgan). It is not surprising that a variant from the norm of establishment

Christianity should develop in a distant colonial hinterland, where three centuries of imperial rule had still imposed little more than a veneer. Yet the doctrinal differences between Pelagius and Augustine were not great, and were aggravated by misunderstanding and arguments at cross-purposes.

The faith of Pelagius was that Christ's injuction "Be ye perfect as your Father in heaven is perfect" (Matthew 5: 48) was meant to be taken seriously, and that God had endowed people with free-will for moving towards this aim. Augustine's experience of conversion had left him convinced that God's predestined intervention alone could bring fallen man to a spiritual condition of "precarious convalescence", dependent on constantly receiving the "medicine" of grace. Despite this difference, in his first years as a Christian, Augustine's approach had been much the same as that of Pelagius, in living to create a dedicated elite of *perfecti* - not unlike those he had known among the Manichees - to bring the Church as a whole nearer that spotlessness and absence of wrinkles proclaimed in St. Paul's memorable simile.

When Pelagius came to Rome he had been shocked by the laxity and low moral standards among many who were leading or accepted in Church circles. His call for change produced a remarkable response, particularly among the young and among wealthy men and women. Many of these gave away lands and houses to take part in this apostolic campaign. Stridency and a tendency to fanaticism were not however calculated to appeal to Augustine in his later years when he was trying to instil the rudiments of faith and discipline into a somewhat passive flock, including Donatists deprived of their churches. His concern was no longer just to increase those *perfecti*, who had already formed a nucleus as his *servi dei* - rather to raise, even a little, the moral and spiritual level of those average, respectable lay-people, who were not much different in their mode of life, and even in some of their cult-practices, from the respectable pagans of an earlier day.

Opposition to all that endangered truth, as he understood it, had to be the work of Augustine, not just because he was a bishop and an establishment figure, and so a pillar of the prevailing orthodoxy, but as one standing firmly on the rock of his unchallengeable experience of conversion. So other great figures of the age took up their stand against Arianism, which the barbarians favoured, because by reducing Christ to a lesser figure than the Godhead, they could revere Him as if He were a god or a hero from one of their legends. The Monophysite tendencies of the Copts similarly came under attack. The tragic element in the situation was the antagonism between those expressing themselves in so many varied ways, antagonism sometimes merging into violence. Social and political conflicts inevitably took on a religious colouring. In such circumstances Christianity may have a positive role in helping subjected people to freedom. But among those who are supposed to be brothers and sisters in one faith, dissensions aggravated by state-power have produced inquisitions, ferocious persecutions, and wars - and the eventual enfeeblement of the faith which the violence has been intended to protect. Only in recent years, in the face of the inhumanity and bankruptcy of state-violence in imposing ideological orthodoxies, have people moved in a widening awareness to mutual tolerance and fruitful dialogue.

CHAPTER SIX

THE END OF CIVILISATION IN THE WEST
AND ITS RENEWAL

1. Landowners into Bishops: *Christians take over administration in the disintegrating Western Empire. Peacemaking: Paulinus of Nola; Sidonius Apollinaris; the role of the bishops; immigrants and anarchy; Christian missions.*

Government service and the army were losing good men to the Church. At Milan Ambrose had been obliged by popular acclaim to exchange his governorship of the province for the bishopric of the city. Augustine's decision in the Milan garden turned him also from secular ambitions to leadership in the Church. Another was Victricius, who gave up an army career to become Bishop of Rouen. He influenced Paulinus who had been set on a brilliant administrative career, but even more decisive for the latter was his encounter with another former soldier, St. Martin of Tours, who cured his eye trouble besides strengthening his faith.

The heir of vast estates in Gaul and Italy, Paulinus was brought into the highest level of the imperial service by Ausonius, his tutor at Bordeaux University. Ausonius, also a wealthy landowner, had been made a Consul, thanks to having been tutor to the Emperor Gratian in the years before he came to the throne. Through this connection with the Court he helped to launch Paulinus on his career, first as a junior Consul, then as Governor of Campania, the province in Italy where Paulinus owned Nola and surrounding estates.

At this point, aged 26, already known as a gifted poet, Paulinus had within his grasp all that the world could offer of success and fame. Three years later he married Therasia, from another landed family of Gaul, one of a growing number of ladies of wealth and position who devoted their lives to furthering the faith. The marriage strengthened Paulinus in a decision to renounce his career and devote his whole time to serving Christ in an obscure situation, as free as possible from worldly cares. He disappeared to estates which he owned in Spain, later returning to Nola, where he looked after the shrine of the former Bishop, St. Felix, eventually becoming Bishop there himself.

Paulinus turned a deaf ear to the pleadings and queries of Ausonius. After several years of silence he replied to his old tutor's letters with a poem declaring that the gods of Olympus have yielded to Christ as the source of inspiration and new life.

"Hearts consecrated to Christ give refusal to the Muses, are closed to Apollo ... Now 'tis another force that rules my heart, a greater God that demands another mode of life, claiming for himself from man the gift he gave, that we may live for the Father of life."

Men of the stamp of Paulinus could undertake great and heroic work for the Church even when their grasp on the faith was far more tenuous than his. When the Church became official and the pagan temples were closed, many people at all levels of society conformed outwardly, continuing their old way of life. The beneficiaries of the change which had wrecked the cities were the great country landowners. The State had increasingly interfered in local government, imposing ever heavier taxes, until the middle class was ruined, and the only voting possible, in these once flourishing democracies, was what people could do with their feet. The landowners could escape much of the taxation, and could utilise the manpower and property of those who fled from the cities - and this flight increased as the cities became subject to siege or sacking by roving barbarian bands. In the villas, which they sometimes fortified, landed families could maintain their comfortable way of life, particularly on estates which were off the main routes followed by war-bands and armies. Rome might be sacked by Goths and Vandals, corn-ships cease to sail and war-bands ravage and destroy, but on the estates of a magnate like Sidonius Apollinaris, and in other quiet areas of Gaul, country life continued for the wealthy with its amusements and sterile literary exercises.

"As we turn the pages of Sidonius, we seem to feel the still, languid oppressiveness of a hot, vacant noontide in one of those villas in Aquitaine or Auvergne. The master may be looking after his wine and oil, or laying a fresh mosaic, or reading Terence or Menander in some shady grotto; his guests are playing tennis, or rattling the dice-box, or tracking the antiquarian lore of Vergil to its sources. The scene is one of tranquil content, or even gaiety. But over all, to our eyes, broods the shadow which haunts the life that is nourished only by memories, and to which the future sends no call and offers no promises."

It was only the actual intrusion of the invaders and immigrants into their living-space which evoked the kind of responses exemplified by Sidonius, Until then the atmosphere was rural peace and gentility, with church building and founding monasteries as the main concerns of religious people. The gentry had little thought for such events until battles and sieges were raging nearby, and big blond Germans "breathing out leeks and ardour, Great friendly souls with appetites Much bigger than your larder", were taking up residence as their uninvited guests and neighbours.

Born in the year Paulinus died (431 AD), Apollinaris Sidonius was of similar background and standing. When raised by his father-in-law the Emperor Avitus to be Prefect of Rome, he mingled with the great senatorial families, but otherwise most of his life was passed on his wide estates in Gaul. In 471 or 472 AD he was called by the people of Auvergne to be their bishop and protector, not long before the last Emperor in the West was deposed (476 AD).

A bishop took on many roles, in association with the civil power, or superseding it. He visited prisoners, and put pressure on the magistrates to treat suspects and condemned people with humanity. A bishop would often try cases himself, or act as mediator between parties. Speed and absence of corruption made episcopal courts attractive to litigants. A bishop too had wealth to administer, from the lands which (as in the case of Sidonius) he might own himself, and from Church lands and property. These tended to increase, since in the Christian Empire the Church could receive donations and legacies, while being forbidden by law to alienate them. People in need could look to the bishop for help.

In fact in all matters the people regarded the bishop as their protector, against the exactions of the central or local government, and against the barbarians. With German or Frankish chiefs he could parley, or if that failed he could organise the defence. This fell to the lot of Sidonius during the long-drawn siege of Clermont by Euric - summer sieges during several years, while the surrounding lands were ravaged and scorched. With his brother-in-law Ecdidius the defence held out, the hungry being fed by the latter's munificence, as well as by Sidonius himself. Eventually a committee of bishops arranged the surrender of Auvergne to Euric, in exchange for keeping him out of territories elsewhere. The disgust of Sidonius was great. He suffered two years in captivity, and had the greatest difficulty in securing the return of some of his estates, pleading after long delays in person at the chieftain's court.

At this point the new is clearly superseding the old. The Church has become a power in the land. The great landowners, whether as laymen or bishops, take over the leading roles along with the kings or dukes who emerge from the chiefs of the war-bands. The towns dwindle in importance - such as they have is usually as seats of bishops. The self-sufficient manors, with the estates of abbeys and convents, become the basic economic units, with trade mostly limited to barter and local exchange. Protection is by the lord and his men-at-

bishops. The self-sufficient manors, with the estates of abbeys and convents, become the basic economic units, with trade mostly limited to barter and local exchange. Protection is by the lord and his men-at-arms. The feudal knight replaces the legionary. Chivalry with a Christian flavour becomes the ethos of knightly behaviour and romance. The Middle Ages have dawned and a new culture is born.

Similar events took place in Africa. The Vandals overwhelmed Spain and - commandeering a fleet - began taking over North Africa as well. The Vandals were Arian Christians, but little Christian brotherliness was in evidence as they pursued their conquest of Roman Africa. Catholics and Donatists lacked the unity to resist.

An expansion of the Christian outreach, followed by pauses and even contraction, is noticeable during the time of Augustine. His conversion had come at a moment when the Empire's stability had been restored, and with it a degree of vitality. Along with other converts he was on the attack, even if the attack was more against other brands of Christianity than in converting the un-evangelised tribes beyond the frontiers.

Not that others neglected this work: Paulinus praised Victricius for making the Channel coast safe by converting a local tribe, and other friends received praise for missionary work elsewhere which was producing similar results. Ambrose backed a mission to the Allemanni as a means of making them peaceful - a "strategy which came too late" for saving the Western Empire - as indeed could be said of modern overseas missions as a means of creating a peaceful Euro-dominated world. But with or without missions, the faith continued to spread, in some cases through prisoners of war.

After the first shock of invasions and migrations there was a strong recovery of the morale and missionary thrust of the Church, which increasingly came under Roman Catholic leadership in the West. In the East, Christians and government, Church and State worked on the whole harmoniously together, leading on to the strong, though politically subordinate position of the Church, which before long called itself Orthodox. It too developed a potent missionary outreach.

Comment: Sidonius Apollinaris and his German neighbours. (p. 283)

2. Pioneers of the new civilisation: *Jerome; dedicated women; translating the Bible; moral challenge.   Reactions to the   sack of Rome: Jerome; Augustine;* The City of God. *Leo, a new type of statesman; Huns and Vandals.*

In Western Europe the Church, and particularly the monastic movement, played an essential part in saving what was left of civilisation and bringing on its new phase, Latin Christendom ("the West").

Augustine's contemporary Jerome (347-420 AD), of a well-off professional family of Stridon in what is today Yugoslavia - the town itself was destroyed in the Gothic invasions - was, like Augustine, one of a group of young people who, at school and university, had their fun in the usual way: parties, girls, entertainments. Jerome was a more flamboyant character whose warm affection for friends was offset by bitter quarrels with those who disagreed with his convictions or mode of life. Brought up in a Christian home, his faith only became meaningful through an experience of conversion which he passed on to his sister. Did his parents disapprove of their assertive youngster's way of thrusting not only his new-found enthusiasm for religion but also his ascetic practices and commitment to celibacy on their daughter, with divisive consequences in the home? Anyway there was a quarrel and Jerome broke with them, his life now centered on a group of friends who had reached the same convictions as himself. They lived together as an "informal religious community", in the same way as Augustine and his friends after his conversion.

This relatively tranquil life did not long suit a personality like Jerome who tended to the extreme in whatever he did. He left for a couple of years of masochistic self-repression in the desert of Northern Syria. His life there, however, differed from that of the hermits scattered around the area, whose crude practices of self-immolation shattered his idealism concerning the eremitical life - for Jerome had his prized library with him, and was visited by friends and a succession of copyists (perhaps monks from a nearby monastery) to help in his intellectual work. Jerome was a voracious reader, who, despite a vow made in consequence of a startling dream, was never permanently to abandon his enjoyment of the classics, and was shortly to make his name as a translator and interpreter of Scripture, and a bellicose controversialist. Coming from the border-zone between the Latin West and the Greek-speaking East, Jerome acquired sufficient knowledge of Greek to be at home in that language, and in the desert made a start in mastering Hebrew, a far more difficult task which he more than once almost gave up, learning his letters anew and "studying to pronounce words both harsh and guttural." He persisted as a way of taking his mind off the lustful desires which otherwise continually assailed him.

Returning to Italy, Jerome settled at Rome as an aide to Pope Damasus, drafting letters on theological and other matters, and taking part in the high society by no means disdained by that worldly but efficient pontiff. In that society there were a number of people, particularly ladies of the noblest and most wealthy families, who had rejected the comforts and display of their position (through reading the *Life of St. Antony*, and visits by Athanasius and his successor Peter to Rome), and had adopted a life of asceticism and celibacy. Marcella, a widow of long-standing, had renounced a second marriage and devoted her mansion in the fashionable Aventine district as a centre for a group of girls and women where a life of prayer and Bible-study could be pursued together - one of the informal monastic communities which were springing up in Rome and elsewhere. Jerome soon found himself much in demand as a teacher of these eager students. The home of Marcella's friend Paula, also a widow, was another such centre or house-church, and to her and her daughters Jerome became the spiritual director and teacher. "Our studies brought about constant meeting together, this soon ripened into intimacy, and this in turn produced mutual confidence." Jerome, with his highly-sexed and deeply affectionate nature, found enormous satisfaction in these relationships, but they raised the breath of scandal against him, despite his strictness in maintaining celibacy and observing all due propriety. When Paula's eldest daughter, after a worldly marriage and a merry widowhood, was - still young - converted to the full ascetic and religious life, and then died suddenly, the scandal became a storm. At this point Jerome's patron and protector Pope Damasus also died, and he was virtually expelled from Rome by a Church committee of inquiry ("the Senate of Pharisees", he called it).

From being lionised as an up and coming leader of the intelligentsia and a possible future pope, Jerome was rejected not only because of his friendships and his pushing of the ascetic ideal on to others, but also because of the enmities he had made by his biting tongue and satirical blasting of theological and other opponents. He left Rome, but not before arranging to meet Paula and her equally dedicated daughter Eustochium *en route*, so that they could together proceed to the Holy Land. These two, "whatever the world may think", he wrote, "are always mine in Christ."

After an extensive tour of the sacred sites in Palestine and of monastic communities in Egypt, they settled down at Bethlehem near the church built by Constantine, the ladies in a convent and Jerome in a monastery, both of which they founded and financed. There Jerome continued his vast output of letters and other writings, above all his translation of the Bible into Latin from the original languages. This had been made possible by his continued study of Hebrew - at Rome he had persuaded a Jewish friend to loan him secretly books from the synagogue, which he copied. He carried through his massive task on the Bible with the help of erudite Jews and visits to the fine church library at Caesarea. The resulting Latin version (the Vulgate) superseded the much less adequate translations which had already appeared, and provided the scriptural foundation for the extension of Christianity throughout the West.

Educated and often wealthy women played a large part in these developments. Eustochium took over the convent at Bethlehem when her mother died, and one of Paula's granddaughters (also Paula) succeeded Eustochium. Marcella received, in the informal convent of her home, Marcellina, the sister of Ambrose. Melania of the famous Anician clan, with her daughter and granddaughter, were also pioneers in the ascetic life. The road system, still functioning if sometimes precarious, made possible visits, in Italy to friends like Paulinus and Therasia at Nola, or further afield partly by sea, to Augustine at Hippo or Jerome and the ladies at Bethlehem - visits supplemented by an often copious correspondence creating a network of well-known and articulate people throughout the Roman world.

Before the Western Empire ended, the Church had become a parallel or supplementary system of government to the State with authority that often went far beyond that of the official ruler. The need for such authority was brutally demonstrated by Alaric and his Goths sacking Rome in 410 AD, while the feeble Emperor Honorius was hiding away behind the marshes and defences of Ravenna. On that occasion the Church had been able to save much of its treasures, and its buildings were spared, thanks to the fact that the Goths were Christians, although they were scarcely regarded as such by the Catholic inhabitants, since they were Arian heretics. Further, Alaric had his men under sufficient control to withdraw them from the city after three days, when they left, burdened with loot.

Alaric's sack of Rome was a shattering blow for Jerome. Some friends were dead, some captured. For days and nights he could think of nothing but the catastrophe. "Who could believe", he wrote, "that after being raised up by victories over the whole world Rome should come crashing down?" Augustine's response was more philosophical. While setting himself in *The City of God* to disprove the charge that the christianisation of the Empire was the cause of the disaster, he proclaimed the view that the fate of even the greatest states (or "cities") paled into insignificance alongside the eternal existence of the celestial City which was the true home of men, and whose attainment after life was the proper motive for righteous living and care for justice in matters political and social. Augustine expresses contempt for empires acquired by violence and lust for power, and quotes a story about Alexander and a pirate to this effect. "The king asking him how he durst molest the seas so, he replied with a free spirit: How darest thou molest the whole world? But because I do it with a little ship only, I am called a thief: thou, doing it with a great navy, art called an emperor!"

"Remove righteousness, and what are kingdoms but great bands of brigands?" asks Augustine. But in so far as states are ruled with some order and justice they have their own peace, sharing in the natural peace of the universe ordained by the Creator. As in the State, so in the Church: both the saved and those rejecting salvation are found, but "such as fear and follow the true law of God" make the Church a manifestation of the celestial City, even if it shows forth that City's full glory only intermittently here below.

While directing men's gaze heavenward, Augustine did not detract from the importance of rulers, whether lay or religious, striving to achieve justice and righteous dealing in their work. Augustine makes no call to reject responsibilities in order to contemplate things heavenly, no suggestion of merely waiting for death to bring about the soul's transition to the celestial realm. His thought was otherworldly in its emphasis on the life hereafter being one of goodness, truth and love, but it also echoed down future ages with a challenge to realise these values in every activity of mundane life. This was a necessary corrective at a time when flight from what seemed an increasingly evil and decaying world had an enormous appeal for many - though paradoxically those who were most determined on seeking their salvation by retreat often contributed most in creating the society which was to come.

Augustine died at a moment (430 AD) when the Vandals, following on the Goths, had broken through to Spain and North Africa, and were besieging his own city of Hippo. The Goths, and to some extent the Vandals, were tribes who had already gained much in the way of civilisation from Rome - not all encounters on the frontiers had been bloody, and the Goths particularly had lived alongside of Romans within the frontiers as *foederati*. The long hair and trousers of their menfolk were taken over by teenage Romans and young men as the height of fashion, a vogue not unlike long hair and jeans today. The Huns were more thoroughly alien, more recently arrived from the further parts of Asia. The impression they created must have been similar to that of the Russian army as it entered the lands of Central Europe on the heels of the retreating Germans in 1944 or 1945. To the observer in Czechoslavakia the Russian army was a vast horde "without a beginning and without an end. And finally the rearguard: miles and miles of small light carts drawn by low Cossack horses ... a flood from the Steppes, spreading across Europe."

In the days of Attila this human flood had only been diverted from Constantinople by enormous bribes - destruction of entire cities and the massacre or enslavement of the inhabitants had been the Huns' normal practice. Turned back by a combined Roman and Gothic force at Châlons in 451 AD, they entered Italy and menaced Rome. Despite the shock of Rome's violation by Alaric 42 years before, its defences remained inadequate, with slaves or other fifth columnists within the city ready to abet the enemy. When Attila was preparing his attack the only chance of avoiding an even worse disaster lay in diplomacy. Pope Leo I, with two leading Senators, confronted Attila at his camp. "The pressing eloquence of Leo, his majestic aspect and sacerdotal robes, excited the veneration of Attila for the spiritual father of the Christians." Attila was reminded that Alaric had not long enjoyed his exploit: within a year he had died. Whether it was from superstitious fear or other motives, Attila refrained - and anyway died shortly afterwards.

A similar attempt was made by Leo three years later, when the Vandal king Genseric was threatening Rome. This time Leo was not successful, except in extracting a promise that there should be no incendiarism, massacres or torture, but looting took place for fourteen days with considerable damage to buildings and taking of captives for ransom or slavery.

Had it not been for such authority as the Church and its representatives could exert, and for the mitigating effect of its welfare work, the disaster would have been much greater. The captives who were transported to Carthage (the Vandal base) were succoured by the bishop, Deogratias, who sold church plate to ransom some of them and helped others in any way he could, converting two churches into hospitals for those suffering from the effects of their enforced passage to Africa. In Rome too such aid and welfare as could be organised for the stricken inhabitants who remained there was entirely in the hands of Leo and his staff, the churches - as at other times of need - being turned into depositories for food and alms, and distribution centres.

As civilisations touch their nadir, great men are thrown up who change the course of history - on one level the prophets, teachers, sages and founders of faiths, on another the statesmen such as Augustus or Constantine. At the dead period in the West - "the day when heaven was falling, the hour when earth's foundations fled" - these roles were combined in men like Leo, leaders at once spiritual and temporal, buoyed up by an immense confidence in God, statesmen who dealt with kings and emperors in a harsh world where responsibility for the Church meant reaching out into politics, diplomacy and economics, since slavery or freedom, life or death, were the overriding issues. Although the background of such men is the old world that is dying, they represent in their lives the new world that is coming to birth.   Both in their deeds and words there is something fresh and dynamic.   Instead of being moulded by a crumbling culture, the culture has to change to accommodate *them*. The live cells of their followers are the growing-points of the new civilisation. In our case we too are beginning to reach that point of decay and deadness where the light that such people bring into the world shines out against the gloomy background of anxiety, disorder and disaster.

Under Leo the authority and prestige of the Roman Church increased, in contrast with the dwindling power of the State in the West, weakened by foreign generals competing for power while using their imperial nominees as pawns, expendable when no longer useful. Leo died in 461 AD, before stability returned for a time under Odovacar and Theodoric, but by then he had succeeded in bringing the Papacy to a position of pre-eminence throughout the former and still existing provinces of the Roman Empire. Though not without challenge from Antioch, Alexandria and Constantinople, Rome was recognised as the premier see, the claim for primacy being strongly stressed by Leo as the successor of St. Peter.

Leo was a powerful personality whose clarifications of doctrine concerning the divine and human nature of Christ were acceptable even to Greek-speaking ecclesiastics whose talent for metaphysical hairsplitting usually gave them the lead in these highly debateable questions. It was a triumph for Leo when his "Tomes" were accepted as the correct definitions of doctrine at the Council of Chalcedon, and he put relentless pressure on bishops and the eastern Emperors to deal drastically with anyone who challenged their validity.

The tradition of straight talking by clerics to emperors had been set by Basil in his dealings with Valens, and also by Ambrose, who had brought the last Emperor to hold sway both in East and West, Theodosius I, to his church at Milan to do public penance for a punitive massacre at Thessalonica. Leo's letters to the eastern rulers left them in no doubt as to the action which he pressed them to take against the "unrestrained madness and blind wickedness" of anyone challenging the conclusions of Chalcedon, "sowing lies by the vessels of wrath ... with diabolical purpose." To bishops his language could be even stronger, in exhorting them with various metaphors to deal with "the filthy puddle" or "deadly disease" of heresy. Equally if they evaded their competence or took questionable action without his knowledge or consent, his strictures could be extremely severe. "I am quite dumbfounded, beloved brother, and I am also sorely grieved that you brought yourself to be so savagely moved against someone ... For we made you our deputy, beloved, on the understanding that you were engaged to share our responsibility, not to take plenary powers on yourself."

In morals he was also a forthright speaker in his challenging sermons and letters, for purity of life, abstinence, and the rejection of anger and lust for vengeance, as the condition for a caring heart and generous giving to those in need. "Make this winter's fast fruitful to yourselves in bounteous alms," is his message to his flock, who should rejoice in so doing, just as they should rejoice at Christmas that "for us has dawned the day of ever-new redemption."

Comment: Stridon and Aquileia; Pope Leo I (the Great). (p. 283)

3. **Rome: heritage and growing point**: *Benedict and monasteries: Cassiodorus: continuity in administration; conserving the literary heritage.*

Not long after Leo died, the last Emperor of the West, Augustulus, was pensioned off by the German general Odovacar, and his insignia sent to Constantinople (476 AD). Odovacar ruled with the aid of civil servants from the old professional families. The Senate, though reduced in numbers, still met, and took its responsibilities seriously as the governing body for Rome itself, in matters like the water-supply. Consuls were still elected annually, though without the powers of old. His successor Theodoric, though he took power by violence, gave Italy another period of order and reasonable government, settling his Goths peacefully, by agreement with the landowners, on their estates, which had been depopulated by war and plague. An Indian summer ensued for Italy and some of Rome's neighbouring provinces, while government appointees continued to hold office, the civil service continued to function, and the Senate continued to meet - all under the aegis of the King (the title assumed by Theodoric). A somewhat shadowy allegiance was accorded to the Emperor at Constantinople, whither both Senate and Church sent resident representatives. Grain and wheat continued to be supplied from southern Italy and Sicily to provide the weekly dole for the citizens, and for their amusement wild beast hunts were staged in the Amphitheatre and chariot races in the Circus. An African monk visiting the city as the century ended could scarcely conceive how the heavenly Jerusalem might outshine its glories, despite the depredations of Goths and Vandals, and the decay of ancient temples.

To some of the inhabitants, however, life might seem **rather** different from the rose-tinted vision of an enthusiastic tourist from a distant African township. This at least was the case with the young Benedict (480-543 AD). Education, a well-to-do family, the possibility of a professional career in the peaceful Ostrogothic state - all these advantages had to be rejected as too much part of a corrupt society, with its materialistic values and low morals, which more than a century of Christianity as the state religion had so far not much altered. Benedict was still only a boy, or at most a very young man, when he decided to quit Rome, where he was studying, and seek the good of his soul by rejecting "the world". The story went that his nanny accompanied him to his first retreat some 40 miles away, where he joined a group of like-minded men, but after a short time decided to live in solitude. Although so young, Benedict's well-formed personality enabled him to stand the rigours, physical and psychological, of a lonely life in the wilds at Subiaco, the grounds of one of Nero's deserted palaces. Resisting the usual temptations - he nearly abandoned his retreat for a girl who had previously attracted him - he persisted, helped by another hermit nearby from his meagre store of food. Before long other young men came to join him, so forming the live cell of a movement which was to spread throughout Western Europe.

Benedict left Subiaco when unwanted visitors - especially some loose women sent by ill-wishers - became too much of a nuisance. He retreated with a group further into the country, settling at Monte Cassino, the site of the famous abbey which was to be built and enlarged by future generations of his followers. Like other such pioneers - Pachomius, Basil, Jerome - Benedict had a sister, his twin Scholastica, who founded a convent nearby: a kind of partnership, though they met only once a year, the last time being shortly before they died within a few days of each other.

Benedict effected, it has been claimed, "a revolution in the moral attitude of man". He certainly carried into the coming civilisation of the West the changing attitudes and heightened awareness of human needs which was the best of the heritage from Athens and Jerusalem. He helped to shift the motivation for a dedicated Christian life from the aim of self-mastery by austerity as a means of gaining heaven to that of letting an awareness of God's love be the moulding force - with work (gardening and doing the chores) as well as prayer, worship and study, with care for others, to take up the energies of mind and body. He helped to mould the work-ethic of future generations, changing attitudes radically in respect of work in general and household chores in particular, regarded hitherto as only for slaves, and in the poorer homes for women. When Duke Godfrey of Lorraine found his brother Frederick washing dishes in the monastery kitchen and told him sarcastically that it was a fine occupation for a count, he replied "You are right. I ought indeed to think myself honoured by the smallest service for the Master." The fruit of such examples appeared after many centuries in washing-up and other household chores becoming fairly normal work by husbands in some countries of the West - a facet of Western civilisation which makes it, in this respect, almost unique.

With his keen appreciation of the right motives for a dedicated life, Benedict could sense the exhibitionism or masochism of anyone making a demonstration of austerity. To one cave-dwelling hermit who had chained his foot to a rock he said "if you are really Christ's servant, don't let an iron chain be your fetter, but the chains of Christ." The practical commonsense which was the keynote of his Rule led to its being adopted by most Western monastic communities in subsequent centuries. Benedict, in "this least of all Rules which we have written for beginners," did not stress the need for a harsh discipline, but sought to bring about self-conquest through "the enlargement of the heart and the unspeakable sweetness of love" arising from "running in the way of God's commandments" - a change which would come from joy and devotion rather than from self-mortification. After rising through various degrees of humility,

"the monk will presently arrive at that love of God which, being perfect, casteth out fear: whereby he shall begin to keep, without labour, and as it were naturally and by custom, all those precepts which he had hitherto observed through fear; no longer through dread of hell, but for the love of Christ, and of good habit and delight in virtue."

Nonetheless, rising through the degrees of humility to the sixth ("being content with the meanest and worst of everything") and the seventh ("believing oneself in one's inmost heart to be lower and viler than all") was nothing if not challenging, involving among other things confessing to one's Abbot all evil thoughts and secret sins. There were the long early services, which meant rising in the dark at 3 a.m. winter and summer, and the other six services each day - all the psalms were said or sung in the course of a week, besides much Bible-study and prayer, including at meal times, when silence was required. In fact silence was a general rule, times for conversation being minimal, with jesting and buffoonery outlawed. Punishments - excommunication or even beating, especially for children (15 and below) - were fairly severe, and strict rules governed the receiving of letters or presents, which needed the Abbot's permission, as did travel (no stories to be recounted on returning!). For enforcing the renunciation of private property bed-searches were mandatory.

Heavy responsibility was left with the Abbot for "bestowing all pastoral diligence on his unquiet and disobedient flock, and employing all his care to amend their corrupt manner of life, showing forth all goodness and holiness by deeds rather than his words" (this did not exclude "bodily strikes" for the hard of heart and disobedient). Benedict warned against those who took the tonsure but continued worldly lives, and fulminated against the Gyrovagi or hippie-type wandering monks, who continued to be the bane of the movement all through the Middle Ages, "staying in different cells for three or four days at a time, ever roaming, with no stability, given up to their own pleasures and the snares of gluttony."

The other aspects of the Rule which made it generally acceptable was the sensible care for the health of the members. Unlike the rejection of personal hygiene by Egyptian hermits and monks, and even by those from a cultivated stratum of society like Jerome and his lady friends, cleanliness was enjoined, particularly in the kitchen, where washing of feet for those going in and out was obligatory as well as the weekly washing of towels. Everyone, except the sick or those with more important duties, was expected to help in preparing and serving food - two cooked dishes for the daily meal (children to receive smaller helpings), and a pint of wine for all except those who aimed at the spiritual renewal of abstinence. Labour was expected from the able-bodied in the fields, and help in getting in the harvest. For the sick there was a special apartment, with meat and baths as required; and for everyone adequate clothing and bedding was specified. Though fasting as well as restraint in eating was encouraged to bring the body under full control, there was no masochistic maltreatment of it.

Magnus Aurelius Cassiodorus Senator, born about the same time as Benedict, survived much longer, until the age of 96 or even 100. He came of several generations of distinguished civil servants and administrators. His great-grandfather had defended Sicily against the Vandals. After being chief legal adviser and head of the civil service under Theodoric, he followed in his father's footsteps to the highest position, Praetorian Prefect, under the Queen-regent Amalasuntha and her son.

While in government service Cassiodorus regarded himself as "a part-time Minister of Culture" as well as an administrator. He was in the habit of including philosophical or historical observations in the directives he sent out, and liked to show his knowledge of natural history and other subjects. He prefaces the royal confirmation to Jews in Genoa of all the privileges conferred by "the foresight of antiquity", by opining that "the true mark of *civilitas* is the observance of law; it is this which makes life in the community possible and separates man from beasts". When he is chivvying Theon (*Vir Sublimis,* according to the inflated titles of the day), the official charged with supplying the purple dye for the royal robes, he digresses on its qualities and the shell-fish that produces it. Orders to curb the riotous behaviour of fans at the races lead on to a detailed description of the Circus where they take place, with antiquarian observations. A call to arms compares this mobilisation of young men to the hawk thrusting "her still weak and tender young ones out of the nest" so that they have to fly - all this among detailed directives about taxes and audits; repair of walls, buildings and aqueducts; provision for the royal table and supplies for famine areas; assurances to officials about pay during sick-leave and that sick-leave must be taken when needed (with notes on beauty-spots for convalescing); increasing teachers' pay; supplying mosaic-workers for Ravenna; stopping bribery at papal elections and setting the fees to be paid by appointees to Church posts, etc., etc.

He had a high appreciation of the civilising effects of the arts. Asking his colleague Boethius to find a musician to send to Clovis, King of the Franks, he digresses about music in its various modes and forms, and points to the influence the *Citharoedus* could have, "going forth like another Orpheus to charm the beast-like hearts of the barbarians."

Theodoric's reign ended in bitterness and bloodshed, Rome's leading Senators, Boethius (almost unique in his generation for his studies at Athens) and his father-in-law Symmachus being executed on groundless charges of treason. A ray of the declining civilisation shines from the prison of Boethius, where he wrote *The Consolation of Philosophy,* "a golden volume" (in the words of Gibbon) "not unworthy of the leisure of Plato or Tully, but which claims incomparable merit from the barbarism of the times and the situation of the author."

Theodoric's death in 526 AD was the signal for Italy's descent into the dark age which was now overtaking the West. Church difficulties aggravated an unstable political situation, with fighting and assassinations among his successors. Theodoric, though an Arian, had hoped that the freedom he gave to his Catholic subjects would be accorded to his co-religionists in the East. In this he was disappointed. Not only were Justinian and Theodora taking a hard line to impose their own forms of belief in the East, but they were determined to re-establish the Catholic monopoly in the West and make sure of having an amenable pope. These considerations and the desire of reintegrating the West in an empire as extensive as in its greatest days, were the motives which led them to send Belisarius, a general of genius, to reconquer North Africa and Italy. The wars that followed, first with the Goths, then with the Lombards, wrecked Italy, and left it divided between those areas and cities under the Exarch (the Emperor's representative at Ravenna) and those under various Lombard chieftains who took the title of Duke (*Dux*).

Cassiodorus reached the pinnacle of his career as Praetorian Prefect seven years after Theodoric died. As long as the Gothic regime lasted, he kept at his post in the administrative capital, Ravenna, faithful to his vision of an Italy under a partnership of Romans and Goths. He was frustrated in this aim when Belisarius captured the city. He left for Constantinople, returning fifteen years later, when the war had ended with Italy precariously reunited to the Eastern Empire. He settled down on his estate at Squillace in Southern Italy, where he established a monastery of which the centre-piece was his library.

He had tried to carry out some of his educational ideas before his retirement. During his last period at the Ostrogothic court he had worked with Pope Agapetus to establish the beginnings of a university at Rome, on the model of the famous library at Alexandria which was the centre of higher education there, and of a more recent foundation by Jews at Nisibis (a Persian city, formerly Roman, in Northern Syria). He had tried, he said, "to raise funds to endow Christian Schools with paid professors", as an alternative to the schools of pre-Christian type with their old-fashioned syllabuses. He and the Pope at least succeeded in creating a library, but this was dispersed or destroyed in the course of the Gothic wars. He spent some of his time at Constantinople on an exposition of the Psalms (*Expositio Psalmorum*), in which he expanded a study of St. Augustine's to give deeper understanding of their part in the daily services of the monasteries. "From the sea of the psalms, copious with its waters, I confined and led off narrow rivulets."

Now at a pleasant spot on his estate near the sea he founded, in 540 AD, his monastery college for studying theology and secular literature, which he named Vivarium after the fish-ponds constructed among the rocks. There he brought his books, adding to them over the years. The principal work, apart from prayer, of the monks was not agriculture as at Cassino, but studying and copying books: the routine was educational as well as devotional. The regulations were not those of Benedict's Rule, but owed more to John Cassian, a contemporary of Jerome and Augustine, who spent some years in the monasteries of Egypt before founding his own communities in the south of Gaul. The pre-Christian classics were not to be neglected, and only those monks whose interests lay elsewhere than in study were to take up gardening and agriculture (specialist works were available on these subjects). When it came to physical effort, said

Cassiodorus, the work of the scribe, "if he writes correctly, appeals to me most."

For helping his student-monks he wrote the *Institutiones*, introductory handbooks which he prepared "driven by divine caring ... under the Lord's guidance", in which he surveyed the relevant literature, and gave detailed advice on techniques of study, on spelling, and on the binding and care of books. He reminded the student-monks of the importance of the cause entrusted to them, "the serving of Christians, the guarding of the Church's treasure, the lighting of souls."

This was not the only monastery where such work was done: reading and copying had been among the activities of the monasteries of Pachomius, and they formed an important part of the programme at the Lucullanum monastery near Naples. What distinguished Cassiodorus in his foundation was the systematic direction which he gave, surrounding himself with a group of translators (from Greek) and grammarians, to prepare and collate the manuscripts. He helped to assemble and edit the entire text of Jerome's translation of the Bible.

What happened to his library and the college in the years after his death is not known, but his writings were disseminated throughout the medieval libraries of Western Europe. At the nadir of the West's decline, Cassiodorus gave a new impetus to serious study; to maintaining the Classical heritage; and to stimulating the eventual revival of letters and the arts. In the selection of his official correspondence (*Variae Epistolae*), which he published as propaganda material for the failing cause of Romano-Gothic partnership, and as self-justification for his part in it - not without blowings of his own trumpet - he shows himself pompous and verbose, but his later writings are often direct and to the point. Was this the consequence of the change from a prestigious official job to doing the work of his heart - educational and cultural work for younger people? It was a deeper change, perhaps, than could be expected from the change of situation, and more to do with the spiritual development of the man, fortunate in having a second life of some fifty years after his professional career was over. A man of two lives, he also links two epochs: the ending of the Western Empire (being born just after its demise), and the coming of the new Western civilisation, signalised by the pontificate of Gregory the Great.

4. **Gregory: the change from old to new**: *The Rome of raids and ruins becomes the centre of a new civilisation. Expecting the Apocalypse. Welfare work, miracles, missions.*

Rome, captured by Belisarius, then by the Goths, and changing hands several times, remained as the sixth century ended within the Exarchate under Constantinople, but its garrison was weak and rarely paid. Once, when captured by the Goths, all the inhabitants, reduced to a pitiful remnant by plague, famine and massacre, had been forced to evacuate the city while looting went on unhindered for a month. Though still surrounded by the walls built when her troubles began three centuries before, Rome was but a shadow of her greatness.

> "The laws, the monuments, even the historic recollections of the past gradually fade from memory. The temples fall to ruin. The Capitol, standing on its solitary hill, still, it is true, displays the sumptuous monuments of the greatest Empire ever known to history. But the Imperial Palace, although enduring in its main outlines, a colossal labyrinth of halls and courts, of temples and a thousand artistic chambers resplendent with precious marbles, and still here and there covered with gold-embroidered hangings, is but a haunted and deserted fortress from which all semblance of life has passed away. One little corner alone remains inhabited by the Byzantine Dux, a eunuch from the court of the Greek Emperor, or a half-Asiatic general, with his secretaries, servants and guards.

> "Silent and deserted, the sumptuous Forums of the Caesars and of the Roman people have already fallen into the obscurity of legend. The theatres and the huge Circus Maximus, where the chariot-races, the cherished and last remaining amusement of the Romans, are no longer celebrated, grass-grown and filled with rubbish, moulder to decay ...

> "The vast Thermae [baths] of Imperial times, no longer supplied by any aqueduct, useless, forsaken, and already mantled with ivy, resemble ruined cities in their vastness and desertion. The costly marbles have already fallen, or been ruthlessly stripped from their walls, and the mosaic pavements grown loose and disjointed. Some ancient chairs of light or dark marble, and splendid baths of porphyry or oriental alabaster still remain in the beautifully painted halls, but one by one these too are, for the most part, carried away by the priests, to serve as episcopal chairs in the churches, as receptacles for the ashes of some saint,

or as fonts in the baptisteries. A few, however, together with numerous statues, still remain unheeded, to be shattered and overthrown by falling masonry or buried for centuries in the dust."

The Senate no longer meets, the successions of Consuls, unbroken since ancient times, is ended, but the pattern had already been set by Pope Leo I a century before for Rome's resurgence, and the resumption of her role as the centre of civilisation and order in the West. As Byzantium after her dark age created another empire through the radiating spiritual power of her missionaries and monks, so did Rome under men like Benedict, Cassiodorus and Gregory I. These Romans, from professional and aristocratic families, were steeped in the past, but they carried the best of this past forwards into the future.

Among these men Cassiodorus was exceptional in having some vision for the future. Gregory no more than Benedict had any intention of building something that would last - no idea of saving civilisation or creating a new one. Like St. Paul and the early Christians, he thought the world would shortly end anyway. This is the constant theme of his sermons and homilies; it appears in his letter to a king, Ethelbert of the Angles, and in his *Dialogues* addressed to the people.

"Our Redeemer announces the evils which must accompany the old age and decadence of the world ... Since we have seen some of these predictions happen, we have reason to fear that the remainder will soon arrive ... Everywhere we hear sounds of grief and groaning - cities destroyed, fortresses overthrown, fields depopulated, the land turned into a solitude. No inhabitants remain in the country, scarcely anyone in the towns, and still until today what is left of the human race is smitten without cease ... What is therefore pleasing in this life, my brothers? Rome, former mistress of the world, is now a place of suffering and ruin."

The background is of raids, murders, kidnapping, enslavement.

"Wild hordes of Lombards unleashed from their own native land descended on us ... In this land of ours the world is not merely announcing its end, it is pointing directly to it. Our seeking of the things of heaven must therefore be all the more urgent, since we know that the things of earth are quickly slipping from our grasp ... The world struck as it is with countless scourges, worn out with adversity and daily lamenting its woes, what other message does it din into our ears but that we should cease loving it?"

Born into one of the senatorial families, which for several generations had been Christian (and had produced a pope, Felix III, who may have been his grandfather), Gregory yet had no interest in making a career either in government or the Church. Aged 13 when the Gothic wars ended, he passed his student days in the fragile peace imposed by Byzantium, when some state-maintained teachers were re-instituted. Justinian's successor, Justin II, appointed him Urban Prefect of Rome, which, along with Naples, Liguria, and areas around Venice and the foot of Italy, still (the 570's) recognised Byzantium's sway, as did Sicily and the other islands. A Church appointment followed: he was made Deacon of one of Rome's seven districts, charged with relief and charitable work. But neither of these experiences, in an important government post and as a welfare administrator, nor seven years as the Pope's ambassador at Constantinople, encouraged him to continue in diplomacy or administration.

Before his sojourn at Constantinople he had embarked on the ascetic life of a monk. On his father's death he had devoted his inheritance to charitable purposes and founded monasteries, six in Sicily and one in the family mansion at Rome. His mother, sisters and aunts, dedicated to the same life, were in different houses. He lived for a time as a simple monk in his monastery of St. Andrew's. He was a great admirer of Benedict, who died about the year he was born, and whose Rule was well-known at Rome through the monks who had fled there from Monte Cassino when the monastery was wrecked by the Lombards.

It went against the grain to accept the papacy on the death of Pelagius II, but duty overrode his desire for the contemplative life, deeply though he regretted the choice he felt he had to make. "One who is submissive to the divine disposals ... ought both heartily to avoid the duty of ruling and unwillingly obey."

To Theoctista, sister of the Emperor Maurice, he wrote:

"I have lost the deep joys of my quiet, and seem to have risen outwardly while inwardly falling down", and later he wrote to the Bishop of Antioch: "What tribulations I suffer in this land from the swords of the Lombards, from the iniquities of the judges, from the press of business, from the care of subjects, and also from bodily affliction, I am unable to express either by pen or tongue."

Despite the enormous amount of business which Gregory now had to undertake, he still contrived to live the monastic life as far as possible with his *familia* of fellow-monks, among them his personal aides. He had brought some of these companions with him to Constantinople, in order to have a base in this little community dedicated to prayer and contemplation from which he could carry out his diplomatic duties in "the world". Now at Rome the routine of the monastery merged with the public Mass, which he reorganised as a focus for the spiritual life of the city, with pageantry and "Gregorian" music. When in sufficient health he attended these services, which might take up to three hours a day. But he was dogged by ill-health, perhaps the effect of his austerities, and was practically bed-ridden for his final years.

In the quality and volume of his work he exemplified the best of the Roman tradition, in fact excelling the achievements of his civil service predecessors, while setting an impeccable standard of integrity and concern for others. His expectation of an imminent, apocalyptic change no whit diminished his application in grappling in a highly practical way with the tasks that he had to undertake. These were, on the material level, the defence of Rome and negotiating with the Lombards (who repeatedly besieged the city), in securing supplies of food and ensuring it reached those in need, and in trying to maintain the water-system and buildings; and on the spiritual plane, caring for his flock in Rome and far afield, selecting the best men available as bishops and other clergy, overseeing their work, directing missions abroad, and exerting the primacy of his see and his authority as the successor of St. Peter.

The Church was far the biggest landowner in Italy. Noble families had turned over houses and estates to the Church when their leading members adopted the ascetic life or emigrated to the East. Bequests multiplied. Galla, daughter of the murdered Symmachus and last of her line, as a young widow gave her vast estates near Rome on which monasteries and churches were built. The lands under Church control comprised much of the Campagna bordering the city, and of Southern Italy and Sicily, including the estates of Gregory's family which he had made over, and where the Lombard Dukes had not penetrated. Gregory made detailed inventories of Church property, and kept careful accounts of the income and supplies they produced. The peasants, though tied to their land, had their holdings and the amounts of grain-tax noted in the register, while Gregory sternly opposed embezzlement by local officials and provided a new lot of cattle, sheep and pigs to any peasant who lost his animals through crop failure or other adversity.

He appointed agents, "rectors of the patrimony", to administer these properties, and closely controlled them with deacons or sub-deacons sent from Rome. To these he gave spiritual responsibilities in addition to their administrative duties, which were concerned to a large extent with ensuring the food supplies for Rome. He also vigorously tackled the Emperor's representative, and even the Emperor himself, in demanding that promised supplies of food and money should be sent.

Welfare work in Rome was carried out with the same efficiency and care. There was a monthly provision of supplies, not unlike the old dole of imperial days, but directed to those in need, not just to those who could claim a right - corn, wine, cheese, vegetables, bacon, fish and oil, as well as materials for household needs like dyestuffs and even some luxury items. Three thousand nuns, many of them refugees, received money for their bedding and daily upkeep, giving their help in return.

"I believe that but for these women", Gregory wrote, "not one of us could have survived the Lombard swords." An equivalent of the "meals on wheels" system operated - meals sent by couriers "to the sick and infirm throughout the streets and lanes of every district of the city", with dishes from Gregory's own table "to those of higher rank who were ashamed to beg." The names of all recipients, in Rome and throughout Italy, were noted in the register kept in the administrative bureau of the Lateran (the former palace which preceded the Vatican) with details of the amounts of aid and the dates when they were due.

Gregory also personally took care of families outside Rome whom he knew - wheat to be sent to an aunt, with money to buy shoes for her boys; two widows who were to have specific supplies of wheat; an old friend who had married after briefly becoming a monk, and whose young daughters Gregory promised to look after when he became ill and they were in danger of being harassed by creditors. He gave instructions for the sale of church plate for money to redeem captives from slavery, among them English boys of 17 or 18 "who may profit from being given to God in monasteries", with provision for a presbyter to accompany them from France in case they fell ill and might die, and so would need baptising on the way.

This care for people's spiritual and material needs was only part of Gregory's wider concern, to spread the Gospel as thoroughly as possible, and bring deepening of faith to clergy and laity everywhere he could. His *Book of Pastoral Rule* was an entirely new look at the way in which bishops and others with the cure of souls could carry out their work. His sensitiveness to different kinds of people - he speaks of "sagacious insight" - is shown in the sections on how to admonish people who are presented as opposites: poor and rich, joyful and sad, goodnatured and envious, simple and crafty, etc. As for those who have to do the admonishing they "should show themselves to be such that their subjects may not blush to disclose their secrets to them", and if the hearing of such secrets is likely to give rise to temptations, "the pastor is the more easily rescued from his own temptations as he is more compassionately distressed by those of others." A reminder that one is "on a par with the very brethren who are corrected" may also help; under no pretence should this ministry be turned to "the purpose of domination." The *Pastoral Rule* shows Gregory giving content to the title he most prized, "servant of the servants of God".

Gregory maintained the links he had made with Constantinople during his embassy there. Although he had kept as far as possible when there to his monastic life, he had also moved in the highest society making numerous friends, many among well-placed ladies. A great deal of his correspondence was with friends and officials, as well as with the Emperor Maurice and his wife and sister. He well understood the value of feminine influence, and frequently exhorted the Empress and other ladies to put in words with their husbands to support his requests, whether for military or financial aid, or concerning some ecclesiastical matter (the claim of the Patriarch of Constantinople to be regarded as the senior primate was constantly cropping up as a bone of contention). He made a powerful humanitarian request to the Empress Constantina to take up the cause of the inhabitants of Corsica, so oppressed by the rapacity of government officials that they were selling their children into slavery - "how one ought to feel for the children of others is well-known to those who have children of their own."

As so often in the events of this period a key part was played by women. In dealing with the Lombards, of whom Gregory could use the harshest words as they ravaged the country and besieged Rome, he soon found an ally in Queen Theodolinda, who had been converted to the Catholic faith. "How your Excellency has laboured earnestly and kindly, as is your wont, for the conclusion of peace we have learnt from the report of our son, the abbot Probus ... For you may be assured, most excellent daughter, that for the saving of so much bloodshed on both sides you have acquired no small reward. On this account, returning thanks for your goodwill, we implore the mercy of our God to repay you with good in body and soul here and in the world to come. Moreover, greeting you with fatherly affection, we exhort you so to deal with your most excellent consort that he may not reject the alliance of the Christian republic."

For Gregory the defence of Rome had to be largely a do-it-yourself affair. The Emperor had installed a garrison, but - against Gregory's bitter opposition - most of the troops were withdrawn by the Exarch to protect the line of communication from Ravenna to Rome. In any case the soldiers were rarely properly paid, and though some commanders were good, others exploited their position to make money by such means as selling supplies on the black market.

Gregory's frustrations were great when (as he wrote to the Emperor) from the walls of the city they could see Roman captives being taken away manacled to be sold as slaves in France. At another time the Exarch undercut his negotiations, which were at the point of success, and sent a report to the Emperor which made him appear as an ill-advised bungler falling for Lombard trickery. So it was a matter of great relief when real peace became a possibility, thanks to the good offices of Theodolinda and the percolation of Christianity through the court to the people. It took another century and a half before the Lombards were properly christianised and settled, to become later, as part of the new Italian people, leaders of Europe as bankers and businessmen, pre-eminent in the arts and graces of civilised living.

The civilising outreach of the Church radiated through the surrounding countries. Much of Gregory's correspondence was with the rulers of Gaul, now increasingly known as Francia (France) since Clovis and his Franks had secured control over a large part of the land. The conversion to Christianity of Clovis and his court, however superficial, brought France into Gregory's spiritual realm.

And beyond France lay Britain, where the Angli had set up their kingdom. So to that distant province of the Empire, lost 200 years before, Gregory sent the mission under Augustine, Abbot of his St. Andrew's monastery, with a band of monks recruited from France. They discovered their ally, like Theodolinda, in Bertha, King Ethelbert's queen, brought up as a Catholic of the Frankish royal house. In such ways was the spiritual empire extended which, under the leadership of Gregory and his successors, was replacing the old and now ruined Empire of the Caesars. With the faith came literacy, monasteries, churches (the earliest ones sometimes old ruins restored or pagan temples adapted for Christian use), Latin and vernacular literature, the arts, and eventually the glories of romanesque architecture. Before long in England the monks and saints from the south linked up with those from Ireland, Wales and Northumbria, who had maintained their faith from earlier times during the troubled centuries. By the end of the seventh century, monks from the British Isles who became missionaries and teachers were in the vanguard of those spreading Christian faith and culture, with heroic labours, sufferings and journeys, throughout Western and Northern Europe.

Comment: Gregory's complaint about exchanging the contemplative for the active life; Emperor Maurice and styles of address. (p. 283)

CHAPTER SEVEN

THE MEDIEVAL EQUILIBRIUM AND THE MODERN "HELLENISTIC" WEST

1. The medieval period of equilibrium and cultural transmission: *the three civilised areas of West Eurasia: Baghdad as heir to ancient culture, which passed westwards to North Africa and Spain.   Scholars from Constantinople augmented the movement which culminated in the Renaissance and Reformation, and the Scientific Revolution.   Christian dynamism played a part in this evolution, as in that of the medieval city or commune.*

A brief period of equilibrium between the three civilised areas of Western Eurasia set in around 1000 AD. These areas were Byzantium and its dependencies, the Islamic Caliphate, and the Latin West. During this period the heritage of the older civilisations was preserved, passed on and eventually augmented as communications were re-established and became safer and more rapid. This applied to the more regular use of the Silk Route across Eurasia, and even more important, to the development of ocean-going shipping, both by the Arabs and the Chinese.

The nodal point of this Medieval world was the Abbasid Caliphate, heir of the last world-religion, Islam, to come to birth through the travail of Antiquity. The Caliphate at Baghdad gathered in Greek science, philosophy and mathematics, preserved in the Syriac language at places like the medical school at Gundeshapur, founded by Nestorian missionaries under the patronage of the Sassanid Persian Emperors. Baghdad was heir of Greece, Syria and Iran, and also received the advanced mathematical learning (numerals, arithmetic and algebra) from India.   It drew on the high civilisation of Afghanistan and Turkestan, where cultural and religious streams from all quarters had their confluence, while Muslim savants went as far afield as China.

As the Caliphate declined, Baghdad ceased after three centuries to be the centre of civilisation. Its culture passed westwards to Sicily and Spain, thence to be absorbed into the growing culture of Western Europe as these territories were reconquered for Christendom.

Spain around 1000 AD was the place where pre-eminently the flowering of civilisation came through the merging of diverse streams, in an environment where Christian, Muslim and Jew could mingle on an equal footing and together build up a genuine "republic of letters". In areas where Muslims were dominant and Christians were officially second-class citizens, Christians were still free enough to maintain their own religion and culture, with a distinctive architecture for their churches. And when Toledo was taken back into Christendom the university was not destroyed, but became a multi-cultural school of learning and languages, frequented particularly by scholars from Paris and elsewhere in the north.

Christian dynamism had its part in scientific advance as it did in social change. For men like Roger Bacon "the ultimate value of science was the service of the Church" - even though his superiors in the Franciscan Order attempted to suppress his genius. Lecturing, during his period of freedom, at Paris or Oxford, he was in touch with translators from Toledo, who had been there to work with Muslim and Jewish scholars in turning the books of Greek and Arab philosophers and scientists into Latin.

Theological clashes gave rise to heresies, and massive attempts to formulate a new world-view: al-Ghazali for the Muslim world and Aquinas for Christendom. The scientific heritage, as it came to Western Europe, inspired Grosseteste and Bacon to develop the experimental method, while Leonardo Fibonacci of Pisa, who owed his learning to Muslim scholars in North Africa, heralded the rise of the new mathematics. This led on to the Renaissance and Reformation, and the Scientific Revolution of the 17th and 18th centuries.

In Sicily too, where the Arabs had seized the island from Byzantium, to be conquered later by the Normans, a fruitful mingling of cultural styles developed. Here the Greek strain merged with the Islamic and Christian, with resulting glories such as the churches of Palermo and the cathedral of Monreale. The opening into Italy channelled the Arab and Greek learning to universities in the peninsula, enriched by scholars who brought much of the heritage of Ancient Greece direct from Constantinople both before and after its conquest by the Turks in 1453.

As well as playing an essential role in the universities of Spain under both Muslim and Christian rule, Jews elsewhere in Europe were making an important cultural contribution. Their schools, notably in the Rhineland, had already taken on something of the character of universities by the time of the First Crusade, when such institutions had not yet appeared among the Christians. A high cultural awareness among the Jewish communities was maintained by the international correspondence of the rabbis, dealing with all questions regarding the Torah and its application - a correspondence which strengthened the Jews as a supernational element in contrast to the nationalism (eventually racism) which was beginning to develop, and which added to the religious bigotry in the pogroms perpetrated by the Crusaders as they passed through Germany, and in the expulsion of the Jews from England and elsewhere. But even the massacres and persecutions did not cloud the conviction of the great poet of that epoch in Spain, Judah ha-Levi, that "Israel is to the nations as the heart to the body - not a nation to the nations, but a vitalizing element to them all."

Cordoba, the home of Judah ha-Levi, outshone the other cities of Europe, literally with its street lighting, and with its baths - an inheritance from Rome, as was its bridge across the Guadalquivir. Further north, cities - though materially less advanced - were already resplendent with cathedrals and churches, the outward and visible signs of evolving communities, not unlike the Greek city-states, but different through their Christian inspiration.

The type of government which developed in many cities of Western Europe, in which a proto-democratic element existed, was the commune. A similar system at Novgorod and Pskov in Northern Russia was brought to an end in the adverse circumstances of Mongol invasions and wars. But particularly in the wealthy cloth-producing Low Countries such communes flourished.

The medieval city was "a community of communities in which the same principles of corporate rights and chartered liberties applied equally to the whole and to the parts. For the medieval idea of liberty, which finds its highest expression in the life of the free cities, was not the right of the individual to follow his own will, but the privilege of sharing in a highly organised form of corporate life which possessed its own constitution and rights of self-government."

It is noteworthy that this part of Europe where the communes flourished most strongly is the region where the embryo of today's European Community appeared - Benelux (Belgium, Netherlands, Luxembourg).

The medieval equilibrium, in a geographical sense, was upset by the invasions of Mongols and Turks, which blocked the land route to China. But Arab and Chinese inventions, notably the compass and astronomical tables, opened the ocean routes, and made possible the hazardous voyages by West European seafarers to China round Africa and India. Columbus, trying to reach China by going round the world, discovered America instead. So began the modern "Hellenistic" era when the findings of science applied to technology eventually transformed industry, communications and warfare. Western Europe was the nodal point of this development, because here all the streams of thought, all the inventions of the ages coincided.

Europe, as the 16th century opened, was in a situation similar to that of Europe in the Hellenistic Age - only geographically the areas are reversed. The West corresponds to the Greek-speaking region, divided into numerous states and statelets, many of them in endemic warfare with one another. The East has an expanding Roman-type state in Russia, where the Moscow Grand-Duchy had spearheaded the expulsion of the Mongols (Tatars), and was about to take over the imperial role from the defunct regime of Byzantium. It was long locked in warfare with the Turkish Empire, based on Constantinople - the heir of Persia and the rest of the Middle East, reminiscent of Rome's age-long conflict with Parthia and its Sassanid Persian successor.

In the relations of Church and State there were also similarities with Antiquity. Whereas Muscovy took over the Roman tradition of a priesthood bound up with the State, both supporting and dependent on it, in the West the Greek tradition of philosophical thought continued, arousing religious questionings. These were coloured in the Renaissance and Reformation by the spiritual upsurge, which (as in the Hellenistic period) brought about profound changes in religion, politics and eventually all areas of cultural and social life.

The rise in the West of monarchical and colonising states in the 16th and 17th centuries preceded or accompanied the rise of empires. In Hellenistic times it was Macedon, the Seleucid kingdom, Carthage and Rome. In the 17th century it was the Habsburg Empire, Brandenburg-Prussia, France, England and Spain. Only those cities which were in a particularly strong position to resist the encroaching monarchical or imperial power, by virtue of their geographical position or history - often both - were able to maintain their freedom. Venice succeeded by becoming, for a time, an imperial power herself, while the cities and cantons of Switzerland found strength in confederation, as did those cities and provinces of the Netherlands, once their freedom had been secured against the power of Spain. Successful resistance against powerful neighbours was also maintained by Hansa cities and German and Italian statelets. In some of these places and in the larger states where the reformed religion took hold and was successfully defended, republican and democratic tendencies were strengthened.

2. **Millennial movements**: *Joachim of Fiore; Franciscan "spirituals.*
Medieval millennial revolts.

As in the ancient Hellenistic Era we are again living at a moment when we think that the world may shortly end. "Our world", that is to say mankind's habitat, may be destroyed in a nuclear Armageddon or by environmental depletion and pollution. But whereas in our case we think of annihilation - a full stop to human history - the older view was that the end of the world would be the beginning of a new heaven and a new earth. This vision was proclaimed by the Hebrew prophets and with stupendous imagery in writings like the Book of Revelation. It was a view distinct from that of the Greeks, who regarded history as repeated cycles of the growth and decay of states and nations: they did not expect a golden age to come, but looked back to one in the remote past.

Apocalyptic themes have been dominant at times of imminent or actual disaster, of catastrophe and revolutionary change. They have accompanied great changes in the social and political order. Although the world did not end as expected in the time of Jesus or Gregory, the "world" with which people were familiar *was* ending, and a new one taking its place. For the Jews of the time of Jesus it was the ending of the semi-independent Jewish state with its temple-ritual at Jerusalem: the destruction of Jerusalem and the dispersion of its inhabitants. For Gregory and his contemporaries it was the ending of the Greco-Roman "world".

St. Augustine re-stated these ideas in *The City of God*. With the Resurrection Christ had begun reigning over His Church, both the living and the dead. Those who had stood firm throughout all the persecutions "and had not worshipped the Beast" would live and reign with Him "for a thousand years" (quoting Revelation). All history, in fact, was seen by Augustine in periods of a thousand years, each comprising ten generations, from Adam to the flood, and so by way of Abraham, David, and the Babylonian Captivity to the birth of Christ, this last event initiating the current period of his day, though its duration could not be calculated like others. At its end Satan (Antichrist) would be loosed briefly before the seventh period, "our Sabbath", when God would rest and mankind would rest in Him.

Millennial ideas persisted during the Middle Ages, no longer associated however with the world ending but with the world changing. The ideas were expressed most vividly by Joachim da Fiore (1135-1202). Born into a professional family - his father was a notary at the court of the Norman kings of Sicily - he went as a young man on an official visit to Constantinople. While there he was shocked by the way the plague ravaged his companions. He changed his way of life, went on to Palestine as a pilgrim, and became a monk in the Cistercian order, a reformed version of the Benedictine. For a time he combined the labours of an abbot with writing theological commentaries and a work of prophecy, *Expositio in Apocalypsin*, but finding the need for greater quiet he moved ever further into the mountains of Calabria with a small group of friends, to continue his meditations. The seven days of Creation suggested seven periods of history, but overlaying this was another, the triple division into the Age of the Father (the Old Testament), the Age of the Gospel and the Son, and the Age of the Spirit, when contemplation, the fine flower of monasticism, would become the way of mankind.

> "The third status will be towards the end of this world, not cloaked in the letter but in full liberty of the Spirit. Then, once the pseudo-gospel of the son of perdition and his prophets has been ejected and destroyed, those who teach justice will be like the splendour of the firmament, and like stars in endless eternities."

Already revered as a prophet in his life-time (he was summoned from his retreat to a colloquy at Messina with Richard Coeur-de-Lion on his way to the Third Crusade), Joachim's teachings were taken up by Franciscans and others after his death. When St. Francis of Assisi died in 1226, his followers split into those who observed the original strictness of the Rule, with its insistence on literal poverty, and those who adopted a more relaxed mode of life. The former found in Joachim's writings a prediction that the new age would be brought in by a dedicated order of monks, whom they took to be themselves.

This revolutionary idea of a new age to be brought in by a dedicated group has persisted through European history - and has provoked opposition and persecutions. Peter Olivi proclaimed that the new age which he and the other "spirituals" were bringing in would purify "the carnal Church" of its corruptions. His writings were censored, and the Church authorities went on to find matters for condemnation in Joachim's works, though four popes had supported him in his life-time.

Catastrophes like the Black Death or other visitations of the plague brought hopes of a mighty change from a situation which seemed intolerable. Since one of the signs of the coming Millennium was supposed to be the conversion of the Jews, pressure backed by terror was applied to this end - hence the massacre of those who held out against forced conversion, adding its grim tally to the pogroms already committed by the barbaric hordes straggling across Europe as Crusaders *en route* for Palestine.

Whereas Joachim, meditating in his mountain retreat, was far removed as could be from perpetrating violence or aggression, it was by no means always so with those gripped by his ideas. Feelings ran high among peasantry oppressed by their lords, or unemployed and low-paid workers in the towns, contrasting their lot with that of wealthy guildsmen or merchants. A charismatic "prophet" preaching the imminent Millennium could rouse a powerful following of men and women, prepared both to inflict suffering and to suffer themselves in the time of "woes" which would precede the thousand years of peace and well-being. They were prepared to fight literally against Antichrist, often represented in the later Middle Ages by the Pope, and against his supporters the clergy - especially the bishops and higher clergy who were regarded as being in the same camp as the wealthy laymen, given to "luxury and avarice."

These movements rose to a crescendo in the fifteenth and sixteenth centuries, when the Turks were pressing against Constantinople and shattering the chivalry of Central Europe on the plains of Hungary - and when, with Suleiman's conquest of Egypt, the entire Mediterranean was threatened. For years the Taborites of Bohemia held out, with their fortified places and laagers of ox-wagons, against the rulers and baronage of the land. A hundred years later (1534-5), Münster, a principal city of North Germany, was taken over by Bockelsen (John of Leyden), Jan Matthys, and other revolutionaries who set up their millenarian kingdom; a regular siege of a year or more by the Bishop and his allies was needed to overcome them, but not before a reign of terror and famine had diminished the inhabitants during a regime of war-communism and enforced polygamy.

3. **Pietism and its outreach**: *Three main streams: Germany and the Netherlands; France; England and America. Roman Catholic Pietism; St. Philip Neri; St. Francis de Sales; Jansenism. Pietism's outreach in England: the Wesley brothers; Wilberforce.*

Münster gave the Anabaptists (for as such they were usually known) a bad name, at a moment when the vast spiritual upsurge of the Reformation was on stream, but the gathering power of the movement showed itself more among those, sometimes called Quietists, whose concern was for personal change and seeking the "inner light" of God's guidance, with meetings for prayer, Bible-study and mutual improvement. It meant applying Christ's words "the kingdom of God is within you" - the believer should be "so walking on earth, that he doth in a sort carry his heaven with him." The "divine seed", the indwelling Spirit of Christ, could perfect a man's nature - this was the real change, the essential revolution, all else, including the form in which those called of God should meet or worship together being secondary.

This is the beginning of the Pietist movement - a quiet and on-going revolution which can often appear as affecting only the lives of individuals and families, but which in fact has formed the main stream of dedicated Christian living in Western Europe, or rather in "the West" as a whole. This stream early divided, running in various regions, sometimes underground, but welling up to provide the dynamism and mystique for effective action at crucial moments in society and politics. In recent times the confluence of three major streams of Pietist tradition, in Continental Protestantism, Roman Catholic radicalism, and Anglo-American evangelism, made possible the first great act of statesmanship in Europe since the end of the Second World War, the creation of the European Community.

Like all movements arising out of the Protestant Reformation, Pietism was strongly Bible-based. It looked to the change of heart, the experience of being re-born "in Christ", as the starting-point of new life which then demanded total commitment to following God's will and way. In practice, reading and meditating on the Bible were part of prayerfully "waiting on God" in quietness for guidance in the details of daily living as well as for perceiving purpose and design - a sense of calling - in a person's life. Pietists cherished the example of those they regarded as great Christian souls of the past, whose type of life they believed should be the norm for the present. With little interest in dogma, an emphasis on "heart" rather than "head", and an openness regarding ritual and church order, they were the pioneers of ecumenism. The "gathered" Church of the spiritually reborn had no visible bounds, transcending doctrinal distinctions and the cult-forms of different Churches.

Often with a strong historical sense, Pietists viewed preceding ages in the manner of Joachim, though with a different conception of periods. For them the first Age - a "golden" one - was the era of the New Testament, when gospel Christianity flourished; Constantine brought in "the fall" - the period of nominal Christianity; and the present epoch, in which Pietists were to play a major part, was one of restitution, and reconciliation between God and Man. Whatever the prospects for the third Age, Pietist historical sense was sound in recognising an affinity between their type of dedication and that of the early Christians, as also that of the minority who remained whole-hearted in their practice of the faith when the still largely pagan masses flooded into the Church after Constantine decreed its officially privileged position. As for the third Age, Pietists regarded it as a time of revelation and deeper insights, to be consummated by the hoped-for Second Coming of Christ. In general there has been among Pietists "an overpowering sense of the impending breakthrough of God" during this third and final stage of history, along with a conviction that responsibility is laid on every person constantly to maintain spiritual fitness in a disciplined style of life.

Pietists seldom took political colours; often persecuted, they tended towards non-resistance, but offset this apparent passivity by a strongly evangelical orientation and a readiness to undertake and support missionary efforts. As time went on their spirit infused the political aspects of English Puritanism, and later, in all Western countries, it provided much of the dynamic for social and political reform. Their conventicles, collegia, or house-groups provided fertile growing-points for democratic practice, and eventually brought men and women from this background into leadership in politics, and in numerous activities of charity and reform.

In 17th century England the infusion of Pietism in Puritanism appears in Cromwell's friendliness towards George Fox, founder of the Society of Friends (Quakers). Pietism and the millenarian convictions that went with it were central for the Fifth Monarchy Men of Cromwell's army and of many from the "independent" Churches whose representatives Cromwell summoned to the Barebones Parliament. At its opening he said:

> "I confess I never looked to see such a Day as this ... God manifests this to be the Day of the Power of Christ ... I say you are called with an high calling. And why should we be afraid to say or think, that *this* may be the door to usher in the Things that God has promised; which have been prophesied of; which He has set the hearts of His people to wait for and expect?"

The Barebones Parliament dissolved itself before the Millennium arrived. But the demands for greater equality and genuinely representative government, which were voiced in the debates of Cromwell's army at Putney, continued as a ferment to bring about eventually radical changes.

Cromwell illustrated those ambiguities in Christian attitudes which persisted since ancient times. Whatever strain of Pietism there was in his outlook was offset by the encouragement he drew from the God of battles in the Old Testament. The message of caring for one's neighbour and people in general is also to be found in the Old Testament, but religion as a force in power-politics, often as part of a fervent nationalism and as the ideological cement of the State, has played a more obvious part in the history of Europe, both West and

East, than has the often unregarded leaven of those active in the Pietist tradition.

Germany and the Netherlands were the regions where Pietism particularly flourished. It owed much to the saintly Johann Arndt (1555-1621), for many years Lutheran pastor at Celle in Hanover, and his much read and translated *Wahres Christentum* (True Christianity). This book continued to influence Christian families down the ages: "I gained from my mother a love for Arndt", said Albert Schweitzer (born 1875).

"Christ must grow and come to life spiritually in me", wrote Arndt. "Since I am created a new creature out of Christ, I must also live and walk in him. I must be with him in exile and misery. I must walk with him in humility and the rejection of the world, in patience and meekness, in love. I must forgive my enemies with him, be merciful, love my enemies, do the will of the Father. I must be tempted with Satan and I must also conquer. I must, for the sake of truth, which is in me, be slandered, rejected, despised, attacked, and if necessary I must suffer death for his sake as have all his saints, as a witness to him and all the elect that he was in me and I in him and that I have lived through faith."

Arndt was "indefatigable in reconciling those at enmity, rousing the lukewarm, reminding the careless of their duty, encouraging the disheartened, cheering the disconsolate, instructing the ignorant, and rebuking the perverse." His later follower, Philipp Jakob Spener (1635-1705) became known as the leading pastor in Germany, with some years as Court Chaplain at Dresden, then with a parish at Berlin. August Hermann Francke (1663-1727) from Lübeck, took a leading part in Spener's renewal movement; as a professor at the newly founded University of Halle in Saxony (1691), he made of it the principal centre and disseminating point for Pietism throughout the Continent and America. His astonishing energy in creating educational and charitable institutions, as well as a press and publishing house, was matched by his influence on Count Zinzendorf, the revitaliser of the Moravians, and on Henry Muhlenberg, most prominent of those pastors who were sent from Halle to America, from the mid-18th century onwards, at the request of German-speaking colonists there. Through Muhlenberg and others of the Halle persuasion the Puritan tradition was transformed into "the kind of new-life centred evangelicalism" typical of America.

While Pietism stemmed from the Protestant Reformation, a similar but distinct tradition of Roman Catholic piety came down from saints such as Philip Neri, Francis de Sales and Vincent de Paul. Philip Neri (1515-95) left his home in Florence aged 18, after turning down a good job in his uncle's business, to go to Rome. There he lived for two years with a Florentine customs-officer, who gave him an attic room and a meal a day in return for tutoring his two small sons. He spent long hours in prayer, sometimes in the Catacombs, visited the sick and taught poor people. After courses in Philosophy and Theology he sold his books and began an apostolate, standing at street corners to talk with young Florentines of the quarter.   An attractive personality, known from his childhood for his "singular modesty, piety and affectionate heart", he soon gained a following, while continuing his night-time devotions, during one of which he had an experience like that of St. Francis of Assisi receiving the stigmata.

"Well, brother, when shall we begin to do good?" was his salutation, as he set off with the young men to visit hospitals or churches, interspersed by breaks for hymns in the local Italian. He also held simple services or prayer-meetings for them in his room. He became well-known for these initiatives in evangelism, so different from most religious practices at a time when the Churches had become formalist and in part given to worldliness under popes who often behaved like secular princes rather than Vicars of Christ.

After some years he was persuaded to enter the priesthood, continuing his apostolate mainly through the confessional - he had the gift of reading men like a book. His meetings were transferred to a specially built room called the Oratory - meetings which were "a great novelty at the time": three half-hour talks usually given by laymen, "interspersed with vernacular hymns, reading and prayers ... His object was to make religion attractive, especially to the young.   At the carnival or in holiday season he instituted musical entertainments and the acting of religious dramas, the origin of the modern "oratorio." Inevitably opposition was aroused among those who were challenged in their old ways by this "most unconventional of saints", but he was encouraged by the great reforming Archbishop of Milan, St. Charles Borromeo. Pope Gregory XIII gave formal approval to his communal group of clergy, which he had started with five followers, known as the Oratorians. To the end of his life he continued as "the Apostle of Rome", daily receiving princes and cardinals, students and poor people, in the loggia of his flat above the "New Church" of Santa Maria in Vallicella which a grateful public had built. To each person he gave advice for their particular needs - sometimes also healing their physical ills - and there he died in his eightieth year after a last full day of confessions.

Another Catholic tradition originating with St. Ignatius and his Society of Jesus (Jesuits) was the background of St. Francis de Sales. Born in 1567 at the castle of that name near Annecy in Savoy, he was educated at the Jesuit School at Paris, followed by further study at Padua. Though heir to the family honours, he declined a brilliant marriage proposed to him by his father, instead entering the priesthood in the diocese of Geneva, where he eventually became Bishop (actually based at Annecy, because Calvin and his followers had taken over at Geneva). As a powerful preacher and lecturer he was invited to give the Lenten sermons at the royal chapel of the Louvre, where the King (Henry of Navarre) in vain pressed him to accept a bishopric in France. Still at Annecy he published his highly influential *Introduction to a Devout Life*, and revived the monastic spirit by his encouragement of Madame de Chantal and her Order of the Congregation. He continued to preach until the last week of his life in December 1622.

The daily routine of Francis - Bishop at the early age of 32 - was to rise before 5 a.m., spend an hour meditating, followed by two hours study and reading, before Mass at 9 a.m. The day was usually passed in preaching, hearing confessions, visiting, and writing letters. He believed in being readily available "like a fountain in the market-place." Sick people were sometimes cured, apparently through his presence. He encouraged Drama in the form of Mystery and Miracle Plays, and stimulated adult education. His concern was for the laity. Even Chantal's Order of the Congregation had this orientation, in that the sisters originally - and unusually for those days - spent time in work among the sick. His *Introduction* was written "to instruct those who live in towns, in families or at court."

The advice in his letters is always sensible and down-to-earth: to Chantal he counsels against "vain and useless eagerness ... bustling eagerness". To another correspondent he comments on objections made by her father and husband to her "devotion ... I don't know: maybe you were too eager and fussy about it ... We must if possible avoid making our devotion a nuisance." In the *Introduction* he suggests "an hour every day, some time before the midday meal, in meditation, and the earlier the better, because then your mind will be less distracted, and fresh after a night's sleep; but do not spend more than an hour unless your spiritual director expressly tells you to do so."

In tolerant Holland Catholic and Protestant Pietism flowed together. The Dutchman Cornelius Jansen (1585-1638) initiated the reform movement which took his name. He worked closely for many years with the friend he made at Louvain University, Du Vergier de Hauranne, who became Abbé of St. Cyran. Jansen's movement was inspired by his study of St. Augustine, but his book *Augustinus* about the saint's teachings aroused the same kind of theological conflict (especially on the question of Predestination) as had blazed in the 4th century. The hallmark of the movement was the deepening of personal piety and "a rigoristic moral attitude." The Oratory founded in France by Cardinal de Bérulle on the model of that of Philip Neri was so near Jansen's movement in spirit that it came under suspicion from his opponents. But despite public dissensions the real unity of these movements was shown in the founding of the Jansenist lay community at Port-Royal des Champs in 1633 by Angélique Arnauld, a "spiritual daughter" of St. Francis de Sales. The "sociétaires" of Du Vergier were also strikingly like the fellowships of priests in the Oratory, as were the conventicles of Jean de Labadie (1610-74), inspired by the house-churches he found in Holland. Labadie and Antoine Arnauld (Angélique's brother), and well-known laymen of the community like Blaise Pascal, were leading figures in the later movement, which came under persecution by Louis XIV.

Royal intolerance - the revocation of the Edict of Nantes, the "dragonnades" in the Cevennes, and the suppression of Jansenism - left the way clear for the atheism and man-centred rationalism which turned the democratic upsurge of 1789 into the nightmare of the Terror in 1793.

In England persecutions under Charles II failed to repress the spiritual upsurge. Though George Fox was immured under the leaking roof of a tower in Scarborough Castle and Bunyan was imprisoned at Bedford, the Quakers and other movements flourished, even when excluded from cities by the Five-Mile Act and forced into semi-underground existence.   The parents of John and Charles Wesley, in their impoverished rectory, highly esteemed the works of Francke, and John found his faith renewed (after his frustrating missionary experience in America) through the Dutch Moravian, Peter Boehler, who had been ordained by Zinzendorf.

John and Charles Wesley, with George Whitefield, were outstanding in bringing to people at all levels, including multitudes in the neglected mining and industrial areas, a faith and discipline which revolutionised their lives. The group of undergraduates, B.A.'s and young dons who met in John Wesley's rooms at Lincoln College, Oxford, was one of the originating cells of the movement - they were the "Holy Club", nicknamed Methodists. The other cell, through which Wesley's decisive experience took place ("conversion" only in the sense of Luther's, following years of committed Christian striving), was the group at Boehler's London home. Boehler helped Wesley through his inner struggles and doubts towards a deeper faith in Christ, and at a meeting of the group Wesley felt his heart "strangely warmed". It was for him the beginning of that peace and joy which he had scarcely known while practising his previous ascetic and duty-driven faith.

The Moravians assembled regularly in "bands" or "choirs", to exchange experiences, study the Bible, pray and sing. Such groups, characteristic of revitalised Christianity, reproduced the fellowship which their members saw in the Church of the Acts and the Epistles, and this was carried over into Methodism and the Evangelical Movement. These "live cells" reappear as the class-meetings which John Wesley organised for those who had responded to the preachings, enlivened by the new kind of hymns composed by Charles. Here there was a friendly environment - new spiritual homes like the ancient congregations or *collegia* - not only in the "class" groups but also in the many other live cells connected with churches which came into existence in the great 19th century upsurge. Through these groups many found not only a new way of life in concert with others, but an entire education both in writing and speaking, which often brought them to leadership in the nascent trade unions and in politics.

John Wesley (1703-91) was an extraordinary phenomenon as preacher, administrator, scholar. After his conversion experience in 1738, being denied usually the opportunity of preaching in churches, he followed Whitefield in open-air preaching - also first at Bristol. He regularly preached at five a.m., having risen at four, to crowds which might be as large as 20,000 or even 30,000. During fifty years he travelled 250,000 miles, mostly on horseback, and preached 40,000 sermons. One of the greatest of hymn-writers (as was his brother Charles), he also wrote numerous books, including grammars of English, French, Latin, Greek and Hebrew, an English dictionary, histories of Rome, England, and the Church from earliest times - many of his writings and handbooks being designed for the itinerant preachers whom he trained or inspired. He gave away during his life-time to charity all the money accruing from sales of these books, £30,000, a huge sum in present day currency.

A remarkable "live cell" was that of William Wilberforce and his friends. Whether or not they were relatives, as some were (or became so through marriage), they regarded themselves as "part of a large united family", with all the easy informality of close kinship, living in each other's homes, several of which were at Clapham, then a leafy village three miles from London. In their campaigning to abolish the slave trade and eventually slavery itself, and in promoting other notable reforms - including Wilberforce's great aim of reviving Christian morals and manners throughout the land - "they assembled as frequently as possible to breakfast at each other's houses, or to discuss plans far into the night." They worked together on documents and evidence, making out their case for presentation in Parliament or publication in various forms, and in so doing pioneered modern methods of propaganda with pamphlets, lectures, press articles and posters, with meetings and anniversaries, societies and subscriptions, and with a strategy for preparing petitions with thousands of signatures to bring public opinion to bear on the authorities at critical moments. In these campaigns women took a major part, opening the way to their eventual full participation in public life. Much resulted from the interviews with leading figures - interviews which, in the case of Wilberforce, were often planned not merely to gain a supporter but to win the man, Prime Minister or peer or whoever he might be, to a faith as radiant as his own.

Comment: Quakers on mission; Holbach; Whitefield; Moravians; Wilberforce and friends at Clapham. (p. 284)

CHAPTER EIGHT

CHRISTIANITY'S RIVALS (1)

1. Reason, Nature and the World-Spirit: *Newton's view of the cosmos: effect on religion. Rousseau; Wordsworth. The French Revolution. Hegel.*

The effect of the Scientific Revolution of the 16th and 17th centuries on the ideas of some educated people regarding the universe had been as great as that of Thales and other Greeks in devaluing the mythology of Olympus and the gods of ancient Rome. Isaac Newton, born in the year that Galileo died (1642), presented a view of the cosmos and how it worked which made older theories obsolete. As a Christian, he regarded the expounding of God's glories through his scientific and mathematical discoveries as the most important aspect of his work. But his description of the universe suggested to other intellectuals that it was a contrivance which may well have needed a Creator to set it going, but whose participation in its working was otiose.

This encouraged a watered-down type of religion, in which God had little or nothing to do in any direct way with the affairs of mankind, or - in the minds of some - rendered religious belief altogether unnecessary. This surmise had a considerable vogue in France. Voltaire was among those professing a vague deism; for him the Church was something "infamous". Holbach was a thorough-going atheist. These with Diderot and other "philosophes" played their part in pulling down the old regime - preparing the ground for the revolution which came to France in 1789.

For the philosophers of the Enlightenment, Reason and Nature supplied an alternative to the old religion. Rousseau's faith was in "Nature" - to let Nature have her way in moulding the child and the young adult while keeping them clear of the corrupting influences of society. In this he comes near to Wordsworth, who was

"....well pleased to recognise
In Nature and the language of the sense
The anchor of my purest thoughts, the nurse,
The guide, the guardian of my heart, and soul
Of all my moral being."

Rousseau was steeped in the Classics, but in spirit was, like Wordsworth, a romantic, seeking the quiet life as a guest in various country houses, an idyllic existence (the word recalls Theocritus). He also recalls another great figure of the Hellenistic decadence, Plutarch, whom he greatly admired - parts of *Émile* are Plutarchian in spirit. But whereas the *Moralia* were the expression of Plutarch's character, the same could scarcely be said of *Émile* in relation to Rousseau, who avowed that he was not writing the book to excuse his faults, "but to prevent my readers from imitating them."

Brought up in Calvinist Geneva, he was escaping from a sense of sin in which ostensibly he did not believe, though he confessed (in his *Confessions*) some misdemeanours. Man was born good, he proclaimed, but was corrupted and enslaved by the system. With the right education and a changed social and political structure, man - enlightened by Nature and the intuitions of the heart - would live a life of antique republican virtue under a government like that of early Rome or his own Geneva, both of them semi-rural city-states where magistrates and assemblies truly represented the people. But without sin there was no need of a Saviour, thus removing the basis of a genuinely Christian faith, though Rousseau states his adherence to "the spirit of the Gospel" and admires "the wise author of the universe", who has given us "conscience to love the good, reason to know it and freedom to choose it."

"Man is born free but everywhere he is in chains" was Rousseau's dictum which provided a rallying-call for the Revolution. Semi-religious cults of Reason, Nature or Patriotism were staged (some even before the altar of Notre Dame, with a good-looking young woman to represent the deity of the occasion). Robespierre's abortive "Cult of the Supreme Being" was designed to supersede these others, following Rousseau's recommendation in his *Social Contract* that "it is essential for the State that every citizen should have a religion to make him love his duties."

For many the French Revolution seemed the beginning of the kingdom of heaven on earth. It marked "the reconciliation between the divine and the secular...All thinking beings shared in the jubilation of this epoch." So said the philosopher Hegel: "the consciousness of the spiritual had become the essential basis of the political fabric." "Bliss was it in that dawn to be alive," sang Wordsworth,

> "But to be young was very heaven! - Oh! times
> In which the meagre, stale, forbidding ways
> Of custom, law, and statute, took at once
> The attraction of a country in romance!....
> Not favoured spots alone, but the whole earth,
> The beauty wore of promise, that which sets
> (As at some moment might not be unfelt

Among the bowers of paradise itself)
The budding rose above the rose full blown."

The dream faded into the light of common day with the Directory and Napoleon. What had gone wrong? Hegel proposed an answer - the dialectic: everything changed into its opposite. Despotism changed into democracy, and democracy into demagogy; lawlessness gave way to dictatorship. But the World Spirit dominated all, fulfilling itself in history, for when the thesis changed into the antithesis (the terms being borrowed from the Greek description of dialogue), the synthesis which followed combined elements of the two former situations at a more advanced level.

Hegel did not leave God out, even if he did not identify Him exactly with the World Spirit. "The nature of God to be pure Spirit", he asserted, "is revealed to men in the Christian religion...'Be ye perfect, even as your Father in heaven is perfect'. Christ enforces here a completely unmistakeable requirement. The infinite exaltation of Spirit to absolute purity is placed at the beginning as the foundation of all ... Nowhere are to be found such revolutionary utterances as in the Gospels ... The next point is the development of this principle; and the whole sequence of History is the History of its development."

But by asserting the fulfilment of God's purposes for mankind in the State, whose "truth" lay in its power, Hegel was providing the ideology for Bismarck and all other exponents of *raison d'état*. Each state in pursuing its particular interest would inevitably be in conflict and even at war with other states, and (said Hegel) to try to deal with conflicts by legal arrangements and arbitration was utopian. It was only a step for a later philosopher like Treitschke to glorify war as "an institution ordained of God ... In war nations reveal their genuine strength, physically, morally and intellectually ... The hope of driving war out of the world is not only senseless, it is deeply immoral."

Though using the words "Christ", "God" and "Spirit", these thinkers were not providing a channel for the spiritual upsurge in a genuine Christian sense - the sense of Jesus who refused to join the Zealot movement with its aim of re-establishing the Jewish state by violence, instead calling for loving the enemy, going three miles when asked to go one, and forgiving wrongs seventy times seven. Hegel and Treitschke were prophets of the nationalism which canalised an overwhelming part of the century's spiritual upsurge.

Comment: Holbach; the Directory; Hegel; Treitschke. (p. 286)

2. **Marxism**: *Marx's reinterpretation of Hegel; the Judeo-Christian apocalyptic in this-wordly form; Feuerbach and historical materialism; ambiguities;* The Communist Manifesto - "Workers of all lands, unite!"; *Engels and the withering of the State.*

Marx, who imbibed Hegel's teaching, did not mention "Spirit" or God as moving history on towards ultimate fulfilment. How events could be moving in a purposeful way without a mover (for purpose involves will, and will is a function of personality) was a question evaded by Marx. This metaphysical flaw in the basis of his theory showed up when events turned out differently from the prognostications which the theory indicated, or when attempts were made to remodel society in accordance with it. Nonetheless its appeal was immense. Those who responded saw themselves as having significance in a world-historical process which they could move forward by their efforts and dedication.

Marx himself was a thoroughly dedicated man, who endured poverty and hardship in devoting himself to the truth as he saw it. At one time in London the privations which he and his family had to suffer were such that a much loved son died in childhood and two other children in infancy. His commitment lent power to his words, and was shown in his actions, notably in organising, with his equally committed friends Engels and others, the First International Working-men's Association. Determined to be unlike other philosophers who only explained the world, Marx's complete dedication to forwarding the revolution which he believed would change it, had, and still has, the power to arouse a mighty response. Marxism has been an effective channel for the modern spiritual upsurge, capturing and changing to a greater or lesser degree millions of mankind. The same utter dedication to accomplishing the revolution, abandoning any activity, hobby or interest which might stand in the way, was similarly the secret of Lenin's leadership.

Marx took over from Hegel the idea of progress through dialectical change. But whereas Hegel believed that the dialectical development of *ideas*, especially through increased awareness of the way God or Spirit works in the world, was the key to progress, Marx asserted that the dialectical process through the conflict of *classes* was the means whereby humanity was being brought towards its goal. In the ancient world the appeal of Christianity was the offer of personal salvation both in the present and in the heavenly post-apocalyptic realm, as well as fellowship in the community of those who accepted the teaching and dedicated themselves accordingly; the political dimension, in the call for freedom with peace and prosperity, which had been the Hebrew Prophets' message - "the idea of progress in the broadest and most exalted sense" - had practically disappeared. But Marx's message was entirely this-wordly: the revolution which would mark the end of what he called "pre-history" would bring in the new era, when social conflict would be ended by the coming of the classless society, in which "the free development of each is the condition for the free development of all".

Though derived from a religious tradition, Marx's philosophy was anti-religious. He took over from another philosopher, Feuerbach, the description of religion as a branch of anthropology. There was no God who had made man, but man had made God (and all the gods and godesses) as symbols of natural forces and expressions of human personality. Feuerbach, to his own satisfaction at least, proved that "theology is anthropology."

> "While reducing theology to anthropology, I exalt anthropology into theology, very much as Christianity, while lowering God into man, made man into God....In religion man contemplates his own latent nature ... The mystery of the love of God to man is the love of man to himself."

Marx's theory of historical materialism involved some ambiguities and mental sleight-of-hand. Was it work, men's labour adding surplus value to the material, which was the source of progress (a large part of *Capital* is devoted to explanations of surplus value in the formation of capital)? Was it changes, many of them resulting from capital-formation, in the conditions of production and the appropriation of the product? Or the effect of such changes in making "social relations" appear as "relations between things" instead of "personal relations", such as had at least been the case - despite class oppression - in the feudal order, between lords and serfs? Was it the alienation which was the consequence of this de-personalising of human relations? Or was it merely the dialectical element in class relations?

The Communist Manifesto indeed expressed a doubt: the conflict might end in "the common ruin of the contending classes", but there was a strongly confident note in the claim that history was moving on towards a decisive moment - the equivalent of the Apocalypse - when the new era would begin. The tension between the working-class and the capitalist bourgeoisie (between the "social relations" of production imposed on the workers by factory discipline, and the "property relations" of the capitalists controlling distribution) would become so great that there would be an explosion. These property relations would so fetter the productive forces that they "had to be burst asunder", in the same way that at an earlier stage the feudal property relations had become fetters and were broken. So now, with the increasing organisation and solidarity of the working-class, aided by modern communications, especially railways, the fetters imposed by the capitalists, who had deprived the workers of all property except their labour and had forced them to the verge of subsistence, would be "burst asunder", and "the whole superincumbent strata of official society" would be "sprung into the air."

Marx invited the dispossessed proletariat to speed up history by uniting and agitating with this end in view - they would be joined (as had happened in the French Revolution period) by some of the dominant but doomed class, in this case dispossessed or far-sighted members of the bourgeoisie. As for those who thought they could maintain the capitalist system in the face of periodic crises of slumps and mass-unemployement due to over-production, they were vainly trying "to roll back the wheel of history." There was no question of the workers sitting back and letting the dénouement come: they were to join actively in the process. They had nothing to lose but their chains, and they had a world to win. "Workers of all lands, unite!"

Marx noted the paradoxical aspects of European decadence: "On the one side industrial and scientific powers have developed which no former period of history could have imagined; on the other side there are symptoms of disintegration surpassing even the well-known terrors of the later Roman Empire.. In our time everything seems to be pregnant with its contrast....We know that the new form of social production, to achieve the good life, needs only new men."

Much in Marx's analysis of social and economic development was profoundly perceptive. More perhaps even than Augustine in setting new norms of thought for subsequent generations, Marx changed the thinking of educated, and even uneducated people, throughout Europe and the world. He fathered sociology and economic history as academic disciplines, revolutionised economics, and remoulded much else in philosophy and virtually all subjects under the heading of "humanities". But the actual application of his theories in the politics and social life of Europe and other continents has been at best disappointing and at worst disastrous.

The success of Marx and his followers in gaining their world-wide response was due in large part to the role which Marx took on himself of a modern prophet denouncing injustice and pronouncing doom on its capitalist and bourgeois perpetrators. Perhaps something of this Old Testament quality was the legacy of his Jewish forbears (he could also praise those, like the factory inspector Leonard Horner, who exposed horrible abuses in long hours overworking children and women - also men - and the evasion by employers of such regulations as Parliament was beginning to impose for reducing working hours and improving conditions).   There was also the promise of an egalitarian order in which there would be no more oppression and poverty, because the exploiting class would be overthrown, and the proletariat, as the modern version of the Chosen People, would come into their own.   No longer would the apparatus of the State be necessary, since it only existed as machinery for repressing and controlling the proletariat.   As Engels put it,

> "the interference of state power in social relations becomes superfluous in one sphere after another, and then ceases of itself. The government of persons is replaced by the administration of things and the direction of the process of production.   The state is not 'abolished', it withers away."

Comment: The religious element in Marxism; Feuerbach; Engels. (p. 287)

CHAPTER NINE

RUSSIA: VLADIMIR, PETER AND LENIN

1. **Russia's time-lag**: *Peter's Revolution: religion and culture from Byzantium; early links with the West; retarding effects of Mongol occupation; autocracy. Moscow the "Third Rome"; joint functioning of State and Church; parliamentary type Zemski Sobor: its waning, along with neo-Byzantine culture in reign of Alexis. Church reform and the Old Believers. Peter's forcible westernisation; St. Petersburg; defects of over-hasty reforms: "an inert patient".*

Russia is different from the West, but is nonetheless a part of Europe, suffering from the same kind of ills that afflict the rest of the Continent. It differs in scale, merging into a vast empire stretching across the landmass of Asia. Without well-defined boundaries, the original land of the Rus grew along mighty rivers - Volga, Oka, Don, Dnieper - which brought both raiders and traders. Varangian Vikings from the north imposed on the Slavs around Kiev the first recognisable state. By the 10th century its links with the rest of Europe were strengthened by Vladimir the Saint who accepted Christianity for himself and his people, and by the marriage of his son Yaroslav to a Swedish princess, of his daughter to the Polish king, and of Yaroslav's three daughters to the kings of France, Hungary and Norway.

Russia differed from the West also in that its civilisation came from Byzantium. With Constantinople honey, furs and slaves were the staples of trade, and from there came religion and culture. The great city crowned by the basilica of Hagia Sophia made a dazzling impression. The embassy sent by Vladimir in 988 reported of "the place where the Greeks worship their God", that "we knew not whether we were in heaven or on earth, for on earth there is no such vision nor beauty, and we do not know how to describe it; we know only that there God dwells among men."

As in the West, monasteries provided growing-points for the spiritual life of the people, originally small groups of celibates who settled in forest clearings and other remote spots. Their ideals of holiness were the extreme forms of asceticism favoured in the Eastern Churches, as represented in the lives of such as Simeon Stylites on his pillar. Culturally their influence was less than that of monks in the West, because their particular form of austerity made many of them regard reading as an indulgence: there was no Cassiodorus to

stimulate monastic learning and copying. In any case books were
scarce and those who could read the Greek originals few. Bishops,
always chosen from the monks, could do no more than they to raise
the cultural level. As for the ordinary clergy (who had to be married),
they lived like the peasants to whom they ministered, and as a rule
were equally ignorant. Pagan superstitions survived, and magical
powers (formerly attached to cult objects and rituals) were attributed
to icons, signs (two fingers, not three, to make the sign of the Cross)
and ceremonies. Not that genuine holiness was absent: Russia too
produced her saints.

Kiev, the seat of the Metropolitan, became a place of churches,
monasteries and palaces: its splendour was rivalled only by the
mother-city itself. At the same time another centre, Novgorod, in the
north, prospered on the Baltic trade and its links with the Hansa cities.
Like them it developed forms of self-government - its people had a say
in choosing their rulers.

As in other European countries of those times, the cities
contained but a tiny fraction of the total population. Peasants
everywhere were the majority: though illiterate, their lives hard and
precarious, they still developed a folk-culture deeply infused with the
piety brought by the Greek Orthodox missionaries. The difference
between peasants in Russia and those in the West was that there were
fewer links with the landowning aristocracy - no manorial system to
bring them into some kind of reciprocal relations with them. As time
went on their freedom of movement was curtailed - a first step
towards serfdom.

Nonetheless Russia was evolving, despite the differences, in ways
which did not set the country too far apart from others further west.
The event which cut it off and retarded it for some two and a half
centuries was the Mongol (Tartar) occupation. The mounted hordes
from the east had little difficulty in overcoming the rival princes
whose internecine conflicts had long been weakening Kiev (1240), and
though they did not bring the same destruction on Novgorod, they
enfeebled it by the long years when they forced it to be their tributary.

Whatever beginnings of democracy might have existed in towns
like Novgorod and Pskov, the future was set for autocracy. This was
the most obvious legacy of the Khans of the Golden Horde, and
indeed was the only type of rule possible for the princes of Muscovy
in building up their power and imposing order on their ill-defined
domains. They took advantage of the Tartars' occupation by being
their tax-gatherers, counting on their backing in case of disputed
inheritance.

Mongol rule was "indirect", leaving responsibility to the local
princes and Church authorities. The country stagnated, until the

Moscow ruling house became strong enough to be a challenger. Townsfolk and peasants, tired of the constant infighting of the other princes, rallied to it, providing sufficient support to cause the Mongols eventually to withdraw with scarcely a fight (1480).

The autocratic regime of Muscovy, even before this achievement, took over the attributes of both the Khanate and the Byzantine Caesars, as well as the latter's title (Czar or Tsar). This was appropriated soon after Constantinople fell to the Turks (1453), when Ivan III married Sophia (Zoë) Palaeologos, niece of the last Emperor, who had died in defence of the city. Zoë brought the ways and style of the Byzantine Court to Moscow, whose ruler also took over the double-headed eagle and completed his claim to empire over all the Russians with a bogus genealogy going back to Augustus. The same idea was expressed in a letter from the Abbot Philotheos of Pskov to Ivan's successor, Vasily III: "Our Illustrious highest ruler...is the only Tsar over the Christians in the whole world, the guide of the holy, godly throne of the holy, ecumenical, apostolic Church, which, instead of in Rome and in Constantinople, is in the blessed city of Moscow ... Know, thou Christ-lover and God-lover: all Christian empires have passed away and have been brought together into one Empire of our Ruler, according to the prophetic books, that is the Russian Empire. Two Romes have fallen and the third stands, and a fourth there will not be."

Moscow as the Third Rome played a part in shaping ideas about the Orthodox Church in Russia and its role in the world, but with the revolution of 1917 the orthodoxy became Marxism-Leninism and the Communist Party replaced the Church as the agent for defending its (Marxist) "truth" and spreading its message. In Byzantine days as soon as a tribe or its ruler accepted Christianity it was deemed to have accepted the Emperor ("Caesar") as its sovereign, along with the Patriarch at Constantinople, both being joint heads of the Church in a society where Church and State were indivisible. Similarly in the lands which came to be known as Russia, missionaries who converted a tribe brought it to recognise the sovereignty of the ruling prince at Kiev, who was associated with the Metropolitan representing the Patriarch. When Moscow became dominant and its ruler declared himself Tsar he succeeded to the claims of the Byzantine Caesar. The Metropolitan at Kiev was replaced by a Russian Patriarch, and eventually (1589) the patriarchate was transferred to Moscow.

Transferring the patriarchate was the work of Boris Godunov, at that time Regent after the traumatic last years of Ivan IV (the Terrible). The strengthening of ties between Church and State helped him to gain the throne on the death of Ivan's sickly sucessor, an achievement also due to his system of spies and secret agents, predecessors of the

KGB. This system and the fearful punishments meted out to opponents of the regime followed the frenetic - even demonic - example of Ivan, whose black-robed Oprichniks scouring the land had terrorised nobles and commoners alike, extracting money from those who were lucky to escape dispossession of estates or death by torture. Not that repression under Ivan or Boris sufficed to spare the land the ensuing Time of Troubles.

The end of the Time of Troubles came about with the election of a Tsar in 1598 by the Council of the Land (Zemski Sobor) which for a short time took on the role of a parliament. Tsar-making fell to its lot again a few years later with the election of Michael Romanov. But the House of the Nobles (Boyarskaia Duma) failed to gain a position like the English House of Lords, while the partly elected Sobor could only send petitions to the Tsar. It was convenient for Michael's sucessor, Alexis, to continue summoning the Zemski Sobor for matters like making and financing war, but its competence was limited by the ignorance or incapacity of its members, who represented practically only the State services and urban taxpayers - at the Zemstvo of 1648 half of them were illiterate. The Zemstvo of 1653 was the last one to be called. It was another instance of an institution wilting before it had matured enough to form the basis for a constitutional regime. But in this respect the tsardom was little different from the "Benevolent Despotisms" of Austria and the German states, in an age when England, Holland and Switzerland were exceptional in moving towards democracy with some legal protection for human rights.

Alexis was still half in the Middle Ages, with a life of devotions and ceremonial, of hawking and hunting, of unco-ordinated administration for his extensive realm, and an ill-trained army for his periodic wars. When he died in 1676 the West was beginning its "Enlightenment" phase, while Russia was a long way behind. Mediaeval civilisation had come and gone, with its feudalism different from Russia's, its ideals of chivalry and courtly love and the art and literature which they inspired. So too had the Renaissance passed Russia by, along with the Scientific Revolution of the 16th and 17th centuries. Such revival of learning as there was took place at Kiev, where Greek studies of Church writings were pursued, leading to attempts at bringing the Russian Church, on points of detail, into line with the Orthodox practice of Constantinople.

These reforms had little to do with the inwardness of faith and fundamental matters of belief, so that any analogy with the West's Reformation is not in the reforms as such, but in the self-sacrificing, almost Puritan spirit of its Old Believer opponents. The dissidents comprised large numbers of merchants and peasants, and some of the best of the aristocracy. The saintly Archpriest Avvakum was martyred, a fate from which those of noble birth were not excluded, the most famous being the Lady (Boyarina) Morosova, incarcerated with her sister and their friend, declared to be mentally ill (a precedent for modern practice) and finally with her two companions put to death by harsh treatment and a starvation diet. But such resistance failed to lead to the kind of fruitful dialectic which, in some countries of the West, enlarged the liberty of the subject and strengthened parliamentary institutions.

The reign of Alexis marked the final phase of neo-Byzantine culture, the last period when a certain harmony existed between ruler, aristocracy and people, all linked together by a common faith and the rituals over which Tsar and Patriarch jointly presided. As in Byzantium - a legacy of ancient days - the Tsar was both priest and king. With the Patriarch, the higher clergy and the state officials, his role was to maintain the Orthodox faith and with it order and justice on the pattern of God's rule in heaven. Government ordinances and religious injunctions were indistinguishable: aid to regions afflicted by epidemics or other calamities was in the form of ceremonies and processions with icons, ordered by the Government and carried out by the priests. Everyone - nobles, officials, townsmen and peasants were the Tsar's servants, and from them he exacted service "of persons" in government and army, and "of goods" through taxation.

The Old Believer schism broke the consensus, and added a further dimension to the gap which was already developing between the government and its asssociates at the top and the mass - largely peasants - below. The complicated system of precedence whereby the government controlled the nobility was proving unwieldy. New ideas were seeping in from the West by way of the "German Quarter" of Moscow and the newly-annexed Ukraine (1667), where Kiev had revived as an intellectual centre with its Slavo-Latin Academy. A crisis of identity was developing - an aspect of the decline of the Muscovite culture which was masked during the reign of Alexis by the continuance of the old rituals.

Peter's break with the past was thorough and uncompromising. Government and its edicts were secularised. The Church was reduced to a department of state by the abolition of the patriarchate, which was replaced by a committee (the Holy Synod) under a lay procurator.

Peter was a Tsar like no other. As a child he had a taste of the West since with other children of the court he had been instructed in foreign languages. When adult, seven-foot tall, he "wore no crown nor walked in purple, but, taking axe in hand, would thrust pipe between teeth and toil like a plain sailor." He dragged Russia violently into the 18th century with a programme of westernisation. For Peter it was "do-it-yourself". He learnt the ways of the West from the foreigners in the "German Quarter" of Moscow, then, travelling incognito with a few companions to Holland and England, he (and they) worked as apprentice carpenters and shipwrights. On return he would spend the first part of every day in his workshop.

Up to a point it worked. Nobles and gentry had to wear Western clothes. Beards had to go, even if the Tsar had to cut off some himself. A civil service on German lines replaced the older haphazard ways. A bureaucratic class was created. Those rising to the highest grade were ennobled, and with lands and serfs began displacing the boyars as the leading aristocracy. Instead of one there were several printing presses. A newspaper was started.

Peter's new capital, St. Petersburg, built at an appalling cost in human lives on the bogs of the Neva as it flows into the Gulf of Finland, symbolised the opening to the West. His founding of the city has been compared with Constantine's founding of Constantinople: the creation of a city which shifted the centre of gravity of an entire culture. The scale of it was vast among the wide water-ways of the river and its canals, parks, palaces, churches, government buildings - like Peter's own palace and those of his successors in the surrounding country, everything was designed to impress and to demonstrate that Russia had "arrived".

Peter brooked no opposition. A revolt which began when he was abroad was quelled with barbaric brutality and executions, in which he took part.

From his earliest days he had played at soldiers, drilling his young companions. To create an efficient army and navy was his overriding concern. He brought in expatriates to train the army, as well as for all kinds of specialist work, and he put himself through all the grades of service. Power was the objective, and for this the work of modernisation provided the substructure. After initial defeats he succeeded in overcoming his toughest opponent, Charles XII of Sweden, who commanded one of the finest armies in Europe (1709). Russia came to the fore, quite suddenly, as a Great Power, with an empire stretching as far as the Pacific.

The limiting factor was the pace of change, frenetic and sometimes haphazard - many reforms and institutions were later discontinued or fell out of use. It was as if an amateur genius in a hurry was wielding the surgeon's knife on "an inert patient....almost an insensible corpse." Spontaneous movement, a real dynamic change among the people, did not exist at the time. Peter's work made such a movement less likely in the future, as later reformers, from the Narodniks to Gorbachev, discovered.

Those affected by the reforms were a relatively small number with access to the schools and colleges founded by Peter and his successors. There were some of the old aristocracy together with new men from rising families, such as those which owed their advancement to the distinguished military service of one of their members. The gap which already existed between the peasantry with their primitive culture on the one hand and the small upper crust on the other was immeasurably widened. The peasants in most provinces were gradually forced into serfdom, and Russia became two nations which scarcely understood one another. When French became the first language for many of the elite this was sometimes literally true.

2. **The intelligentsia and reform**: *The intelligentsia: interest in ideas and culture rather than business: role of the State in industry; Slavophils and Westerners: ideas of by-passing the capitalist stage. Alexander II: motives for reforms; from openness to repression. Student revolutionaries: Narodniks: "going to the people": the religious element; Lord Radstock's evangelism; "Renaissance" and "Reformation". Nihilists: destruction of existing order - revolutionary dictatorship: Zaichnevsky, Nechaev, Tkachev, Lenin. Cultural unity with the West. Fin-de-siècle.*

Almost cut off from the roots of its original culture and religion, the elite tended to be dazzled by the material brilliance and superficial rationalism of the "enlightened" Western upper class. It could not easily penetrate to the springs of that culture, and no longer found much spiritual nourishment from the Orthodox Church. Freemasonry came in to fill the void, as did later the Narodnik movement, Protestant evangelicalism and Marxism.

Another constraint on reforms was the lack of associations, whether private or public bodies, to fill the gap between the government and the lower classes. In fact the way Peter reimposed the obligation of service tended to break such ties as already existed on a local basis. His intention was to move society from the static system to the more dynamic pattern of the West, where State and private bodies developed strategies and techniques for agriculture and eventually industry, with a view to exploiting progressively all resources and utilising the new inventions which the advance of experimental science made possible. But whereas in the West the capitalist entrepreneur, with his neo-Stoic or Protestant work-ethic, made an early appearance, establishing companies for trade or industry, in Russia the intelligentsia were more interested in culture in the narrower sense than in business.

The intelligentsia, educated along Western lines in the schools and universities which gradually came to be established from the 18th century onwards, were distinct from the old Church-educated minority, who still existed in the senior levels of the Orthodox Church. Unlike the West, where even rural parsons in some countries were highly educated, the village priests of Russia were usually at the same cultural level as their peasant flocks. But with the opening of the universities to others than the nobility, the sons of village priests came to be an important element among the Western-educated elite. This also was the case with sons of serfs who had managed to buy their freedom, or those that were liberated in the mid-19th century reforms - as well as scions (especially illegitimate) of the nobility. A professional class came into existence: officials, clerks, doctors, teachers, artists - including women who sometimes had opportunities for higher education in advance of those in the West.

Some of this educated minority started businesses, or like the railway-building Sergius Witte brought their entrepreneurial gifts into state undertakings. But it was not until the later 19th century that a capitalist bourgeoisie began to take much part in development. By then the tradition of the State undertaking this role was well established. The Industrial Revolution, when it eventually overtook Russia, came through the State promoting enterprises of all kinds, and particularly railway-building. The State Bank (1860), and the banks which it controlled, did more than just put up the finance, but like Gosplan in later days directed the planning, and through their managerial personnel supervised the development and functioning of the projects.

The Jews, foremost among initiators in commerce and industry in the West, were excluded from such activity until the end of the century in Russia and her Polish domain. Nobles also rarely saw business as their calling, while others from backgrounds which in the West produced businessmen and entrepreneurs, in the East belonged to the tradition which placed contemplation - the realm of ideas - on a higher level than that of work. This went back to the origins of Russian culture, when the Church had the monopoly of education and monks were among the few who were educated. Work was not equated with prayer (*laborare est orare*) to the same extent as in the West, though the monasteries which sprang up in remarkable numbers especially in the 14th and 15th centuries were "full-time centres of work and prayer", and vastly extended the area of cultivation. For those following the hesychast tradition the ideal was not the cloistered and laborious monk, but he who early left the monastery for the hermit's life of ascetic contemplation - the ideal established by such as the 4th century Syrian St. Isaac practising *hesychia*, the stillness and silence which makes possible "the journey inwards into the heart."

Ideas fascinated the newly-educated young of the 19th century - ideas from France, and when France was blocked off by Nicholas I because of its revolutionary ferment, ideas poured in from Germany. Young Russians, who still had a religious background, were attracted by Hegel, or by secularised versions of Christian and Jewish thought. The Catholic radicalism of Lamennais, the socialism of Fourier and Proudhon, mingled with the ideas of Feuerbach and Marx. The mixture was explosive, as ideas were formulated in revolutionary aims.

Here the question of identity embarrassed the intelligentsia: were they of the West, and should they encourage Russia to evolve along Western lines towards parliamentary democracy ("liberalism") and laissez-faire capitalism? Or should its direction be determined by those institutions of the Russian peasantry: the local community (*obshchina*) and its organising body (the *mir*)? The Slavophils, who dominated thought in the 1830's, emphasised Russia's distinctive heritage, and believed that these peasants' institutions could be so developed that they might bypass the stage of capitalism, with its gross inequalities and suffering, and move Russia into a new social and economic order with a special brand of political freedom. This, they averred, could even become the ideal which could attract the West, and prove its salvation when adopted universally.

The idealism, repressed by Nicholas I, became increasingly westernised by the time Alexander II succeeded him in 1855. Despite its vast army, Russia had suffered defeat in the Crimea. In organisation and technology it was out of date, and its economy could not sustain its position as a great power. The fundamental economic reform, it was clear, had to be the liberation of the serfs - something which had long since taken place in the West, and which had been more recently achieved in Central Europe. Politically there were hopes for "liberal" reforms, but Alexander's manifesto (1861) for serf-liberation at once sparked off the nationality question (the Polish revolt), as well as raising difficult issues, notably the heavy burdens placed on the now nominally free peasantry in order to secure compensation for the landowners. In some places there were serious peasant disorders.

Relative openness regarding the public - the equivalent of *glasnost* - had been the policy of Alexander on his accession. The censorship was largely dismantled and foreign travel again permitted. But with the growing rift between Government supporters and its opponents, repressive measures were soon reapplied. While many continued to support the Tsar in promoting legal reforms, including trial by jury, and the setting up of the Zemstvo committees for local affairs, others took a highly critical or frankly hostile line. Extremists

("Nihilists") believed that fundamental change was impossible as long as the autocratic system remained in place, but even when they suceeded in killing Alexander (1881) they paradoxically continued to place their hopes on his sucessor.

Before the first attempts on Alexander's life (1866) two trends were marked in the revolutionary movement. This was dominated by university students, who were encouraged by emigrés of an earlier generation, notably Herzen and Bakunin. After the repression and police control of the universities under Nicholas, the freedom permitted by Alexander had made possible numerous organisations: those aiming at a certain autonomy or "self-administration" - control by students, many of whom were showing interest in peasant life and the *obshchina*, with an intention of uplifting the peasantry and politicising them; and those that were concerned with creating dedicated groups for destroying the existing order.

Students might belong to either tendency, or change from one to the other. Already in 1858, three years before the Liberation Manifesto provoked a new phase of unrest among students (and older critics of the regime), reactionary measures were beginning to be applied against the considerable freedom gained in the "glasnost" period when students were taking over universities and organising mass demonstrations. "Liberal concessions had allowed the growth of a movement and a state of mind which aimed at seizing the initiative from the authorities.....No longer was Alexander concerned to allow (within limits) free public opinion; now he had to curb its extreme features." Most forms of censorship returned and restrictions on foreign travel were reimposed.

For the extremists the Tsar's legal reforms were merely tinkering with the issues (trial by jury was withdrawn in political cases in 1878 following the acquittal of Vera Zasulich after shooting, but not killing the commandant of the St. Petersburg gendarmerie - she was only saved from immediate re-arrest by people surrounding her outside the court). The attempted assassination of the Tsar in 1866 by the student Karakozov had unleashed the "white terror" of the following years, which ended what was left of support to Alexander by the "liberals" among the intelligentsia.

Nevertheless those students who believed in non-violence did not abandon the cause. "The people" had not so far reacted enough against the inadequacy of the reforms - many of the peasantry were still strongly pro-Tsar - hence the movement for "going to the people" took wings. Several thousand students, men and women, eager "to pay the debt" which the educated classes owed the peasantry, descended on the villages in the summer of 1874. "Ethical motives played a crucial role....Sometimes this was expressed in religious terms - a religion which gave a more or less symbolical form to their aspirations for purity and total sacrifice", with a leaning towards asceticism - "we must be as clean and clear as a mirror." The aim was for private life to disappear, to be "transformed into the life of the group and (at least ideally) into the life of the people." In villages where the students were accepted, the experience brought to mind "scenes of the first century and the times of reformations ... discussions till after midnight, an overwhelming feeling of solemnity, and choral singing of revolutionary hymns."

The movement was unorganised and chaotic. The peasants were surprised by these urban youngsters descending on them, and often suspicious, even reporting them to the police. The Narodniks were easy prey for the Third Section and other agents of government repression. Half were imprisoned, some were executed, while others were driven to madness and premature death by brutal treatment in prisons or psychiatric hospitals. The movement was broken, and, for many, violent protests took the place of non-violent dissent.

The Narodnik movement occurred at the same time as the evangelical movement in the West, sharing in a spiritual upsurge common to both parts of Europe. Seen in this light, Russia's "Renaissance" was accompanied by "Reformation" - a time-lag of three centuries. But once the catching-up process began it went fast. Its Renaissance in literature, art and music - the humanities in general as well as in science - fused with the high culture of the 19th century West. On the religious level its Reformation developed along lines which resembled the campus movement in the West. The Narodnik "going to the people" was not unlike those evangelical campaigns which at the same period were sweeping through American campuses and British cities.

While the younger generation had been going to the people, their seniors among nobles and gentry were exposed to a different "crusade", the one-man foray into the salons of St. Petersburg by Granville Waldegrave, third Baron Radstock. As a young man Radstock had been swept into the evangelical movement, which had penetrated the British establishment through such people as Wilberforce and his Clapham friends. During a visit to Paris he had met some Russians, and - continually "waiting upon God in the minutest details for direction and guidance" - found himself in the company of "a certain Grand Duchess" who invited him to St. Petersburg (1874). Weak and ill, his health returned as the train crossed the frontier. With open invitations from many of the highest in the land, it was a time of intense activity, "ten to fifteen hours each day in going from house to house." There were many among the leading families "famishing for truth" and spiritual nourishment which their own church failed to supply.   But when "these new religious ideas...were put into practice, cutting at the root of fashionable life, turning ball-rooms into prayer-rooms, occupying the great nobility with the poorest and most hated classes, stretching out loving hands to Nihilists and Socialists and filling the common people with new desires ... first wonder and then fear gathered force."   Influenced by those who rejected the challenge, the Tsar (not without some agonising, it appears) commanded Lord Radstock to leave the country, while two of the most committed and responsible men whose lives had been changed were exiled. This action on the spiritual and moral level paralleled the Tsar's political failure, in delaying until too late his move towards a constitutional system - the last chance, as it turned out, before repressed demands for change led to his assassination, and a generation later to violent revolution.

Among the so-called Nihilists there were many groups.   At the height of the student unrest in the early sixties, P.G. Zaichnevsky, imprisoned for operating a private press for revolutionary propaganda, produced a manifesto, "Young Russia", proclaiming the need for "a revolution, a bloody and pitiless revolution, a revolution which must change everything down to the very roots, utterly overthrowing all the foundations of present society and bringing about the ruin of all who support the present order."   On the positive side the revolutionaries would set up a dictatorship, with elections (from which "the supporters of the present regime" were to be banned - "that is, if any of them are still alive").   Among other reforms Poland and Lithuania were to be given complete independence, and every other region was to be given "the chance of deciding by a majority vote whether or not it wishes to form part of the Russian Federal Republic."

The western idea of a revolutionary dictatorship, stemming from the experience of the French Revolution, was taken up and developed by Petr Tkachev and Sergey Nechaev.   Nechaev escaped the white terror by joining Bakunin at Geneva, who encouraged him to be the revolutionary *par excellence*, whose characteristics are shared in Dostoevsky's *The Possessed* between Pyotr Stepanovitch and Stavrogin. The nastiest episode in that book, the murder of Shatov after being summoned to dig up the clandestine group's printing press, is based on a similar crime perpetrated by Nechaev against a student whom he falsely claimed to be collaborating with the authorities.   Betrayed and handed over to the tsarist police, imprisoned and flogged, Nechaev's "ruthless, violent dignity" so impressed some of the soldiers guarding him that they "gradually became his audience, his admirers, and often his subordinates."

Associated with Zaichnevsky and Nechaev was Petr Tkachev, much influenced by Karl Marx. Believing that violence was inevitable in the transition to a socialist state, his main concern was to found an organisation of professional revolutionaries. He did not share the hopes of some Marxists elsewhere that an evolving capitalism would eventually give way to the further stage of socialism almost painlessly, but believed that in Russia the revolutionary minority had to strike its decisive blow before capitalism had become irrevocably entrenched. His was one of the greatest influences on V.I. Ulyanov, who as Lenin took on the role of creating, from the so-called majority (Bolsheviks) of the Social Democratic party, the group who would be capable of seizing power after the fall of tsardom.

Under Alexander III there was another period of repression, repeating the pattern which under Nicholas I had followed the relatively liberal regime of Alexander I. Another pattern was repeated as the new century opened: just as a disastrous war had preceded the reforms of Alexander II, so the disastrous war with Japan preceded the revolutionary upsurge of 1905 and the subsequent reforms, notably the institution of the Duma as an embryonic parliament. The agrarian reforms of Pyotr Stolypin encouraged the increase of peasant proprietors and the outmoding of the *obshchina* system.

Though the attempts of Nicholas II (1894-1917) to shore up the autocracy were doomed to failure, westernisation with railway-building and industry was bringing the economy into the rising capitalist tide of Europe and America. As the century ended, literature moved into a fin-de-siècle mood with Tolstoy's mordant criticism of Russia's social ills and pseudo-modernisation (as he saw it) in *Resurrection*, and the plays of Chekhov suggesting - as was indeed the case - that the day of the leisured class and of tsardom was ending.

Social and political criticism appears in the paintings of the later 19th century, while spiritual depth is evident in artists like Kramskoy with his "Christ in the desert" (1872). Historical subjects had increasing appeal, and as part of the search for the roots of the authentic Russia were painted with dramatic realism. Outstanding is Surikov's "Boyarina Morozova", with the lady's gesture of defiance against oppressive authority. The essential Russia could also be portrayed in a work like Repin's "Protodiakon", in which a whole element of traditional life, the village clergy, is summed up. In his best-known work, "The barge-haulers of the Volga", a student is included, hailed by the dissidents as symbolical of themselves.

It was the time of revolutions in painting as well as in politics. In the arts the Russians were overtaking and even passing beyond their Western confrères. The irony in Serov's "Pacification", drawn during the 1905 revolution, cannot be missed (soldiers are being decorated, standing at attention in a line, while corpses lie around). Serov resigned from the Academy on witnessing the massacre of

Bloody Sunday from its windows, in protest against the authorities who controlled the Academy while so brutally thwarting the aspirations of the people.   His sardonic touch is evident in the portraits of some of his aristocratic sitters.

Another contemporary, Vrubel, must be classed among the great, not only as a portraitist, but for the power with which he presented transcendental themes ranging from his modern-style icons of Madonna and Child to his series of "The Demon", suggesting the massacres of warfare and the genocides which Evil was to inflict on Europe in the following century.   A pioneer of cubism, he was followed by truly revolutionary figures like Kandinsky, expressing a deep spirituality through his colour-symbolism.   Women, notably Natalia Gontcharova, were among these leaders of the European avant-garde, who with artists like Malevich continued far into the realm of pure abstraction.   Meanwhile Diaghilev and the designers of décor took the West by storm with their settings for superb productions of opera and ballet.

Comment: Russia's religious heritage; "Nihilist"; Herzen; Bakunin; Lord Radstock; Zaichnevsky; Nechaev; Tkachev. (p. 287)

3. **Marxism-Leninism**: *Lenin's utopianism in* State and Revolution; *Marxist ideology replaces orthodox religion. Anti-Church measures. Stalin's relaxation.*

"We are not Utopians", said Lenin in *State and Revolution*.   "We do not indulge in 'dreams' of dispensing *at once* with all administration, with all subordination."   In fact the dictatorship of the proletariat would impose "iron discipline, supported by state power of the armed workers", until gradually all bureaucracy would "wither away", being replaced by a new order in which everyone in turn would perform "the functions of control and accounting".   At that stage "the state will be able to wither away completely, when society applies the rule 'From each according to his ability, to each according to his needs', i.e. when people have become so accustomed to observing the fundamental rules of social intercourse ... that they will voluntarily work *according to their ability* ... There will then be no need for society to regulate the quantity of products to be distributed to each; each will take freely 'according to his needs' ... The whole of society will have become a single office and a single factory, with equality of labour and equality of pay."

Despite his denials, Lenin's projection of the classless society was a version of the millennial dream, however different "the single office and the single factory" is from Joachim's vision of the third *status*, when the world would become a vast monastery of prayer and praise. The Judeo-Christian apocalypse of a new order contingent on the ending of the world has become a material order of the here-and-now. The cycle of civilisation rising and falling would end with the creation of this "order without quotation marks, when the need for violence against people in general, the need for the *subjection* of one man to another, and of one section of the population to another will vanish, since people will *become accustomed* to observing the elementary conditions of social life *without force* and *without subordination.*"

Besides re-expressing Marx's ideology, Lenin set himself to train dedicated cadres of professional revolutionaries, the equivalent of the austere Franciscan "Spirituals", whose avowed role was to bring in the new order for mankind. These triumphed in Russia in 1917, suppressing the vigorous Christian upsurge of the period between the overthrow of the Tsar in March and the Bolshevik coup in November - an upsurge made possible by the ending of the monopolistic control exercised by the Orthodox Church. The impact of Marxism was increasingly felt in Europe, as well as in China and elsewhere, producing its martyrs and heroes, such as those who died in the Spanish Civil War and many another conflict. When established in Russia, or as the creed of Moscow-supported parties and cliques, its tenets were elaborated and defined by the Party ideologists, with all the rigour of fourth century theologians. And as in those days, all who embraced variants were ruthlessly persecuted as heretics - as indeed were all opponents of the officially approved ideology and the policies which its application involved.

According to Marxist dogma religion has to be eliminated. As Lenin said:

"Marxism always regarded all modern religions and churches, and every kind of religious organisation as instruments of that bourgeois reaction whose aim is to defend exploitation by stupefying the working-class ... This is the A.B.C. of *all* materialism, and consequently of Marxism. But Marxism is not materialism which stops at the A.B.C ... Its aim must be to eliminate the social roots of religion."

In attempting to impose an atheistic faith on Russia as a monolithic state in which the Communist party replaced the Orthodox Church, the Bolsheviks and their sucessors were faced by insuperable obstacles. Marxism-Leninism was accepted by only a small minority as an ideology with moral imperatives, in place of Christian and other faiths, especially in recent years. The entire apparatus of the state and its enforcing agency, the KGB, has been inadequate to secure the desired results through coercion, and though education has been a potent weapon in inculcating atheism, it is doubtful whether there are more agnostics or atheists today than there would have been if the ordinary processes of industrialism and urbanisation had been left (as in the West) to produce their effects.

These educational efforts together with the persecutions may indeed have had the contrary effect since as late as 1975 it was reckoned that "at least" 20% of the population were actively religious - a considerably higher proportion than in the West.

Marx and Engels had believed that religion would "wither away" along with the rest of the mental superstructure of the bourgeois state, once its substructure had been replaced by Communism. Engels had warned that attempts to inculcate atheism in place of religion, instead of waiting for social change to do its work, might be counter-productive, and this has proved to be the case. The attempt to abolish Sunday by instituting the five-day week had to be abandoned, and the secular ceremonies designed to replace rites of passage - baptism, confirmation, church-weddings and funerals - have had (except for weddings) little appeal.

It has been traditional for governments to impose their orthodoxies, and this has been the case throughout Europe until ideas of toleration began to make headway some three centuries ago. Russia has been exceptional only in continuing to impose a regime of orthodoxy, Marxism-Leninism with stress on atheism, so long after their practice has been abandoned in the West - another instance of time-lag.

Taking over church and monastic property and cutting off all financial support were among the first acts of the government set up by Lenin and the Bolsheviks in November 1917, though almost at the same moment a Church Council restored the patriarchate, and vast demonstrations at Moscow and Petrograd welcomed the newly elected Tikhon as Patriarch. To undermine his position and weaken the Orthodox Church (which under the Provisional Government had been purged of its more corrupt senior members), splits among the believers were encouraged, culminating in recognition of a breakaway group, the "Living Church" as the official body. Church buildings themselves being now government property could only be leased back for religious purposes by the request of not less than twenty parishioners, who had to undertake payment of priests' salaries and other expenses. But in the great majority of parishes both in towns and country districts this provision was either ignored or such pressure was put upon believers that they were deterred from joining the committees, so that churches not only became disused, but were often destroyed if not turned over to secular use or converted to "museums of religion and atheism".

By 1939 closure and destruction of churches had reduced the number in use as places of worship to a bare hundred throughout the whole of the Soviet Union, in place of the 54,174 at the time of the revolution. By that date all seminaries had been closed, as well as every monastery and convent (originally over a thousand). Of the 163 bishops, those who died were not replaced; 66 had been exiled; others had been murdered or had been killed by inhuman treatment in penal camps. Only seven were left in occupation of their sees.

A respite was gained by Hitler's invasion. Church leaders unreservedly backed the war effort, and even raised enough money to equip a fighter squadron and tank division. There was a surge of faith at this moment of the country's greatest need. Stalin allowed some relaxation in the harsh anti-Church laws; a few seminaries were reopened and a remnant of monks and nuns allowed to reoccupy their old quarters. By 1947 there were 74 bishops, 30,000 clergy, eight seminaries, 67 monasteries and convents, and about 10,000 "working churches." There was also some improvement in the position of Baptists and other minorities, though Jews were again at risk through the antisemitic campaign mounted by Stalin shortly before he died (1953).

The relative improvement in the Church's position, particularly that of the Orthodox, allowed the Government to use it for attracting support to itself. The enthronement of Patriarch Alexis in 1945 was celebrated with much splendour, and (attended by representatives from Britain and elsewhere) provided such an opportunity; it was followed by his spectacular tour of the Middle East. But the attempt to make Moscow the centre of world Orthodoxy by summoning a conference there in 1948 was opposed by the Oecumenical Patriarch at Constantinople.

CHAPTER TEN

THE CHRISTIAN CHALLENGE IN THE WEST

1. **The 19th century upsurge**: *the Christian challenge: Ludwig von Gerlach vs. Bismarck. French radical Catholicism; Anglo-American evangelicalism. Alphonse Gratry. John R. Mott: "the evangelisation of the world in this generation." Henry B. Wright. Robert Speer: "Absolute standards of Jesus."*

Statesmen of Christian outlook, like Gladstone and Lord Salisbury, hoped that the "Concert" of European states, originating from the wartime alliance against Napoleon and the Congress system which succeeded it, could resolve conflicts by consultation and diplomatic means, and that the kind of co-operation achieved in dealing with Turkey could point the way to permanent arrangements. Part of these might be the acceptance of arbitration, and to this end an international tribunal was required. The Russian initiatives (in line with Alexander I's Holy Alliance scheme a century before) in calling the Hague Conferences of 1899 and 1907 failed to bring about disarmament or obligatory arbitration in the face of German opposition and inadequate support from Britain and other states, but it did result in setting up the Hague Arbitration Tribunal, and later the International Court. International Law, pioneered by the Dutchman Grotius in the 17th century, consequently gained in importance. The Inter-parliamentary Union was formed by MP's from different countries, to bring pressure on their governments for policies such as arbitration and disarmament.

Quakers had long expressed their convictions in a determined anti-war stance. There were those in the same Pietist tradition among the Prussian aristocracy who brought their convictions into politics: one of these, Ludwig von Gerlach, tried but failed to win his friend Otto von Bismarck to these ideas.

Bismarck had experienced a Christian conversion, but its effects were limited to his private life. In politics other norms, those of *raison d'état*, prevailed: to be swayed by any principles other than that of serving the interests of the State, no matter what one's personal predilections, smacked of disloyalty to the ruler and country which one served. When Gerlach challenged his aggressive policies, warning him against "the hideous and mistaken doctrine that God's holy ordinances do not apply to the sphere of politics, diplomacy and war ... as though these spheres were governed by no higher law than that of patriotic egoism," Bismarck broke off his friendship and secured his dismissal from his high judicial post.

Bismarck's triumph over von Gerlach implied the rejection of any belief such as Gladstone's that there was a divine order which was being progressively realised among men - a divine order which, in European terms, was to be perceived in the Concert - "the highest and most authentic organ of modern Christian civilisation" (as Gladstone called it), supported by an enlightened public opinion which he believed was coming into existence. Bismarck sneered at "Professor" Gladstone and his ideas of the Concert: he did not agree with Gladstone that there was a "public law of Europe" which reflected the divine ordinances of society, and which it was the business of the powers working in concert to promote. The most that Bismarck's pallid version of Christianity did for him was to "confirm his belief that the best one could do was to prevent disorder from gaining ground."

This, after achieving control not only of Prussia but of all Germany, defeating Denmark, Austria and France in the process, Bismarck proceeded to do. During his last two decades of power he devoted himself to limiting conflicts and creating a system in which the existing order would be maintained. But peace was not Bismarck's main objective. It was power, and this was what he bequeathed as his legacy. Power became increasingly the proccupation of his successors, to the exclusion of any greater creative idea, which a genuine acceptance of Christianity would have involved.

Besides German Pietism, exemplified in von Gerlach, other streams in the same tradition were French radical Catholicism and Anglo-American evangelicalism. To whatever persuasion they belonged, there were dedicated men and women whose aims were no less than revolutionary and whose strategic action and impact on politics brought them into the realm of statesmanship. There were also those who were men of affairs and politicians by profession, shaped by a Christian background, and committed to realising their principles in practice to the point where they achieved a level of statesmanship beyond the usual art of the possible.

Felicité de Lamennais was one of those in France who were determined to reverse the drift away from the Christian faith which was a feature of the revolutionary period. He became one of the known leaders of the Catholic reaction of the early 19th century - his *Essai sur l'indifférence en matière de religion* aroused immense enthusiasm among the religiously-minded who were looking for a renewed strengthening of throne and altar, the ancient bulwarks of society. At Rome he was warmly received by Leo XII, with a room at the Vatican and the prospect of becoming a cardinal. But a few years later his ideas were revolutionised. Instead of championing the authority of pope and monarch he was preaching the virtues of liberty: separation of Church and State, freedom of education, of the press, association, conscience.

The change of regime in 1830 provided the opportunity to publicise this new liberal, radical Catholicism in a paper, *L'Avenir*, whose motto was "Dieu et la liberté." He was supported in the venture by another liberal abbé, Henri Lacordaire, and by Charles Montalembert, whose education had begun in England, where his father, a refugee from Napoleonic France, had married an English girl. The three friends also opened a school, unauthorised and uncontrolled by the Government, a challenge to which the Government's riposte was closure and a fine. They then made a bizarre attempt to revolutionise the papacy itself and so gain backing in the highest quarters by winning Gregory XVI to their ideas, but their visit to Rome was unproductive. After being kept waiting for many weeks, they were put off with trivialities in a brief audience, and their views were finally condemned in an encyclical. *L'Avenir* had already been discontinued, and Lamennais outwardly conformed, but, disgusted by papal support for the crushing of Poland by Russia and Austria, he again shook the public with his *Paroles d'un croyant*.

This cry from the heart, in Bible-style verses reminiscent sometimes of Ezekiel, sometimes of Revelation, even stopped the printers as they paused to discuss it while setting up the type. The poetic refrains persisted as challenges in the mind: "Nous crions vers toi, Seigneur", "Jeune soldat, où vas-tu?" To a public brought up on Voltaire, Diderot and other exponents of Enlightenment teaching, the apocalyptic, prophetic note was new and disturbing. "Let him who has ears hear, for the times approach ... I understood that there had to be a reign of Satan before the reign of God ... the reign of Satan is accomplished, and the reign of God will be accomplished also ... For the human race it will be like another birth." Lamennais' call for social justice rings out - a fair return for work done, no more poverty - a vision of peoples breaking their chains while a tempest shakes the trembling nations.

Lamennais supported striking workers and other forms of action against oppression. One of his writings landed him in prison with a fine of 2,000 francs, but the regime itself disappeared in yet another revolution, that of 1848, when he was elected as a Deputy to the Constituent Assembly. Lacordaire was also elected, though he shortly withdrew, realising that his channel to the public was through his sermons and lectures, of which he had given a famous series to capacity congregations at Notre Dame. Montalembert had however found his platform in the Assembly, first in the Chamber of Peers after he inherited the title of Count, then in the Chamber of Deputies, to which he also was elected in 1848.

The stream of lectures, speeches, sermons and writings by these men and others - together - with the publicity occasioned by repression - familiarised people with the conception of Christianity (though not necessarily the Church) as a force for freedom, justice and equal human rights. As regards the Church itself, this attempt to detach it from the camp of reaction had some success: signs of change were shown in the early "liberal" phase of Pius IX's reign, and the encyclical *Rerum novarum* and other statements of Leo XIII.

The most obvious difference between developments in French Catholicism and Anglo-American Protestantism is in the proliferation of Churches, sects and all kinds of associations characteristic of the latter. This was a marked feature of England during the Puritan era, and the Pilgrim Fathers and other pioneering settlers carried the same spirit to America. Several of the colonies restricted the public practice of religion to the forms decreed by their establishment, but eventually these restrictions were eroded, and complete freedom became the norm in the Thirteen Colonies and their successor, the United States of America.

This situation encouraged the multiform growth of Christianity - the Great Awakening in the eighteenth century, and the exuberant surges of the nineteenth and early twentieth centuries. This "incoming tide" was part of a world-wide advance: the new life in the USA and Europe stimulated missionary enterprise on a scale never seen before, and this could be carried out with a degree of protection, and with well-developed transport and communications, under the aegis of the Euro-American imperium.

Millenarian thinking was an added stimulus. This had affected America from the moment of the earliest contact between the Old World and the New - it had been a motive for its discovery, since Columbus believed that the Spanish sovereigns had a messianic role in sponsoring his voyage to "the new heaven and the new earth" on the other side of the Atlantic. The English founding fathers and many of their sucessors believed in "the American dream" of building a fully Christian society in places like New England and Pennsylvania. The fact that the frontier was being pressed ever further westwards encouraged the notion that the frontier of Christendom could likewise be extended by spreading the Gospel throughout the world "as the waters cover the sea."

America was the place where it became normal for members of different Protestant denominations to work together, and to seek whenever possible co-operation with Roman Catholics - the seed of the ecumenical movement which burgeoned towards the end of the nineteenth century. In the evangelising and missionary tradition of both British and American Protestants - legacy of Continental Pietism and English Puritanism - the action and leadership of lay people was marked. Around the camp-fires of the American revivals, especially in districts of the ever-moving frontier, distinctions of denominations were blurred, ordained ministers were few, and theological questions ceased to seem important.

In evangelising endeavour there was a special relationship between Britain and America, with close connections going back to colonial times, so that the two countries acted and reacted continuously on each other. Methodism through Whitefield and Wesley had an immense impact on America, and from America there came Moody and Sankey. Their mission to Britain of 1873-4 reinvigorated the faith of many and made a multitude of new converts.

Among those who responded to Moody was Henry Drummond, then a student at Glasgow, impressed by the preaching but more by the after-work, when he was drawn into helping men who came to the "inquiry room". Later, when Professor of Natural Science at the Free Church College at Glasgow, he made his mark not only as a teacher, but through his writings in which he expressed his Christian ideals in terms of the still novel doctrine of evolution and of his own scientific findings. His weekly meetings for students in which he expounded these truths, with great clarity and a strong challenge, were filled to capacity. On visits to the USA, mainly for speaking engagements on the campuses, he worked with Moody who started summer conferences on his estate at Northfield, Connecticut, after the encouraging response (despite initial rowdyism) to a mission at Oxford and Cambridge.

With Drummond there is a reaching out to the world. Visiting China, he saw the vast needs in a sub-continent whose civilisation was disintegrating, and realised that a strategy was required, going beyond the limited possibilities of individual missionaries each working to their own plan, like "casual sharpshooters bringing down their man here and there," instead of "a carefully thought-out attack upon central points, or by patient siege planned with all a military tactician's knowledge."

A sense of strategy became one of the distinctive marks of the Anglo-American campus movement, along with a concern not only to effect conversions but to ensure that they were thorough enough to lead to full Christian commitment. This conviction that strategies for spreading the Gospel could be found through openness to God's guidance arose in the context of missionary endeavour. The warrant for this was to be found in St. Paul who had set his heart on bringing his message to Rome - though at the same time he was open to other leadings whose strategic implications might not seem so obvious, as in responding to the call to Macedonia. In later days a similar sense of strategy had been shown by Gregory the Great in directing missions to the various tribes of the Empire's invaders.

The Anglo-American campus movement spread to the Continent towards the end of the century, but independently there had been similar developments at the Collège St. Stanislas in Paris. This had provided the first platform for Lamennais' colleague Lacordaire, whose fame as a lecturer and preacher came through his courses there in the 1840's.

At that time the college was under the direction of Father Alphonse Gratry. A brilliant student at school and the Polytechnique, Gratry had carried off all the prizes, but, shaken by a succession of spiritual experiences, had renounced a career and all wordly ambitions to devote his entire life to God. After a period of strict seclusion and fasting he felt called to join five other young men at Strasbourg, a "live cell" where, sharing their inmost thoughts and everything else, a "union of heart and mind" was achieved. Gratry's gifts were not long allowed to blossom unseen, and there followed strenuous years of teaching during which he almost killed himself with his exertions, before he became Director of St. Stanislas in 1840.

His vision was "to lift up the world, the family, the entire human race, to a truer life such as the Gospel brings", with faith that this "divine power of rebirth", every act of will and heart, all prayer and self-giving, release power which spreads throughout the world and becomes part of the motivating force of the universe. In the Gospel there is a "science", the way to transforming society. "Life, time and money" had to be dedicated "to suppress evils which lead to poverty, hunger and death" - evils such as "men dying of hunger in the midst of cities gleaming with luxuries, their corpses, together with the refuse of last night's orgies, exposed at the doorsteps of houses."

Perturbed about the situation in Europe as the Crimean War came on, he appealed for a Christian nation to set its course "for peace and not war as the honour and glory of peoples." If one nation could do this we should see great things - the divine power "filling the world and uplifting it."

For this "supernatural strength" was needed. "The master says: Change yourselves. What is impossible for men is possible for God ... possible, conceivable, necessary in a sense. It is a radical change. A transformation, a regeneration."

The way to go about this is to listen to God, who is speaking by the inner voice to everyone, children and adults alike. In order to listen we must be quiet, in such silence as is not enjoyed even by a

studious man, who - when not directly listening to people - is spoken
to by all sorts of writers, many of them "useless", or by "the perturber
of all silence, the profaner of all solitudes, the daily press, which
comes each morning to take from him the purest of his time, an hour
or more." But having secured a time of silence before every distraction
and conversation, victory must be won over "the inner talkativeness
of empty thoughts, of restless desires and entrenched prejudices" - one
must cease to be "the slave of oneself" and of the time in which one is
living.

"'What does it actually mean to listen to God?' you ask ... Here
is the answer. You will write." St. Augustine's words are recalled: "Is
your memory capable of keeping all that your mind has seen? - No,
it certainly is not. - So you must write." You must make the effort of
describing the whole range as well as the evanescent details of this
inner panorama. And if you feel that your health and strength are not
up to it, you must pray for mind, soul and body to be a single,
harmonious instrument attuned to the inner inspiration. You must
take your pen - don't think of the critics and others -just write, in a
few words, the naked and unadorned truth. "Write for God and
yourself ... When the soul meditates quietly and hears something from
God, peace and joy flood in."

For Gratry his mother-tongue was the perfect instrument for
noting the words of God. A master of the written word (he gained the
coveted honour of election to the Academy), he insisted on the need
for acquiring style as "the word in the most exalted sense" ... the man
and his soul "set in the light." He was doubtful if English was
adequate for the purpose - it needed improving: "the harshness of its
words and the circumscribed stiffness of their meaning, the nullity of
its grammar, its relative poverty of inflections, its monosyllabic
tendency, its difficulty in poetry, the feeble echo of its words when
expressing great meanings." But, whatever the language, the need was
to devote time, and particularly the first part of the day, to enabling
the soul to develop, to "find itself." The most precious gift which the
morning quiet time can bring is to open the resources of the soul and
mind, "putting the whole man in movement."

After his time at St. Stanislas, Gratry helped to re-establish the
Oratory of France, suppressed during the Revolution, along the lines
of its original, inspired by St. Philip Neri. Though a devout son of the
Church, at the end of his days he contested the intention of defining
the dogma of papal infallibility at the Vatican Council of 1869-70. His
protest was of no avail, and he withdrew to Montreux, where he died
in 1872.

Besides Moody's Northfield conferences, a major influence on the American campuses was the Young Men's Christian Association - another instance of British initiative finding large fulfilment in America. It was started by George Williams in 1844, growing from a prayer-meeting of twelve men in a London drapery business where he worked. Besides providing educational and social facilities, it was a strongly evangelical body, and the evangelical aim dominated the numerous branches of the Student YMCA which were established in North America.

The Student YMCA provided the leadership and a forum for visitors like Kynaston Studd, a well-known cricketer and brother of one of "the Cambridge Seven" who devoted themselves to missionary work in China. Invited by Moody to tour American campuses, his talk at Cornell encouraged John R. Mott to devote himself to the work in which he was the leading figure for two generations. Mott's life had been shaped through visits to his home of a Quaker preacher and a Methodist minister, whose vision for the young man brought him from helping manage his father's lumber business to the university. There he became the moving force on the campus, through his effectiveness in "individual work with individuals as the real power through which decisive, life-changing work of a permanent character was to be done." He was put in charge of all the student work in North America under the auspices of the YMCA, and became committed to furthering missions overseas through attending Moody's "summer school" in 1886 when a hundred students came forward as future missionaries - the nucleus of the Student Volunteer Movement. In the following years he travelled widely, and during a world tour in which he touched deeply the lives of hundreds of young people, he laid the ground-work for linking together all such bodies in the World's Student Christian Federation, whose object was "nothing less than the uniting of the Christian forces of all universities and colleges in the great work of winning students of the world for Christ" - and this was a means towards achieving the dominant aim of "the evangelisation of the world in this generation." Not that this meant an intention to convert everyone, but "to give every person of this age an opportunity to accept Jesus Christ." This watchword, he maintained, "emphasised as has no other one thing the urgency of the world's evangelisation...an awful necessity because without it millions will perish."

For him students were "strategically the most important group in the world", and he saw their task in military terms - "an army of well-furnished God-called volunteers", and spoke of battlefields and forts. One of his books was *Strategic Points in the World's Conquest*. His primary aim was "not to get great numbers of men, but to get the ablest, strongest men, those who in any walk of life would be leaders", and he quoted Drummond: "if you fish for eels you catch eels; if you fish for salmon you catch salmon." So clear was he on his priorities that on one occasion he declined an invitation to meet Kaiser Wilhelm II of Germany because it would have jeopardised his engagements with students, and he refused the pleadings of the American President Woodrow Wilson to accept the embassy in China.

In 1910 Mott chaired the great missionary conference in Edinburgh, where practically all denominations except the Roman Catholic were represented - a conference which sought to realise the vision of the 18th century missionary pioneer, William Carey, for planning unitedly to bring the Gospel to the world.

A millenarian note is evident in Mott's watchword, for in Christian tradition preaching the Gospel throughout the world was a condition precedent to the Second Coming. The changes consequent on this action at this "decisive hour of the world's history" would be "the enthroning of Christ in the individual life, in family life, in social life, in national life, in international relations, in every relationship of mankind."

The vision was broad and general, with no specific strategy for ending particular social evils in the way that Wilberforce and his Clapham friends had set themselves to abolish the slave trade and slavery, or Lord Shaftesbury had led the country and Parliament in abolishing child-labour and reducing working hours in mines and factories. Though "the social gospel" did in fact have a powerful appeal for many Americans, for Mott the concern was primarily for a new international order. Converting students on the scale he had in view was, he maintained, "helping to unite the nations by stronger and more enduring bonds than arbitration treaties, because it is fusing together by the omnipotent Spirit of Christ the students who are to be the leaders of nations." National distinctions were being eroded within the federation he created - among its students "there is no Britain and no America, no France and no Germany, no China and no Japan, but Christ is all in all."

In the Atlantic-spanning tradition of these upsurges, Mott carried his message to British campuses with considerable effect. He spoke to crowded meetings - it was reckoned during a week in 1908 at Oxford that almost the entire student body of 3,000 attended, with three lectures for dons, a meeting for women, and at the conclusion a closed gathering of 230 men "selected from the 21 colleges with reference to their powers of leadership." The Muslim students were not neglected - he had a breakfast with them, while the rowing men and other sportsmen gave him a lunch at Vincent's. During this visit a "large number" of undergraduates requested interviews.

In Mott's later life such personal encounters might tend to be squeezed out by public occasions and committees, but there were others with whom he worked who had made a science or "art" of "soul-surgery".   At Yale Henry B. Wright - who also came to his commitment through Moody's Northfield conferences - developed new approaches to students, culminating in his book *The Will of God and a Man's Life Work*, a study course in 26 lessons.   "God has a plan for every human life," he wrote.   "God has a plan for the development of the world which extends to all departments of life and to all spheres of human activity."   After teaching Classics for some years, a special Chair of Christian Methods was created for him.   He and his wife set up their home near the campus in order to provide a convenient haven of hospitality.   His period of prayer and Bible study before breakfast was the secret of his effectiveness, but he also kept his mind alert during the day for "luminous thoughts", which he jotted down in a notebook to be acted upon at the appropriate time.   He treated these impulses with respect, for he was convinced that through such thoughts God could guide a person in his life and calling, if "the receiving instrument" was kept clean.

In this context he quoted another Northfield recruit, Robert Speer, who in his book *The Principles of Jesus* set forth the four "absolute standards of Jesus ... No man who through the deliberate act of surrender of the human will to absolute standards of purity, honesty, unselfishness and love, has once felt the coursing of these immortal powers in his spirit, can ever after find any experience of this new life tame or commonplace."

Comment: Alexander I and the Holy Alliance; Bismarck and Ludwig von Gerlach; Dwight Moody;   Alphonse Gratry; Henry B. Wright; Stamina and approach of Mott on campaign; absolute standards and decline of moral order in the West. (p. 289)

2. The 20th century challenge: *Marc Sangnier; "Crypte" and "Sillon"; deepening democracy. Moral collapse in Europe after World War I. Frank Buchman: origins, strategy. "World-changing through life-changing."*

The Collège St. Stanislas continued to be an active propagator of Alphonse Gratry's ideas long after he resigned.   A student of a later generation was Marc Sangnier, who had early been introduced by his grandmother to Gratry's *Les Sources*, one of her favourite books.   With two or three friends, seeking like Gratry an *âme commune*, Sangnier started a lunch-break discussion group.   The crowd of students, jostling each other as they surged into the basement room (the "crypte" which gave the movement its first name) was stirred by the conviction "of a great task to accomplish - to bring about the coming of God's reign on earth as it is in heaven, not only in the close intimacy of hearts but in cities, nations, the entire world!"

This adolescent enthusiasm, a millennial vision like that of the youthful John Mott, might have evaporated with growing maturity, but it was supported by lecturers, one of whom founded a "Union pour l'action morale" which besides Catholics included Protestants, Jews and "spiritual free-thinkers." One of Sangnier's friends, Paul Renaudin, founded the paper *Le Sillon*, proclaiming in the first issue that he and his colleagues were "like the seed which keeps watch under the furrow (*le sillon*) during the winter and ripens in silence, confident of the harvest of the coming summer." A few years later, in 1899, the Crypte merged with the *Sillon* and took the latter's name as part of the growing Christian-democratic movement.

The millennial overtones struck a chord with many people as the new century began. The dedication of Sangnier and his friends matched the need of the hour. When he moved on to the Polytechnique the meetings continued: open meetings attended by former Stanislas students and others including some "blouse bleu" workers (in craft occupations), and smaller meetings for the twenty or thirty "responsables" - times of silence and prayer, of Bible-reading and "meditating aloud together, to strengthen and encourage ourselves."

Sangnier, embarking on a military career, had his first experience as an enlisted soldier in barracks, sharing a room with several conscripts who kept him and themselves awake with a "mauvaise conversation" about "amour", until "I put my head out of the blankets and began: 'Now I would like to speak a little, and tell you what I understand by Love.'" After talking at some length he could not sleep, but rose next morning "with a smile of confidence", and before long gave another talk, this time to the other student cadets in their common room. One of them responded, "opening his entire soul to mine." The army, Sangnier maintained, should ideally be "une grande école nationale", and he put this thought into practice when he and another close friend of "Crypte" days were given a free hand by their commanding officer, when on garrison duty, to counter boredom among the troops by "des conférences morales."

This course for soldiers prepared the friends to launch the *Instituts populaires* as the centre-piece of a great educational programme, based on study-circles which spread throughout France: by 1905 (when Sangnier had renounced his military career to devote himself full-time to this work) there were 640 study-circles with another 130 run by other bodies but linked with the Sillon. Sangnier calculated that workers accounted for 80% of those attending the courses, which were for the most part not specifically religious, but dealt with subjects of general cultural interest, as well as professional training, musical occasions, and plays. But, with the help of worker members, the Institutes and circles were certainly oriented in a Christian direction, towards a "mutual popular education", through which an "apostolat" would be undertaken by both workers and former students - all unpaid volunteers - for realising the Sillonist vision of social, national and international change.

Sangnier was no organisation man, and liked to think of the Sillon as "a life, a ferment, a spirit": one was in it to the extent that one shared in the *âme commune*. Since "today more than ever we are suffering from division and dream of unity", unity must be the aim, both between classes and between countries - and this (it was Gratry's teaching) must start with oneself. An "ideology" - "the cause" was crystallising, "engaging the heart equally with the mind, and with action as the integrating element." It was a new dimension of democracy, "deepening its ideal". The vision was of a future "if we deserve it: a new and deeper manifestation of Christ, in a new condition of society, in a regenerated world."

It was a bold attempt, at the height of the secularising anti-Church movement, to bring about a "social transformation", not merely reforms (which the Sillonists also supported) such as old age pensions, but new structures through applying the co-operation principle in economic affairs, such as workers' participation in management. Sangnier saw the opening decade of the century as an opportunity to win practising Catholics who could "animate a movement of the whole French people", directing them "towards a new society" by ways which were neither those of Marxism nor of laisser-faire liberalism.

Like other initiatives of this order the movement soon ran into opposition. Attempts to break up Sillonist meetings were countered by recruiting some members into the "Jeunes Gardes", who in their uniforms (following the Salvation Army and the more recently founded Boy Scouts), were given a semi-military training, and acted as bouncers and stewards. But the most serious opposition and the heaviest blow came from Rome, when the fate of *L'Avenir* was repeated by Pius X's censure of the movement for being under lay direction. It was a shattering blow, though Sangnier recovered and the movement was re-launched as the Ligue de la Jeune République, with *La Democratie* replacing *Le Sillon*. But two years later in 1914 the situation changed with the outbreak of war.

To men of Mott's convictions the war had come as a fearful shock. They had been relying on the apparently secure world framework of law and order organised and dominated by Europe, in which to operate for carrying out their evangelising task. Now that order had been shattered, and, among other consequences, Russia - in extent and potentiality one of the greatest fields for this endeavour - had been withdrawn into the camp of militant atheism. The war also shattered "the easy, optimistic complacency", as Sherwood Eddy, one of Mott's fellow-workers put it, "of ... a fictitious evolutionary social development towards millennial utopias." Mott was disconcerted by "the frightful moral collapse" occasioned by the war, while the YMCA, which had been the main vehicle of his work, was no longer in the running to repair the evil. Having devoted itself to welfare for the troops, it became in peace-time, with its hostels and similar services, an unrevolutionary part of the system.

Mott's work therefore in part had to be done again. The other part, to which he personally paid much attention, was the ecumenical movement, and this had an important influence in changing the attitude towards their sister-Churches of those who were already convinced Christians, and duly established its institutional organ in the World Council of Churches. But this was a somewhat different work to that originally envisaged by Mott, that "deep, all-pervasive and even revolutionary work wrought by the Spirit of the living God."

Though Mott lived on until 1955, his mantle in respect of this part of his work fell upon Frank Buchman. Buchman was remarkable, not only for the way in which he developed the "art" of changing lives and encouraging commitment particularly among the younger generation, but for the strengthening of his conviction as the world crisis deepened, that a *strategic* approach was needed if humanity was to be "turned God-ward" and civilisation saved - a strategy which was for "everyone everywhere", going well beyond winning students as the vanguard of the new age. This conviction and his faith in the unlimited possibilities in every individual, led eventually to a strategy for contributing to the resurgence of Western Europe and of countries overseas like Japan.

If Buchman was optimistic about individuals, he did not share the illusions of the pre-1914 years that the spread of Christianity by itself would lead to the solution of world problems. Christianity would only be effective in this sense, he believed, if its challenge reached right down to the root motivations of individual lives, in matters of sex and the desire for security, and in the urge to gain power and control over others. Further, the number of people so changed would have to be considerable - he called for "a hundred million listening" (to God), if mankind was to follow another way than its "historic road to violence and destruction."

Frank Buchman originated from those Pennsylvania Dutch families whose ancestors, mostly from Switzerland and the Rhineland, had migrated to America in the 18th century. These influences played their part in shaping his outlook. He had some contact with the campus movement during his student days, but his main concern had been social work, visiting hospitals, prisons and workhouses. After graduating at a Lutheran seminary (1902), he managed a hospice in Philadelphia looking after boys taken into care. His method of getting the boys up on Sunday mornings "was not to scold, but to announce there would be pancakes on the table at 9 sharp." But his ideas about the kind of food boys should have caused differences with the supervisory committee, who accused him of extravagance. He resigned, with frustration and bitterness which only disappeared when, on a visit to England, a speaker at the evangelical Keswick Convention brought before him "a vision of the Crucified."

Thereupon he wrote letters of apology for his resentment to the hospice committee and asked their forgiveness. The "new sense of buoyant life" impelled him to share his experience with others. At this point he took the post of YMCA Secretary at Pennsylvania State College. Working with Mott, Wright and others, who came over to campaign with him, his impact was considerable. In his second year pratically all the students attended their meetings, and a large number came on to the Northfield Conference in the vacation.

After six years at Penn State Buchman went to India in 1915 to help in the mission to students under YMCA auspices. His work there with the YMCA Secretary Sherwoood Eddy convinced him that the mass-approach then fashionable in evangelistic campaigns was unproductive - like "hunting rabbits with a brass band." Progress would only come by "individually dealing with men." He by no means abandoned Mott's objective of "making Christ regnant" in the world on all levels, social, national and international, but was convinced that only conversions carried through on a person to person basis could be effective. His vision was enhanced by his time in China, at a period when leading personalities such as the American-educated Sun Yat-sen were more open to Western influences than ever before or since. Sun had been the first President of China after the Manchu Empire fell in 1911, and though his power had waned amidst the increasing anarchy in the country, there seemed to be a chance that he or his associates, who were mostly Christians at any rate in name, could be inspired to undertake a work of spiritual reform to provide the moral infrastructure for the nation.

It was a strategy which went far beyond the thinking of most missionaries in the field. Buchman's vision was clear even if the difficulties which would have discouraged anyone of a less confident and buoyant nature were too readily discounted. Though the immediate outcome was disappointing, due in part to the opposition of European missionaries who were challenged in their comfortable assumptions and personal shortcomings, Buchman never lost this vision of "world-changing through life-changing." He gradually built up his "force" or team, mostly from graduates and undergraduates on both sides of the Atlantic, until the depression of the early thirties provided the opportunity for him to break out into wider fields of endeavour.

A journey to Latin America in 1931 brought home to him the full challenge of Communism.

> "Communism and Fascism have created the greatest crisis in the history of the Christian Church since the catacombs. What does this entail? A whole new orientation in the presentation of the Church - go out into the streets, highways and hedges. Not our conception of the Church, but the answer the world needs ... Develop the ordinary man. The Devil gets him if we don't."

With this conviction the wheel had come full circle, from the Spiritual Reformers of Luther's day, and their Quietist or Pietist sucessors living out their intense Christian experience in families and small communities. Now it was necessary to create a new framework within which the Christian life could be lived - within which perhaps *any* ordered life could be lived, since already people feared that another conflagration like the Great War might mean the end of civilisation and the return of the Dark Ages.

Hence the note, struck even more strongly by Buchman than by Mott, that while the work of evangelising - "life-changing" - must go on, and more urgently than before, it must pave the way for a radical change in the whole civilised order of mankind. The world was at a turning-point - the idea was in the air: in no sense the monopoly of Communists and Nazis. "Is it to be God's light of a new day for Europe and the world; or is it to be the fading light of a doomed civilisation? The world faces this historic choice." He called men and women to the same experience as that which had transformed his own life, and so cease being "part of the disease" and become instead "part of the cure."

By the 1930's he realised that if decline and catastrophe were to be averted and the world moved instead towards a new era, it could only be through a profound change in the leadership as well as in the "ordinary man." There was indeed a spectacular response as people packed the British Industries Fair building at Birmingham, Oslo City Hall, the Castle of Elsinore, and the Groente Veiling at Utrecht. A campaign in Canada early in 1933 which attracted thousands encouraged thoughts of similar moves in Germany, but by then Hitler had taken over. Any ideological force except Nazism was excluded, or at least kept under strict surveillance. Attempts by Himmler to win Buchman's Oxford Group raised false hopes that change on the part of the leadership might make Germany "a front-line of defence against the antichrist of Communism." Buchman's limitless faith was such that for him nobody should be written off. It was only after an interview with Himmler that he was disillusioned, and realised that a different strategy was needed to deal with the "demonism", as he now saw it, which had gripped Germany (1936).

Comment: Frank Buchman's experience at the Keswick Convention; Sun Yat-sen. (p. 292)

CHAPTER ELEVEN

CHRISTIANITY'S RIVALS (2)

1. **Nationalism**: *nationalism vs. internationalism and pacifism; religious patriotism; bellicism vs. international socialism. Militarist propaganda;* Our Island Story; *Boy Scouts; imperialism, insecurity and power.*

To most of those enjoying the sunshine on beaches and mountains at the beginning of August 1914, as well as the far greater number who could not afford holidays, what they read in the papers came as a bolt from the blue. Whether it was called jingoism or patriotism, nationalism was leading to disaster.

In Europe generally nationalism was a surging and often passionate emotion, in which clergy as well as lay people shared - patriotic sermons were the expression of an attitude as common in Britain as in Germany, France, or Poland and other countries in Central and Eastern Europe whose people were striving for liberation. It captured much of the upsurge which otherwise went into more clearly spiritual channels, and was often fused with a form of religion. It recreated on a larger scale something of the spirit of those independent cities (or communes) of the Middle Ages, which had been not unlike those of the ancient world. By the end of the century it had become an "all-demanding, all-excusing nationalism ... linked to the belief that the state was a living organism which was more than the sum of its citizens", and that the citizens "could only fulfil themselves completely within it, so that it had an overriding claim on their loyalty and obedience."

This variant of the spiritual upsurge achieved its hideous climax in Fascism and Nazi racism. The other main competitor to Christianity was Marxism. This was the ideology of the German Social-Democratic Party (SPD), and was a large element in the socialism of France and Britain, though in Britain especially there was a strong Christian infusion owing to the Methodist or Evangelical background of many Labour leaders, notably Keir Hardie, the first Labour M.P. In Germany the ruling classes feared the already powerful SPD, which in 1912 became the largest party in the Reichstag. The expectation that a war would enable them to curb the Socialists was a strong encouragement to the influential *Sammlung* - the alliance between some industrialists and East Prussian Junkers, who aimed at keeping the urban working class in an inferior position, deprived in the Prussian

Landtag of equality of voting rights, and in the Reichstag of any possibility of hoisting the SPD into power. By the winter of 1912-13 this group was hoping for war as a "saviour" - nothing would be left of the 110 Social-Democrats at the next election, it would be the end of Jewish Social-democracy (the antisemitic note is significant).

When the crisis came the Social-Democrats were in fact solid with the *Sammlung* and other nationalist groupings. In the Reichstag the party voted almost unanimously the war-credits. The internationalism and anti-militarism of the Second International, to which the SPD was affiliated, was never more than skin deep, and the same applied to the trade-union organisations of the member-countries. Nationalism and xenophobia divided the delegates to the Second International's congresses. Though an Anglo-French initiative by Keir Hardie and Edouard Vaillant forced on to the agenda of the 1910 congress a proposal for a general strike for preventing war, German opposition rendered it impracticable. It was only a tiny group of militants of the Second International who had enough enthusiasm for anti-war policies to outweigh their national loyalties and preoccupations. The outlook of the work-force in every land was determined by nationalist attitudes and mental stereotypes of the hereditary or current enemy. The hollowness of socialist pretensions was demonstrated in the week before the war's outbreak in 1914, at an emergency meeting of the International Socialist bureau, and the conference of Belgian trade unionists which was attended by French and German fraternal delegates. The question of anti-war action was deferred to a future conference, partly because the urgency of the crisis was not realised - but it was clear anyway at Brussels that Legien (Germany) and Jouhaux (France) did not have a united mind on the subject.

Nationalist feeling had been deliberately worked up in Germany and Britain by their respective Navy Leagues, in order to gain public backing for the large financial appropriations and consequent tax demands required by the "naval race", amplified in Germany by the equivalent army organisation, the Wehrverein, from 1912 onwards. But the success of these organisations, especially the highly efficient German ones financed by Krupp and other firms with a stake in armaments, their propaganda fed through all the media of the time and by a host of school-teachers and academics, was only assured because it struck a highly responsive chord - and a much more responsive chord than that of class solidarity. It did not prove difficult for the Navy League and the Wehrverein to convince most of the industrial working class that there was a deadly danger from reactionary Tsarist Russia, and for this reason they had to support the war.

Nationalism was fed into children from the earliest days. It was the theme of books like *Our Island Story*, which must have gone into many thousands of British homes and schools in the opening years of the century. This compote of myth, anecdote, verse and history is recounted in a vein of unfailing appeal to the young readers at whom it was aimed. The old favourites reappear: St. Gregory in the Roman slave-market "gently puts his hand" on the "curly heads" of the English children there - "Nay, not Angles but angels they should be called"; Arthur and the Round Table; Alfred and the cakes; Good Queen Bess - they are all there. The seamy side of empire is naturally disregarded; the glorious deaths of Wolfe, Nelson and other heroes are recounted; under missionary influence the Maoris give up cannibalism and their chiefs acknowledge the overlordship of "the great White Queen", with "cheers from both the natives and the white people." General Havelock and "his brave soldiers" raise the siege of Delhi, and he and Outram march on to save the beleaguered ladies and their menfolk at Lucknow. Wolfe's exploit is followed by the poem beginning

"Not once or twice in our fair island story,
The path of duty was the way to glory."

To do justice to the authoress of *Our Island Story* she also produced *A History of Germany* for the same age-group, because - although "no story, of course, can be so brave and splendid as our own 'rough island story' ... yet in the history of other nations there are things worth knowing." And she hoped that knowledge of the "brave deeds" and the struggles for freedom by Germans would "dispel the clouds of suspicion and set us free from preparing against attacks that are in truth contemplated by none of us." These last words she quoted from Lord Haldane, whose mission to Germany in February 1912 failed to halt the naval race and head off the threatening war.

Even so promising a creation as the Boy Scouts, perhaps the best thing to come out of the South African ("Boer") War of 1899-1902, had its nationalist side, with its motto "Be Prepared." This, as "B-P" (same initials - Lt.-Gen. Robert Baden-Powell) pointed out, was connected with "emperor" (from the Latin *im-parere*, to prepare), and so with "empire". By then (1908) the King had become King-Emperor, "and we are all working to back up our King." B-P's *Scouting for Boys* was a work of genius, admirably targeted on its objective, since it arose out of the author's experience of soldiering and the open-air life on the Indian North-west Frontier, Afghanistan, and parts of Africa, notably Mafeking in Cape Colony, which he successfully defended during the siege of October 1899 to May 1900, employing boys as messengers and scouts.

Nationalism as expressed in this handbook was tantamount to a religion, since it meant putting "the good of the country *above everything else*" (B-P's italics - compare the German national anthem "Deutschland über alles"). This was the answer to the decadence indicated by those who were saying that the country was "already on the downward grade", though he admitted that it was "near to the parting of the ways." While disbelieving that "our empire will fall to pieces like the great Roman Empire did, because its citizens became selfish and lazy, and only cared for amusements," he reverts several times to the need of taking to heart the lessons of Rome's decline. The empire, he says,

> "fell at last, chiefly because the young Romans gave up soldiering and manliness altogether; they paid men to play their games for them, so that they themselves could look on without the fag of playing, just as we are doing in football now. They paid soldiers to fight their battles for them instead of learning the use of arms themselves; they had no patriotism or love for their grand old country, and they went under with a run when a stronger nation attacked them.

> "Well, we have got to see that the same fate does not fall upon our Empire. And it will largely depend upon you, the younger generations of Britons that are now growing up, to be the men of the Empire. Don't be disgraced like the young Romans who lost the Empire of their forefathers by being wishy-washy slackers without any patriotism or go in them. Play up! Each man in his place and play the game. Your forefathers worked hard, fought hard, and died hard, to make this Empire for you. Don't let them look down from heaven, and see you loafing about with hands in your pockets, doing nothing to keep it up."

The mention of heaven as the abode of the empire-builders arose from B-P's Christian faith. "No man is much good unless he believes in God and obeys his laws. So every scout should have a religion." On this point B-P was refreshingly ecumenical, including in religion, besides different Christian denominations, "every God believer" such as Jews and Muslims.

Baden-Powell was an optimist. The "magnificent Empire", he maintained, was "only at the beginning of its development", and he saw it as the expression of Britain's historic role - "all powerful for the good of the world." This belief he shared with many of his contemporaries like Lord Cromer, who opined that "the special aptitude shown by Englishmen in the government of Oriental races pointed to England as the most effective and beneficent instrument for the gradual introduction of European civilisation into Egypt", which he virtually ruled for 24 years.

The other side of the coin was British pride and superiority. In one of the plays in *Scouting for Boys* suggested as suitable for acting, John Nicholson of Indian Mutiny fame browbeats Mehtab Singh (who declines to take off his shoes as a mark of respect): "you forget that you are dealing with a Briton - one of that band who never brooks an insult even from an equal, much less from a native of this land."

Though agreeing with everyone who wanted "to see the abolition of the brutal anachronism of war", B-P was in fact one of the most effective exponents of that "political culture" in which the leading states of Europe shared, based on the assumption that violence was normal in the relations of civilized states, and that "each nation, after climbing laboriously to the zenith of its power, seemed then to become exhausted by its effort, and sit down in a state of repose, relapsing into idleness, studiously blind to the fact that other nations were gradually pushing up to destroy it."

This outlook was matched in Germany, where "curricula in primary and secondary schools were designed to educate obedient patriots, steeped in the military heroics of the German past, convinced of the inferiority of other nations, and prepared to accept war as a positive aspect of international affairs." School textbooks in France expressed a similar ideology, even if those of the two countries naturally indicated a different hereditary enemy. The shock of defeat in 1870 and the loss of Alsace and Lorraine had been deeply humiliating, and the consequent bitterness and hatred directed against Germany permeated all forms of thinking and writing, from literary and academic works to school text-books.

In such books the national myths and history were instilled into children, with their respective heroes from Vercingetorix to Napoleon and from Hermann (conqueror of Varus and his legions) to Bismarck. All this contributed to "the mood of 1914", the upsurge of tribal-nationalism, which made the conscripts march cheerfully to war and the women to press white feathers on civilians. The Poles, Serbs and other suppressed nationalities similarly cherished their myths and history, while the aristocrats of the Habsburg Empire, which held so many of these nations in thrall, sought emotional security in loyalty to their ageing monarch, and military security in their obsession to control or crush Serbia.

Comment: Professor Sir Michael Howard on the causes of wars. Social-Democratic party of Germany (SPD); Second International: Robert Baden-Powell. (p. 292)

2. **Nazism**: *antisemitism; Nietzsche: the will to power and the superman; Hitler's schooling and postwar indoctrination: perverted mysticism and Aryan mythology. Hess, Haushofer: millennial ideas; Himmler: the Black Order; Rosenberg:* The Myth of the Twentieth Century.

In the war of liberation against Napoleon and in the subsequent struggle for unification, nationalism in Germany had become something of a religion, ousting the parochial patriotism of the princely states. Bismarck's victorious wars and the declaration of the German Empire in 1871 brought a crescendo of national feeling, which alongside similar emotions in France and Britain burst into a blaze in 1914. But in the thirties Germany was ripe for an ideological revolution. The high hopes of 1914 had ended in the frustration of defeat, the humiliation of Versailles and the post-war upheavals. Two million dead and thousands of maimed had not yet produced a land for heroes to live in. The French occupied the Ruhr, the inflation wiped out savings, and with the slump from 1929 onwards there came mass unemployment.

Marxism was the doctrine of the powerful Social-Democratic Party, which kept to the parliamentary rules of the Weimar Republic, but the Leninist version of Marxism provided the ideological thrust for the smaller but highly militant Communist Party. Communism was a religion for many: its "myth" had supplied the spiritual basis for revolutionary action by those who had taken power in Russia, and were now striving to take over Germany. But for many Germans an even more potent myth was compounded of virulent racial ideas which gained strength from Wagnerian romanticism and Nietzschean philosophising. The moral and spiritual malaise diagnosed by Nordau in the nineties had become a psychic disease by the twenties.

Fascism, which triumphed in Italy, put the stress on the nation as the decisive factor in history, but with Nazism it was race, and this gave rise to crude neo-Darwinian theories that the fittest and best racial specimens should be born and brought up, with the corollary of killing off those who were not wanted, the Jews in particular but also Gipsies, the elderly and feeble-minded. As for the Jews, there was more than just hostility to them as an alien, non-national element. In Nazism all sorts of irrational ideas became attached to Jews as "the poison people", and this went right back in German history, perhaps to the days when the Jews were a more civilised element among the rather backward and barbaric Teutonic peoples and among the Slav peoples of Eastern Europe. Once the Jews had gained their freedom through the liberating laws especially in Prussia in the 1860's, they often achieved positions of eminence in the professions, in the world of business, finance and banking, and were an easy target for the hostility of the small man such as the shopkeeper who saw a Jewish-owned chain store threatening his livelihood.

Both Fascism and Nazism were looking to national regeneration and the will to power, the building up of armed might, the preparation for war and conquest, but it is the irrational element which stands out in Nazism. German romanticism had nurtured a strain which Nietzsche developed, not merely the "God is dead" phrase, by which he meant that Christianity was dethroned, but his assertion that other forces were coming to the fore. Nietzsche's Superman could not really be confused with the Führer or leader, though this kind of connection was made, but his ideas were part of a trend in literature towards a perverted kind of racial mysticism, a religion of blood and soil, even if in the minds of many it was covered with a Christian veneer. There were visions of a new Reich, a political community of believers whose form of worship would be this revived and re-militarised German paganism. Already in the mid-19th century these people were beginning to look for a Führer and were propagating a particularly vile kind of antisemitism, along with idealisation of war.

Myths which had inspired the pogroms of the Middle Ages were resuscitated, such as the murder of Christian children for ritual purposes, and a world-wide conspiracy to demoralise, weaken and take over the inhabitants of the earth. The forgery purporting to be notes of a meeting of these conspirators, "The Protocols of the Elders of Zion" (in reality a concoction by the head of the Okhrana, the tsarist equivalent of the KGB) circulated as a potent antisemitic weapon. When these myths and fabrications came into contact with the racism of Hitler "the result was an apocalyptic vision not only of contemporary politics but of all history and indeed of all human existence."

Not that all Germans were affected. Hitler never had a clear majority of the electorate behind him. But forces for nurturing this evil had built up over the centuries: a feeling of insecurity behind ill-defined frontiers, often overrun by the French on the west and threatened by Russians and other Slavs in the east; the horrors and miseries of the Thirty Years War; the difficulty of creating a national identity in a land cut up into a multitude of states; the sense of frustration of a potentially great nation lagging behind while others became world-powers. And then the trauma of bloodshed, hunger and collapse which in 1918 had ended Germany's bid for security amd dominance.

With the mass unemployment of the thirties Hitler's movement went from strength to strength. It appealed to the narcissistic self-worship which afflicted many - worship of the body as a blond racial type, projected in athletic display and nude art-forms. This was mingled with a streak of savage and sadistic self-assertion, the Aryan man's alternative to masochism in his condition of psychological malaise and economic insecurity. Dark forces of destruction were linked with Wotan, the ancient pagan god whose very name meant wrath.

Ich liebe die hektischen, schlanken
Narzissen mit blutrotem Mund,
Ich liebe die Qualengedanken,
die Herzen zerstochen und wund.

Ich liebe, was niemand erlesen,
was keinem zu lieben gelang;
mein eignes urinnerstes Wesen
und alles, was seltsam und krank.

(I love the slim, hectic Narcissus
with its blood-red mouth.
I love thoughts of torment
and wounded hearts that bleed.

I love what no other has chosen,
what none has been able to love;
my own most inward being
and everything strange and sick.)

This sickness was exemplified in Adolf Hitler, product of inadequate parents and a frustrated ambition to be an artist. The Vienna where he spent his early years was suffering from the same psychological ills as Germany, with a similarly poisonous antisemitism. Active service in the war had been a liberation; all the greater was Hitler's frustration when it ended in defeat. But discovering in himself demagogic powers of the highest order, Hitler soon built up a sizeable following in Bavaria, with which he attempted the coup of 1923.

This landed him in prison, but as a political prisoner he was accorded remarkable freedom to receive guests, and food and drink to entertain them. Rudolf Hess became a close companion, bringing with him the occult beliefs and practices of the semi-secret Thule Society.

Hitler had been impregnated with these ideas since school-days at the Abbey of Lambach, decorated with swastikas by Abbot Theodore Hagen. Hagen had his own cryptic interpretation of the Bible, especially Revelation: he had acquired his ideas while travelling in Asia. One of the monks, Adolf Joseph Lanz, left Lambach and the

Christian faith to found the occultist Order of the New Templars. He claimed to work with superior beings, and his review "Ostara", which sometimes printed editions of 100,000, was "devoted to studying the heroic and virile race which proposes to transform into reality the teachings of race-science in order to preserve the noble race ...in the purity of blood and virility." "Ostara's" antisemitic, anti-socialist and pan-German doctrines were absorbed by Hitler. As a young man in Vienna in 1912 he began writing a book (though perhaps never getting further than the title-page): "The German Revolution", decorated by a swastika.

Various streams converged in the making of the myths of Nazism. There were similarities with the Gnosticism of the Ancient World - the belief that the real God is not the God of Jews, Christians and Muslims, but a Being revealed most fully in man. This "Self" is always in process of becoming, going beyond its existing bounds towards the evolution of a super-Self represented by a leader who is to move the cosmos into a new era.

The immediate source of these ideas in the mythological hotchpotch of Hitler, Hess and other ideologists was in Central Asia and India. Madame Blavatsky, Annie Besant and others popularised theosophical ideas in the West by their travels and writings, and were followed early in the 20th century by Karl Haushofer, who thought he had found the mysterious land of Thule somewhere between the Pamirs and Himalayas. Thule was supposed to be the source of Vril, an energising power which was to strengthen the resurgent Aryans under their superhuman leader for conquering and transforming the world. According to a sect in Gujarat, who had the swastika as their symbol and whose ideas Haushofer studied, the next thousand-year cycle of world history was being initiated by the superior Being with the aid of the Aryans.

All this might have evaporated as the maunderings of unhinged personalities had not Haushofer joined forces with a bogus Baron von Sebottendorf, who had absorbed similar ideas in the Middle East. Sebottendorf founded the Thule Society as an offshoot of Freemasonry; Haushofer joined its lodge in 1917 at Munich, where he was Professor of Geopolitics ("space is power") at the university. One of his most assiduous students was the ex-service officer and pilot, Rudolf Hess, who became his "Scientific Assistant."

Sebottendorf's aim was to found a militant sect committed to carrying out his racist ideas in practice: an "order" not merely militant but also military, of dedicated initiates around a divinised guide (Führer). It had the swastika for its symbol and 'Sieg Heil!' for its watchword. Among its sinister activities there were parodies of, or parallels with religion. The Faust-like covenant with the powers of darkness parallels the covenant of Israel with God, or (in a personal way) that of a Christian with his Lord. These forces, deployed by Sebottendorf and his followers, were designed to transform a man - forces which were trans-human, "operating beyond the ordinary physical, moral and intellectual limits", the very powers of Satan. The yoga-like practices and other forms of psychic training were later adapted for those SS personnel who were directed to operate the extermination camps and similar undertakings; they were initiated into "the mysteries of evil" and taught "to adore a man, to hate pity, and to die for an idea."

The ramifications of Thule, connected with the equally ultra-nationalist and antisemitic "German Order", were numerous. Among the groups with these leanings at Munich which it infiltrated and supported was the German Workers National Socialist Party (NSDAP). Hitler, still in the army as a "confidence man" (*V-Mann*) in the Education and Propaganda section, investigated it and became a member (November 1919).

Bavaria and its capital Munich had recently been restored to a semblance of order after a short spell of communism and several other chaotic governments, and the local Reichswehr command was doing all it could to train activists and set them working among the public to strengthen the anti-communist stance. Hitler was one of those who had been trained in special courses for this work, where he had shown his demagogic talent. On these courses he met several Thule leaders, including Haushofer; also the dramatist Dietrich Eckart, who became his friend and partner. Another lecturer, Gottfried Feder, who equated capitalism with Jewish power, became one of his most effective propagandists, and a talented young officer and course-mate, Hermann Esser, became for many years his right-hand man in the Nazi Party.

These, with Ernst Röhm and other ex-service colleagues, formed the original "cell" which, attracting men like the young Baltic German, Arthur Rosenberg, grew like a malevolent cancer in the German body-politic, eventually destroying it. Hitler was accepted as the leader for whom Esser and Eckart were looking: a man with the charisma "to radiate mysterious and irresistible appeal to a crowd, paralysing the critical faculties of the individual." Hitler and his friends were convinced that a new party was needed in order to spread their ideas. They took over the NSDAP, built it up, and made it a formidable engine of power.

With Hess, Haushofer and Eckart, Hitler spent long hours in his two-room suite in the modern Landsberg prison. He underwent a kind of conversion, accepting the Thule doctrine that a new "spiritual millennium" was beginning, with himself as the destined leader, endowed with all powers needed to displace Christianity and bring the nations into subjection. Those who knew him recognised the change in the man after his Landsberg experience. After he was released, his speeches, prepared by trance-like communings with occult forces, came forth with a torrent of words which were received as inspiration by his hearers. There was something of the medium about him - his personality was "doubled" on these occasions.

The millennial appeal was powerful. At this turning-point in history "Providence" had decreed that he should be "the great liberator of humanity." Mankind was entering a new "solar period" when a process of change that had been going on for thousands of years was approaching its completion. The turning-point for humanity was the emergence of a new type of man, a mutation in the biological, scientific sense. "Imagination is needed in order to divine the vast scale of the coming order."

His appeal was primarily to those - a select minority - who were ready to be initiated into these grandiose conceptions and the accompanying way of life. The Templars and the Grail were the prototype: the Grail of "pure blood." The masses represented the civilisation that was sinking; they would have to be worked on, but they could die. Winning the owners of wealth and the governing classes was important, but the way to do this was not through myth or millennial visions but (in Rauschning's paraphrase) through "business advantages, erotic satisfaction, and ambition, that is to say the will to power."

The reduction of Hitler's sentence from 5 years to 9 months meant that *Mein Kampf*, begun in jail, had to be finished later. With the re-launching of the party, other figures gained an ascendancy: Goebbels, Himmler and Heydrich. Of this evil trio Himmler was the most thoroughly steeped in ideology, drawn particularly from Germanic myth. He literally worshipped the spirit of the early medieval Emperor Henry I, conqueror of the Slavs, annually spending hours at his tomb, whence he received psychic power, with subsequent apparitions of his hero. When the Nazis took over the government and it became possible to use the slave-labour of the concentration camps, Himmler rebuilt the ruined Wewelsburg Castle as the centre for the Black Order, his revival, in a new version, of the Teutonic Knights who had won East Prussia from the Slavs. Wewelsberg was also a shrine for the elite SS of the Order: sombre rituals were performed echoing Himmler's inherited (but rejected) Catholicism, blended with Germanic paganism.

He was obsessed by the Siegfried story and myths like the Holy Grail, believing he had discovered its secrets which bestowed cosmic, irresistible powers. Other castles provided training for the SS, based on these myths, together with those of blood and soil. The real horror ensued when, during the war, Himmler carried out plans for transforming the whole of Germany and its annexed territories into a Jew-free Aryan Utopia on the model of his Black Order.

Nazism was in fact as much a religion as the Mithras and other cults which had canalised some of the spiritual currents of ancient times. The Nazis were not just copying Christian rites when they staged the Party Days at Nuremberg, with grandiose ceremonies, turning the stadium into a cathedral - they were the rites appropriate to their perverted form of faith. The word 'Reich' had religious connotations, harking back to medieval concepts when the "Holy" German Reich was regarded as representing God's kingdom on earth. Their Reich had its martyrs, notably the sixteen dead in Hitler's 1923 coup, for whom twice-yearly memorial services were staged which would have done honour to the saints. Its millenarian prospects - the Reich of a thousand years - would fulfill the prophecies of old. Hitler was both High Priest and Saviour, sent by "Providence" to fulfil the destiny of the Aryan race - all others would bow down or be destroyed. The nation-community which he led was a re-paganised Church.

Thus was created a potent myth, an *idée-force* or motivating idea, which by raising images in the minds of impressionable people, often quite young, and endowing these images with a kind of psychic dynamism, could impel many millions to support disastrous and inhuman policies, plunging Europe into bloodshed and committing unspeakable barbarities. As Hitler said in *Mein Kampf*, it was not rational arguments which would sweep the masses into such action, but an all-embracing fanaticism. To create this was his work. In his speeches the words "Deutschland! Deutschland! Deutschland!" could be thundered forth with mystical overtones. So was re-created "the new yet old blood-myth", about which Alfred Rosenberg, the Nazis' "philosophical" ideologist, wrote his wordy *The Myth of the Twentieth Century* - "the myth of blood and of the soul, race and self, people and personality, blood and honour" which "must penetrate, bear up and determine the whole of life. This new-old myth is the reawakening of the spiritual cell-building centre" - the "centre of the people's and the race's honour" (*das Zentrum der Volks- und Rassenehre*). Whatever the precise meaning of this expression, it was linked with the call for a mighty effort of will, "the 'Alone, I will' of Faust, a commitment of faith in the new era."

The "cells" of the movement were the cliques and gangs of conspirators who fashioned their "heroic heathendom" under the leadership of the Pseudo-Messiah. This was the high water-mark of that flood of irrationality which submerged the Weimar Republic - "the murky waters seeping from all sorts of groups with their private myths, uniting to form a mighty stream". Many of these groups were of homo-erotic tendency. As one prophet of Nazidom put it, the national ideal was to be achieved "in the love for each other of splendid and beautiful young men of Germanic race". Whether homosexual or heterosexual, the ideology did not rely on the family as its main cell-building component - the family, according to Rosenberg, "nowhere was the cause nor the most important support" of the state. The germ-cell was the *Männerbund*: the union of men "singlemindedly aiming at some particular goal".

By 1932 demonstrations of brown-shirted SA and the black SS, riots, provocations, and all kinds of violence against Communists and other opponents had reduced parts of Berlin and other towns to something like a state of civil war.

"Hate exploded suddenly without warning out of nowhere; at street corners, in restaurants, cinemas, dance halls, swimming-baths; at midnight, after breakfast, in the middle of the afternoon. Knives were whipped out, blows were dealt with spiked rings, beer-mugs, chair-legs or leaded clubs; bullets slashed the advertisments on the poster-columns, rebounded from the iron roofs of latrines. In the middle of a crowded street a young man would be attacked, stripped, thrashed and left bleeding on the pavement; in fifteen seconds it was all over and the assailants had disappeared".

The police could still control a Nazi demonstration by a strength of two to one - if they so decided - but in January 1933 the Nazis were in power, ruthlessly clamping their system on the country.

Comment: Vril; Haushofer and the Aryan homeland; the author's views on Nazism as a student and as an "exchange teacher" in Nazi Germany. (p. 293)

CHAPTER TWELVE

TOTALITARIAN EMPIRES AND DISSENT

1. **German martyrs**: *cf. Rome: ideological persecution. Pastor Schneider; Alfred Delp, S.J.; Dietrich Bonhoeffer; Helmut von Moltke.*

The kind of empire which the Nazis created was based on militarism and militarised industry. This had been foreseen by Burckhardt, who had added that Germany could only survive through "something great, new and liberating - it will have its martyrs". On all these points he was prophetic. Besides military might the Nazi state depended on ideological rectitude. As in the Roman Empire, the authorities were bound to view askance any religion or ideology that could not be accommodated with its own, and would persecute such of its members as would not recognise the claims of the State or deliberately challenged its policy.

Belonging to the wrong race was another signal for persecution. The Jews were to be harassed, expelled, and (for those remaining) annihilated. Communists were imprisoned and murdered, the Social-Democratic Party was destroyed, its leaders brutally treated. As for Christians, the promotion of German-Christianity was a way of destroying the real faith by permeating it with racial doctrines, to the point where Christ was represented as an Aryan and the Old Testament declared irrelevant. Many clergy of the Evangelical Church were prepared to compromise with the German-Christians and their so-called reforms, with inadequate "leaders" being thrust upon them as bishops, though others were encouraged by Karl Barth's resounding "NO! to both the spirit and letter of this doctrine".

Some freedom of action was secured by courageous bishops, like the Protestants Meiser and Wurm and the Catholics von Galen and Faulhaber, who from time to time protested, but with little effect, about the treatment of Jews, Gipsies and the infirm. Some protesters, like the former U-boat commander, Martin Niemöller, were imprisoned. Some who refused military service, like the Jehovah's Witnesses, were also sent to concentration camps.

There were indeed Christian martyrs in the mould of those who refused to make obeisance to the Roman Emperor as a god. Of these was Pastor Paul Schneider, who spoke out openly against the regime for its anti-religious stance. Imprisonment and warnings had no effect on him. He refused to accept release on conditions, though asked to consider his wife and six children. "I know why I am here", he said. "Do you think God gave me children that I might only provide for their material welfare? Were they not entrusted to me so that I might safeguard them for eternity?" Refusing to take off his cap when the swastika flag was raised, Schneider was stretched on a rack and given 24 strokes of the whip. Immured in a wet and gloomy cell, he was strung up by his arms to the bars of his window for hours at a time.

"His hands could be tied higher and higher behind his back, forcing his head into a bent position. The Agony of the Cross was being re-enacted, but not as a single, awful ordeal .... Day after day, and week after week, as he fined down to a broken, bruised skeleton, clad in rags and with his body crawling with lice ... he prayed aloud, in a resonant voice which carried across the parade ground filled with its human scare-crows ... 'Jesus said - I am the resurrection and the life'".

He died of torture and maltreatment, just before war broke out.

Among other Christian leaders who were killed by the Nazis were Alfred Delp, Dietrich Bonhoeffer and Helmuth von Moltke.

Alfred Delp, S.J. (1907-1945), a convert to Roman Catholicism who had entered the Jesuit Order, was one of the Kreisau Circle who did not survive. He was arrested in July 1944, and although in no way involved in the attempt on Hitler's life, was "tried" before the notorious Roland Friesler in the People's Court and executed.

"Our own crime", he wrote, "was that of heresy against the Third Reich ... Anyone who dares cast doubts on the Nazi system is of course a heretic - and former judgements on heretics are child's play compared to the refined and deadly retribution practised by these people ... My offence is that I believe in Germany and her eventual emergence from this dark hour of error and distress, that I refused accept that accumulation of arrogance, pride and force that is the Nazi way of life, and that I did this as a Christian and a Jesuit. These are the values for which I am here now on the brink waiting for the thrust that will send me over ... Germany will be reborn ... It may be that even this shambles in which we are now living, this devastation swept by bitter winds of fate, is the destined place and hour of a new holy night, a new birth for humanity in its search for God".

One of Germany's younger theologians, he writes of "creative dialogue" with God, and goes on:

"The realm of the personal God is heaven, that is to say, it is the sum-total of all that man considers to be his life's greatest happiness. Fulfilment and more. It is not primarily a place or a period in time or anything like that. It is fundamentally God himself - a conscious union with Him.   Anyone who has achieved that union is in heaven. It is a union that uproots all our limitations and destroys our previous habits if we are fortunate enough to begin to experience it here on earth ... Man will have to re-learn, much more positively and intensively than before, that life leads from the personal dialogue with God to the actual personal encounter and the experience of unity with God. He will have to learn that this is his heaven and his real, his only, home."

A greater contrast could hardly be found between Dietrich Bonhoeffer's ministry to children in a poor district of Berlin, and the methods of the Hitler Youth. Recently ordained at the age of 25, Bonhoeffer was directed (in addition to his job as a student chaplain) to take over a confirmation class in one of the poorest districts of Berlin. He found 50 boys "making an indescribable din". By simply standing quietly for several minutes, and then telling them a story, he gained their attention and before long their complete confidence. He took the boys through the full preparation for confirmation, even leaving his home in the fashionable Grunewald suburb to rent a room in the same district as his pupils. He devoted his free evenings to them - they came invited or uninvited. He played chess with them, taught English, and took them youth-hostelling at weekends - an exercise in community living which gave point to his talks on "the Holy Spirit in the community". Following the confirmation he took some of the boys to his parents' country house: for these slum-dwellers it was "like a journey to the end of the world." He gave up a visit to the Holy Land and with the money provided a weekend shack for his pupils in the rural outskirts of Berlin.

Bonhoeffer belonged to the professional establishment of Germany. His father was the leading academic in psychiatry and neurology. His mother came of a family which had married into the aristocracy: among the relatives with whom they kept close touch were the Yorck von Wartenburgs, one of whom, Peter, played a major part in the conspiracies against Hitler, and paid with his life after the *attentat* of July 1944. Her father had been a chaplain to the Kaiser Wilhelm II, whom he took to task for referring to the working-class as "canaille" - after which the Kaiser's displeasure necessitated his retirement from his court functions. Christian culture and readiness to stand for principles was deeply ingrained in the large Bonhoeffer family.

This family, and Dietrich in particular, were among those who early perceived the evil in National-Socialism, and the danger to their country if Hitler gained power. "Will it not be all up if we do not immediately become quite different?" he asked in 1931 - "talk differently, live differently?" A year later, although the pro-Hitler vote at the second election that summer dropped from 38% to 33%, he predicted that there was little time left. "The story of the destruction of Jerusalem by pagans is beginning to have a terribly close significance for us." He challenged the false religiousness among fellow-Christians that was simply a cover for "doing what we want", which in political matters furthered an unbridled lust for power, playing one nation off against another. When Hitler gained power in January 1933 and proceeded to enforce antisemitic decrees, Bonhoeffer led the opposition to the "Aryan paragraph" excluding those of Jewish descent from the ministry, and later became one of the founders of the Confessing Church in the opposition to the national (Reich) Church which, in the hands of the German-Christians, had accepted Nazi racial doctrines.

Time as a student in America, and as pastor to the German congregations at Barcelona and Sydenham, strengthened Bonhoeffer's ecumenical convictions. He became a leader in the ecumenical movement, and a close friend of one of its British promoters, George Bell, Bishop of Chichester. He had a hard struggle to open the eyes of colleagues in the movement to the mistake of compromising with Nazism by accepting as valid representatives at their conferences the "German-Christian" nominees of the Reich Church. As a member of the Confessing Church he was not allowed officially to exercise his ministry, though he succeeded for several years in directing an illegal seminary for training ordinands in a disused country house at Finkelwalde in Pomerania, and later at a place even more remote from Berlin, thus escaping the attention of the Gestapo.

Finkelwalde and its successors represented a new type of monastic community, a resurgence of that form of the "live cell" which had played such a part in regenerating civilisation in ancient times. Not that Finklewalde was in competition with the Roman Catholic monasteries which still existed in Germany: in fact when forced to give up his teaching Bonhoeffer passed several fruitful months in the monastery of Ettal.

Not only the teaching, but the way of life at Finkelwalde differed considerably from a theological course at a university or ordinary seminary. There were no servants - everyone, including Bonhoeffer, undertook the domestic work. He instituted a quiet half-hour at the start of each day and meditation on a specified text - which was such a novelty for the students that most were lost to begin with in finding how to use the time effectively. There were some grumbles, as also when he advocated confession between one another before Communion. Along with this there were games, expeditions to the nearby coast, much fun and especially music - Bonhoeffer's proficiency at the piano had at one time made music seem a possible profession for him.

Bonhoeffer's *Life Together* presents in a few pages the quintessence of his experience at Finkelwalde.

"The community of the Spirit is the fellowship of those who are called by Christ ... Within the spiritual community there is never, nor in any way, any 'immediate' relationship of one to another, whereas human community expresses a profound elemental desire for community, for immediate contact with other human souls, just as in the flesh there is the urge for merger with other flesh ... Spiritual love, however, comes from Jesus Christ, it serves Him alone; it knows that it has no immediate access to other persons. Because Christ stands between me and others, I dare not desire direct fellowship with them".

But - never afraid of paradoxes - Bonhoeffer adds that despite these limitations on the community-building power of marriage, family and friendship, these associations have to be "projected into the spiritual community." When later he became engaged and was shortly after imprisoned, his perceptions on this point were sharpened: "You can hardly imagine how I long for everyone", he wrote to his fiancée. "After these long months of solitude I have a real hunger for people."

In the rural parts of Pomerania, Bonhoeffer was supported by the Confessing Synod of the Old Prussian Church which would have no truck with the flawed Reich Church. The Old Prussian Church counted among its members solid Junker families, some of which, like the von Gerlachs of a previous generation in their opposition to Bismarck's non-Christian *raison d'état*, could not accept the anti-Christian doctrines of Nazism. Of these members of the aristocracy "of the best kind, standing up to the last for truth and for right", was Ruth von Kleist-Restow, whose numerous grandchildren filled her town house at Stettin in term-time, and whose country house, not far from Finkelwalde, was always open to Bonhoeffer and his friends. Provisions from her farms and other gifts tided the seminary through periods of shortage until the Gestapo closed it. Before long all her four sons had been killed at the front, and three of her grandsons, sharing the fate of many of Bonhoeffer's pupils. Bonhoeffer's introduction into this circle brought him into touch with relatives, some of whom like Fabian von Schlabrendorf were involved in the abortive putsch of July 1944. It was to one of Ruth von Kleist's granddaughters that Bonhoeffer became engaged just before his arrest in 1943.

It was Bonhoeffer's deliberate decision to be fully involved in his country's trials and tribulations, when he could easily have been an observer from afar. Friends had invited him to America in the summer of 1939, on the understanding that he wished to stay there as a theological lecturer. But in the knowledge that war was about to break out he resigned his engagements and returned to Europe just before war began.

"I have made a mistake in coming to America", he wrote to one of his sponsors.

> "Christians in Germany will face the terrible alternative of either willing the defeat of their nation in order that Christian civilisation may survive, or willing the victory of our nation and thereby destroying our civilisation. I know which of these alternatives I must choose; but I cannot make that choice in security".

Bonhoeffer's imprisonment was the consequence of his participation in the resistance, through a network in which his brother Klaus and other near relatives were involved, notably his brother-in-law Hans von Dohnanyi. Dohnanyi's ability had led to his rapid promotion as a civil servant in the Ministry of Justice, despite his refusal to join the Nazi Party or its front-organisations, and he was already as a young man a judge of the Supreme Court at Leipzig when Admiral Canaris, head of the Abwehr (the army's intelligence and counter-espionage service) asked him to join his staff on the outbreak of war in 1939.

More important than its counter-espionage activity, the Admiral's organisation was the nerve-centre of the plots against Hitler. The close relation between the two brothers-in-law made Bonhoeffer privy to the activities of the Abwehr network, and eventually (after being obliged to relinquish his Church work) he was enrolled officially on its staff.

In taking on this work Bonhoeffer had no intention of becoming a martyr. For him it was a pratical matter: "if he, as a pastor, saw a drunken driver racing at high speed down the Kurfürstendamm, he did not consider it only or his main duty to bury the victims of the madman, or to comfort their relatives; it was more important to wrench the wheel out of the hands of the drunkard". For this he was prepared to forgo his priestly functions, to pray for the defeat of his country, and support those plotting to kill Hitler as the first step towards restoring lawful government and ending the war. As a courier for the Abwehr he made several visits to Switzerland and Sweden, ostensibly to use his ecumenical contacts for gaining information which would help the war-effort, but in reality to further the plots to remove Hitler and gain Allied support for these plans.

This meant working undercover, with deliberate deception of the Nazi authorities. Bonhoeffer was able to play his part in the resistance until arrested, along with Dohnanyi and others, in April 1943. The plotters against Hitler faced a series of disappointments. After the capitulation of the Sixth Army at Stalingrad, support for them throughout the army became more widespread, but Hitler seemed to bear a charmed life, escaping several attempts to kill him, culminating in his surviving with no more than bruises the bomb which Claus von Stauffenberg exploded in Hitler's underground war-room at Rastenberg on 20 July 1944. His death should have been the signal for an uprising organised in part by the Abwehr. Its failure gave full control of security to the Gestapo and the SS. Most of the plotters were rounded up, tortured and executed.

Bonhoeffer, already in prison, was not directly implicated, but he was moved to closer confinement in the Reich Security Office, then to Buchenwald, and was eventually executed at Flossenburg shortly before the war ended, in April 1945. His Brother Klaus and brothers-in-law Hans Dohnanyi and Rudiger Schleicher were also killed at about the same time.

During the first eighteen months of his imprisonment, in the military gaol at Tegel, his friendly interest in people, including the gaolers, had somewhat unusual consequences. To several hardened and foul-mouthed soldier-warders he became a confidant, to whom they went for advice in their troubles. During air raids the staff felt safer if they could be near him: he exuded confidence and peace of heart.

While in Tegel Bonhoeffer wrote the theological letters which made him famous. A rising theologian before the war began, a pupil of Harnack and a friend of Karl Barth, his reputation had been enhanced by his book, *The Cost of Discipleship*. In it he had denounced the dispensing of grace on the cheap, "the deadly enemy of our Church".

"We are fighting for costly grace ... Cheap grace is the preaching of forgiveness without requiring repentance, baptism without Church discipline, Communion without confession, absolution without contrition. Cheap grace is grace without discipleship, grace without the Cross, grace without Jesus Christ, living and incarnate. Costly grace is the treasure hidden in the field; for the sake of it a man will gladly go and sell all that he has".

In his letters he goes further. He counsels against a false dependence on God, using Him as a means of escape from the world's sufferings: "God would have us know that we must live as men who manage our lives without Him." The bald statement is really part of a paradox:

"Before God and with God we live without God. God lets Himself be pushed out of the world on to the Cross. He is weak and powerless in the world, and that is precisely the way, the only way, in which He is with us and helps us ... Christ helps us not by virtue of His omnipotence, but by virtue of His weakness and suffering ... Man is summoned to share in God's suffering at the hands of a godless world".

Bonhoeffer's call is for faith in God "who conquers power and space in the world by His weakness" - faith, not reliance on churchly "religion", not "in the first instance bothering about one's own needs, problems, sins and fears, but allowing oneself to be caught up in the way of Christ", in a world that is "coming of age". We hear again the echo of Joachim da Fiore: the world, Bonhoeffer believed, was moving out of the age of "religion" into the age of "Jesus, the man for others". His concluding word is that "it is not for us to prophesy the day, but the day will come when men will be called again to utter the word of God with such power as will change and renew the world".

The last glimpse of Bonhoeffer is on his knees, just before his execution, during those mad April days as the Reich "of a thousand years" was foundering. One of his poems was a personal prophecy:

"Come now, solemnest feast on the road to eternal freedom,
Death, and destroy those fetters that bow, those walls that imprison
this our transient life, these souls that linger in darkness,
so that at last we see what is here withheld from our vision.
Long did we seek you, freedom, in discipline, action and suffering.
Now that we die, in the face of God himself we behold you".

Before his arrest one of Bonhoeffer's journeys was to Norway with Helmuth von Moltke, another Abwehr agent. The occasion was the attempt by Vidkun Quisling, appointed by the Nazis as Prime Minister after their occupation of Norway, to bring the Church into a condition like that of the "Reich" Church in Germany. Fjellbu, Provost of Trondheim Cathedral, one of the main resisters, was removed from office, whereon the bishops refused to officiate within the framework of the state Church. Then, after a decree setting up a version of the Hitler Youth, over a thousand teachers resigned, followed by all the pastors. Bishop Berggrav, the initiator and inspirer of this action, was arrested. What impressed Bonhoeffer was this almost united resistance by the Norwegian clergy and teachers, along the lines of the action which he had vainly proposed at the height of the Church struggle in Germany. In the event Quisling was ordered, from Berlin, to put Berggrav under house arrest instead of bringing him before a "People's Court", and generally to backtrack on the aggressive Church policy.

The journey to Norway was one of the rare occasions on which these two leaders of the resistance met, though they had many links with other resisters, especially those who had been brought into the Abwehr like Adam von Trott, and relatives of one or the other who were also involved, like Peter Yorck (Moltke's cousin) and Hans Dohnanyi. Moltke was brought into close contact with Dohnanyi as both were working in the Abwehr's legal department, Moltke having trained as a lawyer, with the specialism of International Law. His mother was English and this made it natural for him to complete these studies at the Inns of Court in London, just before war broke out. Bonhoeffer's friendship with George Bell was paralleled by Moltke's with Lionel Curtis, the initiator of the Royal Institute of International Affairs and a leading advocate for restoring Christian values in politics and international relations. It was at a dinner at All Souls College, Oxford, as guests of Curtis, that Moltke's friendship with Trott began.

In his young years, before Hitler came to power, Moltke had not been especially noted for his Christian faith, but this deepened steadily, as it did with others, through facing the challenges of the Nazi regime. Communists too had faith which nerved them to resist, but with less consistency than the Christians, since the party line, during the period between the Molotov-Ribbentrop Pact of August 1939 and Hitler's invasion of Russia in June 1941, had been to co-operate with the Nazis (even if the latter did not reciprocate). But, in the words of Moltke's biographer, those who started with "a mere attitude of humanist benevolence", but would not compromise with the evil, felt the need increasingly for "an anchoring point beyond the visible world". In Moltke's case, he found (writing in 1942) that "the amount of risk and readiness for sacrifice which is asked from us now, and that which may be asked from us tomorrow, require more than the right ethical principles", and he came to believe that the rehabilitation of moral values in Germany could only be done on a religious basis.

In earlier days the beginnings of "the Kreisau Circle" can be seen in the summer work-camps for young people of different classes and backgrounds, where Moltke met several of his later colleagues. But much of his energy in the twenties went into saving the estate and farm at Kreisau - the legacy of the great-uncle of Bismarck's wars - of which the endowment had evaporated in the inflation, bringing the estates into the receiver's hands.

With the war and his entry into the Abwehr came access to information kept secret from most other Germans: the deportations of Jews, the setting-up of death-camps, the maltreatment of prisoners, and the violation of conventions for governing occupied territory. He strove, at times with sucess, to alleviate sufferings and injustices, by bringing such weight as the law could dispose on officials and officers at all levels, even going so far, against the advice of his friends, as to visit Gestapo headquarters for information about the fate of certain people. He went to Denmark to warn about the Jews in danger of deportation. He did his best to stiffen the resistance of army commanders, and of colleagues and superiors, against allowing the SS and the Nazi security service full rein in occupied territories, and was disgusted by the weakness and hypocrisy of so many "stuffed shirts" who could have taken a stand and failed to do so (though a number were grateful to him for giving a lead, and rallied accordingly). He agonised over these things, losing sleep as he thought about Jews and Russians. "Only one thing is sure," he wrote to his wife in 1941. "The horsemen of the Apocalypse are beginners to what is ahead of us ... Every day brings new insights into the depths to which men can sink".

With Stalingrad and Alamein, and the American entry into the war, it was clear that Germany's defeat was only a matter of time. Moltke began to plan with Trott and others, including some trade union leaders, how to deal with the situation after the collapse. He worked out "Fundamental Principles" for the restoration of sound government.

"The point of departure lies in the recognition of the divine order of things on which human existence is founded ... The main task now facing mankind in Europe is to get this divine order recognised. The solution lies in the resolute and vigorous realisation of Christian values. The Government of the [future] German Reich sees in Christianity the foundation for the moral and religious renewal of our people, for the surmounting of hate and lies, for the rebuilding of the European community of peoples. The free and peaceful development of national culture is no longer compatible with the maintenance of absolute sovereignty by individual states."

The new Reich would have to be structured as part of a European federation.

Such work could be done at weekend meetings in the privacy of Kreisau or of Yorck's Berlin house, and documents could be safeguarded, but contacting anti-Nazis who could take over as local governors on the eventual collapse was a more risky business. As Moltke wrote to Curtis while on an Abwehr trip to Sweden: "Can you imagine what it means to work as a group when you cannot use the telephone, when you are unable to post letters, when you cannot tell the names of your closest friends to your other friends for fear that one of them might be caught and might divulge the names under pressure?" But the risks were worth while. Almost nothing of the talks and none of the documents leaked out to the Nazis, and though some of the circle like Trott and Yorck were killed after the failure of the July 1944 putsch, others like the political scientist Otto von der Gablentz and the jurist Hans Peters survived. In the midst of decadence and disaster, and despite these tragic deaths, seeds were being planted which would bear fruit in due course. As Yorck said: "Even if - as I hope - we are today living through the sensational end of an epoch, we must not overlook the seeds which will enable new life to spring up out of the ruins".

Eventually, following allegations by a spy, Moltke became suspect to the Nazi security service, who seized the opportunity to discredit the Abwehr. He was arrested in January 1944 and remained in prison for a year before being tried by Freisler.

He was not tried for having connection with the *attentat* of 20 July. In fact he had opposed proposals for doing away with Hitler by violence. "We need a revolution, not a coup d'état", he had said, and wrote later that he had disapproved of such measures because "they would not get rid of the fundamental trouble which was spiritual ... Our case histories prove that it is neither plots nor plans, but the very spirit of man that is to be hunted down".

It was during his months in prison and the days before execution that Moltke showed his spiritual resilience. He rejoiced that, at his trial, the case did not rest on accusations of plots "of violence or organised opposition. What was discussed concerned the demands in practice of the Christian ethic, nothing more. And for that alone are we sentenced. In one of his tirades Freisler said to me 'Only in one respect are we and Christianity alike; we demand the whole man!' ...

Of the whole gang Freisler was the only one who knew why he had to do away with me ... Here it was all grim earnest. 'Who do you take your orders from? From the other world or from Adolf Hitler? Who commands your loyalty and your faith?'"

In this last letter to his wife he listed his Bible readings, especially the Epistles to Corinthians.

"No, I am not busy with the good God or with my death. He has the inexpressible grace to come to me and to be busy with me ... You are my 13th chapter of the First Epistle to the Corinthians. Without this chapter no man is really a man ... Without you, my dear, I would have 'had not charity' ... And we have been allowed finally to symbolise this fact through our shared Holy Communion [adminstered by the prison chaplain, a friend and member of their circle, Harald Poelchau], which will have been my last. It is not given to us to see Him face to face, but we must needs be overwhelmed when we suddenly realise that He has gone before us our whole lives through, a pillar of cloud by day and of fire by night, and that in a flash He suddenly lets us see it ... I have simply been the vessel for which God has taken such endless trouble".

"Right to the end", a fellow-prisoner wrote, "he was completely free in soul, friendly, helpful, considerate, a truly free and noble man amid all the trappings of horror". He was executed on 21 January 1945. Freisler followed him to death, in an air-raid, ten days later. Within five months Germany had surrendered, Kreisau was incorporated in Poland, and after extraordinary adventures his wife and children were brought by the British (on the intervention of Lionel Curtis) in safety to the West.

Comment: Martin Niemöller; Karl Barth. (p. 296)

2. **Russian repression**: *Renewed repression under Khrushchev, but rising interest in religion, especially among young people. "Acts of the Apostles" in a labour camp. Spiritual experience in solitary confinement. Anti-Church policies in Georgia and Central Europe, and reactions.*

In the Soviet Union the rise of Khrushchev opened another period of persecution. The Penal Code was revised with punishment of up to five years imprisonment for "organising or leading a group whose activities are carried on under the guise of teaching religious doctrine and carrying out religious rites which entail harming the health of citizens or any other encroachments upon the person or upon the rights of individuals ... and likewise enticing minors into this group". Arrests followed, many monks being among the victims, with imprisonment often in hospitals and mental institutions.   Most monasteries which had been reopened since the war were again closed or converted to other uses, and the seminaries were reduced to three. Children were torn from Christian parents to be educated as atheists at boarding-schools. Young believers were excluded from universities and could expect no promotion in the public services.

Splendidly illustrated books and brochures depicted well-attended churches at Moscow and elsewhere, full since their number was so pitifully small in relation to would-be churchgoers. In 1965 there was only one church per 150,000 inhabitants in Moscow, compared with one per 3,000 before the revolution. For Leningrad the ratio was 50% less. In many towns and extensive country areas there were no churches at all open for worship.   When destruction was planned for the great Cathedral of Christ the Saviour in Moscow, a ring of people surrounded it, to no avail - the soldiers moved in with dynamite. The site was converted to a swimming bath. However some churches are now being returned to local congregations for their rightful use.

One consequence of the ban on evangelising, hardly envisaged by the state authorities, was the revival of sermons in Orthodox churches, with the innovation of a question time on Sunday evenings. This was attractive particularly for young people for whom Marxism-Leninism had lost all meaning. Many were drawn to Fr. Dimitri Dudko's discussions in the Church of St. Nicholas on Preobrazhenka in Moscow during the first months of 1974, when "the church was packed with such a strange crowd that it was hard to believe it was not a youth club". An Englishman who attended a session wrote:

"The immorality of Soviet society, its inhumanity and corruption, its lack of a moral code or credible ideals, means that Christ's teaching comes through to those whom it reaches as a shining contrast. It stresses the value of the individual, of humaneness, forgiveness, gentleness, love ... The loss of these qualities is one of the most disturbing features in modern Soviet life".

It was the last time Dudko was allowed to speak in the church. A month later the KGB removed him.

Though the situation has been changing, all believers have been at risk. After restoring their convent and living in it for some years, the 140 nuns of Ovruch were given 24 hours by the Chairman of the

Town Council to quit, because they were needed as workers in a brick factory - the militia were sent to enforce the order.

The response can be like another chapter of Acts. Georgi Vins, a leading Baptist, did three years in a labour camp, was rearrested in 1974 and sent to a Corrective Labour Camp. On the first occasion he was with his pastor and a young Christian convert, the three of them leaving 17 children to be looked after by their wives. Vins relates:

> "In the barracks where we lived, we three prayed openly by our plank beds. We talked openly about God ... Some of these prisoners stopped smoking and swearing, and even began to pray. All this greatly troubled not only the local camp authorities, but also Moscow.

> "The Camp Commandant once said among a group of officers, and it was reported to us: 'Another six months and half the camp will become Baptists!' Of course he was greatly exaggerating, but the atheists' degree of alarm was very high. At the end of June 1967 a special commission from Moscow arrived in our distant *taiga* camp. In the most categorical way they forbade us to pray and to talk about God. But we could not submit to these demands. One of the brothers told the colonel who headed the commission: "We are unable not to pray and not to talk about God. This is our life. And if you have torn us away from our families and from our homes and brought us to the North so that we would stop praying and believing - it won't happen. Even here we will pray by our bunks and we will serve our God!"

> "The present moment in the history of our church is only the turning of one of the most difficult pages, but not by any means the last one", was the confident assertion of Archpriest Vsevolov Shpiller in a Moscow sermon (1973). "More and more frequently and unexpectedly you meet people of the most varied ages and situations who have gone through deep inner, spiritual, mental and emotional crises, sometimes through tragic conflicts which they have found insoluble in a non-religious framework, who are asking the Church about different things, more and more frequently, more and more deeply, more and more earnestly". And out of the agonies of persecution and oppression comes the most profound spiritual experience.

During his time in solitary confinement Anatoli Levitin developed a routine. At 8 a.m. he would begin walking round his cell repeating the Orthodox liturgy, "inseparably linked to the whole

Christian world". He would pray for the Pope, the Patriarch, the leaders of his own Church. "At the central point of the liturgy ... I felt myself standing before the face of the Lord, sensing almost physically his wounded, bleeding body. I would begin praying in my own words, remembering all those near to me, those in prison and those who were free, those still alive and those who had died ... The prison walls moved apart and the whole universe became my residence, visible and invisible, the universe for which that wounded, pierced body offered itself as a sacrifice ... After this, I experienced an exaltation of spirit all day - I felt purified within". He believed this continuing experience to be due also to the prayers of other Christians giving "living water and the bread of life, peace of soul, rest and love."

The effectiveness of Lenin's atheist policy has been as dubious in Russia's empire as in its home-lands. Outwardly in some provinces and subject states the success has been spectacular, at least in terms of closing churches and monasteries. This is notable in Georgia, Stalin's fatherland, where - after savage persecutions - only 40 churches of the Georgian Orthodox rite were open (there had been 2,500 before the Bolsheviks re-annexed the country to Russia in 1921). The Uniate Church of the Ukraine was also devastated. In the vast areas of Central Asia and elsewhere closure of mosques or their transformation into museums have been part of the policy of weakening the hold of Islam, though the large increase of the population through the high birthrate has impelled the authorities to permit the opening or reopening of mosques since 1977. As for the Jews, synagogues have been shut, the teaching of Hebrew was practically banned, and emigration closely restricted.

In territories more recently incorporated into the USSR the sucess of the policy varied. Minorities have usually been made to suffer more than the Orthodox. To add to their one permitted church the 15,000 Roman Catholics of Moldavia built another with their own hands, but it was demolished by the authorities, and their single priest was harassed and hampered by such means as drafting him into a labour unit (though his outraged congregation prevented this), and depriving him of his driving licence while forbidding visits to the sick or dying without permits for each occasion.

Lithuania had been as solidly Roman Catholic a country as Poland. On occupation by the Soviet Union in 1940 the Papal Nuncio was expelled, the Concordat with the Vatican abrogated, almost all Church property and land confiscated, and state subsidies and pensions ended. Monastic orders were abolished, their buildings confiscated, and monks and nuns deported to Siberia. Nazi occupation made little difference to the situation, and Soviet persecution continued after re-annexation. Bishops were sent as prisoners to labour camps - one was shot, although Jews testified that he had saved their lives from the Nazis - and others died in the inhumane conditions. Of those allowed to return home after Stalin's death, one, the 80-year-old Bishop Matulionis, was allowed to say Mass though not to administer his diocese, but he and another bishop managed to consecrate some others. Khrushchev's arrival in power brought on another period of extreme persecution, with attempts to cause splits by promoting Soviet stooges. Typical was the confiscation of a church whose construction had been authorised by the Government. After being built by voluntary labour and donations it was turned by Government order into a concert hall. But by the Brezhnev period the KGB were still unable to prevent the collection of 17,000 signatures to a petition protesting against restrictions on religious education, the imprisonment of priests, the banishment of bishops and other forms of persecution.

Soviet policy may in fact have strengthened the faith rather than otherwise of practising Lithuanian Catholics (94% in 1940). There was universal rejoicing when in 1989 the Cathedral at Vilnius was returned to the Church. The experience in Poland had been similar, where Catholicism has fused with nationalism as a powerful unifying force for the people, who for so much of their history have been a prey either to an indisciplined oligarchy or division and occupation by foreign powers. The election of Cardinal Woytila as Pope John Paul II, acclaimed even by Polish Communists, and the tremendous response to his visits there in 1979 and 1983, showed with no shadow of doubt where the people's true loyalty lay, while the most publicised act of the secret police, in the shadow of the KGB, the murder of Fr. Popieluszko, presented them with a martyr for their cause.

These events have taken place despite the full treatment on Soviet lines designed to split the Church by setting up pseudo-religious organisations - Pax, Caritas, Veritas - with oppression or removal of the leadership, confiscation of property, harassment or abolition of religious education, abrogation of the Concordat with the Vatican, and attempts to control clerical appointments. In 1953 Cardinal Wyszynski was arrested and confined in a remote monastery. Eight bishops, 900 priests and over a thousand laymen were imprisoned. Such persecution in no way lessened the struggle. The pseudo-Church bodies were discredited. On being freed in 1956 Wyszynski continued the fight, refusing to compromise on fundamental issues, while ready to make concessions as he had previously done in the agreement of 1950, by which he had secured the reopening of the Catholic University of Lublin in return for requesting the Vatican to extend the Polish dioceses westwards to conform with the country's new frontiers (a step towards the State securing legitimation of these acquisitions).

A degree of independence was secured by the Polish Communist Party in choosing Wladyslaw Gomulka as its First Secretary in 1956 in the wake of the rising of that year, without prior consultation with Moscow (it was with difficulty that a furious Khrushchev was mollified). This admittedly narrow margin of manoeuvre was reflected in the position of the Church, relatively strong by comparison with most others under Soviet domination. But this strength was also due to the Church's unity and the character of its leaders, which matched the determination of the people - outstanding personalities like Wyszynkski, a man of "simple patriotism, radiant piety [and] total integrity", and Karol Woytila who, long before he became Pope, had shown his "scintillating talents and profound spirituality" as actor, poet, playwright, sportsman, philosopher, parish priest and university chaplain and professor, as well as a much loved and respected bishop. Having become Pope in one of the most remarkable papal elections of all time, his first visit to Poland in 1979 (an extraordinary event to have been permitted by a Communist regime) brought new life and hope not only to Poland, where it inspired the Solidarity movement, but throughout Central and Eastern Europe. He said, in Warsaw, "Christ cannot be kept out of the history of man in any part of the globe, certainly not in Poland", and called for "a Christian Europe" and for the recognition of the historic links formed through the evangelising of all the Slav nations. At Auschwitz he spoke of "the Golgotha of our times".

By contrast few of the Communist leaders were other than time-servers and careerists. The party became "the resort of the most self-seeking elements of society, who see it as their passport to a successful career, to a high salary, to promotion, to privileged social benefits, and in some cases to licentious conduct, but only rarely as an opportunity for dedicated service to the community".

As elsewhere under Soviet surveillance it was sometimes possible to ignore the behests of the State, which in any case was little more than "the administrative branch of the party". In Przemysl Bishop Tokarczuk could get no answers from the authorities to his requests for appointments and buildings. He then built 150 churches without permission. The method was to have them prefabricated and put up in one night. When the militia came next day to bulldoze them, the entire congregation was encircling the building and the militia could do nothing. On being summoned by the authorities he told them that he would be building 20 more churches in the next three years, on the principle that no one should be more than half an hour's walk from a church.   Similarly Fr. Franciszek Blachniki explained that he developed the "Light-Life" movement by ignoring official prohibitions - no less than 70 written orders - to disband the summer camps which by 1984 had been attended by around 300,000 mostly young people.

The vision is of a leavening process which can radically change the situation, not only in Poland but world-wide.   In Poland many hundreds of groups or "oases" inspired by the movement have sprung up.   The same upsurge or "revolution of the soul" encouraged by the Pope's visits, inspired *Solidarity*.   Its strength lies in the consciences and convictions of its supporters, who must begin, says Lech Walesa, "by putting things right in themselves".   Two months before being assassinated Fr. Jerzy Popieluszko said in a sermon that "the solidarity of the nation had its roots in the call for the return to truth and justice".

In Czechoslovakia the Soviet attempt at splitting the Church was more effective than in Poland.   The pseudo-Church organisation "Pacem in Terris" attracted many clergy who otherwise feared to lose their state licence and with it freedom from the harassment suffered by their less compromising colleagues.   Of these latter Bishop (later Cardinal) Tomasek gave an inspiring example by his steadfastness through three years as a prisoner in a strict regime labour camp, and then under surveillance in a small Moravian parish (other bishops, half the priests, thousands of monks and nuns, together with Catholic writers and intellectuals, were also imprisoned in the early fifties). Harsh controls continued, but a religious revival was noticeable, often as a kind of folk-religion, especially among the younger generation. The largest ever assembly in the country's history, some 250,000 people, gathered at Valehrad in July 1985 to celebrate the 1,100th anniversary of St. Methodius, the medieval evangelist of Moravia. Cardinal Tomasek read the Pope's address, but the Minister of Culture who tried to turn the occasion into a "peace" demonstration was pratically howled down with shouts of "we want the Mass!"

In Hungary and the German Democratic Republic the approach of the authorities was different - much more along the lines of waiting for the hoped for rising tide of affluence to remove the social roots of religion rather than of a head-on clash, while inveigling the Churches into a collaborationist situation like that of the "German-Christians" in relation to Nazism.   The Protestant leadership in the GDR, where Lutherans are in a large majority, were however well prepared to avert this development, since as survivors from the Nazi era, they were able to take their stand on the Barmen Confession which laid down the principles of the Confessing Church of Bonhoeffer, Niemöller and other dissidents.

In Hungary, where the Catholics are more than double the

Protestants, the stand of Cardinal Mindszenty against the erosion of his Church's position in matters like education was what caught the public's eye in the West during the post-war years. After the rising of 1956 the Cardinal took refuge in the American Embassy, and during the long period of his virtual immurement there he could exert little influence on events. The Lutherans were also treated roughly, their leading bishop, Lajos Ordass, being kept under house arrest or in prison until his death in 1978 except for a short period from 1956-8.

Close co-ordination in Church affairs has not in fact been a feature of Soviet policy in countries under occupation. In a general way, particularly in the early years, Soviet policy followed a line of imposing or infiltrating as leaders clerics with some sympathy for Marxism or outright KGB agents (which in practice came to much the same thing), displacing and discrediting the original leadership, while making it understood that whatever the confiscations, restrictions and other such actions to date, worse would befall unless the *modus vivendi* decreed by the State was maintained.

3. **The long arm of the KGB**: *function; recruitment; students; inter-war Cambridge and Oxford; campaign against the Oxford Group.*

In imposing the State's policies on the Churches the KGB was at work not only within Russia proper, but also in its empire and beyond. Its hand, or at least its example, was as evident in the murder of Father Popieluszko in Poland as in the silencing of Father Dudko at Moscow. In the case of the latter, after securing a ban by the Patriarch on his preaching in his Moscow church, the KGB arranged his transfer to a parish three hours journey from the capital, but when his success as a speaker was repeated there - multitudes were flocking fom Moscow to hear him - he was removed elsewhere and finally subjected to treatment in prison with the result that he admitted to anti-Soviet "errors" on television.

This "sword and shield of the Party" with its vast informer network has functioned under different names, now "Committee for State Security", reaching "into every crevice of society" under Soviet control "from the Red Army General Staff down to the most humble village". In 1970 a huge new division, the fifth Chief Directorate, was organised, to deal with dissident intellectuals and samizdat publications, and to suppress ethnic nationalism and the religious upsurge. With glasnost the KGB has been given a new look by the propaganda services. It may have changed in its manner and objectives at home, but it may still be continuing in its former ways

Inside the Soviet Union the KGB could operate openly to divert or contain the spiritual upsurge. More indirect methods were needed in non-Soviet countries under Moscow's control, through conniving priests and politicians as well as the secret police. Beyond these bounds its aims were the same: to infiltrate a body like the World Council of Churches, win leading ecclesiastics to become Soviet supporters, and annihilate (if it could not subvert) any movement which presented a serious challenge. From the late 1930's onwards, the movement which fell most obviously in this category was the Oxford Group (Moral Re-Armament).

Since it could not operate openly in countries outside its control, the KGB had to rely on agents and was largely dependent on locally recruited personnel. No methods were barred, from compromising individuals with threats of blackmail, playing on idealistic motives, or simply by cash payments or other material rewards. The object has been to involve individuals directly or maintain them as "sleepers", encouraging them to attain responsible positions in their countries from which they could operate as agents with maximum effect. A KGB manual containing a section on "The practice of recruiting Americans in the USA and Third Countries" proposed that students should be among the main targets.

> "The financial situation of American students [in Latin American countries], their conviction, and the general operational climate facilitate our work. The fact that some of the students are preparing to enter government service (and in some cases they can be directed towards this type of work) indicates that students can form a basis for organising future networks to penetrate United States government organisations ... For the most part they are independent, are free in their choice of contacts and topics of conversation, and lack sufficient experience in life ... Experience in establishing contacts with and developing individuals in these groups has resulted in the formulation of specific methods and approaches."

Such guidance indicates what was the line of approach to students in other countries and at earlier periods. One of the greatest coups was the recruitment of agents from among students at Oxford and Cambridge between the wars. This was achieved in large part by the ability of Soviet propagandists to appeal to the idealism of the young, while utilising their ambivalent sexual proclivities. Even when platonic, these relationships formed networks, which continued in the persons of those graduating into the highest echelons of public life. Academic circles and university societies like the prestigious

Cambridge "Apostles" were wide open to these influences, which tainted the generations as the 20th century decadence set in.

Homosexuality had become respectable in Cambridge intellectual circles early in the century, when some of the most brilliant undergraduates and younger dons made their passionate feelings for each other part of their philosophy of life. The *Principia Ethica* of the youthful philosopher G.E. Moore was taken as their gospel - or rather its last chapter, "The Ideal", in which he affirmed that "personal affections and aesthetic enjoyments include *all* the greatest, and *by far* the greatest goods we can imagine."

The moral principles of the earlier part of the book were ignored. "We accepted Moore's religion, so to speak, and discarded his morals," wrote J.M. Keynes. Before long the "Apostles" were inducting young men on their looks as much as on their intellectual power or promise, and bending the rules in the process. A notorious practising homosexual, Guy Burgess, could become an Apostle, and utilise to the full the powerful network of the society for pursuing his devious personal and political ends.

In such ways the decadence which Bernard Bosanquet, the philosopher of the generation prior to Moore's, had perceived as already beginning to have its dissolvent effects in the nineties, was becoming more clearly evident in the nineteen-hundreds, coming up to the "climate of treason" of the thirties in which the likes of Burgess and Maclean could flourish.

Life at the old universities, for those who combined "frivolity with the pursuit of knowledge ... was the product of the late last flowering of an empire which was already in decay, but was still strong enough and wealthy enough to support a class which was largely immune to the pressure of material care." A change came with the crisis years signalled by the Wall Street crash of October 1929. Mass unemployment, and the failure of the League of Nations to abolish war between its members, gave a new perspective on the realities of life to the younger generation. When Communist proselytism was at its height and Oswald Mosley was finding new recruits for Fascism, undergraduates were also attracted by the Oxford Group, as were some senior faculty members.

At that time the Oxford Group was the most evident and radical expression of reviving moral and spiritual life in Britain. The campaign waged against it in the 1930's, and against its later manifestation as Moral Re-Armament, is a classic instance of the power of the KGB abroad to counter any movement which challenged the ideological and moral foundations of Marxism-Leninism and the Soviet attempts to win hearts and minds world-wide.

Against the Group an unremitting onslaught was mounted, led

by Tom Driberg. A promiscuous homosexual, and a Communist when at Oxford, Driberg gained respectability as a leading Anglican layman, a Member of Parliament, and eventually Chairman of the Labour Party and a Peer. As a journalist, and from the privileged position of the House of Commons, he pursued whatever line the Kremlin dictated, while supporting other agents and traitors like Burgess, about whom he wrote a book. Committed to his deviant life-style, he had evident reasons for attacking the Oxford Group - especially when it came to be assessed by the Kremlin as "the most prominent association which aims to save Western Civilisation from Communism - a universal ideology [with] the power to attract radical revolutionary minds". That this evaluation differed from that current in the West was not surprising, in view of the sustained campaign of denigration led by Driberg, supported by disinformation put out by KGB agents and their stooges in the intelligence services and the media.

For the KGB the most serious threat from MRA was in the postwar years when the Communists lost their hold on the industrial area - particularly the miners - in the Ruhr, which they attributed to its work. The Ruhr had been regarded (according to the Cominform directive Protocol M.) as a centre of mass struggle, "decisive for the German working class". Now the Communists saw their leadership among the miners decimated, as man after man changed, at work, at home, in their whole philosophy of life. The KGB feared that MRA was starting on its "decisive task ... total expansion throughout the world", by "building bridgeheads on each continent and training cadres capable of spreading this ideology among the masses."

It was often after months of investigation, discussion and experimentation that these miners came to the conclusion that MRA was a more profound revolution than Communism. A turning-point came when a Party official, Willi Benedens, sent to bring two of them back from a MRA conference, himself changed while there, and all three recommended that the Party should investigate "Moral Re-Armament's world-revolutionising idea". From then on Communists were forbidden to attend MRA meetings, but many continued to do so, strengthened in their new approach by changes which took place during the same period among top management in the Ruhr. The honesty, openness and consequent trust on the part of both management and labour in the Works Councils (which the British zonal authorities had set up) made these bodies, both in the Ruhr and elsewhere, centres of genuine co-operation. Freed from Communist domination, they contributed much to the "economic miracle" which ensued.

Comment: MRA's challenge to Communists and Nazis. (p. 297)

CHAPTER THIRTEEN

THE RENEWAL OF WESTERN EUROPE

1. **The statesmanship of reconciliation**: *Sangnier; officials in the French Zone of occupation; Robert Schuman, Konrad Adenauer; Pastor Niemöller and the Stuttgart Declaration of Guilt; the Caux conferences of Moral Re-Armament; Irène Laure; Karl Arnold.*

In the pre-1914 period Gratry's influence was still felt in the sphere of peace-building. In 1867 he supported the Ligue internationale et permanente de la paix, founded in that year at Paris. A generation later the Gratry Society was founded, and reconstituted in 1906, backed by Sangnier and his "Sillon" friends: its aim was an "active commitment to putting Christian principles to work in politics", and especially to proclaim that "the principles of Christian morality apply as much to relations among peoples as the relations among individuals".

1914 had seen the eclipse of all such efforts. Sangnier himself served with distinction at the front. After the war most of his energy went into striving for a peace settlement both just and fair, while working for reconciliation with Germany. He anticipated the European Community in calling for an economic agreement between France and Germany as the first step towards integrating both countries in an international "entente" - but the time for creating the necessary structures had not arrived. It was still a question of creating heart or "soul", *"un nouvel état d'âme international"*, and in striving to do this Sangnier was indefatigable.

As a member of the *"horizon bleu"* parliament (National Assembly) immediately after the 1914-18 war, he took an independent line, often as a lone voice. There and in public gatherings he castigated the self-contradictory policy of suppressing Germany while exacting huge sums in reparations, instead of promoting the construction of a peaceful Europe. He organised vast demonstrations, starting with an international peace congress at Paris in December 1921, the first such occasion to which Germans were invited after the war. Another was held in Germany, at the moment when France was occupying the Ruhr in order to force reparations payment - a policy strongly contested by Sangnier in Parliament. Occasions which he arranged on his estate at Bierville, designed particularly to attract young people, were more than just demonstrations. In 1926 6,000 came for a month of meetings, courses, music and plays (an open-air theatre was built). Three aircraft hangers end-to-end held 20,000 for special meetings, at which, among other things, racism and colonialism were condemned. But Europe had to tear itself in pieces once more before a way could be found to direct such enthusiasm into the creation of new structures for ensuring peace.

Sangnier's brand of radicalism eventually found its political expression in the Parti démocrate populaire (PDP) formed by some of his followers in 1924. Its platform was explicitly Christian, envisaging an improvement in the conditions of the underprivileged and workers, and ensuring the latter a fair share in the running of industry; and a foreign policy "resolutely French" while "definitely favourable to the methods of international collaboration". This was the party which in 1931 Robert Schuman joined, to earn himself in the post-war years the title of "Father of Europe" for his part in founding the European Community. Sangnier held himself aloof from the PDP (he was no longer in Parliament during those years) concentrating his efforts at his Bierville centre on "education in depth, the transformation of individuals", and so sending forth "currents" which later led to the creation by others of new structures in society and politics.

Some of his followers, after using the old "Sillon" premises as a Resistance base during the German occupation, changed their group, "Les nouvelles équipes françaises", into a political party, the Mouvement républicain populaire (MRP), with Sangnier as Honorary President. The party was successful at the polls in October 1945, attracting nearly a third of the electorate. Schuman was one of those elected on the MRP ticket.

Sangnier's vision began to be translated into reality in 1945 when a group of enlightened officials in the French zone of occupation, backed by de Gaulle as Head of the Provisional Government of France and by the Zone Commander, General Koenig, initiated a policy of reconciliation. Economic exploitation of the zone was harsh, but its industry and resources were sufficient to finance an impressive educational and cultural development. Many of the officials were specialists in various branches of German history, administration and culture, and the educational directorate was staffed by men of the calibre of Alfred Grosser, the historian and former Resistance fighter.

Large sums were spent on re-writing and producing history and other text-books. An Institute of European Studies was established at Mainz, which was re-founded as a university after a long period of abeyance; also an interpreters' college at Germersheim, and one of administration at Speyer. In addition eight "popular" universities (Volksuniversitäten) were established, besides four French institutes for music, languages, etc. Non-governmental bodies - Catholic, Protestant, Socialist and others - were encouraged to set up associations for youth, and to hold summer sessions which could be attended by officially sponsored parties of young French people. The scheme developed steadily: 1,000 in 1946, 1,200 in 1947, 2,000 in 1948, and 5,000 in 1949, the year in which the French frontiers were opened to young Germans. Friendships were made, whose fruits were long-term rather than immediate, when those involved came into responsible positions in trade unions, politics and education. The relationships and outlook shaped in these encounters strengthened the new system of partnership which the statesmen were beginning to design. In this way the pioneering work of Marc Sangnier between the wars, now revived on a governmental level, produced historic consequences.

But this was the policy and action of an elite. The mass of French people were still gripped by hatred of the Germans for the humiliations and harsh treatment - sometimes torture and terrorism - which they had suffered under the occcupation. Trade unionists would not attend international conferences at which Germans (though anti-Nazis) were present, and such boycotts occurred on other occasions. A change of attitude had to take place in wider circles if a policy of partnership based on reconciliation could be initiated. Schuman, as Foreign Minister during four and a half crucial years from July 1948, knew he had to wait until enough of the public were ready for such a move. He had experienced the full force of Communist attacks on himself for his background, as a Lorrainer whose homeland had been under Germany, obliging him as a conscript to do non-combatant work during the First World War. "He's a Boche!" and other such insults had been hurled at him in Parliament.

This rowdiness had been part of attempts to curb his effectiveness as Prime Minister during the winter of 1947-8, when strikes, sabotage, derailment of trains and other methods of virtual civil war were practised by Communists in their bid for power. Schuman's strength of character, his tenacity and quiet determination to hold to the right course without appeasement or hollow promises had enabled France to survive the ordeal and settle down to a steady spell of reconstruction and development, as a preliminary to the further task of "building Europe".

One of his first moves as Foreign Minister was to make soundings with Karl Arnold, who was concerned with the Ruhr as Minister-President of the state (*Land*) of North Rhine-Westphalia, in search of a European solution of the Ruhr question. Arnold was - along with Adenauer, Schuman and the Italian Prime Minister, Alcide De Gasperi - typical of the leadership which had been persecuted and suppressed by the totalitarian regimes, and which arose with the breaking of the Nazi-Fascist yoke. Like them a Catholic of sincere faith, he had made his name as a leader of the Christian trade unions and as the chief spokesman of the Centre Party in Düsseldorf, where - after surviving harassment and want during the Nazi era - he became Lord Mayor in 1946. His main themes in his speeches during this period were the need to end hate, and the acceptance of a European patriotism in place of self-centred national egoism.

In October 1948 Schuman went to Coblenz to meet Konrad Adenauer, Chairman of the largest party (the Christian-Democrats) in the *Land*, and soon to be Chancellor of the Federal Republic of Germany. The two men could talk together without an interpreter; they were also brought closer by their common faith, as dedicated Catholics (De Gasperi was another German-speaking frontiersman, of the Tyrol).

At a time (January 1948) when Germans were still normally excluded from international conferences, Adenauer succeeded in obtaining an invitation to the conference at Luxembourg of the Nouvelles équipes internationales, designed to bring the various Christian Democratic parties together. Though officially only an observer, he made a speech which was extremely well received, particularly by his frank admission of Germany's guilt during the Nazi period, and his pledge that he and his party would work for a united Christian Europe. In such ways leaders like Schuman and Adenauer infused their Christian beliefs in their statecraft for reconciling the war-torn countries of Europe.

On another level moves were made from the German side for reconciliation. The initiative came from Pastor Niemöller, encouraged by Bishop Wurm and Karl Barth, at the Stuttgart Conference of the newly-formed Council of the German Evangelical Church in October-November 1945.

> "We say with great sorrow: through us endless suffering has been brought to many peoples and lands. That which we have often testified before our parishes we now proclaim in the name of the whole Church; though we fought in the name of Jesus Christ for long years against the spirit which found terrible expression in the National-Socialist terror-regime, we accuse ourselves of not having witnessed more courageously, not having prayed more faithfully, believed more joyously and loved with greater ardour ..."

The significance of the Declaration of Guilt was heightened by the response of French and other delegates of the World Council of Churches who were present at the conference. It was fitting that such a response could be made through this ecumenical association whose Secretary-General, W.A. Visser't Hooft, had given encouragement and support to Dietrich Bonhoeffer during his war-time visits to Geneva, and had tried to keep open the lines of the German Resistance to the Allies.

Martin Niemöller was one of those Germans of extraordinary courage and endurance, who had stood for his convictions against Hitler, but - unlike Bonhoeffer and others - had survived. A successful U-Boat commander in World War I, he later followed in his father's footsteps as a pastor in the Evangelical Church, and came into prominence as one of the most outspoken critics of the German-Christians and of the attempts by the Nazi regime to foist them on the Protestant Churches as the directing element. With Bonhoeffer he founded the Pastors Emergency League in September 1933, to which by the end of the year, nearly half of the pastors had rallied. A high point of his resistance was his word to Hitler, when in January 1934 the Führer summoned to the Chancellory the leading opponents to the German-Christian take-over, and browbeat most of them - but not Niemöller - into accepting, at least temporarily, the leadership of his stooge Ludwig Müller, the ex-army chaplain who was shortly to be made Reich Bishop. To Hitler's "You confine yourself to the Church - I'll take care of the German people", Niemöller replied: "We too as Christians and churchmen have a responsibility towards the German people. That responsibility was entrusted to us by God, and neither you nor anyone in this world has the power to take it from us".

The immediate outcome was the bombing and ransacking of Niemöller's rectory, despite which he continued to speak and preach his convictions for several years, founding with others the Confessing Church at the Barmen Synod in May 1934, until, along with most other Confessing Church leaders, he was imprisoned in 1937. After several months in gaol he was tried and freed, but before he could go home was sent to Sachsenhausen concentration camp as Hitler's "personal prisoner". He was liberated only at the war's end, miraculously escaping the fate of Bonhoeffer whose last journey to Flossenburg he had shared.

The Stuttgart Declaration was only part of Niemöller's work for reconciliation after the war. Not without opposition from some other Church leaders, he continued this work whose scope was eventually widened when, as Head of the Foreign Affairs Department of the German Evangelical Church, he was able to act (in the words of Bishop Dibelius of Berlin) as "the Ambassador Extraordinary of the German People".

The World Council of Churches was one channel of such efforts - he was warmly welcomed at its Geneva meeting in February 1946 by clergy resisters from other countries, like Bishop Berggrav of Norway. This was one of many occasions when the WCC brought together national leaders, especially of the younger generation, breaking down the isolation of the war years, and through regular meetings and open forums clarifying the ways in which they could take part in the movement for European unity.

Another initiative which blossomed into a major work of reconciliation was the purchase by a group of Swiss in 1946 of the near-derelict Caux-Palace Hotel for refurbishing as a conference centre of Moral Re-Armament. The aim was to explore ways of changing hearts and minds for bringing solutions to national and international problems.

In its village setting in the mountains above the Lake of Geneva, the MRA centre proved a magnet for many of Europe's postwar leaders from all walks of life. For the Germans who came there the transition in the aftermath of war was dramatic. For several years they had been living among the dreary ruins of their cities, in what was left of wrecked and leaky buildings. In the British Zone especially the meagre ration standards were seldom met, and many were continually hungry - as well as cold, since fuel remained scarce. The transition to Switzerland, its cities intact, its villages neat and well-painted, above all to the warm-hearted welcome, the good food, the meetings, and the teamwork with others of various nations, all made their impact. So did the plays. One of these depicted Fredrik Ramm, the Norwegian journalist, whose change had led, before the war, to his about-turn from exacerbating the Greenland fisheries dispute between Norway and Denmark, to initiating conciliation between the two countries with a public apology on the radio for his hitherto divisive attitude - and led on to his leadership in the Resistance, imprisonment by the Gestapo, and consequent death. Seeing this play Reinhold Maier, Minister-President of Württemberg-Baden, was so overcome by shame at the thought of Germany's misdeeds, that he slunk from the hall and threw himself on his bed, completely knocked out. "It was a presentation without hatred and complaint", he wrote, "and therefore could hardly have been of more powerful effect".

Plays had a special part in these developments. Others shown in Washington and London opened the way for the Zonal authorities (except for the Russian Zone) to arrange exit permits for Germans to go to Caux. In 1946 seventeen Germans received permits, among them widows of Resistance leaders. Next year it was possible to bring in 150, and 414 in 1948. Their attendance during the following three years was over four thousand. These included most of those who rose to responsible positions in the Federal Republic during the coming years in politics and the professions, as well as leading trade unionists across the whole spectrum of right to left.

For the Germans this was a crucial moment, when the constitution of the Federal Republic was being worked out, and new political structures on a regional basis were taking shape in the Länder. The change in some of the French whom they met made a particularly powerful impression. One of these was Mme. Irène Laure, who had been a Resistance leader and Socialist M.P. for Marseilles. Disillusioned after efforts in the interwar years to build bridges between French and Germans, her hatred of the Germans became intense during the occupation. She came to Caux expecting it to be a capitalist trap - her suspicion turned to repulsion when she found there were Germans present. She was on the point of leaving when a talk with Buchman left her with the uncomfortable thought, "can you build the new Europe without the Germans?" After three days and nights of agonised ponderings, she stood up in full conference with the words: "I hated Germany so much that I would have liked to see it erased from the map of Europe. But I have seen here that my hatred is wrong. I would like to ask all the Germans present to forgive me".

The effect on the Germans was electric. One of them related that he could not sleep for several nights - his "whole past was in revolt at the courage of this woman". The full horror of the things their country had done came over them. They decided to apologise to Mme. Laure, and publicly admit their shame, while undertaking to work in the spirit which she had shown, to rebuild Europe on new foundations.

Soon after, Mme. Laure was invited to Germany, where she addressed 200 meetings in eleven weeks, making several subsequent visits, eight of them to Berlin, including the time it was blockaded by the Russians. She spoke to many thousands in the Western Zones, addressing the representatives of the Länder parliaments, and meeting the men and women who were coming forward into public life. Others from France went with her, among them two men had who lost most of their families, the one fifteen and the other twenty-two, in the gas-chambers. Such actions played their part in preparing the ground for the political decisions which made it possible for the statesmen to carry through on another level the work of reconciliation, and open a new way towards the future of Western Europe.

Adenauer and Schuman were among those who came to Caux during those years. Adenauer's visit and that of many Germans was against the background of Stalin's attempt to force the Western Allies out of Berlin by means of a blockade. Following a performance of "The Forgotten Factor" he said:

"I consider it a notable deed that in a time when evil so openly rules in the world, people have the courage to stand for good, for God, and that each one begins with himself. I believe - and it is my deepest wish, as it is of all those who have come here from Germany - that the ideas of Caux will richly bring their fruits a thousandfold. This battle is in reality a life-and-death struggle, a battle between good and evil".

Comment: Economic and social factors in creating the Community; Marshall Aid; MRA and the Norwegian resistance. (p. 298)

2. **Jean Monnet**: *new approaches to unity: idealism and economics; American aims; transcending the nation-state; the French Plan of Modernisation.*

The Schuman Plan, which launched the first European Community (of Coal and Steel), provided a new model of association for the countries of Western Europe. Its origins lie in the attempt by the USA after the war to organise Western Europe as a province in its hegemonial area, so that it should be strong enough to stand against its rival imperial power, Soviet Russia, but its genesis was due to the Christian statesmanship of its proponents.

As the Second World War ended, the task of restoring order in a chaotic world, like that which had faced Augustus two millennia before, fell upon the American Government. Roosevelt, with a vain faith in his powers of personal diplomacy, had hoped to win Stalin to acquiesce in a world order secured by "the four policemen", USA, Britain, Russia and Chiang Kai-shek's China. These would have power through the Security Council of the United Nations as the successor to the League. A liberal - more or less free-trade - system would be instituted as the economic basis, with currencies kept stable through the World Bank and International Monetary Fund, which were set up by the Bretton Woods Conference in 1944.

Roosevelt died shortly after the Yalta Conference (February 1945), disillusioned by Stalin's predatory intentions, around which a veil of decency was thrown by promises to observe democratic niceties in the settlement of Poland and the rest of Central Europe. These promises were not fulfilled, and the Soviet Empire, engulfing Poland, Hungary, Romania, Bulgaria, East Germany and the Baltic states, threatened Greece and other countries further west, besides in Asia holding on to part of Iran. Roosevelt's sucessor, Truman, attempted to stabilise the situation by his "doctrine", which pledged support to any country threatened by Soviet domination. The cold war had begun.

This meant strengthening Western Europe as a barrier to Stalin's further encroachment on the "free world". In political terms, the three zones of Western Germany occupied by USA, Britain and France, had to be unified and reconstructed as an autonomous (eventually independent) state, with their zones in Berlin preserved as an outpost within Soviet-held territory. The economic underpinning was assured by UNRRA (the United Nations Relief and Rehabilitation Agency) and by the $3,750m. line of credit to Britain, and from 1948-51 by Marshall Aid.

The aid was launched by Secretary of State George Marshall in 1947 (it took a year for it to come on stream) at the moment when the UNRRA programme was ending and the credit to Britain was running out - a moment when there was an urgent need to sustain the rehabilitation and development policies if they were not to fail through inanition. In effect this applied to Western Europe (excluding Franco's Spain) and Greece, since Moscow forbade those under its domination to participate.

Idealism played a part on both sides of the Atlantic. Rising prosperity and full employment were regarded as the just rewards for the sacrifices and sufferings of war - hence amibitious programmes of development had been taken in hand, entirely dependent on the continued bounty of the USA for the import of capital goods and food. And this was forthcoming, because the hope that swayed the policy-makers at Washington was to create a stronger, more integrated Western Europe, whether or not ultimately a federation. In this, benevolence and the need for a secure barrier against Russia coalesced. There were also calculations about trade. Like Britain in the mid-19th century, so much more powerful economically than any other country, the USA wished to demolish trade barriers and particularly Britain's system of imperial preference. One aim of the Marshall Plan was a free-trade bloc open to the trade of the USA, as a counterpart to the political organisation of its imperium.

A move in this direction was GATT, the General Agreement on Tariffs and Trade, which gradually came into force in the late 1940's. But on the political level the United States of Europe was a non-starter. The West European governments were not prepared to co-operate in a way which would lead to a federation, despite the publicity made by the European Movement with its largely federal aims. The force of nationalism was still too strong: each country was out for itself. Britain and France could sign a treaty in 1947 for security aginst a possibly resurgent Germany, but their co-operation for re-establishing their economies was minimal. When the USA urged them and the other signed-up recipients of Marshall Aid to work out a joint programme for development, all they would produce were individual shopping-lists.   Britain, with the chairmanship of the OEEC (Organisation for European Economic Co-operation - the body set up to administer the aid) showed unshakeable determination to keep it as an intergovernmental association with individual vetoes: supranationalism was regarded as a heresy.

On a basic point of policy Western Europe was in any case divided against itself. On the one hand France and Britain expected to build up their markets and resources at the expense of a Germany which was not only shattered but held down at a low level of economic activity - until 1950 they were steadily dismantling those factories which had survived the bombing. Germany pre-1939 (as also pre-1914) had been the central power-house for the European economy; though absent from her usual markets she could only partly be replaced by her competitors. The bulk of Britain's trade remained overseas, while France lacked sufficient resources and was at times hampered in her recovery by strikes and Communist-inspired unrest. Meanwhile the Benelux countries were clamouring for the restoration of Germany as their main trading partner.

The Americans had hoped to build on a partnership of France and Britain in creating a stable West European entity. When that was not forthcoming, they turned to a possible Franco-German entente. This involved a revolution in the French attitude to the defeated enemy. France's original aim had been a Germany divided up into loosely federated states; coal and coke were to be exacted as reparations from the Ruhr industrial area, whose production was to be strictly controlled, while the other main mining and industrial area in the west, the Saar, was given autonomous status and its economy integrated with France. But there were those among her leaders who realised that another approach was necessary if the post-1918 mistakes were to be avoided, when the humiliation of Versailles was compounded by the re-occupation of the Ruhr in 1923. This attempt to force payment of reparations had inevitably failed, since only an economically restored Germany with a good trade balance could undertake such payments.   Instead the Germans were further humiliated: their bitterness, aggravated by the consequent galloping inflation in which many people lost their savings and livelihood, encouraged the racist nationalism which eventually brought Hitler to power.

Even at the lowest ebb of France's fortunes after her defeat in 1940 there were some Frenchmen who realised that a restored Germany was essential for a stable Europe. A family, who were harbouring Robert Schuman when he was on the run from the Gestapo in 1942, were surprised when he held forth to them for two hours about the need after the war's ending to work for Franco-German unity as part of "building Europe, which we must all do together". There must be no annexations, he explained to another friend at this time - these would only generate further conflicts. "Solutions can only be found in the framework of a unified Europe".

Great acts of statesmanship appear in retrospect to be almost inevitable, but this view neglects the preliminaries in which the need for action is recognised though the way to achieve it remains unclear. Several initiatives preceded the creation of a new structure for Europe, the most dramatic being the proposal by Jean Monnet for a merger of France with Britain at the moment in 1940 when France was being overrun by the German army. This could not be accepted in the chaotic conditions of that time, but Monnet's later proposals led to the launching of the first Community, of Coal and Steel.

Monnet had a way of reflecting during his regular morning walks and mountain holidays, and the results of his pondering were imaginative yet practical ideas, with a fine sense of timing for carrying them into effect. These ambulatory meditations were akin to the morning watch - an essential feature in the life of dedicated Christians. Though not a churchgoer, Monnet came from a Christian home which formed his practice and principles. He could reinforce the conclusion of a memorandum for changing war-time methods of aircraft supply and production by a Biblical quotation, and in underlining the need to enshrine better methods of political co-operation in its institutions, he quotes the Christian philosopher Henri-Frédéric Amiel.

Besides his inspired hunches, Monnet's great asset was his ability to make friends and create teamwork on a basis of trust and openness. He had started life as a salesman in the family firm producing cognac, and he knew from experience that confidence was the essence of a deal. His friendliness was genuine, and thereby created networks across Europe and America composed of "small groups of influential people who controlled the levers of foreign policy, a kind of international party of politicians and civil servants." These were men of the highest calibre, capable of taking wide views and global responsibilities. He also worked on principles. "Experience had taught me that one cannot act in general terms starting from a vague concept, but that everything becomes possible as soon as one can concentrate on one precise point that leads to everything else". Having discerned the point, the next step is to bring others together for joint action.

The "precise point" may indeed be "the difficulty itself ... the very point about which disagreements have come to a head", which can then be used "as a lever to initiate a more general solution ... When you take people from different backgrounds, put them in front of the same problem, and ask them to solve it, they are no longer the same people. They are no longer there to defend their separate interests, and so they automatically take a common view." But even if a common view is not attained, the aim must be (as he said in the context of the European Community institutions) to "direct men's minds to the point where their interests converge" and so "organise the discussion and carry it far enough for everyone to understand and respect the other side's point of view, even if it be rejected at the end of the day". It is hardly possible to describe better the role of the statesman and the process of democracy at its best.

As a young man in 1914 - relegated to civilian work for health reasons - he found access to the Prime Minister, Viviani, bringing to his attention a means of economising shipping and finance for buying supplies, jointly organising their purchase, and pooling with Britain a proportion of the merchant marine of both countries. This led on to tackling, with French and British colleagues, the difficulties in breaking down age-old ideas which both governments and individuals held as to the way each country should organise its war-effort. Stimulated by crises like the devastating effects of the German sink-at-sight submarine offensive in 1917, large-scale organisations were created under Monnet's leadership, notably the Allied Maritime Transport Council.

After the war, as Deputy Secretary-General of the League of Nations, he had much to do with settling the difficult left-overs of the Peace Conference. In this work, as in all his other activities, one key to his success was his readiness to keep in the background and let others have the credit. "Men in power are short of new ideas: they lack the time and information: and they want to do good as long as they get the credit for it ... When ideas are lacking they accept yours with gratitude - provided thay can accept them as their own."

But, working for the League, he soon realised the limitations of intergovernmental co-operation, without an authority which stood above governments. The element of supranationalism had been essential in the war-time co-operation which he instigated, and such success as the League had was largely due to its supranational Secretariat and the acceptance, in certain situations, of the League's role as an arbiter.

He had further experience of intergovernmental work, helping to reorganise the Chinese railways and restore stable currency in Poland and Romania, until with the start of the second World War he resumed his role as co-ordinator on the supply side for France and Britain. This involved continuing contact with the American Government which became even closer after the fall of France, and led on to Lend-Lease and the Victory Program.

His proposal, when France was falling, of joint citizenship and the merging of all possible institutions and facilities, had been considered by Churchill and the Cabinet, and went direct to the French Government in refuge at Bordeaux. The bold concept of pooling sovereignty failed at the time, but Monnet realised that in the post-war period the future of Europe could only be assured by transcending the narrow confines of the nation-state. A measure of supranationalism would be needed in trade and industry for a start. In a memorandum to the Free French Government in Algeria in 1943, he wrote:

"There will be no peace in Europe if States re-establish themselves on the basis of national sovereignty, with all that this implies by way of prestige policies and economic protectionism. If the countries of Europe once more protect themselves against each other, it will once more be necessary to build up vast armies ... Social reforms will be prevented or delayed by the pressure of military expenditure ... The countries of Europe are too small to give their peoples the prosperity that is now attainable and therefore necessary. They need wider markets ... To enjoy the prosperity and social progress that are essential, the states of Europe must form a federation or a 'European entity' which will make them a single economic unit".

This initiative seemed premature when at the war's end the old arrangements of frontiers, customs-barriers and national policies for recovery and development were restored. Monnet accepted that this had to be the starting point for France, and proposed a programme of modernising and re-equipping the country to which de Gaulle agreed. Its success over the following years was due to Monnet's applying the principles of tackling first the difficult problems whose solution would "lead on to everything else", thus arranging an order of priorities whereby sectors such as energy and steel, as they were re-equipped, would enable the same process to be applied to others. By restricting his staff to a small number and a meagre budget, dependent directly on the Prime Minister's office without offering a threat to the power of any minister, his organism continued to perform year after year despite all the changes of governments and ministers - yet exerting a certain authority in directing the whole of France's post-war development. And this was done not by Monnet posing as an expert, which he never claimed to be, but by surrounding himself with a small group of advisers and co-workers: a dynamic "live cell" sharing a common life in a somewhat cramped and old fashioned building but which had - and Monnet regarded it as an absolute essential - a small dining-room so that meals could be had together. He never under-estimated such basic means of establishing the friendliness and trust which alone could make any worthwhile enterprise succeed, and for which no amount of care over details was too much.

In the consultations people from all walks of life were drawn in - employers and trade unionists, officials and academics, those "who were most enterprising and influential in their various fields - they became one huge team."

Monnet's Plan of modernisation was kept going by American aid both before and during Marshall's European Recovery Program, but by 1949 was in danger of arrest due to overproduction in some sectors, notably steel, and questions of marketing and research which could not be dealt with adequately on a purely national level. Several other national economies were reaching a similar point. Only joint planning for key commodities on a supranational basis could maintain the tempo of development.

It was at this point that the parallel crisis came on over the American intention of rearming a resurgent West Germany as a bulwark against the Stalinist East. How, from the French point of view, could the threat of economic domination and renewed aggression by their powerful neighbour be allayed?

3. **Robert Schuman**: *restructuring Western Europe: "apostolate" and the Nazi occupation; imprisonment and escape; character and convictions; the problem of Germany; Monnet's proposals: the Schuman Plan; launching the European Community.*

The Schuman Plan, which resolved both the German and economic problems at the same time, was the brain-child of Monnet and his team. It might have been called the Monnet Plan no. 2, except that Schuman was the one man in the situation with the power to put it into effect, and with the character to carry it through.

Schuman's character had been shaped by the faith he had accepted as a child from his mother (his father had died when he was quite young). His school years were passed at Luxembourg whither his parents had retreated after their Lorraine homeland was annexed by Germany in 1871. Besides the Luxembourg patois he was equally at home in French and German, qualifying in Law after university years in Germany. His mother's death in a carriage accident was a severe shock: at that point he thought of becoming ordained, but a friend persuaded him that "the *lay* apostolate is an urgent necessity ...

the saints of the future will be saints in jackets."

His life was indeed an apostolate, in the sense of service to his fellow-men, though he never thought of himself as a saint, only as "a very imperfect instrument of a Providence which makes use of us in accomplishing great designs which go far beyond ourselves.". It was no ambition which pushed him on to the highest offices. As a lawyer in Metz his integrity and loyalty, together with much shrewdness and power of exposition, won him a reputation as a man eminently qualified to defend not merely the personal interests of clients but the wider interests of the city and eventually of Lorraine itself. For this reason, still in Metz after it had again become French in 1918, he was asked to stand as Deputy in the National Assembly, and he continued to represent Metz or Thionville - a working-class stronghold - with increasing majorities until shortly before his death.

His first call to office came as Under-Secretary of State for Refugees in March 1940, shortly before the fall of France. With the break-through of the German army in May the flood of refugees became uncontrollable by himself or any man. Shortly after the armistice he went to Metz to destroy correspondence which might incriminate people if it fell into the hands of the Gestapo, and also to look after the interests of his fellow-citizens at that most critical time. This courageous step led to seven months in solitary confinement while the local Gauleiter put pressure on him to become a collaborationist. He failed, and moved Schuman to a Black Forest hotel under surveillance, still hoping apparently to win him round by the change of treatment. But the tactic was no more successful, and after some time Schuman escaped to unoccupied France, where - though pursued by the Gestapo and taking refuge in monasteries and friendly homes - he continued his work of looking after refugees. With the liberation of France he returned to Metz where he was re-elected to Parliament, becoming Minister of Finance in 1946.

Stories are many of Schuman's humility, his scrupulous economy and his refusal to trench on the time and goodwill of others for his mere personal convenience. As Minister of Finance he would go around turning out unnecessary lights in the building. He preferred to untie parcels himself, so that the string should not be cut, but kept ready for re-use in a drawer reserved for the purpose. He would not accept the style of living of one of the great ones of the world, and - for the sake of economy as well as simplicity - refused special trains and the company on journeys of all but the most essential retinue. Even as Prime Minister he would travel "in an overfull compartment, where squeezed in a corner he worked all the way to Paris without raising his head". He did not wish to separate himself from the lot of the common man. For ordinary formalities he would join the queue in the Prefecture at Metz, and would go around the town on foot or by bus.

His convictions gave depth to the Christian values of the parties he joined, the PDP and MRP. His ultimate concern was with building Christian civilisation.

"Christ's kingdom was not of this world. That means also that Christian civilisation should not be the product of a violent and sudden revolution, but of a progressive transformation, of a patient education, under the action of the great principles of caring, of sacrifice and of humility, which are the foundations of the new society".

This "patient education" concerned Schuman as much as his parliamentary work. He saw it as part of a "vast programme of expanding democracy ... which finds its flowering in the making of Europe". His vision had much in common with Frank Buchman's and this led to his association with Moral Re-Armament.

Called to the premiership in November 1947, he was the nearest to a saint to occupy the highest position in a great country since the Middle Ages - and the more surprising perhaps that this country was France with its tradition of militant anti-Christian rationalism which had split Church from State, de-Christianised education, and driven out the Jesuits and monks. But this underlines the paradox of the age, during which France had led the Roman Catholic world in fostering missions abroad and producing saints. At this testing moment, with rationing, restricted housing and other post-war difficulties, the Communists were making a dead-set at gaining power in several countries of Western Europe, with France in an exposed position. It needed a man, not only of character and tenacity, but of confident reliance on spiritual power beyond himself, to guide the country through the first terrible weeks of his premiership during November and December 1947.

Later, as Foreign Minister, he was at once confronted with the task of reconstructing Western Europe to include a resurgent Germany. Marshall Aid was already on stream: West Germany was also to benefit from it. Schuman agreed with this policy - but how to rehabilitate Germany so that she could make her contribution to the general recovery, and yet prevent her from regaining strength to the extent that she could once again be capable of threatening her neighbours? The need to solve this problem was made urgent by the even greater threat which seemed to be arising from Russia's expansion into Central Europe - 1948 besides being the year of the Berlin blockade saw the rape of Czechoslavakia. The one hope - and the idea was gaining ground in France - was that if the existing controls over Germany had to be abandoned, an alternative method of preventing her becoming once again a threat to peace might be found along the lines of including her in a federal system for Europe.

Even so the means of doing this were elusive, when the way forward was indicated by the threatening crisis of over-production of steel in Western Europe. Those concerned with this aspect of affairs began to push for a new system whereby the steel industry could be controlled by an international authority for determining production levels and organising a common market. A way of resolving at the same time both the steel crisis and the German question was the brain-child of Jean Monnet - by launching an organisation on a "European" basis (in the event France, Germany, Italy and Benelux), with a supranational authority to integrate and administer the coal and steel industries of the countries concerned. The matter was the more urgent in that Britain and America had called a conference at London for 10 May 1950 to decide how to bring the newly created Federal Republic of West Germany into the Atlantic Pact, which meant that its rearmament was also looming. Monnet's proposal, worked out with his brains-trust, came in the nick of time for Schuman to study it and make his decision during the previous week-end, and then to present it to the Cabinet only the day before the London conference.

What lay behind that moment of decision and its implementation, is hinted at in the description by André Philip, one of Schuman's former Cabinet colleagues and close collaborator: "Often he has tacked about, delayed the decision, tried to dodge the call which was making itself heard in the depths of his conscience; then, when there was nothing more to do, when he was sure of what the inner voice was demanding, he took the boldest initiative and pushed it to its conclusion, equally heedless of attacks as of threats".

Though Schuman was responsible for launching the plan and ensuring its approval by the Cabinet and Parliament as well as by the steel-masters, the Community of Coal and Steel could never have been created without the co-operation of other statesmen who were formed in the Christian tradition: Adenauer and De Gasperi, Jean Monnet, and the Belgian leader Paul-Henri Spaak - men who were capable together of seizing the moment which could change the course of history. Nor could it have proved acceptable to Parliament and the other interests concerned in France - perhaps not in Germany either - without a revolution in public opinion in both countries which prepared the way for replacing inherited hatreds with partnership. Here again the spiritual factor played a part, through the humility, vision and tireless self-giving of a few dedicated fellow-citizens. It was a convergence of spiritual currents: the Christian-based humanism and pragmatism of the Zonal officials and Jean Monnet; the Lutheran-Pietist tradition of Bonhoeffer and Niemöller; the Roman Catholic inheritance of Adenauer and De Gasperi, and its radical tradition coming down to Schuman from Lamennais, Gratry and Sangnier, combining with the Anglo-American stream descending through Moody, Drummond, Mott and Buchman.

These were the creative springs of the greatest act of statesmanship in 20th century Europe. Stalin's rapacity, the Communist menace and American pressure - all played their part in bringing the politicians to their decisions and the public to their support, but without the spiritual factor operating through men and women of character and commitment, their work could hardly have been well-based, with the organism that was its outcome so well adapted for further evolution. The novel economic and political structure which the statesmen initiated, to become eventually the European Community, and within which the age-old enmity of France and Germany was replaced by reconciliation and friendship, may mark the beginning of a new order rather than merely revitalising the old.

Comment: Robert Schuman's concern from early years for the "patient education" of the public. (p. 299)

CHAPTER FOURTEEN

PROSPECTS FOR THE RENEWAL OF CIVILISATION

1. Morals and marriage: *education and intimacy; Martin and Katherine Luther: care for children, and the nuclear family in France and England; debauching manners and morals in ancient and modern times; the response: united families and stable children.*

In the West respectability in marriage has ceased to weigh much with people. But while on the one hand old-time rectitude has given way to looser living, on the other relationships in a wide range of families are shaped by the highest standards of integrity. The paradox is of extra-marital relationships being regarded as normal in many circles, with a high general level of illegitimate births and prenuptial pregnancies, while among other couples deeply affectionate partnerships are evident, with a growing interest in and understanding of the needs of the children.

The situation parallels that in Ancient Rome, when easy divorce and unconventional pairing made the old ceremonies of marriage less important. Today amidst the moral anarchy arising from the rejection of older norms, including marriage itself as a formal and legal estate, it seems that (according to a survey) those couples who marry and stay married "enjoy a more tightly-knit - and in many cases happier - relationship than they used to" - and this may be said even of unmarried couples who stay together. Such partnerships, and the deeper intimacy between couples, may - if they become more common - promise stability and creativeness in the civilisation of the future.

As in the ancient past, deeper marriage relationships came on when girls as well as boys began to be educated. For the upper classes this took place during the period of the Renaissance and Reformation. Between the collapse of the Western Roman Empire and the Renaissance there had been little chance of education for girls, and not much opportunity for boys either. Even if there had been, the type of marriage which probably prevailed over wide areas of Europe did not encourage intimacy. The medieval village of Montaillou in the Northern Pyrenees may not have been typical, but, to the extent that it was, the kind of marriage that prevailed is reminiscent of that in early Greece or Rome: the marriage of young teenage girls, arranged by parents of one "domus" with those of another, with a view to the mutual advantage of their families; boys marrying later, but without denying themselves liaisons which might produce children, who would become servants or day-labourers at the bottom of the social scale. Monogamy was the rule: when a man married he could have only one official wife, though he might - and often did - have mistresses. The priest was supposed to be celibate, but had his concubines, a convenient arrangement since no bride-price had to be paid.

Among the upper classes too, since marriages were arranged, and men anyway married later than girls, there was little chance of close companionship between experienced men in their mid-twenties or more and girls around 13. Changes began with the troubadours who made an ideal of extra-marital love fashionable: the devotion of a man to his lady-love, who was already someone else's wife. The tender sentiments in the songs of the troubadours and the literature which grew up around them began to be transferred to married relationships as well. What started as "an idealisation of adultery" led on to the ideal of romantic love and intimacy in marriage, a process not unlike that in Greece, where the new ideal had been set by the loving relationship between a man and his hetaira.

The beginning of literacy for laymen was also destined to deepen the married relationship, though it was only in a few royal courts and some convents that girls might learn their letters. For boys too, outside courtly circles, education was long the monopoly of the Church, with most students in minor orders and hence (officially at least) celibate. When schools became more common, in the towns, the effect for a time was to increase the gap which tended to exist between husbands and wives, since literacy placed the man on a cultural level from which his unlettered wife was excluded. As in schools, so in colleges and universities, though laymen could be admitted to these normally Church-ruled and celibate institutions, there was no question of women being allowed to matriculate. Abelard giving tutorials to Héloise, niece of the Canon in charge of the school (in effect college) of Notre Dame at Paris, was an unusual situation, and when they fell in love and secretly married, the outcome was a tragedy.

As early as 1400, girls' as well as boys' schools for the laity existed in the prospering towns of the Rhineland, France and elsewhere. By this time it was becoming common for boys to have a Latin-based education at the hands of private tutors or at grammar schools (as they were called in England) without being committed to a "religious", hence celibate life. But there might not be many literate wives. In the 15th century Paston family in England, wives had to get men to write letters for them to their husbands.

Intimacy in the home deepened as education improved. The conjugal family became normal in middle class life, replacing the extended family. Feelings of intimacy and togetherness in the home - a sense of family life - began to develop. In Books of Hours husbands and wives appear working together, and the whole family is portrayed on altar-pieces and funerary monuments. In the home intimacy was strengthened by relegating servants to separate rooms.

Literate wives became capable not only of keeping the family accounts, but of helping their husbands in business. Partnership of this kind reinforced a growing consciousness of the equality of men and women. When love-matches increasingly replaced the traditional arranged marriages, there are signs of more respect and caring on the part of the spouses for each other.

Martin Luther and Katherine von Bora were among the pioneers. She was a lady of noble family, one of a group of nuns whom he had helped to escape from their convent. Katherine not only brought up the children and ran the home, including an aunt, three nieces and students who boarded with them (Martin was a professor at the university) - she also looked after the printing of his sermons and pamphlets, produced vegetables, fruit, pigs and poultry in their garden and later on their smallholding at Zulsdorf (where cows were included), helped her husband in his theological work and restored peace with people whom his roughness had offended. "Between husband and wife", he said, "there should be no question of *meum* and *tuum*. All things should be in common between them, without any distinction or means of distinguishing." When away he addressed letters with designations like "To my gracious girl, Katherine Luther v. Bora and Zulsdorf, at Wittenberg, my darling." He bequeathed her everything, not only because she had been to him "a pious, faithful and dutiful wife, always loving, devoted and beautiful", but also because she kept the accounts and did the budgeting, and would have to pay his debts.

Luther was revolutionary in abandoning his celibate life as a monk and embarking on matrimony in this dramatic way. Though chastity (celibacy) was still maintained for monastic orders and clergy in the Roman Catholic Church, a much more positive view of marriage for lay-people than was current at the time of St. Augustine had been expressed by St. Thomas Aquinas in the thirteenth century. This move away from a negative attitude to "the flesh", with accompanying rigorous asceticism, towards a mode of spirituality which gave the body its due place, notably in marriage, was developed in Roman Catholic circles by such as St. Francis de Sales.

"Love wedded to fidelity gives birth to a confident intimacy", he wrote in the section on "Advice to those who are married" in his *Introduction to the Devout Life*. "The union of husband and wife through devotion is the closest union of all and the most fruitful, and one to be mutually encouraged." He compares the pleasures of marriage to those of eating - both pleasures are justifiable, not necessarily or merely in terms of their primary objects (in eating "to preserve and nourish life", and in marriage "for the procreation of children"), but also when they serve "to promote that mutual friendship and concord we owe one another". At the same time he warns against the dangers of "excess, or perversion of the primary end."

The views of St. Francis are particularly noteworthy, in that he was a man who loved deeply, though he never married and kept strictly to his vow of chastity. He was not afraid of loving - in contrast with the desert-dwelling renunciants of ancient times; his answer to loving, or indeed being in love, was more love. His deepest relationship was with the Baroness de Chantal, sister of the Archbishop of Bourges, at whose house they first met. Jeanne de Chantal, charming, witty, and "a shrewd judge of character", was widowed at 28 with several small children. To Francis she became his "so very dear daughter". Many of his letters to her (as to others of his "spiritual daughters") have survived in his beautiful italic hand, firm to the day he died. One of the earliest (14/10/1604) is a declaration of his particular kind of love:

"From the beginning of your consulting with me on your interior life God gave me great love for your soul. When you spoke to me more openly I felt my love for your soul grow in a wonderful way and this made me write that God had given me to you. I could not, I think, have added to my affection for you in any way, especially when I was praying for you. But now, my dear daughter, a new quality has been added, to which I do not seem able to give a name; I can only describe it by its effect which is a great interior sweetness that I feel in wishing you perfect love of God and all other spiritual blessings ... My affection for you has a special quality which consoles me infinitely, and if all were said, is of great profit to me."

His love naturally extended to the whole family: "I am praying much for our Celse-Bénigne and the little company of girls, and I ask them to pray for me" (some years later the eldest girl married Bernard, the saint's younger brother). Later he writes (1/8/1606):

"I will not try to say how full my heart is for you, but I will say that it is full beyond compare; and this affection is whiter than snow, purer than the sun: that is why I have given it free rein since you left me, letting it have its way."

He exhorts her "to speak frankly ... that is to say as to a soul which God by his sovereign authority has made all yours ...   You would not believe how happy I was to have news of you." Chantal survived him for 19 years. She rests beside him in the chapel at Annecy.

Few deductions can be made from statistics of illegitimate births in relation to the development of "Affective Individualism" and the deepening of marriage intimacy. The 18th century experienced "staggering rates of illegitimacy". The Industrial Revolution, especially in Britain, where people were crowding into squalid housing around factories, may have contributed to this along with French and other upheavals in the latter part of the century. Illegitimacy rates were also remarkably high in Central Europe in the mid-19th century. There industrialisation can scarcely have been a factor, except perhaps in Vienna where more than half the babies were born out of wedlock.

In England, where the illegitimacy rate dropped in the later 19th century, couples usually stayed together. A frugal life on a ten-shilling wage, with a kitchen-garden and a pig for fattening, could be the background of caring and friendly relations among family and neighbours in a farming community such as that described by Flora Thompson. It was not unusual for educated couples to write to each other daily during courtship or absences. Figures who towered over the political scene, like Gladstone and Lord Salisbury, drew strength from the unclouded partnership with their wives and the affection of their children. When such relationships could be taken for granted, confidence was reinforced that the essentials of civilisation were in place.

As the century ended the decline that was setting in was, in Nordau's diagnosis, most evident in the trend towards permissiveness in morals. The failure to maintain standards against perversion and lasciviousness was a canker which could destroy the bloom. As William Blake had written a century before:

"O rose, thou art sick!
The invisible worm
That flies in the night,
In the howling storm
Has found out thy bed
Of crimson joy,
And his dark secret love
Does thy life destroy."

The difference between the ancient and modern situations is a difference of scale, in today's deliberate debauching of manners and morals, not just by those individuals who always appear at an advanced stage of civilisation, to take a rationalist line in criticising and overthrowing the older norms or guide-lines - aided by those who are out to make money by exploiting the seamy side of sex - but also by dedicated devotees of evil. The trivialising of sex in literature and the media, making fornication, adultery and perversion seem part of normal living, marks the nadir of decadence in our culture.

As in the ancient world, what is insidious for shattering the foundations of society is the combination of sexual licence with the cult of cruelty. Pornography, so readily available today, in books, magazines, television and videos, has taken the place of the antique mass-voyeurism of the arena. For the feature of hard porn which stands out is not merely the dehumanising of women, but their exhibition as objects of cruel and sadistic practices. These practices could become compulsive viewing by video on the kind of scale which, with the "games", debauched the populace of Rome. The consequence can be copying, in sadism, rapes and other forms of sexual abuse.

The power of sheer unadulterated evil can never be shrugged off. Video nasties, paedophilia, narcotics - even children's horror-comics, suggestive toys and supposedly harmless games with tarot tables can lead on to occultism and hideous obscenity such as surfaced in inter-war Germany, when Satanism entered politics with Nazism. At that point black magic linked with antisemitism made the Holocaust possible. Wewelsburg Castle, rebuilt by Himmler for initiating the SS into his parodies of the Mass, remains a pilgrimage centre for Satanism. In Britain Satanic rites involving drugs, animal sacrifices and the drinking of urine and blood have been causing "great anxiety" to the National Society for the Prevention of Cruelty to Children: seven of their teams have evidence of children being abused in such rituals.

Happy and united families certainly still exist in Europe and the West. The question is whether there are enough to produce a generation of stable, outgoing and responsible people, able to look after and help those who - through deficiencies in their upbringing - are rootless, disturbed, perverted and self-centred. Are there enough sound homes to produce the leaders capable of saving Europe from disaster by setting a course towards a higher culture, a better civilisation?

The answer is certainly in the affirmative. The facts of decadence may be alarming, but it is the figures of what is going wrong that get into the statistics, not what is going right in the multitude of homes which, because they are going on well, are taken for granted.

In the various surveys of sexual mores which have appeared, one point is absolutely clear - teenagers and young adults who refrain from sexual activity before marriage are in the vast majority of cases from homes where religion is taken seriously - and when they marry, these are the couples whose marriages are likely to last. Often there is a strong spiritual basis for such homes, founded on a common faith and commitment, which - in the multi-cultural cities of today - may be Jewish, Hindu or Muslim, as well as Christian. These homes stand out against a background of disintegration much as Christian and Jewish homes stood out in the decline of the Roman Empire, and can be the growing points of the civilisation and culture of the future.

In a book written for teenagers, and partly by them (published at the height of the "permissive" trend), the two sentences which caught the attention of reviewers were: "The best contraceptive is the word 'No'. It is absolutely safe and has no side-effects - except to make it easier to say 'No' next time." These sentences were singled out as if they were remarkable, yet clearly it is such common-sense that it should hardly be necessary to express it.

Less attention was paid to the context of this statement, which was preceded by a Swedish girl's account of her experience.

"Purity gives you a sparkle and a gaiety that do not have to be put on. It satisfies you deep down and I believe it is the normal way to live. Permissiveness, instead of satisfying, just makes you grab for more and more.

"What do you do when temptation comes? I find I can do one of three things. I can give up and fall. I can try to fight it in my own strength. Or I can turn to God and win the struggle. When I do that, he always tells me to open my heart wider and to think for more and more people. Purity and care for others go together in my life and that is why I think it is progressive. It will answer the decadence in my own country and give us the passion to end starvation in developing countries."

Without this opening of the heart to others the pressures of one's nature may be irresistible, and this applies to any form of sexual temptation. It is a modern version of Augustine's admonition: "We have therefore to guard the sincerity of love towards God and our neighbour; for in this is chastity of mind sanctified."

Comment: girls' education during the Renaissance and later; "the decisive shift" from the "Open Lineage Family" to the "Closed Domesticated Nuclear Family" (Lawrence Stone); Montaillou; the Burgundian law of King Gondebaud about the marriage relationship;

query about the extended family; Martin and Katharine Luther and Katherine's convent-breakout; Luther's views on women's place; romantic love and "Affective Individualism" 1600-1800; "illegitimacy explosion". (p. 300)

2. **Modern decadence**: *cultural comparisons: speed of progress; technology; sterility in architecture; from Classicism to Impressionism; anguish, war horrors, disintegration of personality.   Women and culture; query on "progress"; Albert Schweitzer*: The Decay and Restoration of Civilisation.

An obvious difference between the ancient world and today is the speed of our scientific progress and the immediate application of the findings of research in ever more sophisticated technology. Whereas the steam-engine invented by Hiero of Alexandria remained a toy, the discoveries of modern scientists and inventors have been swiftly used for practical ends. In this respect the 19th and 20th centuries have differed from all that have preceded them in "the cumulative products of scientific research and its utilitarian application, which in its degree is altogether unexampled in the history of mankind".

The fact that progress of a certain kind continues and accelerates can obscure the features of our own decline, since this decline has by no means reached the depths of sterility shown by Rome in the 3rd and 4th centuries AD. Our situation is more like that of the Greeks, whose faith in progress, particularly in technology and medicine, continued from the great age of the 5th century into the 4th BC, in the same way that similar expectations in these spheres have continued from the 19th century into the present. There was however "no falling off in creative energy": it was the age of the greatest orators and philosophers, when new forms of art and literature appeared, with remarkable advances in mathematics and astronomy. But, as in our case, "something at least of the old confidence had been lost".

With us scientific and technological advance continues apace, and the exploration of space leads to amazing astronomical discoveries. Inventiveness in new forms of culture continues - science fiction, impressionism in art and literature, the achievements in film, radio and television - we are far from the cultural barrenness which overcame Rome in the 4th century AD. Where this threatens, and most obviously resembles that of Rome, is in our architecture. In the 3rd century the Classical orders dissolved into plain walls and bare facades, in the same way as our glass and concrete boxes have succeeded the buildings of the 19th and earlier 20th centuries, so varied in design and ornament.

In sculpture Thorwaldsen, Gibson and Bates, with the light-hearted charm of Carpeaux, mark the sunset of a long tradition, though elements of it linger in the ponderous forms of Maillol and Henry Moore. With Rodin something new appears, his "Balzac" reflecting the spirit and personality of the subject by effects of light and shade, optical illusions in the place of clear-cut form; or in the clay-modelled construction of his human figures with a plasticity maintained in the bronze casting and even when copied in marble. This style recalls third century impressionist sculpture, and goes along with the many modern experiments of more or less abstract kind. In this respect too the part played by abstract designs parallels the variety of non-figural motifs in the post-Classical and Byzantine periods, later intensified by iconoclasm and the influence of Islam. The disparate and anarchic trends in today's art are expressive of our own Age of Anxiety - most obviously in the movement of painting as it ruptured the Classical mould, to the further movement represented by Picasso, from naturalism to abstraction and symbolism.

In the nineties Bosanquet had noted how Impressionism typified one aspect of decadence, the concentration on a particular element derived from an old tradition, but so altered and developed as to originate a distinctive trend - a process of change in language as in art. "In decadence words and ideas and forms of art are all dragged off by different minds according to their needs and fancies, the unity of thought and feeling having broken up." But then they are sometimes worked out "with a certain many-coloured novelty and audacity ... the old beauty echoing on and on, but acquiring a new and original note in their very echoes ... as for example when the Greek beauty was touched with Asiatic richness."   The study of light had been a preoccupation of artists like Caravaggio and Rembrandt, but this was taken up - "a fragment of tradition" - and developed to the utmost degree, almost without relation to the forms which the light illumines: Turner's seascapes and sunsets, even something so mechanical as a train crossing a bridge, express light almost in essence, predating Monet's Thames at London or his garden at Argenteuil. In this "pure study of light" Impressionism shows "no narrowing of the imagination", but "places a fresh instrument in its hands and opens to it new worlds to conquer." This concentration on light and colour is reminiscent of those Late Roman mosaics, whose elevation from floor to walls and ceiling made possible an incandescent richness of light and colour by the use of gold and many-hued tesserae.

The oncoming anguish of the age is expresssed by nineteenth century artists like Van Gogh in his self-portraits and his writhing, agonised landscapes, and in Munch's "Scream" of 1893. Almost a century earlier Goya had painted his "3rd May 1808". In his "Disasters of war" and the "dark paintings" of his final phase he presents war and all sorts of nastiness in a totally different manner to academic Classicism.   Another century had to elapse before the cruel wastage and mutilation of young lives came to public consciousness in the terrible years which followed the glamorous expectations of August 1914, but already Goya was portraying war's effects in negating humanity among the stinking corpses, raped women and their wailing children.   The bloodthirsty, sadistic evil is expressed in the "Disparates" (or "Absurdities") - no laughing matter these - and in the leering faces and monstrous satanism of witches' sabbaths and other depictions of the dark side of human existence.   Fuseli too hints at occult forces taking power, but the full dimension of this menace as the nineteenth century opens is left to Goya: the sinister onset of a phase of history, which with its torture, holocausts and military massacres, its terrorism and inhumanity, begins to rival, in the lives and deaths of millions, the miseries of the last century BC.

After Munch's "Scream" there are only a few years to go until Picasso's "Demoiselles d'Avignon" - how far removed from Botticelli's damsels! - and the portrayal of what is within Western man and woman rather than merely what the eye beholds.   In a portrait like "Vollard" of 1909 the cubistic treatment suggests disintegration of personality.   And what has happened to the joyousness of youth in the fractured planes and rectangles of Braque's "Young girl with a guitar"? Freud had already published papers on psychoanalysis (he invented the word) and *The Interpretation of Dreams* by the end of the century, but he was still unknown to the wider public when painters of the Surrealist movement drew their subject matter from dreams and the subconscious - another way of expressing the interior life rather than visible "reality".

The camera has made possible art-forms which Antiquity never knew, not least the cinema and more recently television, in which literature and drama share in novel types of presentation. Photography has enormously extended the range of the visual arts, but in portraiture it necessarily expresses appearance rather than inwardness.   Karsh's "Churchill", like a Roman bust of Caesar or Augustus presents a leader confident in his resolve to fight until victory for his country and empire.   Ten years later Graham Sutherland's portrait, destroyed as unworthy by the sitter's widow, was of a tired Titan whose world, which he had done so much to save, is threatening to crumble about his ears.   The icons of Byzantium may not have depicted men and women in all their "reality", but as in the paintings of many moderns, the inner spirit is what pervades.   In those days it was holiness; today it is more likely bewilderment.

Women have played a greater part in these advances than in any previous civilisation. The principle of equality of man and woman, proceeding from Stoicism and Christ's teaching, had already begun to be expressed during the ancient "decadence" in intimate partnerships between husband and wife, and has been handed on as one of the most important legacies to our own civilisation. In all spheres of cultural and political activity women have had increasing opportunity as they gained greater freedom than their forebears from the near monopolising of their time and energy by long periods of child-rearing and household chores. Not since Sappho have women won such acclaim in the field of literature; in England they did as much as men, if not more, to develop the novel from its epistolary beginnings. In the Western world as a whole, in sport, science, politics, and the professions from journalism to the ministry of the Churches, they have been vying with men. It has yet to be seen whether the changing roles and relationships of men and women, and the new position in the social order in which women are finding themselves, are likely to have a determining effect in improving the prospects for the future of civilisation.

In his inaugural lecture as Professor of History at Cambridge in 1895, Lord Acton could claim that "the wisdom of divine rule appears not in the perfection but in the improvement of the world; and that achieved liberty is the one ethical result that rests on the converging and combined conditions of advancing civilisation." The growing hunger for freedom on a democratic basis throughout the world gives substance to this prophetic utterance. But since Acton electrified Cambridge with these words, faith in progress, whether held by Christians or non-Christians, is no longer an effective ideology.

The Greeks had doubts that scientific and technical progress assisted moral advance. Some thought that the effects would be adverse. This tension between "the belief in technological progress and the belief in moral regress" continued during the Roman period. Such progress, it was recognised, creates new needs, encouraging materialism and corruption, while covetousness stimulates the larger-scale and more destructive wars which advancing technology also makes possible. Our two "world wars" have had an effect in raising queries about progress similar to the doubts about the future provoked by the civil wars and corruption which destroyed the Roman Republic. In Britain, the former workshop of the world, tendencies are evident in the economic system which, as in the case of post-Republican Rome, were symptoms of decadence. Rome, like London, had also been "the banking-house of the world ... speculation was the life-blood of an economic system where production was losing every day and mercantilism was invading everything. Work might still ensure a modest living, but no longer yielded such fortunes as the chance of imperial favour or a speculative gamble might bestow."

The pessimists have a strong case. Burckhardt's prediction that neither Christianity nor anything else was likely to stave off the descent, by way of ever more terrible wars and the accompanying dehumanising industrialism, to the cultural deadness of a Roman-type imperium, seemed on the way to realisation after 1945. Kierkegaard had used the parable of the liner, with the single passenger trying, but failing, to draw the high-living captain's attention to the danger indicated by the white speck ahead ("it will be a dreadful night"). In the post-*Titanic* years B.H. Streeter made another use of the same analogy. "Our world is like an Atlantic liner deprived of rudder, compass, sextant, charts, and wireless tackle, yet compelled to go full steam ahead. There is magnificence, comfort, pulsating power; but whither are we going?"

Streeter, as the head of an Oxford College, was challenging the younger generation in the same way that T.H. Green had roused his students two generations earlier. To Oxford came also, as World War II was threatening, Albert Schweitzer, emerging like some Old Testament prophet from his hospital in the rain-forests of West Africa. His theme, which could have been the title of this book (and was actually that of the book in which he published his lectures) was "the decay and restoration of civilisation". "If the ethical foundation is lacking, then civilisation collapses", was his message. He spoke of "the collapse of philosophy" and the consequent lack of "any real theory of the universe" which was generally accepted. "Ethical progress", he maintained, "is that which is truly of the essence of civilisation ... material progress is much less essential", and may have a good or bad effect on it.

3. **The Gorbachev Revolution**: *Andropov and Gorbachev recognise need for moral revolution; stagnant economy, corruption - comparisons with time of Alexander II; social and political problems; religious and class motivations; falling standards;* glasnost *and proliferation of ideas and discussion groups; prospects for constitutional change; need for economic breakthrough, but difficulties in changing the system; need for change in mental climate and end of one-party state; agriculture; unrest of nationalities and ethnic minorities; Gorbachev's vision of world change; his call for truth, but difficult to accept truth in Soviet history; a precondition for* perestroika.

In the present situation, if Russia resembles Rome, it has followed the ancient exemplar by failing to conquer the rest of Europe. Our civilisation may continue doing what Greece did to Rome: overlay its culture with ours, and penetrate it on every level.

Empires disintegrate as loss of nerve and failure of will set in and increasingly strong challenges arise - the process we have seen most clearly in India during the decades before independence. The Russians have suffered from the same "illusion of permanence" which made the British, like the Romans, think that their empire would go on for ever. With their time-lag compared with the West, the Russians have only just emerged from their "Victorian" era, with Afghanistan as the last example of attempted empire-building. Now the empire itself is dissolving. The only question is how far the process will go. De-colonisation, perhaps disintegration - or the transition to a new type of organisation: these are the options confronting the Soviet Union. The new system could be a "club" like the Commonwealth, or some kind of federation. If it were patterned on the European Community, close association of the two Communities, East and West, in what Gorbachev calls "the common European house (or home)" could become possible.

Today Russia shares most of the social ills of the West: alcoholism and drugs; marriages of which two out of five fail within three years; a high abortion rate; corruption in public and private life, aggravated - in the case of the Soviet Union - by a flourishing black market. But are these symptoms of decadence, or are they characteristics of a developing society which has been dislocated by terrible wars, violent attempts at modernisation and industrialisation, and is now suffering from the technological/consumer syndrome?

The need for change is pressing. After many years of improvement, standards of health are declining as measured by life-expectancy. The population of Russia proper is barely replacing itself (one abortion for every child born). The quality of life remains low, with poor housing, long queues for shoppers and the necessity to pay extra in bribes or tips for so many goods and services. Falling productivity in industry and on state farms necessitates the revolution in attitudes and motivation for which Gorbachev is calling.

For all the costly efforts of Stalin and his successors to industrialise the Soviet Union it has been unable to catch up with the West and Japan. Khrushchev's boast that Russian industry would soon outdo that of the West was backed by attempts (with almost total unconcern for adverse effects on health and the environment) to bring the USSR into the lead in those sectors which loomed largest in his day - coal, steel and heavy industry generally - but are now secondary compared with the high-technology industries of the advanced countries.

The situation resembles in many ways that which Alexander II faced on his accession - a lost war, a stagnant economy, widespread corruption, and a bureaucratic system which stifled initiative and responsible citizenship. "Since Peter the Great", wrote Anatole Leroy-Beaulieu in the 1880's, "power has been systematically applied to suppress every spontaneous movement in the country in order to reduce it to the condition of a robot, an obedient mechanism [like a watch] having no other motor than the governmental spring. The whole administration has been copied from military organisation ... extended to all the details and minutiae of existence in an inquisitorial form unknown elsewhere. From one end of the empire to the other, in local as in central administration, everything has to be done by order ... One feels the effect of this kind of regime, applied throughout generations."

Another author mentions how the Crimean War "had revealed the bureaucratic cancer in all its maligant ugliness. The 30 years of corrupt police government were paying their dividends."

Today the economy, with its graft and inefficiency (though with vast resources devoted to defence) can no longer sustain superpower status. Cuts and more effective budgeting for defence are as necessary now as they were in the days of Alexander II ("we could not afford to go on," his chief adviser Gorchakov had told him, as the Crimean War ended). Though the abolition of serfdom in Alexander's time paved the way for a better functioning economy, it took a generation for the rise in productivity to be significant. As for improvements in morale and the moral basis of society, this was something outside the Tsar's terms of reference.

It is however precisely on this last point that Gorbachev may have an advantage over his reforming predecessor. He has led a life to which no scandal attaches, and has kept free from the blemish of corruption. Alexander came from a background "where sexual corruption had been taken for granted since the days of Peter the Great, where faithful husbands were ridiculed". His doubts and depressions, his "inward contradictions" and his "paralysing moods of helplessness" were certainly not redressed by his home-life divided between the increasingly estranged Tsarina (although with her it had been a love-match) and his mistress Catherine Dolgoruka. Gorbachev by contrast evidently has enjoyed a genuine partnership with his wife since their student days together. "We discuss everything", he has said.

In personality and experience Gorbachev is a highly sophisticated politician - a statesman who has made his way up from humble origins, through university and varied jobs in administration and the Party hierarchy, outdistancing (while sometimes making friends with) possible rivals at every stage. In contrast Alexander was born into the purple, and though he was better educated than any previous Tsar and had gained much useful experience as Crown Prince, his apprenticeship in politics could scarcely compare with Gorbachev's.

It took over 60 years for the failure of Lenin's revolution, as carried on by Stalin and his successors, to become apparent to some of the new intelligentsia who had been formed by the expanding system of education. By the late 1970's Yuri Andropov, who was to suceed Leonid Brezhnev, was among those who realised that another revolution was needed if Russia was to sustain its superpower role. He glimpsed that the basic element in such a change had to be moral, without which the much-needed economic progress and general catching-up with the West had little chance of achievement.

The Brezhnev era had seen growth in GNP and more consumer goods, but this had been insufficient - they had also been years of drift when the defects of the system had not been tackled, hence the flourishing black economy and corruption. Before he took over from Brezhnev, Andropov - a puritan in private and public life - used the KGB, of which he was the head, to begin a clean-up. Highly-placed racketeers were dismissed, some even executed. KGB were sent to confront those, high or low, who were taking time off from their duties to go to the baths or bars. The drive against alcoholism began in earnest (huge queues formed at the relatively few places where drink was still to be had).

For a Marxist-Leninist Andropov was saying some curious things. "We must teach ... an attitude to life in which material goods ... should not dominate a man but serve to satisfy his highest needs. Only the spiritual riches of man are truly without limit. And though you cannot put them in a purse or hang them upon your wall for prestige, that is the sort of accumulation we are for. It is the only one worthy of man, of Soviet man."

Not that Andropov, for all his civilised tastes, was a Western-type liberal. Like Gorbachev, and like the other younger leaders whom he bequeathed to Gorbachev as his team, Andropov was a thorough believer in his ideology, convinced that it could be made to work in the Soviet Union. And as one commentator reminded us, Marxism-Leninism was "an all-embracing system of ideas and values. It takes all mankind and his works into account. It is as possessive as a jealous lover, venomous in its attacks on any system that appears to be competing with it." But being a realist about the defects of the system, and believing that it could be made to work, Andropov sympathised with many of the critics about what was going wrong, and manoeuvred skilfully to divide those who would rally to a programme of reform from those who were irremediably alienated. Jewish emigration was stepped up - which also aided detente with the United States. Solzhenitsyn and some leading dissidents were deported, others were allowed to leave, though many were still in gulags or psychiatric hospitals in even severer conditions than before. Prizes were given for films and books popularising the KGB. With a section of the intelligentsia won over, the danger of the kind of conflict between intelligentsia and government which had helped to wreck tsardom was for the time being averted.

Despite this activity moral change lagged. Corruption was little abated and alcoholism barely repressed, while the hoped-for new sense of responsibility on the part of both work-force and management, with dedication to the job in hand, seemed as remote as ever. Ideas supported by violence had been inherited from Lenin: the Marxist-Leninist ideology (as practised by Stalin) had become the ideology of the State. Andropov failed to realise that the ideology as a description of reality and prescription for rebuilding society did not accord with the facts, and that the socialist Utopia as realised in the USSR was a pretence fostered by a tissue of lies ceaselessly filling the evermore hollow-sounding propaganda.

Andropov's death in 1984, followed a year later by that of Chernenko, left Gorbachev as the strongest contender for power. This he achieved, adding to the chairmanship of the Party (1985) the presidency of the Supreme Soviet (1989). Now (1990), with the Party becoming increasingly discredited and its share in power diminishing, Gorbachev has created his supreme office in the State, the executive presidency. As the latest successor to the tsarist autocracy, he has seen clearly - more clearly than Andropov - the extent of the change needed in the Soviet Union, and especially moral change as the basis for everything else. "Questions of moral order and social justice are being raised ever more sharply and persistently in every layer of our society .... Today our main job is to lift the individual spiritually, respecting his inner world and giving him moral strength ... We must look at ourselves in terms of whether we live and act according to our conscience. In some things we may have gone astray, adopting standards alien to us ... We must begin with ourselves. [The need is for] courage, initiative, high ideological standards and moral purity ... and an ability firmly to uphold the humane values of socialism."

What chances has Gorbachev to succeed?

He must maintain the support of at least a large section of the intelligentsia, the new well-educated stratum of society from which he and his wife come. He must gain the active support of that equivalent of a professional class composed in large part of the scions of the older leadership who have been able to put sons and daughters through the better ("special") schools where learning languages, especially English, is a major part of the curriculum, and which opens the way to plum jobs in culture and diplomacy. These people have been usually more interested in careers which give them an opening to the West, with opportunities for travel, than in politics or administration.

In tsarist days - going back to Nicholas I - it was the new elements in the intelligentsia who tended towards radicalism or even revolution - those who had benefited from the opening of the universities to others than the gentry, such as sons of village clergy, minor state officials and liberated serfs. Linking with the guilt-laden offspring of gentry and aristocrats, they provided the body of the Narodnik and Nihilist movements - eventually also of Marxism. Now, after a hundred years, the same signs are appearing of a radical wing in politics - not necessarily dissidents, for Gorbachev has so far gained support, though by no means uncritical, of some of its members for his reforms. Now (early 1990) an eventual threat to his leadership is coming from Boris Yeltsin, who has opposed the extension of Gorbachev's powers.

"We have to achieve a breakthrough", Gorbachev has said. "Only a highly developed economy can ensure the strengthening of the country's position on the world scene and enable it to enter the next millennium in a manner befitting a great and prosperous country. There is no alternative."

But how to bring about this breakthrough? The centrally directed economy worked badly, but dismantling the system and virtually putting nothing in its place has made the situation worse. Market forces have not taken the place of Gosplan to ensure an adequate supply of consumer foods and housing. Sakharov cited the soap factories which at least produced a fair amount of cheap soap, but now with the recently introduced "self-financing" the managers find it easier to manufacture a small amount of expensive soap in order to make the profit they are required to show - with the result that cheap soap dwindles on the market. Few managers anyway have had much real training in management, or have any grasp of economics. "Capital" is a nasty word, and there is little knowledge of how to use it - the elementary waste of resources is clear to see just by observing in Moscow's suburbs the number of half-finished buildings on which no work is being done for lack of essential materials. Central planning has been cut, but rational allocation of resources has not taken its place. "Profit" is another dirty word, while a concept of "equality" still reigns. Co-operatives or individual traders providing goods or services may be regarded as profiteering "speculators" by those still wedded to ideas of "sullen egalitarianism."

Gorbachev's task was made more difficult when the terms of trade moved sharply against the Soviet Union a year after he took power. In 1985 the USA forced the revaluation of the yen, as a means of breaking one of Japan's major devices for continuing high exports along with protectionism. This was done by vast sales of dollars, which duly forced up the yen's value, though at the cost of depreciating the dollar - by no less than 55% against the yen. Since the USSR's oil sales, denominated in dollars, made up most of its hard currrency earnings, they lost over half their buying power by 1986. This fall was compounded by the fact that the deutsche mark had been obliged to follow the yen upwards - and Japan and West Germany were the two countries where the USSR was doing most of its buying. In consequence "the USSR was having to export nearly four times as many barrels of oil to buy one unit of DM import than it had to only fifteen months before, in January 1985 ... There was going to be no hope of using a crash programme of consumer goods imports as a way to win even temporary popular support for *perestroika*. So reform would have to proceed without that useful lubricant."

Autocracy gave way, after the tyranny of Stalin, to collegiate rule with leaders whose abilities and effectiveness have varied from the geriatric incompetence of Chernenko to the brisk sophistication of Gorbachev. While the relations of Communist Party bodies with those of the State remain vague, the Party maintains some control through the continued presence of the KGB. Elections to the new Congress of Peoples Deputies have been a landmark in change, as have been those within the Party, ousting many incompetent and corrupt old-timers. The vigour of the debates (and the fact of their being televised), in the Congress and in the Supreme Soviet which it elected, augurs well for the evolution of a genuinely democratic system. The tempo has been maintained with elections in the heartland, the Russian Soviet Federated Socialist Republic. Gorbachev's election as Executive President, with powers that make him stronger than almost any Western leader, is matched by the ebbing of power from the Politburo and the Party's hitherto powerful Central Committee which has been a focus of conservatism - not only a brake on Gorbachev's reforms but a threat to his continued hold on power. At the same time the renunciation by the Communist Party of its "leading role" brings the Soviet Union nearer to being a genuinely democratic state, with a constitution which is being gradually elaborated, and - equally important - a legal system which is being reformed.

Large segments of the old system are thus being cleared away, with democratic structures beginning to replace them. The prospect that these may function properly is enhanced by at least one valuable legacy of the Communist regime: completing tsardom's last educational effort in bringing literacy to practically everyone. This has also enabled new leadership to rise from worker and peasant backgrounds. Gorbachev, coming from this background - his father was a collective-farm tractor-driver - illustrates the possibilities of careers open to talents.

There is still the cumbrous, slow-moving bureaucracy, a large part of whose function was to operate the command-system economy. This has been breaking down - so that its commands are no longer sent when needed, or if sent are often ignored. The danger is that too much time may be required before people adapt to operating a free-market economy, with the likelihood of a complete breakdown in supplying the necessities of life.

Successful adaptation implies new standards of honesty. Writing of the bureaucracy a hundred years ago, Leroy Beaulieu singled out corruption as its greatest defect. "From Peter the Great to Alexander III, the administration, the finances, the army - all the public services - have been the prey of peculation, misappropriation of funds, and fraud ... Like a poison or virus, spreading throughout the body social, administrative corruption has poisoned all its limbs, distorted all its functions, debilitated all its strength." Not only the bureaucracy but all walks of life today are suffering from this virus. For obtaining the most ordinary services (for instance in hospitals) bribes or tips are required, often consolidated into regular charges - a sad echo of late Roman decadence. A young mother is quoted as saying "The only experience worse than an abortion is having a baby in a Soviet hospital .... Unless you pay a bribe there will be no anaesthetic, and if you do not pay a rouble a day to the ward attendant you have to clean the space around your own bed and she will not bring you a bedpan ... If you give birth on Friday night or on Saturday, you will not see your baby again until the Monday morning."

A whole mental climate has to change in order to create a market economy. A significant section of the public must move beyond revealing corruption and abuses, to the stage of forming a consensus about how the system *should* work - about policies which should be introduced. The Communist Party, for all the hopes of its hardliners, cannot perform this role. Yet the abandonment of this role means expecting that the oscillations and conflicts of public opinion will eventually produce such a consensus. Is even Gorbachev's leadership adequate to move public opinion far enough in this direction?

The danger is that the revolution initiated from above may (as in the time of Alexander II) lead to a situation in which the authorities (and Gorbachev in particular) lose the initiative - a situation which has already arisen in regard to the Baltic republics and the Central European ex-satellites. A revolution initiated *and controlled* from above is the most difficult of all political feats to perform, as the experience of France after 1789 shows. Extremists on the left or reactionaries on the right may easily take over. Confronted by these dangers the authorities may revert to the harshest repression - the course that

Alexander took after 1861. Growing discontent with the deteriorating economic situation may precipitate any of these outcomes.

A fundamental change in agriculture is basic for economic progress. In this matter ideological principles are at stake. The land which is still in good heart and remarkably fertile is to be found in the relatively small area of cultivation composed of the private plots of collective farmworkers and the gardens and backyards of town-dwellers who possess them (not a large number as most of the latter are forced to live in vast apartment blocks). From these come a high proportion of the Soviet Union's fruit, flowers and vegetables. Until recently the doctrine has been that collectivised state farms are the most productive forms of agriculture, yet in practice this is not the case. A reversion to peasant ownership, or Gorbachev's proposals for long leases to independent farmers, are a move in the right direction. If implemented they could put back heart into neglected or crudely exploited soil. The long aftermath of Stalin's de-kulakization policy might at last be overcome - aggravated as that has been by the wartime depopulation of entire districts which have never recovered.

This resumption of what had been Stolypin's policy during the years 1906-11, of encouraging peasant ownership and family farming, may again transform Russia into one of the great grain-growing and cattle-producing countries of the world - a policy which Lenin admitted at the time was "the quickest development of productive forces, the best conditions of labour for the mass of the population", but which he attacked because its success would thwart his Marxist aims.

A possible comparison is with Constantine the Great, who undertook the mammoth task of revitalising the decadent empire of his day. Now is not the time to make an assesment of Gorbachev. Many years will have to pass before this could be possible. But, realising the basic moral need, Gorbachev has taken a step like Constantine's in ending religious persecution. However, the anti-religious laws still confine evangelism and most kinds of church work in a strait-jacket - they have not been revised or repealed (1989). Lenin's doctrine of atheism as fundamental to the State is no longer being applied thoroughly, but has not been altogether abandoned, though the old argument has been dropped that Communism produces better people than morality founded on religious belief.

As in the case of Constantine, Gorbachev's mother is a Christian. This may have played a part in his attitude, but more important may have been his realisation of the contradiction in trying to raise the moral level of the people while at the same time repressing Christians and Jews, treating them at worst with persecution and at best as second-class citizens, with little chance of higher education, professional advancement or responsible positions in the economy or administration. The contradiction became particularly glaring in the anti-alcoholism campaign, since Christians and Jews are generally sparing in the use of alcohol (as also are Muslims, whose mullahs strongly supported the Government's stand). It is hardly likely that any Party organ will again criticise a book, as did *Kommunist* in the pre-Gorbachev era, for suggesting that a society "without absolute moral standards" could perish.

Returning cathedrals and churches to their proper use is now part of government policy, though such restitutions cannot be expected as a right by congregations requesting them - and if the buildings are returned, the congregations are made to pay for their restoration after years of neglect and misuse. In the Ukraine, where the Uniate Church has been a focus of Ukrainian nationalism, disputes have arisen with its claims for buildings taken over by the Orthodox. The Orthodox Church was given a special position there, with attempts to suppress the Uniate Church (in communion with Rome) - in this respect following tsarist tradition.

This pattern of Church-State relations was originally set by Constantine in making the Orthodox Church a pillar of the State, which continued in Byzantium and Russia. After Lenin's onslaught and the limited reprieve granted by Stalin in the course of the Second World War, a reduced but amenable Orthodox Church has been supporting the State and many of its policies, especially in foreign affairs. This Church is now being called upon to help in morally reforming the Soviet Union. It may enjoy again in freedom the continuation of its spiritual upsurge - its "renaissance" - which took place during the first decades of the century, with its galaxy of saintly leaders and philosophers - Sergiev, Berdyaev, Blok, Frank, Struve, Florensky, Bulgakov and others. After the false dawn of 1917 when the patriarchate was restored, to be followed by the many thousand martyrdoms of Lenin's terror, those who survived suffered prison or exile. Now the Orthodox and other Churches no longer have their light kept forcibly under a bushel, but can shine forth to the world.

In carrying through moral reform the major difficulty has been in motivating people to change. According to Marxist-Leninist ideology the class struggle is the dynamic of all that makes for progress, the determinant of action and behaviour in every sphere. But since the class struggle no longer existed officially in the Soviet Union, the basis for morality in a sense disappeared, and with it the touchstone for distinguishing right from wrong in many areas of life. Some new basis for morality has now to become generally accepted.

Glasnost has been necesary for the first phase, of revealing the inadequacies of the existing situation: not only in respect of the shortages, but of the spate of accidents on land and sea, of which Chernobyl was the first to be fully (though tardily) revealed to public gaze. As former Prime Minister Ryzhkov said: "Tragedies may hound us, but behind every one of them are irresponsibility and immorality". For the next phase, *perestroika* (reconstruction), a complete revolution is required.

Glasnost corresponds to the reduction of censorship and of restrictions on travel, along with legal reform and the restoration of autonomy to the universities, which characterised the opening years of Alexander II's reign. The proliferation of circles for discussing politics, philosophy and literature, and groups for pursuing environmental aims and every kind of interest, suggests that Soviet society, so apparently inert, is showing renewed vitality, as demonstrated by the lively and sometimes heated - if rambling - disputations (hardly debates in any formal sense) in the Congress of Peoples Deputies or the Supreme Soviet. This matches the experience in Alexander II's reign, and again in the period 1905-1917, including the spontaneously formed councils (*soviet*) of workers, soldiers and others, before they were abolished or emasculated by the Bolsheviks. As in those times people can be carried away by utopian visions and unrealisable ideas, but there must be many today educated in technology as well as the humanities, and with a pragmatic cast of mind, who are capable of confronting the manifold - and indeed appalling - problems of their country. One observer sees in the understanding many show of the complex Soviet legal system (subject now to reform), and their determination to stand for their rights as citizens, the basis of a new constitutional order. "The elements of a civil society are now in place", he maintains, in the multitude of informal associations, though they are still "in a state of unstable equilibrium, not being closed down but not being legalised either".

Unless a certain tempo of changes on *all* levels is maintained, the outcome may once again be an increasingly disillusioned public and an increasingly divided intelligentsia. In Alexander II's time reform slowed down as a fight to the finish with the Poles was undertaken, and the divisions between supporters and opponents of the regime intensified. Today unrest from the Baltic republics to Outer Mongolia may prematurely end the reform programme.

In 1983, when Gorbachev (under Andropov) was in charge of the economy he said: "Every new step in the development of the economy inevitably causes profound transformations in social, class and national relationships, in the entire political superstructure". The Gorbachev revolution, as it gets underway, will continue to be regarded in the West cautiously, albeit hopefully. Having gained a breathing-space in the arms race and achieved some modernisation, might he or some sucessor not want to lead a people, now readier to respond, towards adventurous policies for reclaiming superpower status? The possibility of a more efficient USSR, with technological achievements matching those of the West and Japan, entering at some future date into another arms race and so challenging the superiority of the West, is daunting indeed.

An alternative scenario is suggested by the attempts of Russia in 1899 and 1907 with the conferences at The Hague, when similar recognition by the tsarist government of Russia's inferiority faced by Wilhelmine Germany, prompted the attempt to slow down the arms race of those days and perhaps even avert the threat of war. The initiative, to which Britain's response was lukewarm, was swiftly sabotaged by a Germany conscious of its might and beguiled by militaristic aspirations. But had this initiative been supported, the fearful catastrophe of 1914-18 and its baleful consequences might have been averted: world history would have been different. Should not the West now continue to respond to Gorbachev's initiatives, on the ground that he may genuinely intend to help turn the page of history to a new chapter of peace and goodwill for humanity?

"This is a totally new situation", he has said, "which signifies a break with the traditions, the way of thinking and the patterns of behaviour which have developed over centuries, and even over millennia. The human spirit does not adapt to change immediately, that's true for everyone, including us. We have started to change our way of thinking, and to bring many familiar things into line with reality, including things in the military and, of course, the political fields."

On other occasions he has spoken of the need for "constructive and creative interaction between states and peoples on the scale of the entire world."

Whatever the limits of *glasnost*, the new openness advocated by Gorbachev is, according to one observer, designed "to give his empire a new European identity." Catching up has always been only part of the westernising process; even more important has been the assertion of Russia's place and role in Europe, and by extension in the world.

At bottom the search for reality will determine the future, depending on the thoroughness of this search, and how far truth once recognised will be accepted, both for the remoulding of the State and for dealing with Russia's restless empire. What is important is the recognition that problems, whether they are social, political or economic, are at bottom moral, and even spiritual. Gorbachev's language is very different from Lenin's when he speaks of "an interdependent and in many ways integral world" taking shape through competition between capitalism and communism. Through "these dialectics", this "struggle of opposites, through arduous effort, groping in the dark, as it were", a new world, he believes, is being born - in fact "the course of history, of social progress, requires ever more insistently" that this must happen "on the scale of the entire world ... so that civilisation should survive."

It is certainly to be hoped that "history" or God is moving mankind towards this new synthesis or "dialectical unity of opposites". We can hope all things from future history. It is Gorbachev's presentation of the past where clarification is needed. His call is for truth - "moments of truth are needed like air", he says. History is "a serious and responsible science, if one sticks to the truth, of course" - and this is necesary "because we must draw lessons from the past" to build "a scientific policy ... on a strict assessment of reality." We must not be "mesmerised by ideological myths."

Yet this is just the error he may fall into, perpetuating the tradition of "mendacity", as Leszek Kolakowski calls it - "not an accidental blemish on the body of Communism [but] the absolute condition of its health and life." It is not merely a question of revealing more of the horrors perpetrated by Stalin, but of basic historical interpretation since 1917. Gorbachev asserts the right of every nation "independently to choose its own way of life and its own system of government", ignoring the fact that neither Russia itself not the lands under its control *freely* accepted Communism. When he writes of the Russian "people's loyalty to the free choice they had made in 1917" he ignores the fact that it was only a small minority of seats (175 out of 707) to which the Bolsheviks were elected in the Constituent Assembly of January 1918, a few weeks *after* their seizure of power. Had they allowed constitutional developments to proceed, the history of Russia and the world might have been very different, but Lenin had the Assembly forcibly dissolved after one day's sitting. This was part of a process of violence, expropriation and murder for overcoming the "class-enemy" and imposing Communism on the country. Historical revision has proved so difficult that examinations have had to be suspended. New facts are indeed forcing revision, for instance of Gorbachev's presentation of postwar history when "the European states made their choice: some of them remained capitalist while others moved towards socialism". This has been rectified by the revolutions of 1989: the moment of truth had to be accepted that it was only occupation by the Red Army which enabled Stalin to stifle at birth the democratic regimes set up under the Yalta and Potsdam accords, and to continue the forced inclusion of the Baltic states and Moldavia within the USSR.

"Dialectics" may be a possible way of interpreting history, but only if the facts are respected. The Yalta and Potsdam agreements were "democratic" in the sense that they specified free elections in the countries under Russian control, but it was certainly not "the United States, Britain and France" which "sabotaged the accords" (according to Gorbachev's book *Perestroika*) and made a nonsense of the electoral process, instituting Soviet-style governments composed of Moscow's nominees.

Many further revisions of hitherto official history are needed if confidence is to be maintained in the ringing words with which Gorbachev concludes *Perestroika*: "We want freedom to reign supreme everywhere in the world." "Criticism", he says, "should always be based on truth." To accept truth in the place of lies and myths would assist him and all his reforming colleagues in their undoubtedly sincere desire to raise the moral level and economic performance of their country, and contribute to the making of a peaceful, integrated world.

Comment: biographical details of Mikhail Gorbachev and others; the conferences at The Hague, 1899 and 1907; the economic situation in 1989. (p. 303)

CHAPTER FIFTEEN

CONDITIONS FOR RENEWAL

1. **Resolving conflicts: reintegration with nature**: *wars and ideological conflict; rich/poor classes and nations; Robert Carmichael: closing the gap between the developed and developing countries. Social dynamic: co-operation and conflict. Growing points of the new society, ancient and modern: Japan and the Japanese factory. Global civilisation: the world as "our neighbour". Man takes over from nature; reintegrating; the triumph of science.*

The discrediting of Marxism and the waning of the Marxist-Leninist regimes in Europe have diminished the ideological element in the conflict between East and West - except that the term "East" may take on new significance as long as China adheres to its own brand of Marxism. In any case it is abundantly clear that expenditure on ever more sophisticated weaponry, demanding increasingly astronomical expenditure, not only by the superpowers but also their clients and satellites, is far from a rational way of maintaining peace. Although the astonishing growth of productivity in the industrialised nations makes possible rising quantities of both guns and butter, the proportion spent on the guns restricts the butter of education and welfare services to levels considered unacceptably low by many citizens. Meanwhile the standard of living of those high in the economic pecking order continues in ever more glaring contrast with that of the vast majority of people, and this reinforces demands that the amount spent on armaments be cut.

Furthermore there is growing awareness that this is a fact of social organisation not only within countries but on a global scale - that the rich industrial nations have forced down living standards for millions in the rest of the world, or at best maintained them at a very low level, while their attempts to rectify this discrepancy have been pitifully inadequate through schemes like UNCTAD, and when it comes to aid have often been grossly misdirected. Banks and investment institutions in the wealthy countries of the West made huge profits on loans to the third world (as well as to their poorer East European neighbours) in the boom years before 1973, and then by "recycling petro-dollars". When interest rates on many loans rose as a consequence of monetary adjustments to contain inflation, the debt burden overwhelmed most third-world economies. Some loans have been written off and the terms of others revised, but a large proportion of the GNP of these impoverished lands is still claimed as interest. Higher standards of responsibility, such as those set by the World Bank, are being demanded to ensure the urgently needed development of the peoples concerned. President Bush's "globalisation of foreign policy" holds out hope that the USA will return to supporting marketing arrangements such as those on wheat and sugar, thereby reversing previous policies adverse to third world development, while the commitment at the Houston (Texas) Conference of seven leading industrial countries to reduce farm subsidies (July 1990) should - when applied within GATT - bring beneficial results. There are promising innovations in the Lomé Conventions and the related parliamentary assemblies, where representatives from the European Community and the ACP (African, Caribbean and Pacific) countries meet to plan their trade together.

One of the pioneers of these developments was Robert Carmichael, who along with other industrialists from France, Germany and Holland (notably Frederik Philips, President of Philips Industries) paralleled with their innovations the political and economic stuctures which the statesmen were creating. Carmichael was a pioneer in three respects during the postwar period: in Franco-German reconciliation; in bringing new patterns to industry; and in relations between Europe and the less developed world.

Characteristic of such pioneers was his partnership with his wife and unity with his children, which came into his life when, at the end of the war, a British officer serving with the American forces in Paris brought home to him the challenge of Christ's standards. A leading industrialist, he sloughed off the minor good works and committees which had filled much of his time with endless activity, and devoted himself to applying his new principles in his enterprises. One of these was a tile factory which had been brought to the verge of closure by low productivity aggravated by Communist activity among the workforce. A different approach to their leader resulted in his change: he gave up drinking, his home was remade, and he initiated new work-modes in the factory. Before long Carmichael was able to give the workers a self-financing rise of 35%, while devoting further profits to their housing and an insurance fund against unemployment.

He had inherited a firm which a Scottish ancestor had established in Northern France for the manufacture of jute products. While still quite young Carmichael had become Chairman of the employers' organisation of this industry. His opposite number in the Popular Front confrontations in 1936 had been a militant Communist, Maurice Mercier, trade union leader of 800,000 textile workers. The meetings had been stormy, though new agreements had been reached. One lasting gain from the encounter was the education Carmichael received regarding the abysmally low pay of many workers. Meeting Mercier the next time at Caux, twelve years later, he found him to be a man who had begun to change through his war-time experience in the Resistance, and was now changing a great deal more through experimenting with quiet times and absolute standards. A founder of the Force Ouvrière (a breakaway from the Communist-dominated CGT - Conféderation Général du Travail), Mercier was in charge of negotiations for a new deal for the textile workers. In the process he brought many delegations of workers and employers to Caux, representing over seventy firms, and in the favourable climate which this created, the first collective agreements were made covering the entire industry (1951 and 1953). Although an anti-inflationary measure which helped to stabilise prices, this brought an increase averaging 15% to the workers with subsequent self-financing rises of 7% and 8%, while greatly improving other benefits such as pensions and paid holidays. It was taken as a pattern for other industries in France and elsewhere in Europe. Works committees comprising equal numbers of workers and management were set up in which the fullest exchange of information took place, and a programme of plant replacement and modernisation was carried through in time to ensure full competitiveness when France entered the Common Market. In consequence this formerly most strike-bound of industries entered a period of industrial peace, and a powerful boost was given to the upsurge of France's economy.

Carmichael was most impressed on this first visit to Caux, in 1948, by the calibre of the German delegations, while the French were somewhat sparsely represented. He made it his business to remedy this, and as a first step informed members of the French cabinet and administration as to what was going on in Caux. Before long, M.P.'s and members of the armed and civil services were at Caux, while the employers who came were often brought by Mercier and other trade unionists. This development played a significant part in creating the climate in which reconciliation with Germany became possible on the political level.

For Carmichael new perspectives opened.

"1. To think of the world instead of only thinking of my own industry; to take part in rebuilding the entire world and not just to manufacture a product; to satisfy the needs of humanity and not solely respond to those of my country.

2. To work as one of a team, which is not an easy thing for many industrialists.

3. To make myself quiet and to listen ... to allow a thought to take effect, however unreasonable it might seem to be. I need at least half an hour of silence to get rid of the thoughts which my mind stirs up. But then come thoughts which can lead to a situation being transformed.

4. To become a revolutionary ... which means giving everything for an idea ...

For me as an industrialist, this revolution means a fundamental change in the aims of industry. What have we been doing, all of us, during the last half-century? As employers we have worked only for profit, as workers for wages. Today there is a far bigger aim which we must accept - to work all together to satisfy the needs of all and to rebuild the world.

Profit, which is indispensable for the functioning of any enterprise, should not be an end in itself. It ought rather to be the barometer of the well-being of the business, and the fruit of a proper co-operation by those in it working for the benefit of all."

Carmichael was one of the first to point out that industries, declining or threatened in the West, could only survive by uniting "not with the idea of going on an out-dated defensive, but to undertake constructive negotiations with developing countries." Regarding the textile industry, it was necessary to think about it in the world setting, with a view to reaching agreements for fair remuneration to the producers of raw materials, while working out a concerted plan for sharing out the industry among specific countries, and so avoid the ruinous consequences of an anarchic global competition. He challenged his colleagues of the European industry to become "the pioneers of a new economy".

This is what Carmichael pioneered in his own particular sector of jute. During the post-war period new uses for jute were becoming popular, such as in carpeting and wall-coverings, in addition to the traditional demand for sacks and baling material. While the industry had been expanding, supplies had been somewhat disorganised by the partition of India and Pakistan at the time of independence (1947). The growers were left in Pakistan, while the mills were in India - hence India's programme of building up her own jute production caused difficulties for Pakistani exporters, while incidentally diminishing the much needed food-producing areas in India.

The problem first really impinged on Carmichael during a visit to India and Pakistan in 1951. Coming immediately after an inspiring New Year conference at Washington D.C. in prosperous America, the shock of stepping over the body of a starved man outside his Calcutta hotel was a powerful stimulus to further thinking about Europe's responsibilities towards the under-developed world. The thought came to him strongly as a commitment: "You are responsible for the growers of India and Pakistan". To that end the fears and bitterness dividing the countries must be allayed, unity must be fostered, and in the resulting climate of confidence new policies must be forged. An essential step in this direction was building unity among the jute importers and processers in Europe (American imports of jute being minimal). Hence his founding of the Association of the Jute Industry of Europe in 1954, joined by the representatives of fourteen countries.

As Chairman of the Association Carmichael went on another trip in 1957 at the invitation of the Pakistan Government - he was to make eight such journeys in all, although these were not easy for him due to a polio attack when a young man. The Government accepted the principle of price stabilisation, which Carmichael was urging as one of the best ways of helping the producers, who were at the mercy of fluctuations caused by speculators buying up crops and releasing them on the market for their own advantage, and by the activities of middle-men and money-lenders. But to make such a plan work, agreement with Indian growers and buyers was necessary, and with India over this matter the Pakistan Government would not co-operate. It needed all Carmichael's considerable flair for diplomacy (two of his uncles had been the Cambon brothers, both key ambassadors in an earlier epoch), together with his patient care for individuals and the inspired touches which came from his regular morning quiet hour.

For two years while Pakistan tried its own price-stabilisation policy (which failed), the focus moved to Europe, culminating in a conference of the Association of the Jute Industry at Stockholm in July 1959. Patiently getting to know those concerned - it was a help to know their wives too, so these were also invited to the conference - Carmichael now felt himself in a strong enough position to call for a radical change of policy towards the suppliers. But strong objection was taken to this - many of his colleagues in the industry wanted the existing system to continue, since it seemed most likely to keep the price of imported jute low, nor were they much moved by Carmichael's vision of what might be (to use more recent phrasing) a new international economic order, in which fair returns would be agreed on for all those usefully employed in the industry, from the growers in the fields to the sellers of the manufactured product. It was not easy for those who had been concerned merely with raising profits to go along with Carmichael's convictions that the European jute industry could have a part in healing the divisions between India and Pakistan.

"For that to happen it is clear. that the deepest motives of the European jute industry would have to change fundamentally. A new idea should shape our attitude towards these countries, a strong desire to serve them, a real sense of our responsibilities towards the masses of India and Pakistan who are suffering from want while we are well provided."

So heated were the objections to Carmichael's proposals that he felt obliged to tender his resignation as Chairman - which the conference however found itself unable to accept since no one was ready to replace him.   In effect Carmichael's vision was tacitly accepted as the basis of a new policy -"our responsibility as Europeans towards countries like Pakistan and India; in fact the role of jute in the destiny of the world".

This meeting marked the beginning of a kind of shuttle diplomacy, with Carmichael travelling back and forth to Pakistan and India.   The first of these journeys, at the end of 1960, brought agreement with the Asian suppliers on the principle of stabilising the price of raw jute. A year later Carmichael's journey was aimed not so much on matters of business, but to get to know the people. In the atmosphere thus created he was able to arrange with the Pakistani Minister of Commerce the agenda for a conference the following March when details of the agreement were worked out.

The greatest difficulty arose over actually fixing the price of the raw product, which had to be done yearly under the auspices of the U.N. Food and Agriculture Organisation based at Rome. But at Rome too there were helpers, among them a FAO official, Eric Ojala, a New Zealander with whose aid Carmichael hit on a strategy which - almost miraculously, it appeared - brought together the Pakistani representative and the Europeans (despite instructions emanating from their governments in several cases to sabotage any such agreement), so that they unanimously arrived at what all agreed was a just price. This was the start of several years of price agreement and stabilisation, virtually cutting out the speculators, which benefited the return to the growers by an average of 300%.

Such progress has to be fought for continually if it is to last. After some years there was a renewal of speculation and corruption. Carmichael had now retired, but, undaunted, he and his wife returned to the sub-continent and worked for six months at the MRA centre at Panchgani and elsewhere to help bring about the change in people needed to curb these evils. It was his last journey to Asia. In 1973

Robert Carmichael died, but not before he had worked out, in effect, a model for the "stabex" scheme which was eventually to be incorporated in the second Lomé Agreement negotiated by the European Community and the 52 ACP countries.

All this was only one part of the action undertaken by this man, who by any standard would have been regarded as having an exceedingly exacting job. It was possible for him to undertake such activity effectively only because his vision and strength were constantly renewed at the source which he found in his times of quiet. After getting rid of all his minor activities "Robert became a man of prayer", said his wife Hélène. "That was certainly the characteristic of the latter part of his life." He played a major part with Robert Schuman and others in Franco-German reconciliation and in the difficult work of decolonisation which France carried out during this period. As much as anyone he prepared the way with Bourguiba and Masmoudi of Tunisia, and with Guessous and other nationalists of Morocco, to meet in fruitful consultation and negotiation with their opposite numbers among the French. He demonstrated in this and many other ways how a new dimension of living could take people far beyond the ordinary social and political categories, beyond class and race and "the 'isms", towards the creation of a new type of world society.

Every society grows out of the old one. Its embryo can be perceived before the parent order disintegrates. Where Marx went wrong in the opening sentences of *The Communist Manifesto* was in identifying each embryonic order with a specific *class*, oppressed by a dominant class. The growing-points of the new culture, as society collapsed in Antiquity, were not (as he asserted) in the conflict of "plebeians and patricians", but in their co-operation in the burgeoning Church, where upper-class professionals like Leo and Gregory became popes presiding over congregations who first formed a state within the State before taking over the State itself, along with much of its administrative system. Founders of monasteries and their successors, such as Benedict and Cassiodorus, were from similar backgrounds. The monasteries were growing-points of the coming order, in which much of the old culture was preserved while new developments in education, art and architecture were fostered. In the East Basil's monastic and welfare institutions at Caesarea of Cappadocia were a microcosm of a new society, whose principles and to some extent practices eventually permeated the civilisation of Byzantium. In the West landowners provided homes and work for refugees from the towns. As bishops and abbots, they initiated (with other landowners) the medieval manorial system. It is only at later stages, as civilisation advanced, that the conflict of classes appears as an important feature of social change.

The Industrial Revolution shifted the economic basis of European culture on to the power-driven machine; while agriculture naturally continued to provide much of the raw materials and other commodities, it too became mechanised, along with transport, mining, and most other economic activities. Conflict between management (with its "bourgeois" supporters) and labour has indeed fuelled reform movements, with consequent improvements in wages and working conditions, but beyond a certain point it has retarded rather than stimulated progress of this kind.

The renewal, not just the reform of society, is to be found in situations where harmony is established between the two sides of industry. This was shown in 19th century Britain, where - in striking contrast with the exploiters of labour - numerous entrepreneurs, who were heirs of the spiritual upsurges from Quakerism to evangelicalism, made it a prime object to improve their workers' conditions, provide model housing, education, sport and other amenities. In some firms a tradition was established whereby, during slumps, the "bosses" cut their own salaries to keep workers in jobs.

In more recent times the major growing-points of industrial civilisation - the global civilisation of the coming century - have moved from Europe to Japan. There a norm of efficiency, and high quality in the product, have been achieved in the factories and businesses, and this now has to become the norm both in developing countries and the former pacemakers of Europe and America, if their industries are to be viable in the competitive world-market of today.

Japan learnt from Europe and America, then developed new expertise which is passing back to the West. A British firm making cables for a Nissan factory in Britain finds that these products are beset with defects and come slowly off the line, with poor delivery resulting. The management asks Nissan's help, who send two specialists and arrange a week of discussions between the operators and management. "When they returned the assembly line worked perfectly. There has not been a single defective component in ten months." Production increased from 224 to 300 cables an hour. What the manager and his work-force did was to adopt the Nissan philosophy of *kaizen* (continuous improvement), applied by everyone from cleaner to managing director, starting with a new understanding by the operators that the quality of their individual work directly affected the quality of the product - they then came up with their own suggestions for improvements. (*Times*, 3/7/90).

This instance of cultural transmission and re-transmission stems directly, on one level, from the transfer of industrial methods by

Americans who were rejected in their own country, and on another from the spiritual upsurge channelled through the Anglo-American campus movement. The first (and better known) part of the story was due to W. Edwards Deming and J.M. Duran. Deming, a government statistician, came to Japan shortly after the war, discouraged by the lack of response in America to his system of building quality into a product in the course of production, instead of attempting to ensure it was there by inspecting the product afterwards. "His idea was to study each and every part, each and every procedure, and then set statistical controls that would prevent wide variations in quality." "Think quality, don't think price!" was the doctrine preached by himself and his colleague Duran, as they called on management to study the entire process, develop solutions, institute on-the-job training, and ignore short-term profits.

Both the timing and conditions were propitious for this doctrine. Traditionally the Japanese work by a system of consensus, applied at that time by the political and business leadership in place of the militarists, who had previously captured control but had then been forced into limbo through defeat in the war. The vital growing-point was a small group of politicians, bankers and other businessmen, who met in clubs, exclusive restaurants and geisha houses, to shape economic and political strategies.

> "Over dinner, bankers conferred among themselves and with corporation presidents about, for example, the priority needs for capital expansion in shipbuilding, textiles or chemicals. The appropriate cabinet ministers and government bureaucrats were consulted and advised about budget appropriations and legislation. And out of the give-and-take between these elements emerged the compromises which guided the economic development of the country. Although there was often fierce competition between rival companies, it was a process far removed from the strident free market of the Western democracies and was often the despair of the [American] Occupation, which was dedicated to abolishing cartels, monopolies and price fixing. But it worked with stunning success, as the United States discovered to its dismay some twenty years later."

When Deming arrived in Japan in 1946 he met a group of statisticians who arranged a meeting for him with 45 top executives. To many of them his ideas made sense, and by the 1950's were altering work methods throughout the whole of Japanese industry. "Quality circles" were set up in the factories. The principle was to do everything by consensus. In a factory meeting of eight or ten people "you might have the senior technical guy, the product planner, a marketing guy, and then in the back row there's the young technical guys in lab coats ... And after the meeting, all the Japanese get together and the first thing they do is ask the young guys for their opinions. 'What do you think? What should we do?' And that's all good. It helps them grow, and lets them see how their big bosses behave, and their opinions are factored into the decision ... And then you have a young man who understands, is on the team, his loyalty is so high. It can take time."

Good relationships are fostered, not merely among management and between management and operatives, but between the firm, the suppliers of components, and the vendors. The search is for *Dantostu* - the best of the best, in quality and reliability, and in what the customer really wants, and then design "leadership products ... meeting customer needs for performance at lowest industry costs." Much time is spent on training and courses, such as "Leadership through Quality" for managers, and other courses for those at all levels in the firm.

That conditions were favourable to this development was largely due to the same spiritual currents which in Europe were enabling statesmen to create the new political and economic structures. Not long after Deming made his entry into Japan's industrial life, an Englishman, Basil Entwistle, and an American, Ken Twitchell, were entertained (1950) at two successive lunches at the Tokyo Rotary Club, where they met the Chairmen of many of the largest businesses - those who would shortly be directing Japan's "economic miracle".

Entwistle, who had touches with some of Japan's leadership through pre-war contacts, had previously helped delegations - significant in their personnel, though small in numbers - to obtain visas from the Occupation authorities for one of the conferences at Caux, and a similar one at Los Angeles. Through those attending these conferences, and the Rotarians, doors opened to most of the key figures in politics, finance and industry. During the following five months at no less than 50 lunches, dinners and other occasions, Entwistle and Twitchell met a full cross-section of the leaders in all walks of life. A lunch meeting of the Electrical Manufacturers Association was attended by the Chairmen and top management of the four largest companies - Hitachi, Toshiba, Mitsubishi and Fuji. Many of these came subsequently to conferences at Caux and in America. Among them were the Mayor of Hiroshima, and an executive of the Communist-dominated All Japan Metal Workers Union, Katsui Nakajima, who had survived the bomb in Hiroshima after an illness of several months. Nakajima's change from a bitter class-warrior to a consensus-building leader came through his apology for his hatred to

Suzuki, Police Chief of Osaka, who himself became a national figure in creating harmony after shedding his hatred for Communists, Koreans and others.

Change in such men was significant, since the process of consensus was still being disrupted by the Communist bid for power, especially in heavy industry. At the Tokyo Shibaura Co., manufacturing heavy electrical equipment, run by Toshiba, the trade union had almost reduced the firm to bankruptcy by slowdowns, strikes and violence, and though the Occupation forces had intervened to oust the Communists, friction between management and workers continued. To one of the conferences in America came both Toshiba's Managing Director and the Chairman of the union. Other sectors, after being prime targets for Communist activity, became models of consensus and efficiency. Such were Telecommunications and the National Railways, whose management attended conferences in Europe and organised courses for their staff (the Railways shortly developed the fastest train in the world). Wives accompanying husbands to the conferences, and the increasing prominence of women leaders like Shidzue Kato, well-known for her campaign for women's rights, were a new feature of the Japanese scene, as were the occasions which became common of management sitting with labour, opening their books and negotiating their differences. In politics younger leaders, like Yasuhiru Nakasone (later Prime Minister), came forward, while Nobosuke Kishi made his famous Asian tour of reconciliation (1957), humbly apologising in the Philippines and other countries for Japan's wartime record of occupation and oppression.

> "Businessmen began getting to know union men as people, conservatives and socialists stepped out of their normal confrontation roles with each other. Bureaucrats started associating with people who had been only statistics. Lasting personal friendships developed above party, class and point of view, where few had existed before."

Some of those most responsible in national affairs began meeting regularly each fortnight in this spirit - a counterpart of the "clubs" which wielded power in the political parties and business circles, "except that this group was composed of widely differing interests, rather than representing any clique." At a weekend in the Hakone Mountains resort, the men of a Toshiba delegation headed by the Managing Director spoke of personal decisions on drinking, honesty with their wives, and responsibilities as husbands and fathers. Typical of such grassroots changes were the flowering of relationships in the home.

In the rest of the world Japanese products, by their quality and reliability, were taking over markets from their older competitors, and were innovating in fields such as electronics and the silicon chip. If the postwar industrial conflicts had continued to rack Japan at a time when vast new opportunities were opening with the technical advances of the day, it is doubtful whether the electrical manufacturers could have seized the moment as they did. Instead creative partnership, and the new teamwork in industry, not only made Japan a world leader in this sphere, but spilled over into other industries where the economic miracle took shape.

Others from Europe and America came to join Entwistle and Twitchell in Japan. Entwistle left the country in 1958. "Perhaps only those who lived through the postwar years could realise how fragile was Japan's democracy," he wrote, "and how close she came to losing the heart of her traditional culture." Without a new spirit "she would have lost the genius for consensus and group loyalties in the face of looming class war and industrial confrontation ... The changes were more than material and economic. The spirit of the people had been transformed from anxious speculation, unnatural humility and tentative probing to an eager optimism about the future and a confident pride in present progress. During the years of recovery there had been some fierce conflicts, disappointments and confusion, but the Japanese people had shown an extraordinary ability to learn from the past and work together to overcome forbidding obstacles. And more than that, the nation had demonstrated to the world a determination to maintain both the freedom of the individual and the discipline of a tightly knit society to make democracy work, despite authoritarian pressures from within and without. They had reconciled in a fascinating way the rival claims of tradition and innovation, to release an energy soon to command the attention of the world."

A whole range of ideas enters the argument at this point, which goes beyond envy or the mere self-interest of people wishing to improve their own living-standards and the social services on which they depend. The realisation that we are all living in one Global Village has taken root in people's minds. Nearly a century ago Nordau observed that the constant exposure to "the thousand events" taking place all over the world was adversely affecting the nervous system of people. With radio and television this exposure has been enormously intensified. While our nervous systems have perhaps largely adapted to the strain, there has been a positive outcome in the realisation that the whole world is our neighbour. A famine in part of Africa cannot be shrugged off as an event in some far-off country of which we have scarcely heard. There is a sense of involvement in both the weal and the woe of the world as never before: millions can share in a royal wedding or a football final as well as feeling compassion for the victims of natural or man-made catastrophes. As for the latter, anxiety can mingle with sympathy, as seen in the response to the Chernobyl reactor disaster. So also with other events of which the longer-term repercussions only gradually become plain, and which are not contained within national frontiers: pollution, deforestation, and the depletion of natural resources.

Another simile corresponding to the Global Village is Spaceship Earth, as we view ourselves through the astronaut's eyes. Modern technology is drastically changing ideas about our mutual dependence and overrides frontiers in the process.

Radio and television are only two out of a multitude of inventions which have spread from Europe and its extensions ("the West"). The conviction that through science most things can be changed or manipulated has given Westerners confidence and the technical means to subdue other peoples politically and culturally. And indeed the world *has* been transformed and its distances diminished, even if in a manner which threatens its imminent doom, and Western ideas have become dominant throughout the globe. The West has brought every country into the "one world" of ideas, communications and technology. Russia is at present pre-eminent in space, but along with the rest of Europe and the West in general, is faced by the efficient and innovative industry of Japan and other countries of the Pacific. China may well become part of this advancing frontier, leaving Russia and the West, as the Italy of Roman times was left, to play a secondary role to that of its progressive neighbours.

Laurens van der Post writes of the Africa of the Bushmen - the Africa before the coming of the Europeans - as a place where "Nature - that is God's nature - was in charge". A European mode of life, by contrast, was one "where man seemed to be entirely in command." Bill McKibben speaks of "our wholesale alterations of nature. *We* are in charge now whether we like it or not. When God asks, as He does in Job 'Who shut in the sea with doors ... and prescribed bounds for it?' and 'who can tilt the waterskins of the heavens?' we must now answer that it is with us."

Eating the Tree of Knowledge is a parable of Man's use of reason, giving him the power to be "as gods", manipulating nature instead of living with nature. The regularity of nature is now in jeopardy, all those regularities on which Man has been able to count, climatic stability, seasonal change, "normal" rainfall, temperature and sea-level ... Man has been destroying nature as a predictably functioning super-organism. The "clock" can no longer be expected to tick in the same old way - its time will change, and Man will not be able to re-set it.

The clock analogy seemed appropriate for illustrating Newton's theories. Newton did not leave God out, but others did, implicictly or explicitly, with the result that His handiwork has been tampered with to the extent that, in part, it has been rendered unworkable - *and we continue to compound the damage.* Awareness of this crisis must lead to new thinking and living if humanity is to survive. What is needed, for a start, is the sense of integration with the natural environment.

> "Earth of the vitreous pour of the full moon just tinged with
> blue ...
> Far-swooping elbow'd earth - rich apple-blossomed earth!
> Smile, for your lover comes ...
> You sea! I resign myself to you also ...
> Sea of stretch'd ground-swells,
> Sea breathing broad and convulsive breaths,
> Sea of the brine of life and of unshovelled yet always-ready
> graves,
> Howler and scooper of storms, capricious and dainty sea,
> I am integral with you."

For Whitman this integration was of a piece with his devotion to democracy -

> "I speak the pass-word primeval, I give the sign of democracy,
> By God! I will accept nothing which all cannot have their
> counterpart of on the same terms."

He was no romantic escapist, as his devoted hospital service in the American Civil War demonstrated, followed by his moving ode on the death of Lincoln.

Anxiety about the environment in no way detracts from admiration of those pioneers in science, medicine and technology who have made possible a better life for millions and have alleviated so many of the afflictions of mankind. In Antiquity plague became endemic, with resultant large-scale depopulation, since knowledge to control it did not exist. Today medicine has eliminated plague and other killers like smallpox; it may prevent the spread of AIDS, even if it fails to cure it. But since modern threats to health and the environment are so largely man-made and their causes are now understood, they can to some extent be controlled by moral means, and usually more effectively than by prophylactics and technology. At the same time the do's and don'ts, which make for the well-being of the individual and the community, may be simple to expound, but need character to apply. Whether it is the ills of developed countries, compounded by unemployment, alcoholism, drug abuse and racism, or whether it is the hunger and dereliction of the third world, the killing and maiming in senseless "little wars", the stifling of millions of lives by abortion, the destruction of the environment, or the threat of nuclear annihilation - everything which adds up to an "extreme of evil" can only be countered by an "extreme of good."

After summing up the evils from which pre-revolutionary Russia suffered, and living through the revolution itself, Pasternak concluded in the words of Zhivago: "I used to be very revolutionary-minded, but now I think that nothing can be gained by violence. People must be drawn to good by goodness."

2. The democratic alternative to Marxism-Leninism: *Soviet options; 1989 and 1848. Leninist atheism and the suppression of spontaneity. The alternative - democracy based on moral and spiritual values; the approach to conflict-resolution. Gorbachev's move in freeing religion. The restoration of moral absolutes. Starting with oneself: "an inner change of character".*

The Soviet rulers, in allowing more freedom, have to try to reconcile it with authority. When it is a question of a group of nations - which it is in the case of the Soviet Union - the European Community can show a possible way ahead. As primarily an economic community, though inevitably with political implications, and with principles of organisation and control differing both from laissez-faire liberalism and autarchic totalitarianism, it comes to the fore as a new kind of international entity. Whether or not it evolves into a fully-fledged federation, it is clearly in line with the needs and potentialities of the age. What has proved valid for a number of countries in Western Europe may well be equally valid in the Centre and East.

This indeed may be the only hope for a measure of unity in this area which has lived through the most extraordinary year of revolutions in peace-time since 1848. In that year the settlement imposed on the Continent by Britain, Russia and Austria after the previous great war (the Napoleonic), was challenged by a rising of the peoples: governments were overthrown, and democratic constitutions temporarily (in some cases permanently) replaced autocratic regimes. But for the most part the changes that were initiated could not for long be maintained. Too much a "revolution of the intellectuals", some of the governments which it engendered lacked able administrators or charismatic leaders.   In France the reaction brought to the throne another Napoleon, albeit no militarist like his uncle.   In Austria a younger and more vigorous emperor replaced the ageing Ferdinand. When the constitution promised by the Prussian King Frederick William IV in the early revolutionary days was eventually promulgated, it left real power in his hands; he refused the throne of a united Germany with a constitution worked out by an elected national assembly (which was dispersed by force). The Poles had two years earlier tried and failed to throw off Russia's yoke in a rising of violence and bloodshed - to be repeated with equal violence and similar failure in 1863-4. Russia in 1848 sent her army to help Austria quell the revolt of Hungary.

Class and national divisions aborted most revolutions before their leaders' aims were achieved.   Where gains in constitutional government were made, notably in Scandinavia and Switzerland, these divisive factors were at their weakest, though an older cause of division - rival creeds - had played a part in Switzerland's civil war a year before.

Will there be a re-run of history? A dismal scenario could result from the revitalised nationalism of Russia's republics and ethnic groups: those of the Baltic region, Georgia, the Ukraine, Armenia, and perhaps the largely Muslim territories of Central and Eastern Asia. The demand of Moldavia to be reunited with a Romania freed from its Ceausescu oppressors, and of the German Democratic Republic to merge with its western neighbour, might in times gone by have triggered a European (or even world) war, in the way that Serb aspirations lit the fuse in 1914, igniting an explosion which changed the frontiers in Central Europe after vast bloodshed - to be repeated a generation later.

De-moralisation engendered by these wars, with their massacres and genocides, their famines, and the loss of so many among the finest of the youth - all this has added to the decadence of our days. If the worst-case scenario is the consequence of the present upheavals, the future for Europe and indeed the planet (already environmentally threatened) is bleak indeed.   Such conflicts would not have to "go nuclear" to provide many of the effects of a nuclear war - this would be done by a few bombs on nuclear power-stations, with consequences like Chernobyl which could spread far beyond Europe itself.

However the hope that history's next chapter will be different is strengthened by the example of the West.   The chain of fate was broken when the old national rivalries, persisting like tribal or mafia-type vendettas on a monstrous scale, either died out or were transmuted into ritualised contests of song and sport, after costly repentance and reconciliation - or were contained within the framework of the Community with its structured regulation of the power-aspirations of the member-states.

Gorbachev has appeared, in the waning of the modern "Hellenistic" Age, like Constantine at a similar period of Rome's decline. He may arrest the decadence and even provide the impetus and framework for the eventual burgeoing of a new civilisation. As one of the relatively few students of Law in Russia during his time at university, he had a window on the West which was denied to most of his contemporaries, and gained understanding from such as Locke and Rousseau of the basic elements in democracy. His initial idea, as he gained power in the State, was evidently to make the Marxist-Leninist system work, but the attempt to do so by replacing bits of the system piecemeal with democratic elements has led on, willy nilly, to a much bigger revolution whereby - if anarchy is avoided - the Soviet Empire on which the sun is now setting may be transformed into some kind of federated democracy.

It is not a question of replacing Communism with capitalism - the antithesis is false. Communism of the Marxist-Leninist variety has not worked and cannot work because it attempts to enforce rights and duties with the apparatus of State-power, whereas they can only properly be performed by the spontaneous motivation of individuals and groups. State-power can enforce an *external* action, but this deprives it of the personal "motive and disposition" which would give it spontaneity, "by destroying the spring on which moral action depends." At the extreme limit there can be large-scale operations performed by brutally-dragooned multitudes, such as the building of the White Sea Canal by many thousands of Stalin's gulag prisoners. When such State-pressure operates at every level, to prevent certain types of action and enforce others, right down to the details of personal and private life, it becomes increasingly counter-productive. People can only properly contribute to the well-being of their community or State within a system of rights and liberties which provide "the condition and guarantee of our becoming the best that we have it in us to become ... Every act done by the public power ... can only be justified it it liberates resources of character and intelligence greater beyond all question than the encroachment which it involves."

In the Communist system the slogan "from each according to his ability, to each according to his needs" is shown up to be utopian rhetoric as much as Lenin's forecasts of the spontaneously operating social order in his *State and Revolution*, once the class-enemy had been annihilated.

"Capitalism" is an umbrella label covering the economic system of various non-Communist societies, whereas Communism denotes a social order as well as an economic system. The Communist social order fails in the same way as did Peter the Great's militarisation policy, which as Leroy-Beaulieu pointed out "suppressed every spontaneous movement in the country".

That is of course an exaggeration: the truth is that the area in people's lives for purposive, creative activity, of the kind which can only develop by spontaneous motivation, was drastically restricted. Marxist-Leninism, particularly as applied by Stalin, went much further in so hemming in people's lives right down to the most personal level of faith and convictions, that spontaneity, and the whole-heartedness which goes with it, ebbed away. Spontaneity in literature came under such severe censorship that the resulting works were often suppressed - the only means of circulation being by *samizdat* or publication abroad. In the economy the lack of heart in industry showed up in the shoddiness and shortage of goods, and in agriculture in the loss of "heart" in the land, with the chronic shortfall from the collective farms.

The contrast is not in fact between two economic systems but between two cultures, two types of social and political order, the one authoritarian, the other composed of "an immense variety of ways of life sustained by individuals making their own decisions." The economic system of each is different, dependent on the culture and its accompanying social-political order, not the other way round as asserted by Marx.

The culture which has given birth to genuinely democratic regimes - not make-believe "democracies" of the "peoples" variety - is basically Judeo-Christian. In the words of Robert Schuman:

"Democracy owes its existence to Christianity. It was born on the day when man was called to realise in his temporal life the dignity of the human being, in the freedom of each person, in respect for the rights of each and by the practice of fraternal love for all. Never before Christ had such ideas been formulated. Democracy ... has recognised the primacy of the inner values which ennoble man. The universal law of love and charity has made each person our neighbour ... This revolution has operated under the progressive inspiration of the Gospel which has formed the generations by a slow work, sometimes accompanied by agonising struggles."

Because of this Christian basis of democracy, Communists, like Nazis, in developing their own kind of culture, had to get rid of Judaism and Christianity. For Lenin the propagation of atheism and the destruction of the Churches were prime elements in his strategy, just as for Hitler Christianity and Judaism had to be replaced by a revived paganism of blood and race.

In taking steps to free the Churches and abandon religious persecution Gorbachev has moved towards establishing the basis for a democratic society, and with it for an alternative economic system. This system will be "capitalist" by virtue of abolishing the State's monopoly control of capital (including land and real estate) and labour, though the degree of State control in proportion to that of individuals and non-State bodies would be a matter of gradual evolution: since the economies of all developed countries are mixed, no blue-print is possible as to the relative size of the public and private sectors. Similarly no universal model can be presented for the right balance in matters of welfare between programmes carried out by the State or local authorities and those initiated and carried out by private associations.

On the political level, the alternative to enforced association (as for instance of the Baltic States with the USSR) is the spontaneous impulse of consent, perhaps within a "community" or confederal structure. The use of power, when consent is lacking, can produce a semblance of order, but given the opportunity suppressed peoples demand freedom, to have their own State or join with another. These demands arouse conflicts between national, ethnic and religious communities, such as have always occurred in empires as they decline or dissolve.

Before political solutions are sought there is usually a need for preliminaries. What should be done is actively to search out the underlying elements of conflict, in thwarted aspirations, desires for vengeance, the fear of domination, or ordinary greed and ambition, and strive to deal with these by meeting the human needs on levels deeper than the political or material and deeper than the ideological, viewed in terms of argument and counter-argument. An approach is needed which goes to the heart of the matter - and this is the heart of each person, so far as hearts are accessible - accepting the moral challenge and applying the *essentials* of the great religions as the founders and prophets have proclaimed them: not as dogmatic propositions, but as truths which can set us free. Only so is it possible to move away from the unrealities and irrationalities of theoretical argumentation, and penetrate to the roots in human nature, where change with new motives can build foundations of lasting peace.

The practicalities of this approach on the part of a significant number of people were illustrated with dramatic effect in the reconciliations which made possible the integration of France and Germany in the European Community. In the process the old nationalist clichés whereby French and Germans characterised each other have disappeared and a spirit of partnership has been created. This historic step was born of the Christian culture of Europe, applied in its essentials in the personal and political life of those initiating this development, and in many of their supporters. The freeing of religion by Gorbachev could lead on to a similar mode of conflict-resolution in Central and Eastern Europe.

In the ancient decadence conflicts were evident between paganism and the incoming religions from the east, as well as between these religions themselves, not to mention the dogmatic quarrels which rent the Christian Church. Today there is less conflict between adherents of different religions and dogmas - the dividing line is rather between the worshippers of Mammon and people of religious faith. And in this conflict there has been a tendency, not known in the ancient world, for those of *all* faiths to stand together against atheism and materialism, and within the different faiths to penetrate to their essentials as the dynamic for bringing together the creative minority of mankind to save the planet and remake civilisation. The unprecedented gathering of 100 representatives of various faiths at Assisi through the initiative of Pope John Paul II (October 1986) is an instance of this trend.

Accordingly, on analogy with the Ancient World, the first condition for the renewal of civilisation is the revitalising of religion, not as a source of conflict but of the spiritual power which is the essence of the various faiths and the morality which they teach. For these go together: to love God with all your heart, mind and strength (at least to set yourself to do so) *is* to love your neighbour as yourself. The one intention complements the other. The spiritual dynamic comes from total commitment in pursuit of these aims, taking the absolute for the standard both in devotion to the Almighty and caring for the neighbour in the widest sense of the word. It follows that the restoration of absolute standards in place of those that are relative and situational, in politics and business as in personal life, is another condition for the renewal of civilisation.

Nothing can replace self-criticism and judgement of ourselves and our society by moral absolutes - only so can we evaluate *progress* towards the freedom which offers the highest fulfilment to everyone in mutual caring and service, as distinct from *process* which may really be decline. In this the historian's role is important: "the standards by which we judge should be absolutes", says Sir Michael Howard; "cultural relatives" only mislead.

This renewal of civilisation has to be the work of a creative minority (to use Toynbee's phrase again) - those who are sensitive to the spiritual currents of the age, who commit themselves to restore standards and give leadership. This was the role of the Christian Church in its early, formative days. The changes in society that ensued were at its beginning local, confined to small communities and scattered congregations, but the Christians' vision of transformation was universal. Today if we follow their example our vision and awareness must be global, because the evils threatening Europe and the West threaten equally the planet as a whole.

For this reason the message proclaimed by the creative minority must be in terms which are intelligible everywhere. It must stress the truth that this world-transforming work depends on personal decision and that the person to begin with is oneself.

"The difficult problems with which we have to deal", said Albert Schweitzer, "even those which lie entirely in the material and economic sphere, are in the last resort only to be solved by an inner change of character. The only conceivable way of bringing about a reconstruction of our world on new lines is first of all to become new men ourselves ... Everything else is more or less wasted labour, because we are thereby building not on the spirit, but on what is merely external ... If the ethical is the essential element in civilisation, decadence changes into renaissance as soon as ethical activities are set to work again in our convictions and in the ideas which we undertake to stamp upon reality."

He adds that "we must study the history of civilisation otherwise than as our predecessors did, or we shall be finally lost."

3. **The strategy of world change**: *the Christian leaven in Antiquity and today; the challenge of the prophets; transforming humanity. The world's creative minority: strategy; the role of silence; humanity's zero hour; moral guidelines. The spiritual upsurge in Russia and Central Europe. The lessons of history.*

Civilisations have enormously enriched each other by sharing their achievements in culture and technology, particularly their spiritual heritage. In Europe the heritage from the Jewish people, fusing with the wisdom of Greece and Rome, has developed a certain outlook and attitude which can be termed "Christian". Only a comparatively few Christians in each generation - we think of the saints, both those recognised as such, and those unrecognised - have grasped and lived fully the Christian revelation. Yet the influence of this whole-hearted, even if tiny minority down the ages on the mass of more or less nominal Christians has been to turn them in a more spiritual direction, to leaven them with their own outlook and ideas. This applies also to non-Christians, as Nikolai Berdyaev points out:

"The best type of communist, that is to say the man who is completely in the grip of the service of an idea and capable of enormous sacrifices and disinterested enthusiasm, is a possiblity only as the result of the Christian training of the human spirit, of the remaking of the natural man by the Christian spirit. The result of this Christian influence upon the human spirit, frequently hidden and unperceived, remains when people consciously refuse Christianity, and even become its foe."

A historian of the Roman decadence warns against superficial judgements of Christianity's impact by dwelling exclusively on its failure to bring about a fuller realisation of its ideals. It brought about "fundamental changes" then, and it can bring about yet more fundamental changes now. The working of the Judeo-Christian leaven in the ancient society did not become apparent for several centuries. Its further working in our society today, through transforming motives and attitudes, may bring about changes that are no less than revolutionary, and because history is moving so much faster than in ancient times, the effects should be evident much sooner.

Leaven does its work through the multiplication of the cells which compose it - in our case people. "Civilisation can only revive", says Schweitzer "when there shall come into being in a number of individuals a new tone of mind which will gradually win influence over the collective one, and in the end determine its character." Likewise B.H. Streeter pointed out that:

"History shows that in case of wars, revolutions, strikes and other major conficts, a relatively small weight of public opinion on the one side or the other, or the presence or absence of moral insight and courage in a few individuals in positions of influence, has often turned the balance between a reasonable settlement and a fight to the finish. Modern civilisation can only be saved by a moral revival. But for this it would suffice if every tenth or hundredth person were changed. For each such person raises the level of those whom he touches in the home, in business, and in public affairs."

Whether the leavening influence of Christianity could ever change society to the point where harmonious co-operation and interdependence fully replace class domination and exploitative oppression is a question for the prophet, not the historian. The prophet's role is to project a vision, without which "the people perish", in the sense that, lacking purpose, their lives become disordered and their civilisation disintegrates. The vision is of a new order of living, a leap of imagination which enabled an Isaiah or Micah, some two and a half millennia ago, to project a world where swords would be turned into ploughshares and the lion would lie down with the lamb. It has taken that amount of time and the menace of a nuclear apocalypse for men and women to begin seriously working to create a type of world society where war would become unthinkable.

In those days of newly developed weapons of bronze and iron, technology was already sowing the seeds of the world's ruin and destruction. Today, when technology's advance has led to an even deeper crisis, our perceptions have been heightened. We now realise that the challenge is not only to change in our personal lives, but to effective working together between communities and nations. Starting with home and family, this involves a strategy on a universal scale, with the aim no less than transforming the world.

With this realisation, in the words of André Chouraqui:

"L'histoire a retrouvé son sens et sa droiture.
Au-delà de la nuit l'aube est annoncée,
Au-delà de la mort surgit l'éternité,
Au-delà du mensonge accourt la verité,
Et la lumière assaille au-delà des ténèbres
Les citadelles croulantes d'idoles mortes."

("History has found again its direction and its rightness.
Beyond the night the dawn appears,
Beyond death rises eternity,
Beyond the lie truth comes swiftly,
And beyond the darkness the light assaults
The crumbling citadels of dead idols.")

"We are at this moment", wrote Teilhard de Chardin, "passing through a change of age ... The future will decide what is the best name to describe the era we are entering. The word matters little. What does matter is that ... at the cost of what we are enduring, life is taking a step, and a decisive step, in us and our environment."

For Lévi-Strauss "the fusion of groups previously separated" by conflicts of class or race, "is carrying humanity towards a global civilisation."

Laurens van der Post proclaims "a life full of power which ... reintegrates our infinite diversities for another mutation we cannot yet discern", though first we have to overthrow the "cold and arrogant despotism of reason" and "remake ourselves". God working through nature provides the "energies and forces" with which there is nothing man "cannot change, including himself." Chouraqui echoes van der Post in reminding us that what the prophets of old were proclaiming was not "progress" but a "mutation" - a total revolution of society. His challenge is to personal change in our character and motives, and so to come nearer that level of living which he expresses as "transparent towards God and men, cleansed of all dirt so that the light coming from on high can penetrate and illuminate us."

The pioneers of a new era - almost "a new species of humanity", as Bergson calls them - operate with a sense of strategy. At the dawn of Christianity St. Paul showed this sense, which took him throughout the eastern Empire and eventually to Rome. For these pioneers, spearheading moves towards a future of hope, strategy is not merely man-devised. Through taking time for God or "the inner voice" we may perceive what we should do, how to work and inspire others. Van der Post says that taking part in the "main thrust towards the creation of a new kind of individual" involves an experience as of listening to an inner voice; absolute obedience to this brings "a feeling of happiness almost too keen to endure."

Chouraqui's conviction is that silence should forge regenerated humanity. "We must find men to build the new world ... We must found a new order whose roots would reach down into the still living depths of Israel, Christianity and Islam. The nearer we get back to our sources, the nearer we will be to each other, without ceasing to be intensely ourselves ... I am expecting men who will arise, fully attentive to silence, and ready at the zero hour of humanity."

Truths revealed in silence: the answer to the lies and unreality on which so much of warped human society is based - "the inhuman power of the lie", as Pasternak calls it - not only in the Russia which he depicts, but also in the constant "pressure to co-operate with small lies" in the West. Solzhenitsyn proclaims the same message of silence:

"His inner self demanded silent contemplation, free of external sounds, conversations, thought of work, free of everything that made him a doctor. Particularly after the death of his wife, inner consciousness had seemed to crave a pure transparency. It was just this sort of silent immobility, without planned or even floating thoughts, which gave him a sense of purity and fulfilment. At such moments an image of the whole meaning of existence ... was conjured up in his mind..."

We are reminded of Alphonse Gratry's advice to set aside time in quiet each morning, and - vanquishing "the inner talkativeness of empty thoughts, of restless desires and entrenched prejudices" - to take pen and "write for God and yourself ... When the soul meditates quietly and hears something from God, peace and joy flood in."

For Frank Buchman the silent time after waking, when he gave his mind to "disciplined direction", was "the daily source of creative living and thinking."

> "Radio has given us a counterpart. Whenever we see that instrument, we know that if we tune in, we shall find a response. But many who ought to know better still fail to listen. They must follow their egocentric way still further, continue to talk, talk, talk, rather than learn the great compelling truth, the great symphony that comes to us when we listen."

Beyond a strategy in which we may personally participate there is a strategy transcending our human scale. Events unexpectedly occur which can only be seen, perhaps long afterwards, as part of a vast movement in history. At the deepest crisis of the Hellenistic decadence, spiritual currents from the east renewed life and hope, and saviours, both spiritual and political, appeared.

As the millennium draws to a close we seem to be reaching "zero hour" in our civilisation - a time which could be much more shaking and more decisive than the Cuba crisis of 1962. Whenever it happens - and it may be happening NOW - a decision has to be made by a dedicated minority of the human race to bring mankind nearer to harmonious living, cherishing instead of despoiling the resources of the planet ... otherwise catastrophe will overwhelm us.

Jesus and Paul shared a prophetic vision of a crisis which would be one of extreme intensity. We share in that vision of "the Prince of this world" and the powers of darkness - as exemplified by Nazism - not giving up easily their plans to pervert or annihilate God's creation. There was an "hour" of darkness which Satan had in his power, as Jesus said at the time of his crucifixion, but that power, his disciples believed, received a shattering blow with his resurrection. For them a new reality came into the phrase "thy kingdom come", for this old Hebrew prayer which Jesus incorporated into the one given to his disciples was experienced by them in their own lives. For them, and for all those in succeeding generations who shared this experience, reality came by way of those other words of the Master, "the kingdom of heaven is within you" and "among you".

Christianity triumphed over its rivals because of the quality of commitment, the endurance under difficulties and persecutions of at least a sizeable number of its adherents. Not all Christians refused to make the symbolical offering in front of the Emperor's statue (many conformed to the Government's test and were given a certificate to this effect), but those who stood out on principle, who would not compromise with evil as they saw it, were prepared to suffer martyrdom. This was not death necessarily, or not immediately. Like present-day dissidents they would face the equivalent of the gulag, working in salt-mines in the harshest conditions. They might be maimed in one leg and blinded in one eye to reduce the possibilities of escape. The sheer cold courage and conviction when faced by such a fate are beyond assessment - as they have been again in the case of the martyrs of the modern age.

In a period of confusion, disorientation, alienation, plagues, epidemics, and conflicts of class, nation and race, there is a desire for salvation. So it is today, and so it was during the ancient world's Age of Anxiety. As with early Christianity, a strong appeal is made when its rigorous moral content is stressed, answering the need of many for guidelines for a sound and fulfilling life.

In today's world this applies in a dimension which transcends the boundaries of race and creed (as William Blake perceived 200 years ago):

> For Mercy, Pity, Peace, and Love,
> Is God our Father dear;
> And Mercy, Pity, Peace, and Love,
> Is man, His child and care...
>
> And all must love the human form,
> In heathen, Turk, or Jew;
> Where Mercy, Love, and Pity dwell,
> There God is dwelling too.

Today the reinforcement of the spiritual upsurge is coming from Russia and Central Europe, where the blood of the martyrs and the sufferings of the Churches have produced a new generation of militant, self-sacrificing Christians. One of the unexpected events of history has been the election of a Polish Pope - a Pope who may be the forerunner of leaders from the East, ready to join with others from the West and with all those from every land who have stood out against egotism, lustfulness, and the competitive pursuit of power and money.

The decline of great empires and impressive systems heralds the rise of new cultures, a fresh blossoming of the human spirit. A superficial view over the shifting landmarks of our day will not reward the observer. Only those of fine perception could see in Roman times the growth of a new spirit which could revolutionise the world. In ancient days the issues were not so clear, but we have the lessons of history before us: we have eyes to see and an urgent choice to make. Are we to be among the last generations of a twilight age, or the pioneers of a society such as the world has never seen?

Comment: The Cuba crisis; André Chouraqui; response of the younger generation; author's experience. (p. 305)

EPILOGUE

Extracts from the play *Procès à Jérusalem* by André Chouraqui.

The Rabbi: It is scandalous to see a Jewish author, above all a Jew of Jerusalem, make a stage-play of the Passion of Christ. It would be better to take on something else, for example to explain to us why the Christians have for two thousand years crucified *us* ...

A Muslim: Our holy Prophet Mohammed, in setting the seal on prophecy, has surpassed the teachings of the prophets and Christ, who is, for us, if not the Son of God, at least a prophet ....

The Clergyman: Don't you think it's our disputes, our quarrels, which crucify Jesus Christ, the Son of God? He didn't even ask us to be Christians, but like Moses with the Jews, to do God's will and be examples of righteousness, peace and love ...

The long-haired Young Man: It is your quarrels which are really the cause of the crucifixion of Man and of God. You make out that you are saving the world ... Four millennia after Abraham, three thousand years after David, two thousand years after Christ, thirteen centuries after Mohammed, what have you saved? Whited sepulchres - you have been preoccupied with your quarrels and your ambitions in the guise of religion, more than in saving the world, a world threatened by the nuclear apocalypse or just as surely by slow death from our endless pollutings.

It is due to your faults, your crimes and your failures that God is the real loser in history. The world will be lost unless new men take on becoming real examples of Love. Jews, Christians, Muslims, unite around your sources! Listen, listen to the message of righteousness, peace and love which contains the essence of the appeals sent forth from Jerusalem by your prophets and apostles. Become in truth saviours of a world which is hurtling to destruction, and take Man down from all the crosses of the world.

(Les Éditions du Cerf, Paris 1980, 239, 242-4).

COMMENTARY AND NOTES

Introduction. Regarding what appears to be a profound change taking place in civilisation, Fritjof Capra in *The Turning Point* (London 1983, pp. 7, 14, 15) writes of "social indicators" in periods of cultural transformation: "a sense of alienation and an increase of mental illness, violent crime and social disruption, as well as an increase of interest in religious cultism." He cites Pitrim Sorokin and Lewis Mumford, the latter to the effect that there may have been only half a dozen such periods in the history of the West, preceded by mankind's invention of agriculture, among them the rise of Christianity at the fall of the Roman Empire, and the Scientific Revolution of the 16th and 17th centuries. Capra continues: "It is a transition of planetary dimensions. As individuals, as a society, as a civilisation, and as a planetary ecosystem, we are reaching the turning-point....A thorough change in the mentality of Western culture must be accompanied by a profound modification of most social relationships and forms of social organisation."

Ch.1 (1) Bosanquet represented those people of the 19th century whose staple in education had been Greek and Latin literature, Greek philosophy, and the history of Greece (especially 6th and 5th centuries) and of Rome (especially the last two centuries BC and the first century AD). Such people were in agreement that for the Greeks the period 530-430 BC was the epoch "of the highest possible beauty and value" (Frank M. Turner: *The Greek Heritage in Victorian Britain* (Yale 1981), 29, quoting Matthew Arnold in *Pagan and Medieval Religious Sentiment* (1864).) It was idealised as setting a standard for human achievement and culture. "Their selectivity did not allow them to see it whole....Their Hellenism almost denied the existence of the non-rational, aggressive, self-destructive impulses in humankind." (Turner, 35-6).

This "moral and normative use of the past as a guide to the human condition in the present" (Turner, 15) - as providing a standpoint for viewing the present - was a typical Victorian approach. It was a medium for writing tracts of the times. Turner's section on Matthew Arnold clearly illustrates this point. "Arnold's Hebrews were not Jews but rather contemporary English Protestant Nonconformists. His Greeks were not Hellenes but a version of humanity largely conjured up in the late 18th century German literary and aesthetic imagination ... Arnold's exploration of Hellenism in *Culture and Anarchy* must be regarded as a statement of radical Victorian humanism." (Turner, 21, 29).

Decadence increasingly preoccupied Classical scholars - "the menacing sense of decadence that invaded the public mood towards the close of the century." (Richard Jenkyns: *The Victorians and Ancient Greece* (Oxford 1980, 334)) "Many Victorians, conscious of living in a secondary era, felt they had more in common with "later" periods of antiquity, when culture had passed its acme ... In an atmosphere of apocalyptic jingoism the analogy with Rome acquired a new force: there too had been the braggart architecture, the vast wealth, the decay of morality and religion, the puzzling mixture of decadence and majesty." (Jenkyns, 293, 335).

Jenkyns makes a useful clarification of the word "decadence": "...an ambivalent word: though it often carries connotation of moral depravity, it can be used in a purely descriptive sense to describe a culture that has passed its zenith." (p. 295)

Ch. 1(2): T.H. Green. Professor Turner in *The Greek Heritage in Victorian Britain* (op.cit., 359-364) depicts Green as a lapsed Christian whose faith had "dissolved", classing him with Bosanquet and "many other late Victorian intellectuals who had abandoned the Christian faith." The effect of his attempt to help others to find alternative values to those of Christianity was to "demean the Christian faith".

This is erroneous, the error arising from a misunderstanding of Green's view of the relation of Plato's and Aristotle's philosophy to Christian values. Far from demeaning these values or the faith from which they were derived, Green puts them in a context which is a progression from that in which the Greek philosophers formulated their truths about "the good" - "there are senses", he says, "in which a higher moral standard is possible for the Christian citizen than was possible for the Greek of Aristotle's age." (*Prolegomena to Ethics* (Oxford 1883), p.273) But the formulation itself is as valid for the Christian now as it was for the ancient Greek: that virtue lies "in the conscious direction of the will to the human good", and that "only so far as we are members of a society, of which we can conceive the common good as our own", (p.201) can we be moved to devote our efforts towards it. This "purity of heart" of "disinterested interest in the good" (p.271) is a recognition that the reward of a good act is in the action itself, and makes "a strong contrast with the appeal to semi-sensual motives that has been common, and perhaps necessary for practical effect, in the Christian Church". (p.271)

At the same time his attitude to the Church was not derogatory - far from it. "The Church", he said, is "the witness of Christ in another than the conventional sense: not as the depository of a dogma reflecting but faintly that original intuition of the crucified and risen One, in the light of which the blind Saul saw the barrier between Jew and gentile, between man and God, disappear; but as the slowly articulated expression of the crucified and risen life." (*The Witness of God and Faith* (Oxford 1883), 18).

As in the case of any profound thinker on these matters, Green's conclusions were based on his experience, and it is clear from his writings, especially the two "lay sermons" which he gave to the Balliol undergraduates in his capacity of College Tutor, "The Witness of God" and "Faith", that his experience was such as to give him a deep understanding of St. Paul's conversion on the Damascus Road. With such understanding and consequent commitment, any dependence on the historical record or the need for asserting belief in specific events became otiose. His aim was, as Arnold Toynbee (uncle of the historian) said in the introduction to these sermons, "to establish in them an intellectual position for the Christian faith which should not be called in question by every advance in historical evidence and in physical science." (vi) This aim was the more necessary at a time when the critical approach to New Testament study initiated by David Strauss and others was threatening to demolish faith along with much of the historical basis for it.

Ch.2 (1) The Classical world and the West. Comparisons between events of Greek and Roman history and of modern Europe have often been made, for instance between 19th century Europe, particularly Britain, and the Roman Empire. Gilbert Murray, the leading Oxford Hellenist in the first half of the 20th century, compared Germany to Sparta and Britain to Athens, as the first World War was ending - though he rounded off his analogy with the warning that "such parallels must only be allowed to amuse our reflections, not to distort our judgements." (Gilbert Murray: *Essays and Addresses* (London 1921), 33) I am indebted for this reference to R. Jenkyns (op.cit. 336).

Ch.2 (1) Rome's wars with Persia: After Alexander's death the territories of the former Persian Empire became part of the Seleucid successor states. They became reconstituted as Parthia in 250 BC, which in 224 AD was overthrown by Ardeshir I, who founded the neo-Persian Empire (Sassanid).

Ch.2 (1) America's hegemony was at its strongest in the period immediately following World War II, but there was hesitancy and lack of clarity in American policy. Roosevelt's initiative in laying the ground-work for the United Nations, through which America might exercise leadership, was following Woodrow Wilson's example with the League of Nations (though that had been repudiated by Congress). Beyond this, American involvement in China and Japan made clear the necessity of leadership in the Far East, but in Europe, particularly Central and Eastern Europe, America "consistently refused" (in the words of George Kennan) to make clear her "interests and wishes ... We have refused to name any limit for Russian expansion and Russian responsibilities." (Kennan to Bohlen 3/2/45, quoted by W.W. Rostow: *The Division of Europe after World War II* (University of Texas 1982), 38)

When the Control Council was set up to administer the occupied territories in Europe, the American position "incorporated no clear positive concept of Europe or of the American interest in its structure." (Rostow, 26) Any testing of Soviet intentions, or of confronting them, was hamstrung by Roosevelt's declaration at Yalta that the United States would not keep a large army in Europe, and that its forces would withdraw from Germany within two years.

There were, it is true, men in the Foreign Service who believed that adequately to test Soviet intentions a different stance was needed than "the defensive, uncertain, questioning posture of 1946." (Rostow, 68) Yet, during the period 1944-7, when there was still a fluid situation in Central Europe with large anti-Soviet majorities in elections in Poland and Czechoslovakia, facing the Soviets down, as Truman faced them over their occupation of Azerbaijan in 1946,might well have arrested the Soviet advance, and might even have made a united, if neutralised, Germany a practical possibility. By failing to test adequately Soviet intentions or to confront them, the boundaries of America's hegemony in Europe, determined by Russia's imposition of its "iron curtain", had to be more narrowly drawn than would otherwise have been the case.

With the Truman "Doctrine" (1947) a stand was indeed taken against the extension of the rival imperium of Russia, but the reinforcement of the Doctrine by Kennedy in his Inaugural was negated by his failure to overthrow Castro in the abortive invasion at the Bay of Pigs. The weakness of the American imperium was demonstrated by the necessity the U.S.A. was under of tolerating a client of its rival in its own "backyard".

In Asia similar difficulties arose through the failure in the early stages of the Vietnam war to maintain a clear-cut policy - "it was usually muddled and invariably indecisive." (Paul Johnson: *A History of the Modern World* (London 1983), 631). After the French defeat, the American refusal to endorse the Geneva settlement was compounded by Kennedy's authorisation of the anti-Diem coup. The U.S.A. became increasingly involved, starting with the bombing of the North in February 1965 - "a weak compromise, absolutely characteristic of the irresolution which dogged American policy throughout the tragedy." (Johnson, 632) American involvement increased until nearly half a million troops were committed, while the tonnage of bombs dropped was nearly half as large again as the total dropped on Europe, Africa and Asia in World War II. By the time 900 planes were lost and 30,000 Americans killed, it was decided to run the whole costly operation down, but by then inflation had hit the dollar.

This was in spite of the fact that although her military strength apparently declined relative to Russia's, post-war America was in a class of her own, having amassed three-quarters of the world's gold and huge amounts of foreign exchange. Part of her aim in encouraging other people to liquidate their empires was to open the world's markets to the full blast of American competition. In putting pressure on Britain to end her "imperial preference" system she was only following in Britain's footsteps when, as the dominant economic power of a century before, Britain had imposed a regime of free trade in all the markets where she had the power.

America's insistence on making the £ and other currencies convertible into dollars shortly after the World War ended, provoked a serious hitch in restarting the world's economy, since other countries soon ran out of dollars. But this was rectified by Marshall Aid (see Commentary for Ch. 8), and the dramatic increase of prosperity in which most countries of "the free world" shared during the fifties and sixties was a triumph of the American hegemony. But just as World War I destroyed the efficient but delicately balanced economic system of the previous decades, so another war, that between America and Vietnam, destroyed the post-World War II system. Even without the effects of that war, the American trade balance was being cut by the increasing competitiveness of imports from Europe (especially Germany), Japan, and other countries of the Pacific area. The Government failed to finance the war by adequately increasing taxes or cutting back on its "Great Society" programmes.

Johnson, following Kennedy, had adopted his anti-poverty programme, and set his sights on the goal of a "Great Society" characterised by "abundance and liberty for all, by an end to poverty and racial injustice." (A.L. Hamby: *The Imperial Years: The United States 1939* (London and New York 1976), 304) A massive federal programme was initiated, "the most ambitious example of welfare liberalism to clear Congress since the New Deal" - Medicare, the Housing Act, raising social security benefits, an aid bill for higher education. But Congress was against higher taxes, either for financing this programme, or for paying for the war.

With consequent massive overspending, along with falling productivity and increasing competition, America's trade went into deficit for the first time since the 19th century. Unable to finance this deficit indefinitely out of its diminishing gold reserves, it by-passed the system which it had itself set up (operated by the International Monetary Fund) for defining new parities, and suspended the convertibility of the dollar into gold (August 1971).

Scrapping what was left of the post-war Bretton Woods system meant that the U.S.A. was abandoning its obligation to maintain orderly arrangements for devaluing (or re-valuing) currencies, so that sterling and other currencies were obliged to float, as was eventually the dollar itself, thereby initiating a chaotic period on the international exchanges. This did not affect the American economy too adversely, since it was so strong, while the dollar's value was maintained at a fairly stable level by being the major reserve-currency for many countries. But the "rather brutal, unilateral way" in which the Government made its decisions showed up an America "shorn this time of even the pretence that it was acting in the interests of the world community as a whole." (Edward Mortimer: *Roosevelt's Children* (London 1987), 177).

Cutting the link with gold meant the end of America's control of the world monetary system - "the supervisory role of Washington collapsed." (Johnson 664) "The dream of a Great Society was in shreds." The Vietnam War worsened "every social strain in American life." (Hamby 322) "The American century seemed to have ended only 25 years after it had begun." (Johnson 672)

Further details about the decline of the American hegemony are to be found in Paul Kennedy: *The Rise and Fall of the Great Powers* (London 1988). The "overstretch" experienced by empires at a certain stage afflicted America particularly acutely because of "the plethora of fixed and entangling alliances with other sovereign countries", (359) which she assumed after World War II, while it became increasingly difficult to maintain military power relative to the USSR owing to the rocketing cost of armaments, especially bombers and battleships (442-3) along with falling growth in productivity from 1965 onwards. (434)

On another level America's decline is indicated by the extent of illiteracy (10% of the population), while "with his or her mind numbed with video-pulp and the new electronic folklore, the average citizen is becoming detached from reality." (Charles Bremner: "Is this, like, cultural decline?" - *The Times*, 9/9/88)

The nature of this decline is illuminated by Allan Bloom: *The Closing of the American Mind* (Harmondsworth 1988). He points to the decay of the university as the key area when it comes to decadence. America's great moment came with saving the world in the Second World War - its universities reached their highest point of development in the forties and fifties, with the accession of some of the best academics from Europe who were refugees from Hitler. And within universities the key faculty is Humanities, where Philosophy is taught, and whence it should spill over and fertilise other faculties. Philosophy (subsuming Theology, the medieval queen of academia) must hold this position because it enables people "to participate in essential being", (380) taking them to a vantage point such as is supplied by studying Ancient Greece (Homer and particularly Plato), from which they can momentarily forget, and then enhance their "accidental lives". (380)

The decline of Philosophy in the universities can be dated to the mid-sixties. By then the rot was setting in for other reasons as well, notably the decay of religion, an outcome of the decline of the family. "Attending church or synagogue, praying at the table, were a way of life, inseparable from the moral education that was supposed to be the family's special responsibility in this democracy ... The things one was supposed to do ... were all incarnated in the Bible stories." But now "the dreariness of the family's spiritual landscape passes belief ... Children are raised, not educated." (57) The Bible provided "a vision of the order of the whole of things, as well as the key to the rest of Western art [and] access to the seriousness of books. With its gradual and inevitable disappearance, the ... necessity of world-explanation is disappearing." (58)

Science, having separated itself from Philosophy, marches on, producing ever more modern miracles, among them T/V and the pill. "Parents can no longer control the atmosphere of the home and have even lost the will to do so. With great subtlety and energy, television enters not only the room, but also the tastes of old and young alike, appealing to the immediately pleasant and subverting whatever does not conform to it." (59) And with radio and T/V and the now inevitable Walkman, rock music has come to dominate the lives of the young, with its "one appeal only, a barbaric appeal, to sexual desire - not to love, not *eros*, but sexual desire undeveloped and untutored ... An enormous industry cultivates the taste for the orgiastic state of feeling connected with sex ... The words implicitly and explicitly describe bodily acts that satisfy sexual desire and treat them as its only natural and routine culmination for children who do not yet have the slightest imagination of love, marriage or family. This has a much more powerful effect than does pornography on youngsters," (73, 74) who are emboldened to do such acts by the easy availability of pills, condoms and abortion.

If parental authority attempts to intervene, rebellion results. "Selfishness becomes indignation and then transforms itself into morality. The sexual revolution must overthrow all the forces of domination, the enemies of nature and happiness. From love comes hate, masquerading as social reform ... (74) Of all the experiences of the soul [indignation] is the most inimical to reason and hence to the university." (327) The student rebellions of the sixties were the outcome, abetted by trendy faculty members, when the authorities, yielding to violence, threats and sit-ins, introduced new subjects or remoulded old ones to satisfy the protagonists of anti-racism, anti-elitism, anti-sexism and feminism. "Unlike other revolutionary movements, which tended to be austere and chaste - beginning with the first revolution, 1688, in England, which was really puritan - this one was antipuritanical. The slogan was 'Make love, not war.' Although the similarity of language was exploited, this is very different from 'Love thy neighbor,' which is an injunction very difficult to fulfill. 'To make love' is a bodily act, very easy to perform ... The practices of the late Roman Empire were promoted with the moral fervor of early Christianity and the political idealism of Robespierre ... The students ... were able to live as they pleased in the university, as *in loco parentis* responsibilities were abandoned; drugs became a regular part of life, with almost no interference from university authorities ...; all sexual restrictions imposed by rule or disapproval were overturned; academic requirements were relaxed in every imaginable way, and grade inflation made it difficult to flunk." (328)

Attempts to put Humpty-Dumpty together again have had scant success. The students themselves have deteriorated, and the university can give them little help. They arrive there, often semi-literate, in need of remedial treatment to make up for the inadequacies of their high school education. There is less study of languages. Interest in Europe and its heritage has dwindled, as it has in regard to their own country, "its grandeur and attendant folklore." (55)

Students may be nice but they are "flat-souled". (134) With "liberation" has come lack of passion - and commitment. "When I see a young couple who have lived together throughout their college years leave each other with a handshake and move out into life, I am struck dumb." (123) Even if marriage is undertaken it may soon end in divorce, now "normal ... America's most urgent social problem, but nobody even tries to do anything about it." The results in children, who eventually become students, is "a slight deformity of the spirit ... A large measure of their enthusiasm has been extinguished and replaced by self-protectiveness." (119, 120) The therapy they may have undergone is likely to make worse "the overturning of faith and ambiguity of loyalty that result from divorce" - they are "deafened by self-serving lies and hypocrisies expressed in psuedoscientific jargon." (121)

"Value relativism" has taken the place of absolutes. The "conventions of civilisation" have weakened. Much of the best in married relationships "has simply disintegrated." (124, 126) To restore "our exhausted culture" the "moral supplement" of philosophy is needed to draw strength from "the great remains of a tradition that have grown senile." (206, 209, 135) History too is needed, for we are "like ignorant shepherds living on a site where great civilizations once flourished. The shepherds play with the fragments that pop up to the surface, having no notion of the beautiful structures of which they were once a part ... We need history, not to tell us what happened, or to explain the past, but to make the past alive so that it can explain us and make a future possible." (239) He quotes Rousseau: "Ancient statesmen spoke endlessly of morals and virtue; ours speak only of commerce and money". (304) The study of history may help to "transform men" by "revealing another level of existence." (307, 368)

It is worth quoting Professor Bloom at length, since his comments on American civilisation and the universities can be duplicated from our experience in Europe.

Ch.2 (2) The gods and goddesses of Olympus had a close connection in the popular mind with the well-being not only of individuals but of the city, e.g. Athene with Athens. The decline of the city-state, devotion to which had been "the real religion of the fifth century", involved the decline of the Olympians. (Gilbert Murray, op.cit., 17)

The achievement of Epicurus (b. 341 BC) was, under the impulse of "the blessed Being", to bring together in bonds of affection (*philia*) communities of men and women, including slaves and hetairai - a fore-shadowing of the congregations or churches of the Christians, and like them in their early years with an attitude to marriage that was often negative. (Murray, 128-137) The Cynics (literally those living a dog's life), like Diogenes, had much in common with modern hippies. They aimed to return to nature and the simple life, to "fear nothing, desire nothing, possess nothing." (Murray, 120) Unlike many hippies, however, their purpose was not selfish, but to "bring freedom and salvation to their fellow-men." Before the monk Telemachus brought the "games" to an end by throwing himself into the arena, two Cynic philosophers had attempted the same object by the same act of self-immolation. (Murray, 117-121) There were women Cynics, a famous instance being Hipparchia, a girl of good family who turned down all her aristocratic or handsome suitors, insisting on living with the Cynic Crates, in beggar's clothes.

The further religious changes - of the 3rd century - are characterised by Murray as "the failure of nerve." E.R. Dodds puts them down to "the great social changes which followed the death of Alexander ... The loosening of the traditional political and religious bonds which had attached the citizen to his small city state, and the development of vast monarchies bureaucratically administered, left the individual with an increased sense of isolation and helplessness and forced his thoughts inward upon himself and his personal salvation." (E.R. Dodds: *The Ancient Concept of Progress* (Oxford 1973, 17)) In Murray's words "It is a rise of asceticism, of mysticism, in a sense of pessimism; a loss of self-confidence, of hope in this life and of faith in normal human effort; a despair of patient inquiry, a cry for infallible revelation; an indifference to the welfare of the state, a conversion of the soul to God." (155)

The good man no longer aims to help the society to which he belongs, "but rather, by means of a burning faith, by contempt for the world and its standards, by ecstasy and martyrdom, to be granted pardon for his unspeakable unworthiness, his immeasurable sins." (155)

Ch.2 (2) Seneca: Lucius Annaeus Seneca (4-65 AD), "the Younger" (to distinguish him from his father, a well-known rhetorician and author), though recognised as a Stoic was an independent thinker. His stress on a man's duty to himself and his neighbour encouraged Victorian writers to posit some connection between him and St. Paul, his contemporary in Rome.

Ch.3 (1) Hetairai: Dr Oswyn Murray of Balliol College, Oxford, has supplied the following information:

Hetairai were of course companions for drinking parties, owned by individuals or shared between two or three men; they were often slaves or freed slaves, and always foreigners. Their education therefore bears no relation to the education of citizen women (which in most cities, as far as we can see scarcely existed). *Hetairai* were educated, in dancing, singing, flute playing and the general arts of making themselves acceptable to men: we hear of *mesdames* who ran training schools or callgirl agencies; the most famous of these is described in Demosthenes' speech *Against Neaera* (volume 6 in the Loeb edition) - that was in Corinth, where of course ritual prostitution was part of the cult on Acrocorinth: these temple girls were used at *symposia*. In general it seems to me that the famous centres for *hetairai* were the trading cities, like Corinth, Naucratis in Egypt, or Miletus, and that it is likely that the girls from such places were better trained than from elsewhere. The training was as a result of private enterprise, and for the purpose of increasing the value and desirability of slave girls. The best source for all this is book 13 of Athenaeus: *Deipnosophistae* (volume 6 in the Loeb).

How far Aspasia was really a *hetaira* in this sense is obscure. Certainly strictly she was not a *hetaira*, but a *pallake* - that is a woman taken without the legal form of marriage, but possessing many rights as a permanent companion (including originally the right to procreate legitimate children, though not by Pericles' time - his children were by his own law illegitimate, and had to be given legitimacy by decree). It was the comic poets and her enemies who called her a *hetaira*. The stories told about her in Plutarch's life of Pericles (ch.24) are not reliable, but might suggest that she had indeed once been a professional *hetaira*, with the appropriate education. If she were a well-born citizen, it is hard to see how she could have got any education, and difficult to say what that might have been; though the Ionians were said to allow their women to live freer lives than mainland Greeks. But since the formal education of a man of Pericles' generation would have consisted of the skills suitable for the drinking party and gymnasium plus reading and writing (dancing, learning poetry and composing it, music and sport), perhaps their education would have suited each other. Intellectual pursuits are often more fun if one hasn't studied them formally, which of course the Greeks never did - or not till the fourth century.

Dr. Murray's note leads on to the information about *hetairai* in *Deipnosophistae.*

Athenaeus, a Greek (or Greek-speaking inhabitant) of Naucratis (Egypt) which produced, as he says, "famous courtesans distinguished for beauty" (Bk.XIII, 595-6 in Loeb VI, p.213), wrote *Deipnosophistae (The Sophists at Dinner* or *The Gastronomers)* around 220 AD - some six centuries after Pericles and Aspasia. His book is a kind of conversational encyclopaedia of everything connected with dining well, from menus to flute-girls, with much discursive information largely drawn from literary sources. "I have not discussed courtesans", he writes, "after the manner of Aristegoras ... I do not speak to you of flute-girls just beginning to be ripe, who have very quickly, and for a price, undermined the sailors aboard the freighters, no, I have spoken of the real 'companions', that is those who are capable of preserving strictly a friendship without trickery, ... the only women in all the world who are addressed by the title of 'friendly', or who derive their name from that Aphrodite who, among the Athenians, is called 'the Companion Aphrodite' ... she who brings companions together, male and female; that is women friends." (XIII, 571; VI, 85) "No wonder there is a shrine to [Aphrodite] the Companion everywhere, but nowhere in all Greece is there one to the Wife", says Athenaeus, quoting Philetaerus in *Playing the Corinthian.* "And Amphis in *Athamas* [says]: "Besides, is not a 'companion' more kindly than a wedded wife? Yes, far more, and with very good reason. For the wife, protected by the law, stays at home [the husband could not dismiss her without losing the dowry] in proud contempt, whereas the harlot knows that a man must be bought by her fascinations or she must go out and find another." (XIII, 558-9; VI, 21)

Ch.3 (1) Menander (340-291 BC): the most famous playwright of the Attic New Comedy.

The *Idylls* of Theocritus have been described as a "bucolic masquerade" and a literary tour-de-force - in a similar spirit of make-believe to that of Marie-Antoinette in her rural retreat at the Petit Trianon.

Ch.3 (2) Beryl Rawson, in the first article in *The Family in Ancient Rome* (which she edited - London 1986) throws light on the *familia* as more than "family" in our sense of the word, because - at least among upper-class Romans - a more apt translation might be "household", as slaves and perhaps some relatives would be included. Joint or extended families were rare. "Cicero saw the family unit as a married couple, children, a single household" (p.14, quoting *De Officiis,* 1.53).

Concubinage was frequent, perhaps because of the slave status of one partner when the relationship began - in such cases "concubinage usually worked as an enduring monogamous marriage" (the concept of adultery could be applied in connection with it). It was a relationship recognised by law. Whereas, by Augustus' legislation, members of senatorial families could not marry persons of "freed" status (manumitted slaves), they could have concubines - though not in the house while the wife was living.

Ceremonies of marriage were often observed, though they were not necessary in the "free" marriages which took the place of the older-style marriages such as conferratio, with their awesome weddings. But in these "free" marriages constraints continued, e.g. the wife continued to be under the authority of her *paterfamilias* or guardian appointed by him - though she might have a choice of guardian, or be independent in the sense of not being technically under her husband's authority (which would have been the case according to conferratio and two other forms of marriage, coemptio and usus). Legally these different forms of marriage, putting the wife under someone's potestas or tutela, affected women's rights of inheritance, and of disposing of property during their life-time or by will. Further restraints in this respect were due to the lex Voconia of 169 BC: restraints in matters of inheritance which were placed on women of the highest census. A measure which tightened up these constraints, the *Senatusconsultum Velleianum* promulgated in the early Empire, is treated in Dr. Rawson's book in an essay by J.A. Crook (pp.89 *seq*), who quotes from F. Schulz on *The Principles of Roman Law* (Oxford 1936, reprint of 1951, pp. 569, 571), that it represented "a reaction against the emancipation of women which had been achieved at the end of the Republic".

There was certainly no successful "women's lib" under Rome - Crook speaks of "the continuous and conspicuous lack of emancipation of Roman women" (p.90).

Marriage was monogamous by law, the legal age being 12 for girls, 14 for boys, with first marriages for girls usually taking place by the age of 17 (boys normally a few years later). First marriages were usually arranged. They tended not to last - divorce was frequent. Laws attempted to restrain adultery, though it may have been less common than some historians suggest. Re-marriage was also frequent. Stable unions - the conjugal family with two or three children - were regarded as normal.

Despite the web of legal constraints, and the juridically inferior position of women (based on the male view of "feeble capacity for judgement" (*Propter infirmitatem consilii*: Cicero, *Pro Murrena* 27, quoted p.85)), the home or *domus* was a situation where "many married couples saw marriage as a close relationship between husband and wife" (Rawson, p.30) ... "The concept of 'togetherness' was not altogether hollow or absent". (ibid. 29) "Though the Romans had no word for it, they drew a conceptual circle around the mother-father-children triad and made it the centre of primary obligation." (Richard P. Saller: "Familia, Domus, and the Roman Conception of the Family" in Phoenix, vol.38, Dec.1984 (Toronto), pp.336 *seq*.).

Ch.3 (2) The women's demonstration against the lex Oppia took place in 195 BC. The tribunes M. and P. Junius Brutus were blockaded in their homes to prevent them going to the Senate to veto the abrogation of the law. Two sentences in the speech of Cato ("the Censor") in the Senate, as reported by himself, give the line of the hard-core opponents to this mildly feminist move: "Woman is a violent and uncontrolled animal, and it is no good giving her the reins and expecting her not to kick over the traces...What they want is complete freedom - or, not to mince words, complete licence." (Balsdon's translation from Livy 34, 2-4 in *Roman Women* (op.cit.), 34)

Ch.4 (1) Compulsive viewing of the games is powerfully described by St. Augustine in Book VI, 7, 8 of *The Confessions*, when dealing with the addiction of his friend Alypius - his "madness for gladiatorial shows" - especially how he fell a second time into the habit after once giving it up, and was finally cured of it by his conversion at the same time as Augustine's (Book VII, 12).

Ch.4 (1) The lex Clodia and "bread and circuses": C.S. Loch (my grandfather and Bosanquet's Balliol friend - see Introduction) comments on the lex Clodia in his article on "Charity and Charities" in the *Encyclopaedia Britannica* (supplementary volume 1902, reprinted 1910, also published separately as *Charity and Social Life* (London 1910)): "There could hardly be a more effective method of degrading his [the citizen's] manhood and denaturalising his family. The recipient of this dole was also a voter, and the alms appealed to his weakness and indolence; and the fear of displeasing him and losing his vote kept him socially master of the situation, to his own ruin."

This typically translates into late Victorian terms a situation which differed considerably from the incipient welfare state of modern times against which Loch was taking up arms (on the ground that charity, and specifically the work of the Charity Organisation Society of which he was in charge from 1875 to 1914, should not alleviate poverty at the cost of undermining the character and motives of self-help among the recipients, but should rather strengthen them).

"Not that the Roman corn dole was a welfare system at all in the strict sense. It was not available for all the population ... That notorious idle mob of layabouts sponging off the state is little more than a figment of middle-class prejudice, ancient and modern alike ... What had his vote ever really meant to the ordinary citizen of Rome? If he got a chance to use it at all, it gave him not more than a choice between rival members of the oligarchic faction, which was the only sort of government Republican Rome had ever known." (Alan Cameron: *Bread and Circuses: the Roman Emperor and his People* (London 1973), 3, 4)

It was irrelevant who in imperial times was Praetor or Consul - the Emperor alone counted - "a more accessible and a more responsive patron than ever the Consul or Praetor had proved ... Both halves of Juvenal's antithesis - the past power and present unimportance of the people - were false", because during the Empire they could make their views heard by way of demonstrations at the games and theatre performances. (ibid. 4)

In other words a form of democracy, albeit crude and by no means fully representative, had taken over from the oligarchic system of the Republic. The Emperor, regularly appearing at the games and theatre, treated these occasions like popular assemblies, receiving protests and complaints whether in the form of petitions or in allusive songs and mimes, and notifying changes of policy (even demonstrating such changes, as when Anastasius at Constantinople, "not content with just abolishing an unpopular tax, had all the relevant files burned in the Hippodrome"). (ibid. 9)

While theatre and games provided rough-and-ready opinion polls and a forum for stating government policy, the organisation of the dole had the advantage of ensuring supplies of food for the capital - as long as the system worked. A similar system of "bread and circuses" at Constantinople was modelled on that of Rome, and also appeared in various provincial cities. This system of popular democracy (not to be confused with that of modern totalitarian regimes) developed during the period of decadence, from another system, ostensibly democratic with votes, which had itself become decadent, and which, after serving the aims of the ruling oligarchy, lost the interest even of those who still officially had the right to vote, since they found a better patron in the Emperor.

In the Byzantine period another element came into the circus as the "backdrop against which the emperor could act out in due pomp his role as divine ruler, victor in war, champion of his people, and provider of peace, plenty and games". (ibid. 11) With the organisation of the rival factions of "Blues" and "Greens" there was a further systematisation of the people's "relationship with its rulers, equally compounded of parasitism and riot." (ibid. 1, quoting E. Hobsbawm's description of some Italian cities in the 18th and early 19th centuries, in *Primitive Rebels* (1973)).

Ch. 4 (1) Livy: Titus Livius (59 BC - 17 AD). Balsdon's translation (see reference) is a free one. Juvenal: Decimus Junius Juvenalis (55 - 140 AD approx.).

Aristophanes: "Next to war with other Greek states, Aristophanes hated what he considered decadence. He saw his country threatened with material ruin by materialism, with moral decline by the new trends in thought and literature." - F.L. Lucas: *Greek Drama for Everyman* (London 1954), 368.

Menippus (3rd cent. BC) of the Greek colony of Gadara in northern Syria. None of his satires have survived, except some citations.

Petronius, surnamed Arbiter from his identification with Caius Petronius, "arbiter elegantiae" at the court of Nero, and eventually his victim (65 AD).

The concept of "togetherness" owed much to the Stoics who, like Musonius, believed in the duty of marriage particularly in order to propagate. Since love-making was prescribed only for this purpose another basis had to be found for a relationship lasting beyond the child-bearing age of the wife, and that was friendship, a durable affection. That mutual help and life-long companionship were objectives of marriage, though suggested by Aristotle, was not a commonplace in the Greco-Roman world. "The ideal of tenderness between spouses was, since Homer, always added to the strict matrimonial obligation ... [But] a merit is not a duty ... Affectionate mutual understanding is extolled when it is recorded, but it is not represented as a norm which is presupposed for the institution." (Paul Veyne: "Les noces du couple romain" in *L'Histoire*, no 63, Jan. 1984, 47 seq.)

Pliny the Younger (b. 62 AD), to be distinguished from his uncle, the Elder, who adopted him after his father's death, and was himself a well-known author. The date of his death is uncertain.

None of Calpurnia's letters to Pliny are extant, and in fact no authentic letters from women were known to exist (a famous one, for instance, from Cornelia, mother of the Gracchi, to her son Gaius, claimed to be "the earliest extant prose-writing in *any* language by a woman", has been much altered in the transcription by Cornelius Nepos, as was the way of all Classical historians when they were quoting) - until the recent discovery among the writing-tablets unearthed at Vindolanda (Hadrian's Wall) of an invitation by one army officer's wife to another, to come to her birthday party; an affectionate postscript is written in her own hand. (Journal of Roman Studies, vol. 76, 1986: A.K. Bowman and J.D. Thomas: "Vindolanda 1985: the New Writing-Tablets", pp 120 seq. See also A.K. Bowman: *The Roman Writing Tablets from Vindolanda* (London 1983)).

L. Friedländer *Roman Life and Manners under the Early Empire* (tr. L. Magnus, London 1913) comments on the custom of women eating with men, apparently more usual in Rome than it had been in Greece: "The old custom of women sitting at table had ceased ...; they lay down, like men. In the old days this would have been indecent." (p.248) Upper class women had their own kind of club or assembly, conventus matronarum, an ancient guild of religious origin (p.239).

Decius Magnus Ausonius (310-395 AD) filled high offices in the State (finally Consul of Gaul 379 AD) by virtue of having been tutor of the Emperor Gratian before his accession. Already reputed as a poet, he retired to his estate at Bordeaux, where he wrote epigrams and poems, one of the best-known being "Mosella" about the river of that name.

Ch.4 (2) Lucius Apuleius (2nd century AD) was a native of North Africa. *The Golden Ass* is basically a series of tales strung together, but there is some development of character with the conversion of the hero at the end. *Cupid and Psyche*, which is inserted in it, is like a fairy tale, where the fairies are gods and goddesses involved with mortals, but it has elements of "the ideal romance, flourishing from the first century BC if not earlier ... A stylised, artificial genre in which a highly moral love between boy and girl ultimately triumphs with divine aid over a series of bizarre obstacles set up by malevolent fortune" (P.G. Walsh: *The Roman Novel* (Cambridge 1970), 7). See also Sophie Trenkner: *The Greek Novella* in the Classical Period (Cambridge 1958). The romantic novel continued to develop during the decline of the Roman Empire in response to the "new spiritual and intellectual needs that have arisen in a large part of society" (B.E. Perry: *The Ancient Romances* (Los Angeles 1967), 9), rivalling the obscene Milesian and Sybaritic tales which were also popular during this period.

The Golden Ass is in Latin, though derived from a Greek work. A best-selling romance of later date, in Greek (end of 5th century), is *The Aethiopica* by Heliodorus who was perhaps a bishop (of Tricca in Thessaly), though the presentation suggests pagan authorship. It is a love-story without eroticism, typical of the Byzantine period.

Ch.4 (2) Besides the cessation of municipal gymnasia, other landmarks in the ending of the ancient culture are the closing down of the Olympic Games by Theodosius in 394 AD, and the closing of the School of Athens by Justinian in 529 AD.

Trajan's reply to Pliny about the Christians: "These people must not be hunted out; if they are brought before you and the charge against them is proved, they must be punished, but in the case of any one who denies that he is a Christian, and makes it clear that he is not by offering prayers to our gods, he is to be pardoned....But pamphlets circulated anonymously must play no part in any accusation. For that is the worst kind of precedent and is not in the spirit of our age." (Pliny: *Letters and Panegyricus* (Loeb edition, Cambridge, Mass., 1969), 201, Bk.X, 97 (last sentence varied from Loeb).

Philo Judaeus (b. about BC 15), a Hellenised Jew of Alexandria who was one of the most esteemed philosophers of his time, describes powerfully the persecution of the large Jewish community of Alexandria during the governorship of Flaccus, who took an antisemitic line to curry favour with the half-insane Emperor Gaius (Caligula). After the pogrom which resulted, Philo headed a deputation (40 AD) to Rome of the surviving senators who, as Jews, had special seats on the City Council, but the Emperor refused to give them any satisfaction. (ibid., vol.9: *In Flaccum*; vol.10: De Legatione - the Latin titles are misleading, in that Philo wrote in Greek).

The Romans repressed the Jewish revolts of 68-70 and 131-135 with the utmost brutality and butchery (Josephus, op.cit, 359 and passim), but gave privileges (notably freedom from conscription) to the Jews scattered throughout the Empire. Before Christians were heard of, Jews had already suffered by refusing the Emperor divine honours: in consequence of this in the time of Caligula (38 AD) the pogrom in Alexandria took place. But when Decius ordered sacrifice to the gods (248 AD), the Jews were exempted whereas Christians were persecuted. With Constantine and the accession to power of the Church the position of the Jews (a "deadly sect") worsened. A kind of apartheid, already imposed in Eygpt since the time of Augustus, prohibiting marriage between Romans, Greeks and Egyptians, was repeated in the case of Christians and Jews. (Lane Fox, op.cit., 344, 671)

To what extent were martyrs "the seed of the Church"? Their appeal and that of other Christians are treated by R. Lane Fox. He asserts that martyrs "were not very prolific" (441) - the Church's greatest expansion followed Constantine's conversion, "which owed nothing to martyrs' examples." But commenting on the sermons of the martyr Pionius (250 AD) given when in prison, he says "we can well imagine their impact: like other Christian prisoners, the Elder used his martyrdom to make an alarming case for his faith." (473) Compromise, "by offering incense in front of the Emperor's statue, handing over scriptures, abjuring faith, or eating meat sacrificed to idols, invalidated the essence of the faith, because behind every martyrdom ... lay the self-sacrifice of Jesus himself."

The appeal of Christians and their faith was as much, if not more, through their ethical stance which differentiated them from their pagan neighbours: "the idea of 'doing unto others as you would wish them to do unto you' was not foreign to pagan ethics, but there was no precedent for the further Christian advice 'to love one's enemies'". Unlike pagans, who distributed largesse first to those of their own class, women being last to receive anything, Christians gave equally to all in need - their "'charity' differed in range and motive from pagan 'philanthropy'". (323) Besides their readiness to help plague victims they would ransom captives from the invaders. In the age when the sense of community in the City was breaking down and the law discriminated against the "more humble" citizens, new community was found with fellow-Christians in the local church and in its "world-wide" assembly (*ecclesia*). "All were equal ... In church meetings educated people had to sit as equals among other men's slaves and petty artisans." Women had a noticeably large part, especially in the Church's charitable activities.

The certainty of Christians regarding their faith in an age of uncertainty could be catching: "their God was a God of history, proven in events; above all, he had sent a Son, to redeem men by actions of total selflessness" (261) - the whole idea of redemption being new to all except Jews.

Although there was much falling-away from the high standards of the faith as the years went by, the rigorous training of the first century long continued. Three years "apprenticeship" was the time generally allotted to neophytes, during which their conduct was scrutinised, baptism being eventually given after several final weeks of teaching, exorcism, fasting and confession. Any subsequent lapses incurred banning from Communion, vigils in sackcloth, grovelling and pleading for the brethen's prayers, and confession (sometimes in public). (337-8)

Ch.4 (3) "Federates" (Latin *foederati*): allies by treaty. The Visigoths were neither supplied with proper food nor permitted by the authorities to buy provisions at the ordinary markets. Two campaigns took place, the first resulting in the defeat of the Romans at Marcianopolis (376 AD), the second at Adrianople in August 378. (Gibbon, op.cit., ch.26)

Ammianus Marcellinus (approx. 330-390 AD) was born in Antioch, Syria, of Greek parents, but wrote in Latin. Served in the army on campaigns in Gaul, Germany and the East, before settling in Rome to write his *History of the Roman Empire*. Of this, 18 books are extant covering 353-378 AD - a period during which he had participated in some of the events described.

Katyn refers to the place near Smolensk where in 1943 4,500 corpses of shot Polish officers were discovered. Several thousand Polish officers, who had sought refuge or been captured by the Russians during their occupation of Poland in 1939, had disappeared, apparently because they were an embarrassment to the Russians in their retreat before the Germans in 1941. The Roman authorities similarly "liquidated" a large number of young Goths who had been despatched (in effect as hostages) to various localities in the Empire as part of the agreement permitting the Visigoths to settle south of the Danube frontier in Thrace.

Vandals overwhelmed Spain, then commandeered a fleet to conquer North Africa (430 AD).

Ch.4 (3) What was Constantine converted to? There is his famous vision, at some point before the Battle of the Milvian Bridge (though the account of Lactantius that it was on the night before seems to be erroneous), and in consequence his ordering his troops to paint the sign (*labarum*) incorporating the Cross on their shields. He had evidently had a special feeling for the Sun God, and seems (in the early stages of his conversion at least) to have equated the Christian God with the Sun God. "God", however he may have actually viewed him, became the God who enabled him to win his battles: he devised a prayer for the soldiers which did not specify the God they were addressing (he never lost a battle). In any case, from 312 he identified himself fully with the Christians, and - in addition to endeavouring to secure the Church's unity - showed astounding munificence in charitable giving and the building of churches, besides giving a privileged position to clergy (relieving them, among other things, of the burdens which fell on decurions), and incorporating episcopal courts in the judicial system, as a relatively speedy and bribe-free way of obtaining justice. His regime was one of tolerance. For some years he continued to subsidise pagan cults. He believed there should be one God, one ruler, and so aimed at a consensus being established regarding the One God. "To Christians this God could be Christ, to pagans something less definite." (H.A. Drake: *In Praise of Constantine* (California 1976), 66) His prayer (Eusebius, op. cit., 11, 56) was: "Let those who still delight in error participate in peace and tranquillity to the same degree as those who believe. For the revival of fellowship is for all, and may suffice to lead them into the straight path. Let no one disturb anyone else, let each do as his spirit bids him....For the others...we pray that they too may gain joy through common concord (*homonoia*)." (R. MacMullen: *Constantine* (London 1969), 165) This tolerant approach is very different from

Diocletian's persecution of Manichees as well as Christians in the interests of a pagan orthodoxy as the mystique for a virtually totalitarian state. (MacMullen, 22-23).

Anastasius I (491-518), though one of the most efficient emperors, scores only a few lines in Gibbon (ch.39). An elderly Palace official, he was raised to the purple by the widow of Emperor Zeno (she married him). He strengthened the defences of Constantinople; ended a pointless war with Persia; dealt firmly with Church quarrels, deposing patriarchs and suppressing consequent military revolts; abolished wild beast fights and the mime-theatre (though the latter re-started later); by careful administration and attention to detail rehabilitated the Empire financially, leaving 320,000 lb. of gold in the Treasury, while abolishing taxes which bore heavily on humble craftsmen and merchants and relieving poor peasants with large families by reducing the land-tax, and remitting tax for poor harvest or war-ravages; he also provided funds for the destitute. (A.H.M. Jones (op.cit.), I, 230-237). The figure for the gold reserves given by the authorities is an exaggeration: it means "a large amount".

Florentius: Praetorian Prefect of the East (held this high office for two periods between 428 and 439 AD). (Jones, I, 351)
The "girlfriend" reference (Lane Fox, 669) is to St. Augustine's *Confessions* (Bk III,3) - an episode of which the saint himself was not at all proud!

Ch 4 (3) St. Athanasius (296-373), as a young man embraced the ascetic life, often visiting St. Antony. Elected Patriarch of Alexandria in 326 AD, but was ejected or obliged to flee several times because of the hostility of the supporters of Arius to his orthodoxy as he defined it, in opposition to the Arian heresy. He spent 20 years altogether in exile. His name was given to the Athanasian Creed, although he did not compose it.

The worst faction-fighting in the reign of Justinian (527-565 AD) was actually when the Blues and Greens combined against him in the "Nika" riots of 532 in the capital and other cities. They were eventually put down by the Emperor's elite guards with a massacre in the Hippodrome of 30,000 (according to Gibbon, Ch.40, taking the figure from Procopius) of these exotically garbed, mostly young people. The element of popular democracy in theatre and circus gradually waned; by the 6th century the State had taken over the guilds of actors, athletes, etc., and was financing virtually all public entertainments; the acclamations were becoming ritualised, and the whole proceedings were eventually little more than a part of Court ceremonial. (Alan Cameron: *Circus Factions: Blues and Greens at Rome and Byzantium* (Oxford 1976), 219-20)
The same author rightly points out that divisions of opinion on theological matters were expressions of political differences and rivalries for power (as indeed all forms of ideological conflict almost invariably

are). Ambitious ecclesiastics could further their aims for gaining or maintaining power by way of a theological formula embraced either by Blues or Greens, or sometimes by mobilising monks from the desert "lauras" for street-demonstrations - tactics which the Patriarchs of Alexandria particularly favoured. This "monastic violence" (ibid., 290 seq.) detracted from the peaceful role of monastic communities as growing points of the new civilisation.

Iconoclasm: The movement to abolish image-worship in churches, and eventually the removal of images and pictures (except of Christ) was started in 726 AD by Emperor Leo II "the Isaurian", so called from his birthplace in the Taurus Mountains. The tough, predatory mountaineers of Isauria produced some of Byzantium's finest military manpower, and after the Muslim conquest of Palestine and Syria it was key to the defence of the Anatolian heartland of the Empire on its southern frontier. Leo, says Gibbon, "was ignorant of sacred and profane letters; but his education, his reason, perhaps intercourse with the Jews and Arabs, had inspired the material peasant with an hatred of images; and it was held to be the duty of a prince to impose on his subjects the dictates of his own conscience." (ch.49)

The revival of scholarship during Byzantium's "great age".
Warren T. Treadgold in "The Nature of the *Bibliotheca* of Photius" (Dumbarton Oaks 1980) is informative on the intellectual renaissance from the end of the 8th century, after the sterile period of iconoclasm - "vast progress made by the 9th century revival of learning in discovering, circulating and studying books of all kinds. (114) ... The Bibliotheca was a philological work on a much larger scale than anyone had composed for centuries ... a product of a scholarly revival that was far advanced but was to advance still farther ... a real literary innovation." (115)

Ch.4 (4)   Galla Placidia (390-450 AD), daughter of the last ruler of the undivided Empire, Theodosius, was made virtually a hostage after Alaric's occupation of Rome in 410 AD. She married Alaric's successor Athaulf (Adolf), and after his death Constantius III, who ruled the Western Empire briefly in association with Honorius. On the decease of both these emperors Galla Placidia was in effect Regent of the Western Empire 425-450, on behalf of her son Valentinian III, and was commemorated by the magnificent mausoleum at Ravenna.

Ch.5 (1) St. Augustine and marriage: notes from Peter Brown: *The Body and Society - Men, Women and Sexual Renunciation in Early Christianity* (London and Boston 1990). Augustine's views on sex and marriage were very much his own, and only partly representative of a long-established trend of thought on a subject about which "Christians had disagreed profoundly with each other since the days of St. Paul" (104). Christians like Clement of Alexandria in the 2nd century followed Plutarch, Musonius and others in the Stoic tradition, esteeming marriage and the care of children as part of a well-ordered life. Athanasius (or whoever was writing in his name) similarly presented husband and wife serving Christ together "without distraction" in accordance with "Hellenistic traditions of courtesy, generosity and marital restraint" (135, 255), while even in a treatise *On the preservation of virginity* the 4th century Basil of Ancyra (Ankara) could regard "the profound physical need for interdependence between men and women" as God-given (268).

Christian married partnership could blossom as with Paulinus and Therasia, but marriage was usually presented as estimable to the extent that the sexual drive of the partners was strictly confined and if possible eliminated. Though virginity was generally rated as the most desirable state, "Christian conjugal morality" had to be presented by moderates like Clement as a norm for human relations in opposition to the radical view of the Encratites (*enkrateia* = continence) that intercourse must be abandoned if the indwelling of the Spirit was to be experienced. (58, 92) In some circles baptism would be refused to all except celibates: "only the unmarried had a place in [Christ's] kingdom". (245)

Augustine had much in common with the Encratites, since by the 4th century the asceticism to which he aspired was "invariably associated" with perpetual chastity (202) - though with the hermits and desert-dwelling monks hunger and hardship had often been a greater challenge than eschewing marriage and family, while other than sexual lusts, such as anger, egotism, jealousy and pride had loomed largest as deadly snares. (230, 303, 421-2) By then Christianity had become, in the words of the historian Eusebius of Caesarea, a religion of "two ways of life ... the one is above nature; it admits not marriage" (these were the elite, and ideally the clergy); "the more humble, the more human way prompts men to join in pure nuptials, to produce children," and generally to undertake all kinds of secular activity. (205)

Humanity, in Augustine's view, had inherited a mode of life flawed by "the twisted will" and its accompanying uncontrolled sexual feelings which had marked Adam's fall from grace. (404) Augustine could share with his mentor Ambrose a "vision of a humanity transformed and disciplined" (304), even though this might be blurred in the day-to-day battling with the ordinary sinful humanity of his flock when he became a bishop. Marriage was a social necessity - he had to encourage couples to make it as chaste as possible, while fiercely countering Pelagius and his highly articulate disciple Julian of Eclanum in their presentation of sexual desire and delight as God-given, and "the chosen instrument of any self-respecting marriage ... blameworthy only in its excesses", which could be controlled by a proper exercise of will. (*Contra Julianum*, quoted in Brown 413).

St. Thomas Aquinas (1225-74) on marriage: The relevant passage begins with a discussion of the nature of sexual intercourse in Paradise "before sin was committed". It does not follow, says Aquinas, "in the present state", that being swayed by reason diminishes the pleasurable sensation, "but that the pleasure urge should not clutch at the pleasure in an immoderate fashion; and by 'immoderate' I mean going beyond the measure of reason. Thus a sober man has no less pleasure in food taken moderately than a greedy man; but his pleasure urge does not wallow so much in this sort of pleasure." (*Summa Theologiae*, Ia. 98, 2, from the Blackfriars edition. I am indebted to Fr. Herbert McCabe O.P. for this reference).   This passage is part of a discussion on St. Augustine's observations on marriage.

Ch.6 (1) Sidonius Apollinaris and his German neighbours. The Loeb verison of the poem from which Helen Waddell made her free translation is as follows:

> Felices oculos tuos et aures
> felicemque libet vocare nasum
> cui non allia sordidumque cepe
> ructant mane novo decem apparatus,
> quem non ut vetulum patris parentem
> nutricisque virum die nec orto
> tot tantique petunt simul Gigantes
> quot vix Alcinoi culina ferret.

'I am fain to call your eyes and ears happy, happy too your nose, for you don't have a reek of garlic and foul onions discharged upon you at early morn from ten breakfasts, and you are not invaded even before dawn, like an old grandfather or a foster-father, by a crowd of giants so big that not even the kitchen of Alcinous could support them.' (Sidonius (London and Cambridge Massachusetts 1936), I, 212, Poem XII Ad V.C. Catullinum [to Catullinus Senator]).

Ch.6 (2) Stridon's site is unknown, except that it was on or near the border between the Roman provinces of Dalmatia and Pannonia.

Ch.6 (2) Pope Leo I, the Great (440-461). His doctrinal definitions triumphed at the Council of Chalcedon (451 AD).

Ch.6 (4) St. Gregory the Great, born probably 540 AD, Pope 590-604. The following translation of Gregory's complaint to Peter the Deacon on accepting the Papacy is from Robert Bridges: *The Spirit of Man* (London 1930), no.20. The original is in Gregory's *Dialogues*.

"My unhappy soul, wounded with worldly business, is now calling to mind in what state it once was when I dwelt in my monastery; how then it was superior to all transitory matters, and how it would soar far above things corruptible: How it was accustomed to think only of heavenly things, and though enclosed in mortal body would yet by contemplation pass beyond its fleshly bars: while as for death, which is to almost all men a punishment, that did it love, and would consider as the entrance to life, and the reward of its toil. But now by reason of my pastoral charge my poor soul must engage in the business of wordly men; and after so fair a promise of rest it is defiled in the dust of earthly occupations: and when through much ministering to others it spendeth itself on outward distractions, it cannot but return impaired unto those inward and spiritual things for which it longeth."

Ch.6 (4) Maurice, a professional soldier, Emperor 582-602, was overthrown by the centurion Phocas.

Ch.6 (4) During the period of Gregory's papacy "Rome suffered a metamorphosis and became transformed into a city of cloisters. The metropolis of the universe was converted into a spiritual city, in which priests and monks bore entire sway, and built churches and convents with untiring zeal ... The gradual growth and rise of the spiritual power upon the ruins of the ancient State, under conditions the most difficult, must ever excite the wonder of mankind as one of the greatest transformations in the record of history." (Gregorovius, op.cit.II, 3)

Ch.7 (3) *Quietists:* See R.M. Jones: *Spiritual Reformers in the sixteenth and seventeenth Centuries* (London 1914). Among these reformers the author quotes *Hans Denck* (born in Bavaria 1495, died 1527), who wrote of "the inner witness ... spark of divine life breaking into his soul." A man must "keep still and listen," then "he will hear what the Spirit witnesses within him." This involves losing one's self-will - there is "no other way to blessedness." This "witness" also operates in Jews and heathens. (pp. 18-24) Another reformer quoted is *Caspar Schwenkfeld*, a noble of Silesia (1490-1561), who started by following Luther, but broke with him because he was convinced that Luther was not going deep enough with people to bring about their radical transformation, without which no fundamental change in human society was possible. Persecution by the Lutherans kept him on the move for most of his life from 1527 onwards. He believed that salvation was a moral process of transformation into an inward likeness of Christ: the soul must "receive into itself a divine and spiritual life, having its source in the Being of God and mediated to the soul by the living, inward-working flesh and blood of Jesus." His ideal was "to promote the formation of little groups of spiritual Christians", which at Augsburg and elsewhere took the form of house-groups. (pp.65-83)

   Schwenkfeld's followers called themselves "Confessors of the Glory of Christ." Most of those in Silesia fled in 1720 when a commission of Jesuits was sent to convert them to Roman Catholicism. Some of these made their way in 1734 to Philadelphia in Pennsylvania, where they were known as Schwenkfelders.

Ch.7 (3) Missions abroad were carried out with astonishing faith and courage by Quakers to America, Jerusalem, Alexandria and Adrianople (where Mary Fisher was given a public audience by Sultan Mohammed IV to expound her message).

   There is also the extraordinary story of Katherine Evans and Sarah Chevers told in C.V. Wedgwood: *Velvet Studies* (London 1946), 129 seq. "Women of character and courage, versed in the Scriptures and little else", they were aiming for Alexandria, but as their ship neared Malta they felt their work was meant to be there (1659). Courteously received by the English Consul and local nuns, they were able to "rise up and prophesy in and out of season, more especially at open windows", for 15 weeks before they were imprisoned by the Inquisition. Despite terrible treatment they maintained their morale, and, on the exhaustion of their money, paid their way by knitting stockings and darning clothes for their fellow-prisoners. It was a mystery why they were not tortured or even burnt - instead the Inquisitor tried to provide special food (which they refused). Eventually George Fox and Quakers in England asked Ludovic Stuart, Charles II's cousin and a Roman Catholic priest, to put in a word to the Pope, who ordered their release and they were repatriated.

Ch.7 (3) St. Francis de Sales and Angélique Arnauld. St. Francis was for some time her spiritual director. A number of letters from him to her are printed in his *Selected Letters* (ed. E. Stopp, op.cit.)

Ch.7 (3) St. Vincent de Paul (1576-1660). Born in Gascony, he studied at Toulouse. In his thirties he was captured by pirates in the Mediterranean and sold into slavery, but persuaded his master, a renegade Savoyard, to return to his faith and bring him to France. He became Almoner of Marguerite de Valois, Queen of Henry IV, and formed associations for visiting the sick and prisoners, especially those condemned to the galleys. He founded the Congregation of Priests of the Missons for assisting parochial clergy, centred at the Priory of St. Lazare at Paris. He established the Foundling Hospital at Paris, and the Society of Filles de la Charité, the first unenclosed order of nuns devoted to helping the sick, the poor and outcasts, along with the Order of the Congregation (or Visitation) established by Mme de Chantal with the help of St. Francis de Sales. St. Francis and St. Vincent were friends, and worked together in these undertakings.

George Whitefield (1714-70) came into the circle of the Wesley brothers and their fellow "Methodists" while he was a servitor (a poor student doing menial jobs in college in return for a reduction of fees) at Oxford. On returning from a time on mission with John Wesley in America, his powerful preachings caused him to be excluded by the lax clergy of the day from parish pulpits - so he began preaching in the open air, first to thousands of miners from the Kingswood collieries at Bristol. His voice was so strong and clear that it could reach 20,000 people. He preached over 18,000 sermons to 10m. people, but, being no organiser, all that concerned following up his mission was done by Wesley and his colleagues.

Ch.7 (3) The Moravians were descended from the Church of the Bohemian Brethren, founded in what is now Czechoslovakia in 1467. Though it spread in Central Europe and Germany, by the early 17th century it had been practically destroyed by persecution. Count Nicholas Zinzendorf

(1700-60) gave survivors of the sect parts of his estate at Herrnhut in Saxony, and helped them to reform and reorganise themselves.

Ch.7 (3) William Wilberforce (1759-1833). Concerning his circle, the following paragraphs from Viscountess Knutsford's *Life and Letters of Zachary Macaulay* (op.cit.), 271, 275, are worth adding.

"They were in the habit of either assembling at the same watering-places, during what may be ironically termed their holidays, or else of spending them at each other's country houses, taking with them as a matter of course their wives and children; and it may be remarked that they seem to have ventured upon inviting anyone they pleased to their friends' houses, and to have felt assured that persons, acceptable to themselves, would meet with a cordial reception from their host and hostesses of the entire band of allies.

"Then when the holidays were over, Henry Thornton, Thomas Babington, Macaulay, Mr. Stephen, Mr. Grant and one or two more assembled together as frequently as possible in London for the meals of breakfast and dinner. These men, who followed their own callings with an assiduity which made the world reckon them in that aspect alone as busy men, were thus able to discuss their plans for the conduct of the Abolition campaigns without retrenching the time due to their several professions, and their debates were often prolonged far into the night. They were not only occupied by the welfare of the unhappy slaves, but all kinds of charitable and benevolent schemes ... assisted by advisers ... The weight of continual business was lightened and cheered by sharing it with congenial companions; and the habits of life, thus systematically arranged, served to ensure considerable economy of time and correspondence in days when there were no district messengers, and no telegraph or telephone at the service of busy people.

"Then as the end of the week came round, the friends gathered habitually at the beautiful villas round Clapham Common for the hallowed repose of Sunday; and on these occasions the intimate circle was increased by the addition of a constant succession of companions, who supplied varied interests from the worlds of theology, literature, art, science, and politics, and in some degree served to relieve the tension of minds strained to the uttermost in a single direction ...

"It was in the praiseworthy fashion of those individuals who were characterised as the Saints or the Clapham Sect, to take a very real and keen interest in the rising generation, and to make themselves acquainted with the dispositions and tastes of each others' children."

Ch.8 (1) Paul Holbach (1723-89) was a German who early in life settled in Paris, where his house became a centre for "philosophers", including (for a time) Rousseau. He attempted to find a basis for morality in "naturalism", while condemning all religions. He was kind and benevolent: though strongly against the Jesuits, he befriended them, succouring them in his own home when they came under persecution.

Ch.8 (1) The rule of the Directory marked a stabilising or even reactionary trend in the events of the French Revolution after the enthusiasm and upheavals following the summoning of the States-General in 1789. The Directory took over power from the Committee of Public Safety after executing its leader Robespierre in 1794. Napoleon Bonaparte (1769-1821) as a young general dispersed the mob which threatened its existence (1795), and became First Consul, and Emperor in 1804.

Ch.8 (1) G.W.F. Hegel (1770-1831). During his last years (from 1818) he held the Chair of Philosophy at the University of Berlin.

Ch.8 (1) Heinrich von Treitschke (1834-96). His Prussian nationalism and antisemitism were expressed in his *History of Germany in the Nineteenth Century* (1879-94).

Ch.8 (2) J.M. Roberts in *The Triumph of the West* (op.cit.) underlines this religious element in Marxism. Marx expounded an interpretation of history in terms of the increasing freedom of man from the material factors which determined his existence: freedom in present conditions being largely an illusion, liberation would eventually be achieved through a process of history. But instead of this interpretation being accepted as a system of scientific knowledge, as Marx expected, its historical role has been "not as philosophy but as faith", based on its vision of history. It has had its successes "as an animator and inspirer of men". The outcome of history as "an apocalyptic transformation" is, in Marx's view, the work of God, since "Marx believed in a God, but called him History". Marxism is "essentially a Christian heresy", with a background of the "secularised versions of many once-Christian ideas put forward by eighteenth century philosophers." (79)

Ch.8 (2) Ludwig Feuerbach (1804-72) abandoned Hegelian philosophy for naturalistic materialism.

Ch.8 (2) Friedrich Engels (1820-95) collaborated with Marx on *The Communist Manifesto* (1848) and edited much of his *Das Kapital*, besides writing books, among them *Landmarks of Scientific Socialism* (1878) and *The Origin of the Family, Private Property and the State* (1884).

Ch.9 (2) For the Russian religious heritage see Billington: *The Icon and the Axe* (op.cit.), especially pp.47 seq. "The Muscovite Ideology."

"Nihilist" - the designation appears in Turgenev: *Fathers and Sons* (1861) applied to the student Bazarov.

Alexander Herzen (1812-70) was imprisoned in 1834 for revolutionary writings. Left Russia in 1846, eventually settling in London, where he published his review "Kolokol" (The Bell). One of the greatest influences on a generation of dissidents and revolutionaries, along with N.G. Chernyshevsky (1828-89), who made his name publishing another influential review "Sovremennik" (The Contemporary) and a book *What is to be done?*

Mikhail Bakunin (1814-76) took part in the 1848 rising in Saxony; imprisoned in Russia; escaped from Siberia (in this luckier than Chernyshevsky who served over 18 years hard labour and internal exile); then lived mostly in Italy, France and Switzerland, taking part in revolutionary movements. Joined the First International but was expelled for opposing Marx in 1872.

Lord Radstock's visit to Russia began filling a spiritual void among the upper classes which the Orthodox Church, unreformed, and in part corrupt, was unable to do. The banishing of Radstock and two of his main supporters is analogous to Alexander II's supression of the Narodniks. This attack on Radstock's work prevented it from having the kind of effect on society and government which the evangelical movement had made in England through statesmen like Wilberforce and Gladstone. It is a matter for speculation how far the Zemstvos and other constitutional developments might have been strengthened if the Populist and evangelical movements had been allowed free rein, in which case Russian history, and therefore the history of Europe and the world, might have been different.

Radstock (1833-1913), as one obituary said, "belonged to an age of famous evangelists of a social type and simple spiritual power" - in his case also with "the mind of a statesman", according to many with whom he came in touch. (Trotter: *Lord Radstock* (op.cit.), 72, 106) He declined the career and social life which his position and wealth opened to him. At Balliol under Jowett, with a degree in science as well as in law and history, inheriting his title at 22, marrying at 25 one of the reigning beauties of the aristocracy - travel in America, the opportunity of entering the Diplomatic Service - to many contemporaries he threw all this away to devote himself heart and soul to being a follower of Christ, as he understood his calling. His wife fully shared in what was practically a family enterprise, along with her sisters and his. He no doubt won some converts, though alienating others of his class by handing out tracts when riding in Rotten Row, or taking part in evangelistic campaigns at seaside resorts. But the opposition he aroused was no different from that stirred by anyone who sacrifices career and ease for the sake of challenging his contemporaries in their selfish materialism. "The example of his life pricked many consciences, while he offended the taste of others by his declaration in season and (in their view) out of season of the claims of an entire consecration of heart and life." (114)

P.G. Zaichnevsky (1842-96); S.G. Nechaev (1847-82 - died in prison); P.N. Tkachev (?1842-82 - died in lunatic asylum).

Ch.10 (1) Robert Gascoyne-Cecil, 3rd Marquess of Salisbury (1830-1903). Three times Prime Minister (Conservative).

Ch.10 (1) The Grand Alliance of most European states brought about Napoleon's defeat and abdication in 1814 and his final defeat at Waterloo in 1815. It continued as the Quadruple Alliance of Britain, Russia, Prussia and Austria after the war, but was enlarged by including France and transformed into a "system" for maintaining peace by regular consultation in triennial congresses. Alexander I of Russia tried to instil a religious element into the system by obtaining a pledge that the contracting monarchs should "conformably to the words of the Holy Scripture...remain united by the bonds of a true and indissoluble fraternity" (1815). Britain did not accede to this Holy Alliance. The system of congressional co-operation soon broke down.

Ch.10 (1) Otto von Bismarck (1815-98), chief minister of Prussia 1862-90. Brought about wars with Denmark (1864 - Prussia acquired Schleswig), Austria (1866 - leadership gained in Germany), and France (1870-1 - annexation of Alsace-Lorraine).

Ch.10 (1) Ludwig von Gerlach (1795-1877) wrote in his diary for 30 April 1866, in the run-up to the war which Bismarck was planning against Austria: "Only misfortune can come from the mischievous wrongdoing since 1863, from the present arrogant bragging and threatening, and from the untruthfulness ("audacious mendacity" says The Times) with which, in the desire for foreign possessions, Austria is branded as the aggressor against Prussia and Italy. Perhaps the time is coming when I should speak out openly". On 5 May he sent an article to the *Kreuzzeitung* under the title "War and reform of the Confederation" in which he criticised Bismarck. It was published on 8 May.

On 11 May he was wondering "if I haven't let myself go too deep with Bismarck, and too late" (*ob ich nicht zu tief mit Bismarck eingelassen habe und nicht zu spät aufgetreten bin*). On the 14th he had an interview in which Bismarck "brazenly denied any aggressive attitude towards Austria...he was not an idiot who would involve the country in war, but must act on his own, following his own insight, without anyone else."

The editor's comment is "Gerlach's penetrating warnings rested always on the point that even for statesmen a higher law was more binding than patriotic egoism". He quotes Bismarck: "If I couldn't lie I couldn't be a statesman." (Helmut Diwald (ed.): *Von der Revolution zum Norddeutschen Bund. Aus dem Nachlass von Ernst Ludwig von Gerlach*, Tagebuch 1848-1866 (op.cit.). I, 478-9; editor's comment 63-4).

Ludwig von Gerlach was one of three brothers in Bismarck's circle who took the Pietist view of politics and international affairs. With Leopold (later General) he had been on friendly terms from the days when Leopold was aide-de-camp to Prince Wilhelm (later King and Emperor), as shown in his observations and correspondence in *Bismarck: the reflections and reminiscences of Otto Prince von Bismarck* (tr. A.J. Butler, London 1898). Bismarck understood well enough the idea of carrying Christian convictions into the realm of politics, though he rejected it. "'Pietism' was a word and an idea which were easily connected with the name of Gerlach, on account of the role which the General's two brothers, the President [Ludwig] and the clergyman, who was author of an extensive work on the Bible, played in the political world," he wrote, (II,302) and recounts a conversation with Prince Wilhelm, who had suggested that Leopold was a hypocrite.

"Bismarck: There is nothing of that in Gerlach. In the present day the word pietist has quite another meaning, *viz*. a man who believes in the Christian religion according to the orthodox creed and makes no secret of his belief ...   Prince: What do you mean by orthodox? Bismarck: For example, one who seriously believes that Jesus is the Son of God and died for us as a sacrifice for the pardon of our sins ..." (II,302-3)

But in a letter to Leopold (30/5/57) he explained why it was impracticable to put principles above *raison d'état* - he did not believe it possible "to carry out principle in politics as something whose remotest consequences break through every other consideration." (I,191)   He characterised the General as having "a noble nature", whereas Ludwig "was accustomed to describe me as a Pilate-like character." (I,157)

See also Agatha Ramm: *Germany 1789-1919* (London 1967), 243-4.

Ch.10 (1) Lamennais (1782-1854): *Essai sur l'indifférence*, 1817. Lacordaire (1802-61). Montalembert (1810-70). Their visit to Gregory XVI 1832. Pius IX: Pope 1846-78. Leo XIII: Pope 1878-1903; *Rerum novarum* 1891.

Dwight Moody (1837-99). Descended from a family which was among the earliest settlers (1630's) in Connecticut. As a young business-man he started a Bible class for the waifs of the Chicago streets. The response was such that he gave up a promising career to continue this work full-time. He launched out into campaigns in partnership with I.D. Sankey who provided a distinctive musical element. The first great enterprise of the two men was the mission of 1873-5 in Britain.

Ch.10 (1) Henry Drummond (1851-97). As a student he was captivated by the mission of Moody and Sankey (1873-5), and took an active part in it. After finishing his studies at Edinburgh he became Lecturer (eventually Professor) of Natural Science at the Theological College of the Free Church of Scotland, Glasgow. At the same time he continued his highly effective evangelical work at Glasgow, and - mostly among students - at Edinburgh. Many of his addresses were published in his best-known book (still in print), *The Greatest Thing in the World*.

Alphonse Gratry (1805-72). Director of Collège St. Stanislas 1840-7. Chaplain of the École Normale 1847-52. Joined the contemplative and teaching Oratorians and revitalised the Oratory in France 1852-69.

John R. Mott (1865-1955).

Henry B. Wright (1877-1923)."His classes were made vivid and interesting because they were illustrated with stories of his own experience when face to face with acute problems. He revealed his life like an open book." (George Stewart (op.cit), viii, 5)

The stamina shown by Mott and his associates on campaigns in universities and colleges is remarkable. At Cambridge, following his Oxford visit in 1908, he gave interviews for five hours daily during ten days, besides giving three addresses each day.

During interviews direct dealing with sin was the approach. Mott certainly did not pull his punches in dealing with youth's moral failings, judging from his published talks on "Temptation" and "The battle with impurity." He quoted St. Augustine: "a look, a picture, a fascination, a fall." (Mott: *Addresses and Papers* (op.cit.), II, 357, VI, 34).

Ch.10 (1) Speer's definition of the Gospel ethic in terms of four absolute standards illustrates the coexistence of totally diverse trends within the same culture. His statement was made at a time when "artists, philosophers and scientists were nibbling and hacking away at the absolute standards of the old confident West" - a process which had been going on since "well before 1900" (J.M. Roberts, *op.cit.*,11). Speer and other followers of Moody, notably John R. Mott and Henry B. Wright, were part of what may be regarded as a "Christian counter-attack" (to borrow the title of a book by Arnold Lunn and Garth Lean (London 1969)) in defence of "the supreme, infinite value of the individual soul" (Roberts, 108), with which Christianity had imbued Western culture. The emphasis on absolute moral standards as a challenge for sound living was basic in the Christian teaching of Mott and Wright, as also in that of Frank Buchman, who came during his early years into their circle.

Roberts queries whether this "nibbling and hacking away" brought about decline in the West "in any but a comparative sense." (12) Paul Johnson in his *A History of the Modern World* (op.cit.) is in no doubt about it. He repeatedly states his view of the disastrous effects of jettisoning moral absolutes: "when legitimacy yields to force and moral absolutes to relativism, a great darkness descends". (201) Few of the intellectuals of the left, he says, "had the gritty determination of Orwell to uphold absolute standards of morality, or the experience of the horrors that occurred when relative ones took their place". (336) The Second World War swept off the stage of history "the notion of a world managed by a concert of civilised European powers, within a frame of agreed international conventions and some systems of moral absolutes." (369) Moral relativism "invaded the decision-making of a major legitimate power" (Britain), with Churchill's memo to Beaverbrook of 8 July 1940 initiating mass bombing of Germany - "a critical stage in the moral declension of humanity in our times." (369-370)

The dead in Hiroshima and Nagasaki were, he states, the victims of "a paralysed system of government in Japan made possible by an evil ideology which had expelled not only moral values but reason itself." (427-8)

In contrast, he avers, the belief in the rule of those postwar leaders, notably Adenauer, De Gasperi and de Gaulle, who took over from the dictators, marked a return to "the ascendancy of absolute values." (577)

These observations by Johnson illustrate his thesis of the overturning of the moral order through the work of Einstein on Relativity and of Freud in psychology - a process aided by Marxism and other forms of what he calls "gnosticism" (belief in "a hidden structure of knowledge"). (17) Whereas "the nineteenth century saw the climax of the philosophy of personal responsibility - the notion that each of us is individually accountable for our actions - which was the joint heritage of Judaeo-Christianity and the classical world", the value of the personal conscience was undermined by Freud's teaching on guilt-feelings. (10,11)

Ch.10 (1) Marc Sangnier (1873-1950).

Ch.10 (2) Frank Buchman (1878-1961). A link with the Quietists and Pietists (ch.7 (3)) is his early schooling at Perkiomen Seminary run by the Schwenkfelders (see also *Commentary* under Ch.7(3)) and his later education at Muhlenberg College, Allentown (Pennsylvania).

Ch.10 (2) Sherwood Eddy (1871-1963).

Ch.10 (2) Keswick Convention, initiated by R.P. Smith 1875 for annual evangelical conferences. Buchman described his experience:

"There seemed to be a great distance between myself and Christ, a great abyss, and I knew it was my sin of nursing ill will. That was all. But it produced in me a vibrant feeling, as though a strong current of life had suddenly been poured into me ... A wave of strong emotion, following the will to surrender, rose up within me from the depths of an estranged spiritual life, and seemed to lift my soul from its anchorage of selfishness, bearing it across the great sundering abyss to the foot of the Cross." (Russell (op.cit.), 58; Lily Valley Conference notes (op.cit.)).

Ch.10 (2) Sun Yat-sen (1866-1925). First President of Republic of China 1912. Organized Kuomintang Party. During the anarchic period in China coinciding with World War I and its aftermath, Sun attempted to establish a government for the country from his base at Canton.

Ch.11 (1) Professor Sir Michael Howard has analysed the causes of wars in his book under that title (London 1983). Among his observations are the following:

"The nuclear danger is predictable and controllable. But the 1930's saw the emergence of forces of irrationality which it would rather be neither inappropriate nor hyperbolic to call forces of evil: unpredictable, uncontrollable, still only partially understood." (51) "The Gospels themselves ...faced the fact that at the centre of the Christian religion as of no other great world religion, was the symbol of agonizing and unavoidable suffering. The Christian eschatology, long disdained by liberal humanists even within the Church itself, once again became terribly relevant to human affairs." (51)

Today the need is to go beyond Clausewitz and the older thinkers about war and politics. The State exists not merely to enable its citizens to realise their ethical values, but also to make possible "an international community of mankind." (58)

Ch.11 (1) Keir Hardie (1856-1915). Founded the Independent Labour Party 1893. M.P. 1892-5, 1900-15.

Ch.11 (1) The Social-Democratic Party of Germany (SPD) was formed in 1875 by fusing two working-men's parties (of North and South), of which the latter was Marxist-oriented and became the dominant element under Wilhelm Liebknecht and August Bebel. In 1912 it became the largest party in the Reichstag with 110 representatives.

Ch.11 (1) The Second International Association of Workingmen was founded in 1889 after disbandment of the First International, which had developed its programmes under the leadership of Karl Marx (1818-83). The First International broke up owing to the rifts between different groups, aggravated especially by the anarchist leader Bakunin and his followers. Anarchists were prohibited from the Second International, which united most socialist parties in Europe and had a permanent office, the International Socialist Bureau at Brussels.

Ch.11 (1) Robert Baden-Powell (1857-1941), founder of the Boy Scouts Association. I am indebted to J.B. Joll: *The Origins of the First World War* (op.cit.), 192, for the quotation from *Scouting for Boys*, which led me to this aspect of nationalism.

Ch.11 (1) Evelyn Baring, 1st Earl of Cromer (1841-1917). British Agent and Consul-General in Egypt 1883-1907.

Ch.11 (2) Vril has been defined as "the enormous energy of which we only use a minute proportion in our daily life, the nerve-centre of our potential divinity. Whoever becomes master of the Vril will be the master of himself, others round him and of the world." (Pauwels and Berger, op.cit., English trans., 147). Vril according to this definition is a psychic or psychological phenomenon - hence if Haushofer thought he had found its source in a region of Central Asia which he believed to be the mythical Thule, it could only have been as a discovery of people who, through certain practices, produced this psychic energy.

Pauwels and Berger state that the first mention of Vril (doubtless in Western writings) is in "the works of Louis Jacolliot." In his book *Occult Science in India and among the Ancients, with an account of their mystic initiations and the history of spiritism*, (written in 1866, published in English translation, London 1884), Jacolliot describes himself as Chief Justice of Chandernagua (French East Indies) and of Taiti (Oceania). He does not mention Vril, though the properties of "Agasa" seem similar. "Agasa fluid", he writes, "diffused through nature, puts animate or inanimate, visible or invisible beings, in communication with each other....The being who possesses an excess of this vital fluid acquires a proportionate power, both over animate beings not so highly favoured, and over inanimate beings." (p. 206).

Haushofer certainly believed he had found the original homeland of the Aryans (whom he also specifies as "Germanen") in Central Asia (Karl Haushofer: *Deutsche Kulturpolitik im Indopazifischen Raum* (Hamburg 1939), 184).

Ch.11 (2) Anyone who was politically conscious from the 1930's onwards can hardly have failed to have had some views on Nazism. In my own case, my first recorded opinion is in a letter to my parents written at Oxford in October 1933 (the year of Hitler's take-over), after hearing Albert Schweitzer's lecturers on "The decay and restoration of civilisation." "As Schweitzer says, civilisation is breaking up faster than ever. It won't need another war to show us *that*. It is very interesting drawing analogies from the Hitler regime showing how it militates in every way against the essential conditions for restoring civilisation....It is now possible to understand the great minds of Imperial Roman decadence, seeing the *inevitable collapse* of civilisation, seeing it and being quite impotent to stop it. And they withdrew in on to themselves. But I still think there's a hope - just a chance..."

Experience of Nazism came later during a year as an "exchange teacher" at the Hochschüle für Lehrerbilding (Teacher Training College) at Dortmund, where (to qualify for the training) all the students had to be members of party organisations such as the SA or SS. Along with much warm-hearted friendliness great discussions went on, many of the students being unconvinced about various aspects of the official ideology.

"About three evenings ago", I wrote to my parents, "a tremendous argument started in my room, at about 11.30 at night, between Friedrich Kämper and Friedhelm and Hans, on the subject of whether it was possible to be a good Nazi and at the same time a Christian. When German youth argues it seems to go hammer and tongs at it - none of your gentlemanly detachment and impersonal attitude as is done in England, where it's possible to argue well lying back in an arm-chair - here they always shout at each other, gesticulate wildly, and often not infrequently, apparently lose their tempers. Fried*rich*, it turned out, was an ardent Christian; the other two, especially Fried*helm* who was "in quite a high position in the S.S.", equally ardent non-Christians - not atheists: whether Christian or not most Germans apparently are religious.

"What the issues are exactly, I don't know, though they tell me there's a great fight on between the Church and the State. Friedrich came in to talk to me the following afternoon, and...told me that it was his opinion (and I think of other Christians of Germany), that in the 16th century they had had a great religious leader (Luther), but the country was disunited and they had no great political leader; today the country is united, and they have a great political leader, but no religious leader, and that many people in Germany are hoping for a religious awakening but don't know how it will come." (7/11/36)

The unstinting kindness and hospitality of young and old, and the immense strength of commitment and patriotism, together with much activity that was constructive and praiseworthy, did not fully mask the shadow side of the regime. There were constant reminders of racism and antisemitism: race dominated the curriculum with subjects like "race-science" and "race-geography", while Julius Streicher's obscene publication, *Der Stürmer*, was placarded in front of burnt-out synagogues. An unpleasant surprise was the pervasiveness of the spy system which went so far as the opening of my personal mail. A younger brother had made some jocular comment such as "Watch out - don't get into a concentration camp!", and the next thing was that I found myself being frog-marched by two students in black SS uniforms and top-boots into the presence of the similarly clad Studentenführer (also a student) who demanded the meaning of the outrage.

Ch.11 (2) Theosophy is a kind of Gnosticism: the attempt to penetrate to the knowledge (*gnosis* in Greek) lying behind the manifestations of religions and spiritual experiences in general. As expounded by Mme. Blavatsky (more correctly Blavatskaya) and Annie Besant, this knowledge is largely derived from Indian myths, religions and philosophies, brought into relation with expressions of Christianity in the New Testament, with particular reference to the Gospel of John, some of St. Paul's Epistles, and Revelation.

Behind all religions is "the WISDOM-RELIGION", says Mme. Blavatsky in *The Key to Theosophy* (London 1889). All others, including Christianity, are "but shoots and branches [which] spring from the same trunk." (5) This Wisdom Religion has been preserved "among Initiates in every country", especially India, Central Asia and Persia. The religion is esoteric (secret - only for initiates), whereas exoteric religion is a matter of ritual and public worship. (8) Its transmission is to "the higher Spiritual Self" in ecstasy, i.e. a state of "unuttered prayer". (10) Initiates of the White Lodge of the Himalayan or Tibetan Brotherhood have been the source of the Wisdom Religion for the West; there are other "occult lodges throughout the world, ranging from the white through all shades of grey to black." (Annie Besant in *The Ancient Wisdom* (London 1897), 91). Besant adds in a note (92): "Occultists who are unselfish and wholly devoted to the carrying out of the Divine Will ... are called 'white'. Those who are selfish and are working against the Divine purpose in the universe are called 'black'". She expands this further in mentioning "spiritual evil". (172) "The highly progressed" can follow "the Right-hand or the Left-hand Path ... The Right-hand Path is that which leads to divine manhood, to Adeptship used in the service of the worlds. The left-hand Path is that which also leads to Adeptship [but] is used to frustrate the progress of evolution and is turned to selfish individual ends." This "Black Path" leads to gaining control of "elementals" or "nature-spirits ... a mighty host ... at the head of each division is a great Being, the directing and guiding intelligence of a whole department of nature." It seems that by gaining control from this Being of all or some of the elementals which "administer and energize" this department of nature, "so-called miracles or magical feats are worked." (73)

She states that "the fifth, or Aryan race, now leading human evolution, was evolved from the fifth sub-race of the Atlantean, the most promising families segregated in Central Asia, and the new race-type evolved, under the direct superintendance of a Great Being, technically called a Manu." (431).

It can be seen how an initiate into occultism may be led astray from pursuing "the loftiest moral ideal" (in the words of Mme. Blatatsky - p.25) by way of the right-hand path, and instead may take the left-hand path and so "act selfishly for his own personal benefit; and if he has acquired more practical power than ordinary men, he becomes forthwith a far more dangerous enemy to the world ... Occult qualities or supernatural powers, as alchemy, magic, necromancy, and astrology ... are real, actual and very dangerous sciences." (26) This has been amply borne out on the political level, with Hitler, Hess, Himmler and other Nazis. On the personal level occultism may bring disasters, for instance in married life. "Many happy homes have been broken up as a result of the teaching of spirits, that everyone has a twin soul. The spirits even go so far as to introduce "twin-souls" to each other, after which introductions they are encouraged to leave homes, husbands, wives and children, to live together." Raphael Gasson: *The Challenging Counterfeit* (Bridge Publishing Inc., Valley books, Gwent 1985), 52.

Ch.12 (1) Hans Meiser (1881-1956), Bishop of Bavaria 1933-55. Theophil Wurm (1868-1953), Bishop of Württemberg. Clemens Count von Galen (1878-1946), Bishop of Münster 1933. Michael von Faulhaber (1869-1952), Archbishop of Munich 1917; Cardinal 1921.

Ch.12 (1) Martin Niemöller (1892-1984). Founded Pastors' Emergency League (Pfarrernotbund) 1933; one of founders of the Confessing Church, proclaimed at the Synod of Barmen 1934. Arrested 1937 (Dachau and other camps). Took a leading part in rebuilding the German Evangelical Church after the war, and in reconciliation with former enemies through the "Stuttgart Confession of Guilt" 1945.

Ch.12 (1) Pastor Paul Schneider (b. 1897, d. Buchenwald 1939).

Ch.12 (1) Karl Barth (1886-1968). His *Epistle to Romans* brought him to prominence as a theologian 1919. *Theologische Existenz heute*! 1933 (his NO!). Organised Synod of Barmen with Niemöller and others 1934. Held Chair of Theology in Germany, from 1930 at Bonn, but left for Basle (his birthplace) under Nazi pressure. Championed reconciliation of Germany with war-time enemies, lecturing in ruins of Bonn University 1946 and 1947.

Ch.12 (1) Dietrich Bonhoeffer (1906-1945). As a young theologian came under

Barth's influence. Chaplain for the Evangelical Church at Barcelona 1928-9 and at Sydenham (London) 1933-5. Took a leading part in the Ecumenical Movement, through which became friends with George Bell.

Ch.12 (1) George Bell (1883-1958). Bishop of Chichester 1929. During the Hitler years secured emigration of many Jews and non-Aryan Christians to Britain. Close relations with Confessing Church.

Ch.12 (1) Fabian von Schlabrendorf (b. 1907). Took part in an attempt on Hitler's life (bomb in plane - failed to explode) 1943. After failure of the July 1944 attempt, was imprisoned, tortured, but survived.

Ch.12 (1) Adolf von Harnack (1851-1930). From 1888 Professor of Church History at Berlin.

Ch.12 (1) Vidkun Quisling (1887-1945). On the German occupation, Norway became a one-party state under Quisling's Nasjonal Sammlung 1940. His name became a by-word for a Nazi collaborator.

Ch.12 (1) Eivind Berggrav (1884-1959). Primate of Norway 1937-51.

Ch.12 (1) Helmuth von Moltke (1907-1945).

Ch.12 (1) Adam von Trott zu Solz (1909-44). Rhodes Scholar, Oxford. Jurist. Foreign Ministry from 1939. Killed by Nazis for his part in the attempt on Hitler's life of 20 July 1944.

Peter Yorck von Wartenburg (1904-44). Worked with Claus von Stauffenberg on July Plot 1944. Killed by Nazis.

Lionel Curtis (1872-1955). Developed the concept and invented the phrase "the British Commonwealth of Nations."

Ch.12 (1) The agreement signed between V. Molotov (Russian Foreign Minister) and Joachim Ribbentrop (Germany) on 23 August 1939 opened the way for Hitler's invasion of Poland by giving the Russians a large part of eastern Poland for their share of the spoils.

Ch.12 (1) Otto von der Gablentz (b. 1898) became Director of the Deutsche Hochschule für Politik; Hans Peters (1896-1956) held a Chair at the University of Cologne and took part in drafting the constitution of the German Federal Republic which came into force in 1949.

Ch.12 (3) MRA was a challenge as much to Communists as it was to Nazis, who in a Gestapo report of 1939 attacked MRA as "preaching revolution against the nationalism of the State", seeing it as the National-Socialist State's "Christian opponent". Like the Communists, they were exasperated by the threat of losing their best men - "changing our best young people" (in the words of a Nazi security chief), "winning the idealists" - a threat which made those in MRA "the most dangerous enemies of the State." (Lean (op.cit.), 242-3)

Ch.13 (1) The significance of the policy towards Germany initiated in the French Zone, together with other moves towards reconciliation, has been queried by historians like Professor Milward in *The Reconstruction of Europe* (op.cit.). Milward belongs to the school of thought defined by Charles Pentland in *International Theory and European Integration* (London 1973) which focuses on the economic, social and technological factors: these operate indirectly "to bring about political change...by an incremental process...based on the need to resolve social and economic problems." (p.22) Milward, for example, sees the Schuman Plan as the extension of Monnet's Plan for the modernisation and equipment of France ("the Schuman Plan was called into existence to save the Monnet Plan", p.475), i.e. it was a means of solving certain economic problems, which up to that point had been solvable on a national basis, but which by 1950 could only continue to be solved by an enlargement of the context in which they were tackled.

The other school focuses on "the power, responsiveness and control of political elites and on the political habits of the general public." (p.22) This is the area where "image-advocacy data" operate (in the phrase of Michael Brecher: *Decisions in Israel's Foreign Policy* - Oxford 1974) by means of a range of factors such as "the psychological perceptions of the decision-makers." (Brecher, 5)

Moves on the personal and political levels for reconciliation - which in the case of the Schuman Plan had, according to Monnet (*Memoirs*, op.cit., 310, 392) a "moral" element - reinforce vision, for instance of Europe's role in the world. Such sets of images or ideals can have a powerful motivating force.

Milward in fact is ambivalent, veering from one interpretation to another. He plays down "the acquisition of new and more favourable attitudes towards the idea of European political integration by national voters or populations as a whole", which he characterises as "negligible" - at least in comparison with the role of political elites. Assuming this to be correct, the question remains, what determined the attitudes of these elites, who were certainly (as Milward says) "concerned with matters of future national security" - but they were also concerned with much else. He says himself (p.500) that "European integration...genuinely embodied wider and greater aspirations which elevated the French/German tie beyond a mere traditional alliance. And this in turn gave the alliance a deeper meaning and a nobler purpose for many in the population of both countries, no matter how frequently these beliefs were traduced at government level."

He also mentions that the ultimate intention of the Monnet Plan "was to modernise not only certain sectors of manufacturing industry but the whole country by transforming attitudes of mind." (50) He stresses (55) "the wave of hope for a better world" among people at the war's end, and the wave of enthusiasm for European federation in 1947: the ambitious plans for post-war reconstruction may have been devised "in a sort of dream world where international economic difficulties were largely ignored" - but this again underlines the importance of ideas, rather than suggesting calculated pragmatism.

In connection with the American approach to European integration, he admits that a "set of ideas", though "nebulous" and "imprecise", did provide "a prop of belief in a time of need as well as suggesting a rationale other than the merely technical or strategic for a large programme of aid to western Europe" - a kind of "messianic commitment" or "missionary belief." (59-60) As to the "various European political movements advocating some form of European political integration", these, like the Congress at The Hague in 1948 (which led to the creation of the Council of Europe), exercised "little influence on policy decision and events", but to the ideals of people (particularly in France, Italy and West Germany) "could be attached powerful, if transient political emotions." In the case of Germany "the sacrifice of national interest in a united Europe offered redemption for the awful sins of the past." (392)

For all his slightly sarcastic mention of "the gallery of European saints" (while opining there were many others besides Monnet and his circle, p.396), he stresses the moral qualities and idealism of Robert Schuman. "He had the courage to act quickly ... the courage to seize the moment and translate into reality a complex of vague interrelationships, suggestions and ideas which the fearfulness of others had left trembling on the brink of actuality." (396) He "tapped a vein of hope and idealism which had been buried even more deeply under the common earth of post-war history." (398)

Ch.13 (1) Milward (467) states that an objective of Marshall Aid was the creation of a United States of Europe. But the most authoritative statement is that in the (originally secret) memorandum of George F. Kennan, head of the State Department's Policy Planning Staff, to Marshall of 23 May 1947, in which aid is proposed to "restore the health and vigour of European society" and so counter "the disruptive effect of the war on the economic, political and social structure of Europe." No particular changes in the political structure which it was hoped might result are specified. The American interest is stated as the need to prevent further Communist successes "in exploiting the European crisis", which would "create a serious danger to American security." (Harry Bayard Price: *The Marshall Plan and its Meaning* (Cornell 1955), 21-2)

Ch.13 (1) During the war MRA had both strengthened and was strengthened by the resistance movements, notably in Norway where, according to Bishop Fjellbu (who with Bishop Berggrav led the Church resistance), its coming had been "an intervention of Providence in history".

"We have been fighting more than an armed enemy. We have been fighting godless materialism. The Oxford Group gave us men who helped us to fight for a Christian ideology".

Ch.13 (3) Schuman's concern for the "patient education" of the public is apparent from his early years. As a young man in German-occupied Metz he joined the Union Populaire Catholique Lorraine, which looked to the spiritual unity of Alsace-Lorraine with France, Belgium and Luxembourg. He kept the press-cutting of a meeting in 1913 when the leading speaker said "Vous êtes une école d'apostolat par votre influence et votre vie." Schuman spoke next with a call to study the needs of the workers and to become well-informed about social and political affairs: "Let us be clear about our mission as apostles." Years later the same thoughts reappear in his foreword to the French edition of Frank Buchman's *Remaking the World (Refaire le monde* (op.cit.)).

First the call to mutual education: "What we need, and what is quite new, is a school where, by a process of mutual teaching, we can work out our practical behaviour towards each other; a school where Christian principles are not only applied and proven in the relationships of man to man, but succeed in overcoming the prejudices and enmities which separate classes, races and nations. To begin by creating a moral climate in which true brotherly unity can flourish, over-arching all that today tears the world apart - that is the immediate goal."

Then the practical method, the "apostolate". "The acquisition of wisdom about men and their affairs by bringing people together in public assemblies and personal encounters - that is the means employed. To provide teams of trained men, ready for the service of the state, apostles of reconciliation and builders of a new world, that is the beginning of a far-reaching transformation of society in which, during fifteen war-ravaged years, the first steps have already been taken. It is not a question of a change of policy; it is a question of changing men. Democracy and her freedoms can be saved only by the quality of the men who speak in her name."

(For Schuman's speech of 1913 see Rochefort (op.cit.), 57)

Ch.14 (1) Lawrence Stone (op.cit.) states that the period in post-Renaissance England when girls' education became fashionable in the upper classes was of brief duration, only the middle third of the 16th century. But though the impulse to educate girls may have diminished, educated - or certainly literate - women of middle as well as upper class are not rare in the following century. Stone is of course quite right in pointing out that "generalisations about family change must be qualified in relation to class, status group, literate sector, godly or casually conformist." (10) On the last point, in Puritan families where Bible-reading was important, there would be strong motives for encouraging female literacy (but not necessarily intimate endearments between husband and wife - even first names should not be used, said William Gouge, 1622). (198)

Stone sees "the decisive shift" from the "Open Lineage Family" to the "Closed Domesticated Nuclear Family" as the product of "Affective Individualism" - "the most important change in mentality to have occurred in the Early Modern period, indeed possibly in the last thousand years of Western history." (4,7)

Although specifying Montaillou as "a somewhat untypical, isolated and heretical mountain village ... in the early 13th century", he is in no doubt that until the 18th century in Western Europe "there is no trace of affection in the marital relationship" among the labouring classes, peasants and petite bourgeoisie - which "must reflect a permanent feature of the traditional European society." (103) Even in rich families "expectations from marriage were pragmatically low." (102) Eroticism and romanticism were almost the monopoly of the Court and great nobles' houses. (103)

What was true in Western Europe seems also to have been the case in Central and Eastern Europe. There was (according to Stone) a considerable time-lag in the movement towards "Affective Individualism" in France - even perhaps a century by comparison with England, (387) and this lag may well have been as long or longer further east.

It is a curious parallel with Antiquity that it was during the West's "Hellenistic" Age that intimacy in married partnership developed - the difference being that in the modern West it led on to the feminist movement of which the first signs appear in the 1640's. (199)

Ch.14 (1) Notes taken by the clerk at sessions of the inquisition supply the material for Le Roy Ladurie's *Montaillou* (op.cit.). How far the depositions and answers to interrogations give a fully reliable picture of manners and morals in that particular region is open to question, nor is it clear how far such conditions were general in the rest of Europe. In Burgundy the law of King Gondebaud (about 500 AD) proclaimed that the husband was the protector and not owner of his wife, "compagne de ses travaux, ayant, elle aussi, sa personnalité et ses droits ayant sa place marquée dans l'assemblée de la famille, et donnant ses avis sur les affaires publiques." But later, with the revival of Roman and Canon Law, this changed, the wife being relegated to an inferior position, with the prescription of the husband's right to beat her if she asserted herself against his will. (H. Robin: *Le Droit des gens mariés dans la coutume du Duché de Bourgogne* ((Paris 1900), 7, 10, 65)

Ch.14 (1) The extended family as the norm in Europe (at any rate in the West), before the nuclear family became general, has been called in question. (Michael Anderson: *Approaches to the History of the Western Family 1500-1914* (London 1980), 25)

Ch.14 (1) Martin Luther (1483-1546). His future wife, Katherine von Bora, "belonged to a noble but impoverished family ... who were glad enough to get a daughter provided for by sending her to a convent; [she] had entered [the convent of] Nimtzch when she was ten years old, and had taken the veil when she was sixteen. It was a "family arrangement", practised generation after generation in noble German households....Many of the nuns in this convent, which was reserved for ladies of noble birth, became convinced of the unlawfulness of the vows thay had taken, and wished to return to their homes.

"The ladies wrote to Luther. After some correspondence, the

matter was entrusted to a worthy burgher or Torgau, Leonhard Koppe by name. Tradition says that nine of the nuns, all who dared the venture, met in the cell of Catherine von Bora, who had planned the rescue, on the 4th of April 1523, got out of the window into the court, and were assisted over the wall by Master Koppe, who was waiting for them with a large country cart and some empty beer-barrels. The nuns were put into the beer-barrels, and after three days' journey, part of it through the hostile territories of Duke George of Saxony, they reached Wittenberg safely, where Luther was able to find shelter for them in the houses of some of the most respectable citizens of the town.

"This convent-breaking made a great sensation, and was vehemently condemned. Luther justified it in a telling pamphlet....His letters are full of his successes and failures to get the nine nuns married, Catherine among the rest. The others seemed for the most part contented with the partners proposed to them. Not so Catherine. She was a dignified maiden of four-and-twenty, with a high fair forehead and bright black eyes....."   (T.M. Lindsay: *Luther and the German Reformation* (op.cit.), 193-5)

Ch.14   (1)   While   it   is   true   that   Luther,   as   an   exemplar   of Renaissance/Reformation   man,   was   a   pioneer   of   "Affective Individualism", he was also capable of saying "women should remain at home, sit still, keep house, and bear and bring up children" (could he have said this before his actual experience of marriage?). (Cited by Stone, 203, from *Table Talk*, ed. W. Hazlitt (London 1857), no. 725. The following page references are also from Stone).

Part of the movement to "Affective Individualism", marked in England by "the extraordinary changes in attitudes towards the individual and towards emotion that occurred between 1660 and 1800", (118) was the replacing of the "medieval Catholic ideal of chastity" by "the ideal of conjugal affection" (135) - romantic love having been "regarded by moralists and theologians as a kind of mental illness, fortunately of short duration." (4) Beginning with the Reformation, the trend was towards the married state becoming "the ethical norm for the virtuous Christian". (135) It took longer for the upper than for the middle classes to accept this ideal and (only in the late 18th century) to begin "to channel sex desire into the marriage bond and keep it there" (282) In this trend the romantic novel played a large part: "romantic love and the romantic novel grew together after 1780." (287) But in France husbands continued to have mistresses into the 19th century. (387) (One may add that in certain circles in England it was much the same).

Thomas Jefferson, author of the American Declaration of Independence and third President of the United States, was Minister (i.e. Ambassador) to France 1785-1790. On the morals of the French upper classes he wrote: "Conjugal love having no existence among them, domestic happiness, of which that is the basis, is utterly unknown. In lieu of this are substituted pursuits which nourish and invigorate all our bad passions, and which offer only moments of extasy amidst days and months of restlessness and torment. Much, very much inferior this to the tranquil permanent felicity with which domestic society in America blesses most of its inhabitants." (W.D. Garrett: *Thomas Jefferson Redivivus* (Barre Publishers, Massachusets, USA, 1971), 80)

L. Friedländer: *Roman Life and Manners* (op.cit,) writes (I, 245): "In Paris of about 1750, profligate manners were far worse than in imperial Rome."

Ch.14 (3) Mikhail Gorbachev (b. 2/3/31). Grandfather was founder and chairman of a collective farm; father agricultural mechanic and combine harvester driver, Stavropol Region, North Caucasus. Studied Law at Moscow University (some Latin, Hobbes, Hegel, Rousseau - "the opportunity to gain an insight into a different political culture" - Schmidt-Hauer, op.cit., 49). Returned to Stavropol 1955 with his wife Raisa Titorenko, also graduate of Moscow University, in Philosophy (Marxism-Leninism); in 1967 she completed her doctoral thesis on "New characteristics in the daily lives of the Collective Farm Peasantry (Stavropol)", applying sociological methods unusual in the Soviet Union. Gorbachev rose through the Stavropol Region apparatus to be First Secretary of the Regional Party Committee, 1970. Reputed for raising harvest yields (had been Party organizer for agriculture and qualified as "scientific agricultural economist" by correspondence course).

F.D. Kulakov, Party chief of the Stavropol Region from 1960 onwards, who had supported Gorbachev, went to Moscow 1964 as Central Committee Secretary for Agriculture. Gorbachev replaced him after his suicide (Nov. 1978). Andropov became his patron - Gorbachev had got to know him during Andropov's visits to health spas in the Region, of which he was a native. They campaigned together against corruption. 1979 Gorbachev became a candidate member of Politburo; 1980 full member.

Andropov resigned as KGB head (after 15 years), became Central Committee Secretary for Ideology, International Party Relations and Foreign Policy, 1982. Continued with Gorbachev the anti-corruption campaign, discrediting the Brezhnev clique. Followed Brezhnev as General Secretary on his death, November 1982. During his thirteen months in office "he built a bridge by which a new generation might come to power over the swamp of corruption". (Schmidt-Hauer 95) On Chernenko's death March 1985, Gorbachev was elected General Secretary by the Plenum of the Central Committee.

Ch.14 (3) Leonid Brezhnev (1906-1982). General Secretary on fall of Khrushchev, which he organised, until his death in November 1982.

Ch.14 (3) Aleksandr Solzhenitsyn (b.1918). Writer: *The First Circle, Cancer Ward, One day in the Life of Ivan Denisovich*, etc. Nobel Prize Winner. Expelled from USSR as dissident.

Ch.14 (3) Irina Ratushinskaya (b.1954). Poetess, converted to Christianity, imprisoned as dissident ("subverting the Soviet regime") for 7 years in a strict regime gulag. Released September 1986 and given visa for Britain. Her poems and autobiography are published in *Pencil Letter* (London 1988); *Grey is the Colour of Hope* (London 1988); *In the Beginning* (London 1990).

Ch.14 (3) Andrei Sakharov and his wife Elena Bonner were released from internal exile at Gorky after seven years, in December 1986. He died December 1989.

Ch.14 (3) At Chernobyl on 26 April 1986, reactors at the nuclear generating station went out of control. Staff had been making an unauthorised experiment without proper safety procedures. There was a surge of temperature and a head of steam. Fuel elements burst to give unprecedented emissions of radioactivity. A polluted plume spread across Scandinavia, Poland, North West Europe including parts of Scotland, Northern England and Wales. At least 300 people died, and many others suffered radiation sickness. There was scandalous secrecy for several days before the newly-decreed system of *glasnost* operated. Eventually the wrecked reactor was encased in a concrete "sarcophagus". Large areas of the best agricultural land were made unusable and the water-supply endangered. Chernobyl was evacuated. There is continued toll of genetic and other disorders affecting tens of thousands of people, especially in the Ukraine and Belorussia.

Ch.14 (3) First Hague Conference May-July 1899 (26 states represented). Failed to agree limitations on armaments, but set up Court of Arbitration (Hague Tribunal). Second conference January-October 1907 (45 states represented). "While carrying on the good work of ameliorating the rules and customs of war, the delegates were no more successful than their predecessors in the attempt to establish limitation of armaments and obligatory arbitration." (R.B. Mowat: *A History of European Diplomacy 1815-1914* (London 1922), 289.

Ch.14 (3) The economic situation in 1989 was described by *The Times* (London, 22/6/89): "The budget deficit is running at some 11 per cent of GNP ... Total state debt, according to Dr. Sakharov, is £83 billion. The money supply is out of control. Agricultural reform, including the vital introduction of leases for farmers, is stalled and output is falling ... Losses from state enterprises last year - the first in which "self-financing" was introduced as a principle - are officially admitted to be running at £12 billion a year."

Ch. 14 (3) In *Children of the Arbat* (tr. H. Shukman, London 1988), Anatoli Rybakov has illuminated understanding of Communist morality - or at least has raised questions about it - drawing on his experience as a young man in the 1930's (his book is evidently in large part autobiographical). At that time people could still have revolutionary enthusiasm: "Their hearts swelled with pride. This was their country, the shock brigade of the world proletariat, the embodiment of the advancing world revolution, an island of hope in a world torn by crises, unemployment, moral decline, spiritual poverty. True, they had ration cards and denied themselves everything, but they were building a new world." (36)

Questions arise in the mind of the youthful Sasha Pankratov after he has been jailed on baseless chages in the psychopathic atmosphere of Stalin's regime, as the period of the purges was coming on. In a time of depression something new about the human spirit dawns on Sasha when an unknown prison librarian sends him some books which speak to his condition - the man "had responded to his cry, echoed his prayer, and had shown Sasha an example of humanity, fearlessness and trust." (234) Later, burying a fellow-exile in Siberia, he was "pierced with a feeling of bitterness and joy. He suddenly had a clear sensation of the insignificance of his own misfortunes and sufferings. This vast eternity strengthened his faith in something higher than the values he had lived for so far." (363)

Wondering about the incidents which had led to prison and exile, he remembers that "he had said that what was moral was in the interests of the proletariat. But the proletariat were human beings and so proletarian morality was human morality. And it was immoral to save your own skin at the cost of another's." (441) He is strengthened in his new insight by a fellow-exile, Father Vasily, who persuaded him to take his bed for the night while he slept on the floor - "his was the gentleness of a man who would not be deflected from his duty. His duty was to give whatever he had, and all he had, apart from a bowl of hot water, was a narrow iron bed." (444)

Sasha's ideas may have been uncharacteristic of his generation, as another exile asserted, but he denied this, saying that Lenin also grew up on "the eternal truths", and only encouraged a "particular class morality" because "the Revolution was a war, and a harsh war at that. But in essence our ideas are both human and humane. What for Lenin was temporary and prompted by harsh necessity, Stalin elevated into something permanent, eternal. He raised it into a dogma." (599) Sasha admired the character of other exiles, who "relied on themselves alone, on their own resources, however pitiful, yet they were sufficient to bear all their misfortunes without complaint, and to live in hope." (609) "Even here," he reflected, "people are still upholding the highest human values, and one of those values is compassion ... I don't know much Christian theology, but I think that what moved Lidya Grigoryevna was above religions and ideas, it was the capacity to sacrifice oneself for others. And the fact that it can take place even here, as I said, gives me hope: human feeling has not been killed in people and it never will be." (682)

Ch. 15 (3) The Cuba crisis was the outcome of tension which built up between the Soviet Union under Nikita Khrushchev and the USA under Presidents Eisenhower and Kennedy. Fidel Castro had won power in Cuba in 1959 after three years of guerilla warfare against the right-wing Batista regime. In 1961 Castro proclaimed allegiance to the Communist bloc, annoying the USA with support of left-wing revolutionary movements in Latin America. John F. Kennedy, soon after becoming president in 1960, launched an abortive attack at the Bay of Pigs in order to topple Castro. Soviet support took the form next year of converting Cuba into a nuclear base (1962), from which missiles could be launched against American cities and a large part of the Western Hemisphere as a whole. On discovering by spy-planes what was happening, the USA imposed a naval blockade on all military supplies to Cuba and requested the dismantling of the offensive weapons there.

During a week of crisis (22-28 October), when the world was at the threshold of thermonuclear horror, the wills of the two men who represented the superpowers were in conflict. The nerves of the younger man and his colleagues held. Khrushchev was forced to bow to the ultimatum, and stopped his ships from trying to pass the American warships now "quarantining" the island. He agreed to dismantle the "weapons construction sites" and return the missiles in question to the Soviet Union.

Ch. 15 (3) André Chouraqui (born 1917) originates from Algeria, where his family had been established for several centuries, since being expelled from Spain. Having gone to the top of the academic tree in France with the study of Law, he was deprived of his French citizenship and his right to follow his profession by the Vichy government on account of being Jewish, and fought in the Maquis in a unit which spent its off-duty time studying the Bible in the original languages. His conversion came through Catholics and Protestants, and also through Muslims whom he got to know in the Sahara region - he writes of "the shock of my discovery of God by way of Christian and Muslim spirituality." After practising as a judge in post-war Algeria, he migrated to Israel where for a time he was Deputy Mayor of Jerusalem. He declined the offer of the Presidency of Israel in order to devote himself, besides other writing, to the translation into French of the Bible, both Old and New Testaments, from the original languages.

In addition to the Bible itself, an edition has been published as part of an illustrated encyclopaedia of the Bible, in ten volumes, L'Univers de la Bible. His name as a writer was made in France soon after the Six-day War of 1967 with his Lettre à un ami arabe. His most recent works are an autobiography, L'Amour fort comme la mort, and his translation into French of the Koran.

He belongs to that band of Jewish scholars who have placed Jesus and the New Testament in the authentic Jewish setting, working with Christian scholars who also have been finding a new approach to the Bible and to Judaism, especially (among Catholics) since Vatican II opened new perspectives. Jesus is seen as Yeshua', the spiritual leader and prophet whom the Romans crucified as a dangerous agitator. Chouraqui's experience was of being himself "riveted without hope on the cross with the nails of the persecutors, the same cross" - in Chouraqui's case that of the Nazis - "on which the Roman Empire crucified the nations who dared to resist its law ... I learnt for the first time to see evil in myself ... another self was born in me."

Ch. 15 (3) The response of the younger generation of East and West. Young people have been flocking to the summer conferences at centres like Caux and Taizé, and now large and growing numbers are coming from Russia and Central Europe. (*For a Change*, Oct. 1990, Tirley Garth, Tarporley, Cheshire CW6 0LZ; *Changer*, Oct. 1990, 68 Bd Flandrin, 75116 Paris; *Taizé*, April 1990, Presses de Taizé DL, 726 France; Fr. Roger de Taizé: *Amour de tout amour* (Taizé 1990).

Ch. 15 (3) Author's experience in experimenting with "silence" is akin to that recounted in Garth Lean: *Cast out Your Nets* (London 1990). A memorable outcome of the initial experience was attending a conference in December 1933, about which I wrote to my parents: "The emphasis isn't so much on saving individuals' souls - let alone one's own - but on saving civilisation." As part of the proceedings there was a trip to the House of Commons, where a meeting took place attended by a number of MPs. On that occasion "one of the most significant talks was that of the Hon. C.W. Hambro, President of the Norwegian Parliament, and a very important man on the Supervisory Council of the League. This isn't a crisis which we are passing through, he said - it isn't acute, but a chronic period of degeneration, where civilisation is killed by its own products. He talked about the atmosphere of futility and ineffectiveness at the League, in Geneva - the feeling that the fundamental questions have never been touched, that only the minor and secondary problems have been tackled. He mentioned the insincerity with which debates are usually carried on there, with no sense of the vital issues at stake. It was symbolistic that the new Palace of the League was unfinished - that they couldn't get enough money to allow the artists and the decorators the credits with which to put up wall papers or lay out the lawns and surroundings - that it was a great bare building with a wilderness around it. We have planned too much for the construction and hardly at all for the spirit. He said that it was his experience to come back from a political debate or meeting with a feeling that something was lacking - however successfully the measures had gone through and however right the policy appeared to be. When he got back to his room he always asked himself the question - can all this really touch the spirit of the people?

"That was what real honesty meant in politics. The continual deadlocks in politics are in fact because we have not accepted in international relations the honesty which we demand, or which rather Christianity demands in ordinary life. Absolute honesty in politics would go a long way towards putting right the world's political problems - especially when allied with absolute charity. And there England had very much of the blame to bear, with her previous attitude of 'my country right or wrong': for the principle of absolute love meant no less than considering *other* countries as well as one's own. He said he could see the possibility - he had a vision of all the delegates before a conference sharing together their views and plans in a spirit of absolute honesty and love - and if they did so, how completely different these conferences would be."

These words, which may have appeared visionary at the time, came near to fulfilment 15 years later, when Schuman and the other "Fathers of Europe" conferred together to launch the first Community.

ENVOI

Now for our race our globe
our fragile only ark
swung between fear and hope we ask
what waits in the great dark -
a rendezvous with some new birth,
or the last stand of man on earth?

(From "Last Stand")

*   *   *   *

Yours be the level eye that recognises
millennial Eden notable for its serpents,
Mammon's demesne contesting holy ground,
fatal infections not imported here
by foreign agents, but Cain's parting gift
to the human species.
Yours be the generous hand outstretched to strangers
and neighbours over the fence, or nearer still;
yours be the listening ear, the gift of silence
tuned to the unseen wind, the still small voice.

(From "To Our Grandchildren")

(Lines from "Last Stand" and "To Our Grandchildren" by Michael Thwaites: *The Honey Man* (Aslan Publishing, Braddon, Australia, 1989).

REFERENCES

Introduction
T.S. Eliot: *Notes towards the definition of Culture* (London 1948), 18,26. Paul Johnson: *A History of the Modern World* (London 1983), 4,5. J.M. Roberts: *The Triumph of the West* (London 1985), 11. J.H. Muirhead: *Bernard Bosanquet and His Friends* (London 1935). Obituary in *The Times*, 10 February 1923. Helen Bosanquet: *Bernard Bosanquet* (London 1924). E.J. Hobsbawn: "Marx's contribution to historiography" in R. Blackburn: *Ideology in Social Science* (London 1972). R.C. Mowat: *How Marxism helps and hinders the Study of History* (Oxford Polytechnic papers, 1977). Oswald Spengler: *The Decline of the West* (tr. C.F. Atkinson, London 1929). A.J. Toynbee: *A Study of History* (Oxford 1934-54; revised one-volume edition, Oxford 1972); *Civilisation on Trial* (London 1948).

Chapter 1 - Ancient and Modern Decadence
1. Definitions and comparisons: Bernard Bosanquet: *Some Reflections on the Idea of Decadence* (Bangor 1901), 15. Thomas Arnold: *History of the later Roman Commonwealth* (London 1845), 400,442; *Introductory Lectures on Modern History* (Oxford 1842), 26, 37. Victorian Studies, vol. 28, no. 4 (Summer 1985), Linda Dowling: "Roman decadence and Victorian historiography". Vico: *Selected Writings* (ed. and trans. L. Pompa, Cambridge 1982), 259-266. The quotation about Arnold's ambiguous attitude is from his edition of Thucydides: *The History of the Peloponnesian War* (Oxford 1838), Appendix 1, vol. 1, 521-2. Edward Gibbon: *The History of the Decline and Fall of the Roman Empire* (London 1776-88).

2. The 19th century: progress or decadence: A.P. Stanley: "Whether States, like individuals, after a certain period of maturity, inevitably tend to decay" (Prize Essay, Oxford 1840), 45, 41. W.E.H. Lecky: *The History Of European Morals from Augustus to Charlemagne* (London 1869), I: 126, 147. E.L. Woodward: *The Age of Reform* (Oxford 1938). Matthew Arnold: *Culture and Anarchy* (ed. J. Dover Wilson, Cambridge 1969, first published 1869), 194-5, 210, 95, 159, 49. On education in Germany, Matthew Arnold: *Works* (London 1904), vol.2, second section, p.53, letter to Lady Rothschild, 22/9/65. Geoffrey Faber: *Jowett* (London 1957). R.L. Nettleship: *Thomas Hill Green* (London 1906), 54, 178. *Social Science History*, vol.5, no.3, summer 1981: David Watson: "The Case of British and American Absolute Idealism, 1860-1900" p. 267. *British Educational Research Journal*, vol.8, no.1, 1982: David Watson: "Idealism and Education: T.H. Green and the education of the middle class".

3. Fin-de-siècle anxiety: Helen Bosanquet: *Bernard Bosanquet* (op.cit.); Bernard Bosanquet: *Some Thoughts on the Transition from Paganism to Christianity* (London 1882), 19, 20, 21, 22. Søren Kierkegaard: *The Last Years, Journals 1853-55*, ed. Ronald Gregor Smith (London 1968), 97, 8, 63, 354, 355; *The Present Age*, ed. Alexander Dru (London 1962), 65, 96, 36. Walter Lowrie: *A Short Life of Kierkegaard* (Princeton 1965), 147, 231. Friedrich Nietzsche: *The Anti-Christ* (in

Twilight of the Idols and *The anti-Christ*, ed. R.J. Hollingdale (Harmondsworth 1968)), 118. Crane Brinton: *Nietzsche* (New York 1965), 107. Friedrich Nietzsche: *Thus Spoke Zarathustra*, ed. R.J. Hollingdale (Harmondsworth 1969), 182, 209, 193. *The Letters of Jakob Burckhardt*, ed. A. Dru (London 1955), 170, 147, 207, 107, 143, 211, 151, 202. Jakob Burckhardt: *Reflections on History* (tr. M.D.H., London 1943), 15, 17. Max Nordau: *Degeneration* (tr. from 2nd German edn., London 1895), 2, 5, 7, 21, 33, 40, 41, 190, 556-7, 560.

Chapter 2 - Parallels

1. The Classical world and the modern west: M. Rostovtzeff: *The Social and Economic History of the Hellenistic World* (Oxford 1941); *The Social and Economic History of the Roman Empire* (Oxford 1957). A.H.M. Jones: *The Decline of the Ancient World* (London 1966). *Cambridge Medieval History*, I, (1936) and *Shorter Cambridge Medieval History* (1952). J.M. Roberts: *The Hutchinson History of the World* (London 1976). W.H. McNeill: *The Rise of the West* (Chicago 1963); *The Human Condition* (Princeton 1980). Eqbal Ahmed, M. Razzaz, A. Yusuf, J. Stork: "A world restored (H. Kissinger revisited)" in *Race and Class*, no. 17, 1976. Henry Brandon: *The Retreat of American Power* (London 1972). Ernest Mandel: *Europe vs. America? Contradictions of Imperialism* (London 1970).

2. Political and spiritual salvation in the ancient world: T.S. Eliot: *The Complete Poems and Plays* (London 1969), 189 - "The dry salvages." M. Rostovtzeff: *The Social and Economic History of the Hellenistic World* (op.cit.); *A History of the Ancient World* (tr. J.D. Duff, London 1945). J.L. Myres: *Geographical History in Greek Lands* (Oxford 1953). Sophocles: *The Three Theban Plays* [*Antigone* p. 59 seq.] (tr. R. Fagles, Harmondsworth 1984), lines 503-508. H. Frankfurt: *Ancient Egyptian Religion* (Columbia 1948). M.P. Nilsson: *Greek Piety* (Oxford 1948). J. Hasebroek: *Trade and Politics in Ancient Greece* (London 1933). K. Freeman: *Greek City-States* (London 1950). C.M. Bowra: *Ancient Greek Literature* (London 1933). G.B. Grundy: *History of the Greek and Roman World* (London 1926). John Burnet: *Early Greek Philosophy* (London 1908). G.T. Garratt (ed.): *The Legacy of India* (Oxford 1937). A.J. Arberry (ed.): *The Legacy of Persia* (Oxford 1953). W.W. Tarn: *Hellenistic Civilisation* (London 1952); *Greeks in Bactria and India* (Cambridge 1951). B. Snell: *Discovery of the Mind* (Oxford 1953). Arthur Christensen: *L'Iran sous les Sassanides* (Copenhagen 1944). H.I. Bell: *Egypt from Alexander the Great to the Arab Conquest* (Oxford 1948). *Cambridge Ancient History* III, IV, VI, VII. Gilbert Murray: *Five Stages of Greek Religion* (Oxford 1925), 126-7, 137. Samuel Dill: *Roman Society from Nero to Marcus Aurelius* (London 1904). Seneca: *Moral Essays* I: 4; II: 6, 19, 27 (tr. J.W. Bascoe, Loeb Classical Library, 1928); *Letters to Lucilius* I: lxxi, 37 (p.225) (tr. E. Phillips Barker, Oxford 1932) For Demonax see the writings of Lucian (tr. A.M. Hatmon, Loeb Classical Library, 1913), 149, 173: K. Funk: *Untersuchungen über die Lucianische Vita Demonactis* in Philologus x, Heft 4 (Leipzig 1907). Cora E. Lutz: *Musonius Rufus* (Yale 1947), IV (49), X (79), XI (83).

Chapter 3 - Morals and Married Partnership

1. Marriage contracts and romantic love: Bernard Bosanquet: *The Civilisation of Christendom* (London 1893); *Some reflections on the Idea of Decadence* (Bangor 1901), 7, 17. *Aristophanes*, tr. P. Dickenson (Oxford 1970). Oswyn Murray: *Early Greece* (Brighton 1980). *Greece and Rome*, 2nd series, Apr.1989, vol.36, no.1, David Cohen: "Seclusion, Separation and the Status of Women in Classical Athens." *Thucydides: The Peloponnesian War* (London 1962), Bk.2. Ch.5 (p.126). Athenaeus: *Deipnosophistae* (Loeb/Heinemann, London 1941), vol.6, XII, 571; 558-9, 576-7, 596-7, 607, XIV, 641-2. *Plutarch's Lives*, tr. B. Perrin (Loeb/Heinemann 1916), "Pericles" XXIV. Homer; *The Odyssey*, tr. E.V. Rieu (1946), Bk. VI, pp.102 seq.(Harmondsworth 1946). Sarah B. Pomeroy: *Goddesses, Whores, Wives and Slaves* (New York 1975), 119. Aristotle: *Politics*, tr. H. Rackman (Loeb/Heinemann 1972), V, 1,8. Aristotle: *The Nicomachean Ethics*, tr. F.H. Peters (London 1898), VIII, 6, 12. Menander: *The Principal Fragments*, tr. F.G. Allinson (Loeb/Heinemann 1951), 99, 105. *Menander*, tr. W.G. Arnott (Loeb/Heinemann 1979), I, 227, 301, 315. *Theocritus*, ed. and tr. A.S.F. Gow (Cambridge 1952), I, "Epithalamios", p.145; *Idylls* 11, 18, 27, 28. W.H. McNeill: *Plagues and Peoples* (New York 1976). Polybius, 36, 17. Claude Vatin: *Recherches sur le mariage et la condition de la femme mariée à l'époque hellenistique* (Bibliothèque des Ecoles françaises d'Athènes et de Rome, vol. 260, Paris 1970), 9. R. Flacelière: *Love in Ancient Greece*, tr. J. Cleugh (London 1962); *La Vie quotidienne en Grèce au siècle de Periclès* (Paris 1960). H.D.F. Kitto: *The Greeks* (Harmondsworth 1957). Heliodorus: *The Aethiopica* (tr. with Introduction, Athens 1897).

2. Rome: morals and marriage: J.V.P. Balsdon: *Roman Women* (London 1962), 56, 45, 78. C.W.L. Launspach: *State and Family in early Rome* (London 1908) 191n., 193. J.D. Unwin: *Sex and Culture* (London 1934). Keith Hopkins: *Death and Renewal* (Cambridge 1983). C.S. Loch: "Charity and Charities" *(Encyclopaedia Britannica 1902)*. Livy, tr. B.O. Foster (Loeb/Heinemann 1961). This translation from Balsdon op.cit., 75. Beryl Rawson (ed.): *The Family in Ancient Rome* (London 1986). Mary Beard and Michael Crawford: *Rome in the late Republic* (London 1985). Susan Teggiari: "Roman divorce" (Oxford University seminar paper, 26/11/87). David Noy: "Roman women and arranged marriage" (Oxford University seminar paper, 12/5/88). Harold Mattingly: *Roman Imperial Civilisation* (London 1957). *Musonius* (op. cit.) XIII A (89), XII (87). Plutarch: *Moralia* and *Parallel Lives* (Loeb Classical Library, London 1927). D.A. Russell: *Plutarch* (London 1972). R.H. Barrow: *Plutarch and his Times* (London 1967), 18, 85 (quotation used partly with that in next ref.). Plutarch: *Moralia*, IX, "The Dialogue on Love", 769 A (pp. 427, 431 Loeb); II, "Advice to Bride and Groom", 313 (140), 325 (143), 309 (140). Pliny: *Letters and Panegyricus*, I (Loeb, London 1969), VI, iv, vii; III, iii. H.G. Evelyn White: *Ausonius* (London 1919), I, 72-3.

Chapter 4 - The Impact of the Spiritual Upsurge

1. Roman decadence: Juvenal: *The Sixteen Satires* (Introduction and translation by Peter Green, Harmondsworth 1967), Satire VI,290-3; XI, 297-300; II, 159-163; VIII, 144-6; II, 84-6; 126-7; XV, 110-112; X, 77-81; X, 347-50, 363-4; I, 118. (Peter Green's somewhat free translation creates a difficulty in precisely indicating the lines for reference purposes. For instance, in the last quotation above, Green has distilled his translation from three lines in the Latin (I, 112,113,114) which corresponds to five lines (I, 111-116) in another English version (Everyman, London 1954)). *The Satyricon of Petronius* (trans. and ed. by W. Arrowsmith, Michigan 1962, 90). J.P. Cèbe: *Varron, Satires ménippées* (École française de Rome, Rome 1972). Gilbert Highet: *Juvenal the Satirist* (Oxford 1954).

2. The Christian leaven: Lucius Apuleius: *The Golden Ass* (tr. Robert Graves, Harmondsworth 1950), 279, 284. Pliny: (op. cit.), X, XCVI. A.N. Sherwin-White: *The Letters of Pliny* (Oxford 1966), 708. W.H.C. Frend: *Martyrdom and Persecution in the Early Church*, (Oxford 1965). Hans Lietzmann: *The Beginnings of the Christian Church* (Lutterworth Press 1949), vol 1. B.H. Streeter: *The Primitive Church* (London 1929). Eusebius: *The History of the Church* (tr. G.A. Williamson, New York 1966), I, 4. Adolf Harnack: *The Expansion of Christianity in the first three Centuries*, (tr. J. Moffatt, London 1904), I, 487 - 8, 258. I Corinthians, 6, 9, (New English Bible, Oxford 1970). S. Dill: *Roman Society in the last Century of the Western Empire* (op.cit.), 487. Ferdinand Lot: *The End of the Ancient World* (tr. P. and M. Leon, London 1931), 186. Fergus Millar *et al: The Roman Empire and its Neighbours* (London 1966). Journal of Jewish Studies, vol.50, no.2, 1989: Martin Goodman: "Proselytising in Rabbinic Judaism."

3. Constantine and Byzantium: *Ammianus Marcellinus* (Loeb/Heinemann, Harvard 1939), III, xxxi, 4, 10 seq.. G. Ostrogorsky: "The Byzantine Empire in the world of the seventh century", in *Dumbarton Oaks Papers*, no. 13 (Harvard University, 1959), 20-21. G. Ostrogorsky: *History of the Byzantine State* (Oxford 1968). D. Obolensky: *The Byzantine Commonwealth* (London 1971). N.H. Baynes and H.St.L.B. Moss: *Byzantium* (Oxford 1949). Alfonso Lowe: *The Companion Guide to the South of Spain* (London 1973). H.W. Haussig: *A History of Byzantine Civilisation* (tr. J.H. Hussey, London 1971). Edward Gibbon: *The Decline and Fall of the Roman Empire* (op.cit.) A. Alföldi: *The Conversion of Constantine and Pagan Rome* (tr. H. Mattingly, Oxford 1948). A.H.M. Jones: *The Later Roman Empire* (Oxford, 1964), 400, 1054. St. Augustine: *The City of God* (London 1945). A.J. Toynbee: *Mankind and Mother Earth* (Oxford 1976). C. Foss and P. Magdalino: *Rome and Byzantium* (Oxford 1977). C.W.C. Oman: *The Art of War in the Middle Ages* (Oxford 1885). James Bowen: *A History of Western Education* (London 1972), I, 194 seq. (for late Roman and Byzantine education). Robin Lane Fox: *Pagans and Christians* (Harmondsworth 1986), 669. *Journal of Roman Studies*, vol.78 (1988), Garth Fowden: review of Lane Fox: *Pagans and Christians*. J. Burckhardt: *The Age of Constantine the Great* (London 1949, tr. from *Die Zeit Constantins des Grossen* (Basel 1863)). T.D. Barnes: *Constantine and Eusebius* (Harvard 1981). *Select Library of Nicene and Post-Nicene Fathers of the Christian Church*, I (Oxford 1890). Eusebius of Caesarea: *The Life of Constantine*. Lactantius: *De Mortibus Persecutorum* (ed. and tr. J.L. Creed, Oxford 1984). E.G. Turner: *Greek Papyri* (Oxford 1980) - for ending of Hellenist education in Egypt, 81-4. A. Christensen: *L'Iran sous les Sassanides* (op. cit.). *History*, xxv, no.28 (Sept. 1940), J.J. Saunders: "The Orient and the Graeco-Roman World before Islam". L.M. Hartmann: *The Early Mediaeval State, Byzantium, Italy and the West* (Historical Association 1949). M. Rostovtzeff: *Dura-Europos and its Art* (Oxford 1938). Norbert Elias: *The Civilizing Process* (New York 1978).

4. Art and architecture: R. Bianchi Bandinelli: *Rome: the Late Empire, Roman Art A.D. 200-400* (tr. P. Green, London 1971). H.P. L'Orange: *Art Forms and Civic Life in the Roman Empire* (Princeton 1965), 121-4. Baynes and Moss: *Byzantium* (op.cit.), C. Diehl: "Byzantine Art". A. Grabar: *The Beginnings of Christian Art* (London 1967); *Byzantium: from the death of Theodosius to the Rise of Islam* (London 1966). D. Talbot Rice (ed): *The Dark Ages* (London 1965). G. Mathew: *Byzantine Aesthetics* (London 1963). W. Goetz: *Ravenna*

(Leipzig/Berlin 1901).   T.G. Jackson: *Byzantine and Romanesque Architecture* (Cambridge 1913).   M. Yanagi, E. Takahashi, Y. Nagatsuka: *Byzantium* (tr. N. Fry, Chartwell Books, New Jersey 1978).   Kenneth Clark: *Civilisation* (London 1971).

Chapter 5 - Christian Ambiguities
1. Sex, marriage and the family: L. Duchesne: *Early History of the Christian Church* (trans. C. Jenkins, London 1924), III, 5. St. Augustine: *De bono conjugali* (Of the good of marriage) in *A Library of the Fathers of the Holy Catholic Church, anterior to the division of East and West*, translated by Members of the English Church (Oxford 1847), viii (283). St. Augustine: *The Confessions*, trs. F.J. Sheed (London 1944), VI, 16; X, 6. Matthew 11:19. Peter Brown: *Augustine of Hippo* (London 1969), 248, 212, 181, 62. I Corinthians 7: 31-34.

   2. Monasteries: H.B. Workman: *The Evolution of the Monastic Ideal* (London 1913). *John Cassian (Select Library of Nicene and Post-Nicene Fathers of the Christian Church*, 2nd series, vol. XI, Oxford 1894), bk iv, ch. 27: bk. v, ch. 32; also *St. Basil the Great* (vol. VIII), Letters 82, 223, 265. J.B. Bury: *A History of the Later Roman Empire* (London 1889), I, 208, 317 (for Hypatia). St. Athanasius: *The Life of St. Antony* (tr. R.T. Meyer, London 1950), 33, 37, 67, 77. *The Lausiac History of Palladius* (tr. W.K. Lowther Clarke, London 1918), 54, 113. M.M. Fox: *The Life and Times of St. Basil the Great as Revealed in His Works* (Washington, DC 1939). Baynes and Moss: *Byzantium* (op.cit.).

   3. The State: doctrinal rectitude and dissent: Gibbon (op.cit., edition of 1813), III, 327, 335. St. Augustine: *The Confessions* (op. cit.), VIII, 12; X, 43. W.H.C. Frend: *"Religion and Social Change in the Late Roman Empire"*, reprinted in *Religion Popular and Unpopular in the Early Christian Centuries* (London 1976), XI, 495; *Martyrdom and Persecution in the Early Church* (Oxford 1965); Peter Brown: *Augustine of Hippo* (London 1967); *Religion and Society in the Age of St. Augustine* (London 1972), 203; "The Patrons of Pelagius" (Journal of Theological Studies, n.s. 21, 1970). E.R. Dodds: *Pagan and Christian in an Age of Anxiety* (Cambridge 1965). J.N.L. Myres: "Pelagius and the end of Roman rule in Britain" (Journal of Roman Studies, vol. 50, p.21, 1960). John Morris: "Pelagian Literature" (Journal of Theological Studies, n.s. 16, 1965).   John Ferguson: *Pelagius* (Cambridge 1956). R.F. Evans: *Pelagius: Inquiries and Reappraisals* (London 1968).

Chapter 6 - The End of Civilisation in the West and its Renewal
1. Landowners into bishops: W.H.C. Frend: "Religion and Social Change in the Late Roman Empire" (Cambridge Journal II, 8, 1949), reprinted in *Religion Popular and Unpopular in the Early Christian Centuries* (London 1976), XI, 495, 117. On Paulinus: Frend op. cit, XV, 101 seq. ("The Two Worlds of Paulinus of Nola"). His poem: *Carmen X*, in *Ausonius* (tr. H.G. Evelyn White), Ep.31, lines 20-32. C.E. Stevens: *Sidonius Apollinaris and his Age* (Oxford 1933). S. Dill: *Roman Society in the last Century of the Western Empire* (op.cit.), 194, 214. Helen Waddell: *The Wandering Scholars* (London 1927), 13. A.H.M. Jones: *The later Roman Empire* (Oxford 1964). C.G. Starr: *The Roman Empire* (Oxford 1982). *Cambridge Medieval History*, I.

   2. Pioneers of the new civilisation: St. Augustine: *The Confessions*: book 9, iv,v,vi, *The City of God*, book 4, iii,iv; 18, xlix; 19, xiii-xvii. J.N.D. Kelly:

Jerome (London 1975), 32, 304. *The Principal Works of St. Jerome* (Select Library of the Nicene and Post-Nicene Fathers, VI, 1893), Letters 22 (to Eustochium), 45, 125. S. Dill: *Roman Life in the Last Century of the Western Empire* (op.cit.), 127. J. Stransky: *East Wind over Prague* (London 1950), 22-5. E. Gibbon: *The Decline and Fall of the Roman Empire* (op.cit.),VI, 132. *The Gothic History of Jornandes*, ed. C.C. Mierow (Princeton 1915), c.42. Paulus Orosius: *Historiarum adversum paganos* (Leipzig 1889). A.E. Housman: *Epitaph on an Army of Mercenaries*. T. Jalland: *The Life and Times of St. Leo the Great* (London 1941). P.A. McShane: *La Romanitas et le Pape Léon le Grand* (Montreal 1981). F. Gregorovius: *History of the City of Rome in the Middle Ages*, tr. G.W. Hamilton (London 1900), vol.1. *Leo the Great* (Select Library of the Nicene...Fathers, XII, 1895), Sermon 49,6; 82. Letters 14, 15, 19, 22, 31, 106.

3. Rome: heritage and growing point: Peter Llewellyn: *Rome in the Dark Ages* (London 1971). P. O'Donovan: *Benedict of Nursia* (London 1980). T. Maynard: *St. Benedict and his Monks* (London 1955). H.B. Workman: *The Evolution of the Monastic Ideal* (op.cit.), 154, 156, 148. *The Rule of St. Benedict*, ed. D. Oswald Hunter Blair (Fort-Augustus 1906). The story about the man with the chain comes from Gregory the Great: *Dialogues*, iii.16 (p.144 in trans. by J. Zimmerman OSB, New York 1959). J.J. O'Donnell: *Cassiodorus* (Berkeley/Los Angeles 1979). Pierre Riche: *Les Écoles et l'enseignement dans l'Occident chrétien* (Paris 1979). M.L.W. Laistner: *Thought and Letters in Western Europe AD 500 to 900* (London 1957). Thomas Hodgkin: *The Letters of Cassiodorus* (London 1886), pp.143, 155, 157, 286, etc. Cassiodorus: *An Introduction to Divine and Human readings/Institutiones* (tr. and ed. L.W. Jones, Columbia 1946). *Cassiodori Senatoris Institutiones* (ed. R.A.B. Mynors, Oxford 1937), Praefatio (p.3). Cassiodorus: *Expositio Psalmorum*, Praefatio. U. Hahner: *Cassiodors Psalmenkommentar* (Munich 1973). *Zeitschrift für neutesatamentliche Wissenschaft*, XXV (1926), T. Hermann: "Die Schule von Nisibis vom 5. bis 7. Jahrhundert", pp.89-122.

4. Gregory: the change from old to new: Workman (op.cit). Gregorovius: (op. cit.), I; II, 1, 33. Peter Llewellyn (op. cit.), 96, cited from Johannes Diaconus, *Vita*, II, 24-8. P. Meyvaert: *Benedict, Gregory, Bede and Others* (Variorum Reprints, London 1977). J. Richards: *Consul of God* (London 1980). Christopher Dawson: *Religion and the Rise of Western Culture* (London 1950). Samuel Dill: *Roman Society in Gaul in the Merovingian Age* (London 1926). Gregory the Great: *Homiliae in Hiezechihelem Prophetam* (Turnhout 1971), II. Homilia VI, 22; *Homiliae in Evangelium*, I, 1; *The Pastoral Charge* (tr. H.R. Bramley, Oxford 1874), Pt.1, ch.1, pt.2, chs. 5, 6; *Dialogues* (tr. O.J. Zimmerman, OSB, New York 1959): Bk. I, pp. 14, 25, 46, 51; Bks. II, III, 80, 99, 108, 166, 182, 185 (for quotation beginning "wild hordes of Lombards...."). *Select Library of...Fathers*, XIII, pts. 1 & 2 (Oxford) 1895: Letters, I, 5 (Theoctista); V, 39 (Bishop Anastasius of Antioch); v, 40 (Emperor Maurice); V, 41 (Empress Constantina); VI, 7 (Candidus, Presbyter); IX 43 and XIV, 12 (Queen Theodolinda); XI, 30, 35, 36 (Venantius, Barbara and Antonina, and John, Bishop of Syracuse); XI, 28, 64, 65 (Augustine of Canterbury); XI, 29 (Queen Bertha); XI, 66 (King Ethilbert). Bede: *A History of the English Church and People* (tr. & intro. L. Sherley-Price, Harmondsworth 1968).

Chapter 7 - The Medieval Equilibrium and the Modern "Hellenistic" West

1. The medieval period of equilibrium and cultural transmission: J.H. Pirenne: *Les grands courants de l'histoire universelle* (Neuchâtel 1944). A.C. Crombie: *Augustine to Galileo* (London 1952), 36; *Robert Grosseteste and the Origins of Experimental Science* (Oxford 1953). C. Dawson: *Religion and the Rise of Western Culture* (London 1950), 206. J.H.O. Pirenne: *Mediaeval Cities* (Princeton 1925). Charis Waddy: *The Muslim Mind* (London 1990). I. Abrahams: *Jewish Life in the Middle Ages* (London 1932), 30. H.A.L. Fisher: *A History of Europe* (London 1936). J.M. Roberts: *The Hutchinson History of the World* (London 1976).

2. Millennial movements: Joseph Klausner: *The Messianic Idea in Israel* (London 1956). C.F. Evans: *The Lord's Prayer* (London 1963). Pierre de Labriolle: *La Crise montaniste* (Paris 1913). R.H. Murray: *Group Movements throughout the Ages* (London 1935). John, 16:13. Helen Waddell: *The Wandering Scholars* (op. cit). *Expositio magni prophetae Abbatis Joachim in Apocalypsin* (Venice 1527), Introduction, p.5, col.2. H. Grundmann: *Neue Forschungen über Joachim von Fiore* (Marburg 1950); *Studien über Joachim von Floris* (Berlin 1927). Marjorie Reeves: The *Influence of Prophecy in the later Middle Ages* (Oxford 1969); *Joachim of Fiore and the Prophetic Future* (London 1976). D.C. West: *Joachim of Fiore in Christian Thought* (New York 1975): article by M. Bloomfield: "Joachim of Flora: a critical survey", reprinted from Speculum VII (1932). Transactions of the American Philosophical Society (Philadelphia): N.S. vol.66, part 5, 1976: David Burr: "The Persecution of Peter Olivi", 23. Norman Cohn: *The Pursuit of the Millennium* (London 1961). Eric Voegelin: *The New Science of Politics* (Chicago 1966). K. Löwith: *Meaning in History* (Chicago 1957). St. Augustine: *The City of God* (op.cit), Bk. 20, ch. 7, 9; 22, 30. Revelation, ch. 20. Titus, 1:15. E.H. Erikson: *Childhood and Society* (New York 1950). R.C. Finucane: *Soldiers of the Faith: Crusaders and Moslems at War* (London 1983).

3. Pietism and its outreach: G.H. Williams: *The Radical Reformation* (London 1962). A.G. Dickens: *Reformation and Society in Sixteenth century Europe* (London 1966). H.R. Trevor-Roper: *Religion, the Reformation and Social Change* (London 1967). Thomas Carlyle (ed.): *Oliver Cromwell's Letters and Speeches* (London 1897), III, 62 seq. W.C. Braithwaite: *The Beginnings of Quakerism* (London 1912). R.M. Jones: *Spiritual Reformers in the Sixteenth and Seventeenth Centuries* (London 1914) 8, 76, 77, 78. F.E. Stoeffler: *The Rise of Evangelical Pietism* (Leiden 1965), 85 (citing from Joseph Hall, 1574-1656), 202 (concerning Johann Arndt); *Continental Pietism and early American Christianity* (Grand Rapids 1976), 181; *German Pietism during the Eighteenth Century* (Leiden 1973). *Butler's Lives of the Saints* (ed. H. Thurston and D. Attwater, London 1956), for St. Philip Neri and St. Francis de Sales. Chambers Encyclopaedia (Edinburgh 1908), for quotations about St. Philip Neri. Johann Arndt: *True Christianity* (trans. and introd. Peter Erb, London 1979), 1, 50. *New Cambridge Modern History*, IV, VII. St. Francis de Sales: *Selected Letters*, (ed. E. Stopp, London 1960), 21 (Intro.), 147, 126; *Introduction to the Devout Life* (London 1956), 52. Katherine Brégy: *St. Francis de Sales* (Dublin 1960), 47. W.H. Fitchett: *Wesley and his Century* (London 1906): *Rev. John Wesley's Journal* (London 1906). E.M. Howse: *Saints in Politics* (London 1971), 27. Viscountess Knutsford: *Life and Letters of Zachary Macaulay* (London 1900), I, 253. Garth Lean: *God's Politician* (London 1980). John Pollock: *Wilberforce* (London 1977). Yvette

Wilberforce: *William Wilberforce* (privately printed 1967). E.M. Forster: *Marianne Thornton* (London 1956). Kenneth McAll: *Healing the Family Tree* (London 1982). Ian Bradley: *The Call to Seriousness* (London 1976). William Wilberforce: *A Practical View of the Prevailing Religious System of Professed Christians in the Higher and Middle Classes in the Country, Contrasted with Real Christianity* (London 1797). E. Troeltsch: *The Social Teaching of the Christian Churches* (tr. O. Wyon, London 1931), I, 329 seq. B.R. Wilson: *Magic and the Millennium* (London 1973): *Contemporary Transformations of Religion* (Oxford 1976); *Religious Sects* (London 1970); *Religion in a Secular Society* (London 1966).

Chapter 8 - Christianity's Rivals (1)
1. Reason, nature and the world-spirit: Sir Isaac Newton: *Observations upon the Prophets of Daniel and the Apocalypse of St. John* (London 1733); *Chronology of Ancient Kingdoms Amended* (London 1728). Sir David Brewster: *Memoirs of the Life, Writings and Discoveries of Sir Isaac Newton* (Edinburgh 1855). J.J. Rousseau: *Oeuvres Complètes* (Paris 1824), III: 399n, 244, 204; *The Social Contract*, ch. 8. R.B. Mowat: *Jean-Jacques Rousseau* (Bristol 1938). J.M. Thompson: *The French Revolution* (Oxford 1962) G.H. Sabine: *A History of Political Theory* (London 1963). William Wordsworth: *Lines Composed a few miles above Tintern Abbey* in *The Poetical Works of Wordsworth* (Oxford 1950), 163; *The French Revolution as it appeared to Enthusiasts at the Commencement*, 165. E. Cassirer: *The Myth of the State* (Oxford 1946), 271, for quotation from Hegel on the French revolution. G.W.F. Hegel: *Lectures on the Philosophy of History* (tr.J. Sibree, London 1888), 336-340, 55; *Sämtliche Werke* (Stuttgart 1961), II, 415. E.L. Fackenheim: *The Religious Dimension in Hegel's Thought* (Chicago 1967). *Hegel's Logic* (ed. J.N. Findlay, tr. W.Wallace, Oxford, Oxford 1875). J.M.E. McTaggart: *A Commentary on Hegel's Logic* (Cambridge 1910). M.A. Mugge: *Heinrich von Treitschke* (London 1915), 38, 41.

2. Marxism: J. Klausner: op.cit., 25. Ludwig Feuerbach: *The Essence of Christianity* (tr. M. Evans, London 1881), xi, xii, 289, 33. Karl Marx: *Capital* (tr. E. and C. Paul, London 1930), I, 51; *Revolution and Counter-Revolution in Germany in 1948* (ed. and intro. Eleanor Aveling, London 1896). K. Marx and F. Engels: *The Communist Manifesto* (London 1948), 20, 2, 6, 12, 30. Isaiah Berlin: *Karl Marx* (London 1963). Klaus Bockmuehl: *The Challenge of Marxism* (Leicester 1980). Leslie Newbiggin: *The Other Side of 1984* (Geneva 1983). F. Engels: *Herr Eugen Dühring's Revolution in Science (Anti-Dühring)*, tr. E. Burns, (London 1935), 308. H.J. Laski: *Communism* (London 1927). E. Voegelin: *The New Science of Politics*, (op.cit.). K. Löwith: *Meaning in History*, (op.cit.) 36 (for quotation beginning "On the one side...." from "Die Revolution in 1848 und das Proletariat" in *Karl Marx als Denker* (Berlin 1928), 41). Paul Johnson: *Enemies of Society* (London 1977).

Chapter 9 - Russia: Vladimir, Peter and Lenin
1. Russia's time-lag: V.O. Kluchevsky: *A History of Russia* (tr. C.J. Hogarth, London 1912). Paul Miliukov: *Outlines of Russian Culture* (Pennsylvania 1942). Richard Charques: *A Short History of Russia* (London 1962). B.H. Sumner: *Survey of Russian History* (London 1961). John Lawrence: *Russia in the Making* (London 1957). D. Obolensky: *The Byzantine Commonwealth* (op.cit.), 193. Hildegard Schneder: *Moskau das Dritte Rom* (Darmstadt 1957), 75-6. Philip

Longworth: *Alexis, Tsar of All the Russias* (London 1984). Lionel Kochan: *The Making of Modern Russia* (Harmondsworth 1963). Anatole Leroy-Beaulieu: *L'Empire des Tsars et les Russes* (Paris 1881). Marc Raeff: *Comprendre l'ancien régime russe* (Paris 1982). **2. The intelligentsia and reform:** Kluchevsky (op.cit.), IV, 234. Leroy-Beaulieu (op.cit.), I, 259. Sebastian Brock: *Syrian Perspectives on Late Antiquity*. A.M. Allchin (ed.): *Theology and Prayer* (Fellowship of St. Alban and St. Sergius, 1975): Kallistos Ware: *Silence in Prayer: The meaning of hesychias*, 11. Alain Besançon: *Éducation et société en Russie dans le deuxième tiers du XIX siècle* (Paris 1974); *Présent soviétique et passé russe* (Paris 1980). Franco Venturi: *Roots of Revolution* (New York 1966), 175, 473-4, 502, 292-5 (Zaichnevsky): 387 (Nechaev). Alan Palmer: *Alexander I* (London 1974). E.M. Almedingen: *The Emperor Alexander II* (London 1962). Mrs. Edward Trotter: *Lord Radstock* (London 1914), 207. J.H. Billington: *Mikhailovsky and Russian Populism* (Oxford 1958); *The Icon and the Axe* (London 1966), 53. Nicholas Zernov: *The Russian Religious Renaissance of the Twentieth Century* (London 1963). T.F. Stavrou (ed.): *Art and Culture in Nineteenth Century Russia* (Indiana 1983). Elizabeth Valkenier: *Russian Realist Art, the State and Society: The Peredvishniky and their Tradition* (Ann Arbor 1977), 124. Valentine Marcade: *Le renouveau de l'art pictorial russe 1863-1914* (Lausanne 1971). D. Talbot Rice (ed.): *Russian Art* (London 1935). *Landscape masters from Soviet Museums* (Royal Academy, London 1975). B.A. Pushkarev: *Watercolours and Drawings in Russian Museums* (in Russian, Moscow 1982). N.V. Gogol: *The Government Inspector* (intro. J. Larvin, London 1980); *Dead Souls* (London n.d.). Fyodor Dostoyevsky: *The Idiot* (Harmondsworth 1955), 551; *The Brothers Karamazov* (London 1927); *Diary of a Writer* (ed. B. Brasol, London 1949); *The Possessed* (London 1914). Leo Tolstoy: *Ivan Ilych and Hadji Murad; Resurrection* (all tr. I. and A. Maude, Oxford, various dates). E.H. Carr: *Dostoevsky* (London 1962). A.P. Chekhov: *Plays* (Harmondsworth 1959). W.H. Burford: *Chekhov and his Russia* (London 1948). W. Weidlé: *Russia: Absent and Present* (London 1952). C.P. Pobedonostsev: *Questions religieuses, sociales et politiques* (Paris 1897). **3. Marxism-Leninism:** V.I. Lenin: *The State and Revolution* (Moscow 1972), 46, 88, 93, 75; *On Religion* (Moscow 1981), 18, 21. W. Kolarz: *Religion in the Soviet Union* (London 1961). P. Miliukov: *Outlines of Russian Culture* (op.cit.).

Chapter 10 - The Christian Challenge in the West

1. The 19th century upsurge: Werner Richter: *Bismarck* (London 1964). A.O. Meyer: *Bismarck* (Stuttgart 1949). Helmut Diwald (ed.): *Von der Revolution zum Norddeutschen Bund. Aus dem Nachlass von Ernst Ludwig von Gerlach, Tagebuch 1848-1866* (Göttingen 1970). W.H. Simon: *Germany in the Age of Bismarck* (London 1958), 124-5, 39. K.S. Latourette: *Christianity in a Revolutionary Age*, I, *The Nineteenth Century in Europe* (New York 1970). American Historical Review, vol.90, no.1, Feb.1985: Pauline M. Watts: "*Prophecy and Discovery: on the spiritual origins of Christopher Columbus's 'Enterprise of the Indies'*". Pierre Larousse: *Grand dictionnaire universel* (Paris 1866). F. Lamennais: *Paroles d'un croyant* (Paris n.d.), 8,9,48; *De l'esclavage moderne* (Paris n.d.), 26, 50: *Visions of the People* (trans. of *Paroles* by H.B. Binns, London 1914). *Thoughts from Lacordaire* (Priory Press, Hampstead, n.d.). A. Gratry:

Souvenirs de ma jeunesse (Paris 1874), 161; *Méditations* (London 1889), 89; *Philosophie de la connaissance de Dieu* (Paris 1856), II, 330; *Philosophie de la connaissance de l'âme* (Paris 1857), I, 207; II, 91, 172: *Les Sources* (Paris 1876), ch.l, passim; ch.2,36. W.R. Moody: *Life of Dwight L. Moody* (Kilmarnock 1930). G. Adam Smith: *Life of Henry Drummond* (London 1899), 405. Henry Drummond: *Ascent of Man* (London 1894); *The Greatest Thing in the World* (London 1953). Robert C. Mackie: *Layman Extraordinary - John R. Mott* (London 1965). Basil Matthews: *John R. Mott* (London 1934), 107, 441, 222, 224, 349, 344. C. Howard Hopkins: *John R. Mott* (Grand Rapids 1979). John R. Mott: *The Evangelisation of the World in this Generation* (London n.d.), 16; *Strategic Points in the World's Conquest* (London 1897); *Addresses and Papers* (New York 1946), I, 18; II, 4, 5. George Stewart: *Life of Henry B. Wright* (New York 1925), 72. Henry B. Wright: *The Will of God and a Man's Life Work* (New York 1924), 5. Robert E. Speer: *The Principles of Jesus* (New York 1902). Madeleine Barthélemy-Madaule: *Marc Sangnier* (Paris 1973). Jeanne Caron: *Le Sillon et la democratie chrétienne 1891-1910* (Paris 1967), 56-8, 144, 149. Marc Sangnier: *Autrefois* (Paris 1936), 26, 148, 172; *Dans l'Attente et le Silence* (extract from *Le Sillon*, microfiche Bibliothèque Nationale, Paris, 1905, reprinted in *Autrefois*), 22, 35. Mark Guldseth: *Streams* (Fritz Creek, Alaska, 1983).

2. The 20th century challenge: Sherwood Eddy: *A Pilgrimage of Ideas* (New York 1935), 16; *Eighty Adventurous Years* (New York 1955). R. Chickering (op.cit.), 380, 381. Jean-Claude Delbreil: *Les Catholiques français et les tentatives de rapprochement franco-allemand, 1920-1923* (Metz 1972), 19, 20, 233. J. Caron (op.cit.). M. Sangnier: *Autrefois* (op.cit.). M. Barthélemy-Madaule (op.cit.). D.C. Belden: *The Origins and Development of the Oxford Group (MRA)*, (Oxford University Thesis 1975), 252; J.R. Mott: *Addresses and Papers* (op.cit.), III, 579. B. Matthews (op.cit.), 197, 353. Melvin J. Lasky: *Utopia and Revolution* (London 1977). A.J. Russell: *For Sinners Only* (London 1932), 56, 58. Frank N.D. Buchman: *Where Personal Work Begins* (unpublished extracts and notes from talks given at the Lily Valley Conferences near Kuling, China, 1-13 August 1918). Quotation from an unpublished biography of Frank Buchman. Frank Buchman: *Remaking the World* (London 1961), 3, 144, 78, 79, 15, 65, 41. J.P. Thornton-Duesbery: *The Open Secret of MRA* (London 1964), 64. Garth Lean: *Frank Buchman: A Life* (London 1985).

Chapter 11 - Christianity's Rivals (2)

1. Nationalism: P. Brock: *Pacifism in Europe to 1914* (Princeton 1968). Berta von Suttner: *Lay down your Arms* (tr. T. Holmes, London 1892). *Memoirs of Berta von Suttner* (Boston/London 1910). C.E. Black: *The Dynamics of Modernization* (New York 1966), 77. F. Fischer: *Germany's Aims in the First World War* (London 1967); *War of Illusions* (tr. M. Jackson, London 1975), 38 (for quotation from *Ein verlassener Brüderstamm. Vergangenheit und Gegenwart der baltischen Provinzen, von einem Balten* (Berlin 1899) 212). James Joll: *The Origins of the First World War* (London 1984), 195. Marc Ferro: *The Great War 1914-1918* (tr. N. Stone, London 1973). D.J. Newton: *British Labour, European Socialism and the Struggle for Peace 1889-1914* (Oxford 1985). Michael Howard: *The Causes of Wars* (London 1983). Harvey Goldberg: *The Life of Jean Jaurès* (Wisconsin 1968). Barbara Tuchman: *The Proud Tower, a portrait of the world 1890-1914* (London 1966). J.M. Roberts: *Europe 1880-1945* (London 1967). Jolyon Howorth: "The Left in France and

Germany, Internationalism and War: a Dialogue of the Deaf 1900-1914" in *Socialism and Nationalism in Contemporary Europe (1845-1945)* (ed. E. Cahm and V.C. Fisera, Nottingham 1979); and "French Workers and German Workers: The Impossibility of Internationalism, 1900-1914" in *European History Quarterly*, vol.15, no. 1 (1985). H.E. Marshall: *Our Island Story* (London 1905), 61, 507-8; *Our Empire Story* (London 1908); *A History of Germany* (London 1913), preface. Lt.-Gen. Robert Baden-Powell: *Scouting for Boys* (London 1908), 334, 28, 314, 318, 261, 310, 318, 338, 336. Roger Chickering: *Imperial Germany and a World Without War* (Princeton 1975), 170. The Earl of Cromer (Evelyn Baring): *Modern Egypt* (London 1908), I, 328. Philip Magnus: *Gladstone* (London 1960). Paul Knapland: *Gladstone's Foreign Policy* (London 1935). R.B. Mowat: *Contemporary Europe and Overseas, 1898-1920* (London 1931). Fritz Stern: *The Politics of Cultural Despair* (Berkeley 1961). Raymond Aron: *The Century of Total War* (London 1954). Hugo Hantsch: *Leopold Graf Berchtold* (Graz 1963). Austrian State Archives, Box PA XIX 66.

2. Nazism: Felix Dörmann: *Was Ich Liebe* (poem). René Alleau: *Hitler et les sociétés secrètes* (Paris 1969), 168, 185. Georges Sorel: *Réflexions sur la violence* (Paris 1912), 184. Alan Bullock: *Hitler, a Study in Tyranny* (Harmondsworth 1963). H.R. Kedward: *Fascism in Western Europe* (London 1973). Hermann Glaser: *The Cultural Roots of National-Socialism* (tr. E.A. Menze, New York 1978), 133, 99, 131 (quoting Hans Blüher). Louis Pauwels et Jacques Bergier: *Le Matin des magiciens* (Paris 1960; Eng. trans. London 1971). Hermann Rauschning: *Hitler Speaks* (London 1939; German version, *Gespräche mit Hitler* (Zurich/New York 1940) omits ch. 18 "Hitler himself" ("Hitler Privat")), 270; *Die Revolution des Nihilismus* (Zurich/New York 1938). Theodor Schieder: *Hermann Rauschnings "Gespräche mit Hitler" als Gesichtsquelle* (Rheinische-Westfälischen Akademie der Wissenschaften, Opladen 1972). Alfred Rosenberg: *Der Mythus des 20. Jahrhunderts* (Munich 1930), 665-7, 458, 461. C. Isherwood: *Mr. Norris changes Trains* (London 1935), 130. Ellic Howe: *Urania's Children* (London 1967). Adolf Hitler: *Mein Kampf* (Munich 1932). A. Kubizek: *Young Hitler* (Maidstone 1973). J. Frère: *Nazisme et les sociétés secrètes* (Paris 1974). F. Stern: *The Politics of Cultural Despair*, (op.cit.). E.H. Erikson: *Childhood and Society* (New York 1963). J.C. Fest: *Hitler* (tr. R. and C. Winston, London 1974). E. Vermeil: *Doctrinaires de la révolution allemande 1918-1938* (Paris 1939). Moeller van den Bruck: *Germany's Third Empire* (tr. E.O. Lorimer, intro. M.A. Hamilton, London 1934). C. Ginzburg: "Mythologie germanique et nazisme" (critique of Georges Dumézil: *Mythes et dieux des Germains* (1939)) in *Annales*, July-August 1985. R. Petitfrère: *La Mystique de la croix gammée* (Paris 1962). André Brissaud: *Hitler et l'ordre noir* (Paris 1969). René Guenon: *Le Roi du monde* (Paris 1958). Werner Maser: *Die Frühgeschichte der NSDAP* (Frankfurt-am-Main 1965), 199: French trans.: *Naissance du Parti national-socialiste allemand* (Paris 1967), 70 (for "Ostara").

Chapter 12 - Totalitarian Empires and Dissent

1. German martyrs: Karl Barth: *Theological Existence today!* (tr. R. Birch Hoyle, London 1933), 50. Terence Prittie: *Germans against Hitler* (London 1964), 118. Alfred Delp, S.J.: *Facing Death* (London 1962, first published as *Im Angesicht des Todes*, 1956), 185, 190, viii, 14, 124. E. Bethge: *Dietrich Bonhoeffer* (London 1970), 166, 177, 176, 559. Dietrich Bonhoeffer: *Life Together* (tr. J.W. Doberstein,

London 1954), 22, 25, 99; *The Cost of Discipleship* (tr. R.H. Fuller, memoir by G. Leibholz, London 1948), 37, 38, 18 (poem); *Letters and Papers from Prison* (ed. E. Bethge, London 1971), 417, 360, 361, 160; *No Rusty Swords* (London 1970). W.D. Zimmermann and R. Gregor Smith; *I Knew Dietrich Bonhoeffer* (London 1973), 114, 82. Richard Gutteridge: *The German Evangelical Church and the Jews* (Oxford 1976). A.S. Duncan-Jones: *The Struggle for Religious Freedom in Germany* (London 1938).   Bernard Reymond: *Une Eglise à croix gammée?* (Lausanne 1980). M. Balfour: *Helmuth von Moltke* (London 1972), 177, 173-4, 239-241, 184, 128, 220, 303, 323, 326, 327, 330.   Kurt Finker: *Graf Moltke und der Kreisauer Kreis* (Berlin 1980). *A German of the Resistance: the Last Letters of Count Helmuth James von Moltke* (Introduction by Countess Freya von Moltke and others, Oxford 1974).

2. Russian repression: Archbishop Pitrim of Volokolamsk (ed): *The Orthodox Church in Russia* (London 1982).   Michael Bourdeaux: *Opium of the People* (Oxford 1977); *Religious Ferment in Russia* (London 1968); *Risen Indeed* (London 1983), 26, 43, 58. *Religion in Communist Lands* (Keston College), vol.2, no.6 (Nov.-Dec.1974) for Vins; vol.1, no.3 (May-June 1973) for Shpiller; vol.11, no.2, 1983, 162-3, and vol.12, no.2, 1984, 160-1 for "Light-Life" movement. *The Right to Believe* (Keston College periodical).   Hugh Seton-Watson: *The Decline of Imperial Russia* (London 1964). Trevor Beeson: *Discretion and Valour: Religious Conditions in Russia and Eastern Europe* (London 1982).   Norman Davies: *A History of Poland* (Oxford 1982), II, 615-6, 608, 192. Niels Høberg: *Political Culture: State-Church Relations in the GDR and Poland* (M.Phil dissertation, Glasgow University, 1985). Lord Longford: *Pope John Paul II* (London 1982). Mary Craig: *Pope John Paul II* (London 1982).

3. The long arm of the KGB: John Barron: *KGB* (London 1974), 346, 377; *KGB Today: The Hidden Hand* (London 1983).   Malcolm Muggeridge: *The Green Stick* (London 1975).   Martin Green: *Children of the Sun* (London 1976), 233, 92, 27.   G.E. Moore: *Principia Ethica* (London 1903), 188-9. J.M. Keynes: *Two Memoirs* (London 1949), 82. Paul Levy: *Moore* (London 1949).   For the "intellectual aristocracy" see Noel Annan's article in Studies in Social History (ed. J.H. Plumb (1955)).   Andrew Boyle: *The Climate of Treason* (London 1979). Goronwy Rees: *A Chapter of Accidents* (London 1972). Robert Skidelsky: *The End of the Keynesian Era* (London 1977).   Chapman Pincher: *Inside Story* (London 1978); *Traitors* (London 1987).   Tom Driberg: *Ruling Passions* (London 1977); *Guy Burgess* (London 1956). J.P. Thornton-Duesbery: *The Open Secret of MRA* (London 1964).   Moscow Radio 9/1/53.   *Kommunist*, quoted in *The New York Times* (international edition), 30/4/63. Leif Hovelsen: *Out of the Evil Night* (London 1959), 157. Garth Lean: *Frank Buchman* (op.cit.), 242-3.

Chapter 13 - The Renewal of Western Europe

1. The statesmanship of reconciliation: Madeleine Barthélemy-Madaule: *Marc Sangnier* (op.cit.)   Richard Mayne: *Postwar, the Dawn of today's Europe* (London 1983); *The Recovery of Europe* (London 1970). R.C. Mowat: *Ruin and Resurgence: Europe 1939-65* (London 1966); *Creating the European Community* (London 1973). J.E. Farquharson and S.C. Holt: *Europe from Below* (London 1975). F.R. Willis: *France, Germany and the New Europe 1945-67* (Stanford and London 1965). Lord Pakenham: *Born to Believe* (London 1953).   Louis-Gabriel Robinet: *Koenig, un chevalier* (Paris 1973).   Dietmar Schmidt: *Pastor Niemöller* (Tr. L. Wilson -

London 1959), 147 (for Stuttgart Declaration of Guilt). E. Bethge: *Dietrich Bonhoeffer* (op.cit.). Martin Greschat: *Die Schuld der Kirche - Dokumente und Reflexione zur Stuttgarter Schulderklärung vom 18./19. Oktober 1945* (Munich 1982). Frank Buchman: *Remaking the World* (op.cit.), 9 (Fjellbu). H.W. 'Bunny' Austin: *Frank Buchman as I knew Him* (London 1975). David J. Price: "The Moral Rearmament Movement and postwar European Reconstruction", M.A. dissertation, University of London, 1979. Philippe Mottu: *The Story of Caux* (London 1970). Kenaston Twitchell: *Regeneration in the Ruhr* (Princeton 1981). Reinhold Maier: *Ein Grundstein wird gelegt 1945-7* (Tübingen 1964), 383. Leif Hovelsen: *Out of the Evil Night* (op.cit.). Gabriel Marcel: *Un changement d'espérance* (Paris 1958). Jacqueline Piguet: *For the Love of Tomorrow* (tr. J. Sciortino, London 1985). Rainer Barzel: *Karl Arnold* (Bonn 1960). R.J. Bullen, H. Pogge von Strandmann, B. Polonsky: *Ideas into Politics* (London 1984). Georgette Elgey: *La République des illusions* (Paris 1965), 304, 305, 144. A. Grosser: *La IVe République et sa politique étrangère* (Paris 1961). Journal Officiel (Débats/Assemblée Nationale), vol. XX, 4/12/47, 524 (Communist attacks on Schuman). Konrad Adenauer: article in *New York Journal-Américain*, 31/1/60. Hans-Peter Schwartz: *Adenauer - der Aufstieg 1876-1952* (Stuttgart 1986). G. Lean: *Frank Buchman* (op.cit.), 356 (Adenauer at Caux).

2. Jean Monnet: See previous section; also:- A.S. Milward: *The Reconstruction of Western Europe 1945-51* (London 1984). Pierre Bauchet: *Economic Planning, the French Experience* (London 1964). Jean Monnet: *Memoirs* (trans. Richard Mayne, London 1978), 286, 248, 392, 389, 85, 231, 222, 247. *Amiel's Journal* (ed. and trans. Mrs. Humphry Ward, London 1885) - *Journal Intime* of Henri-Frédéric Amiel. *Encounter*, June 1989, François Duchêne: "First Statesman of Independence" (for quotation "he thereby created networks", etc.).

3. Robert Schuman: See previous section, also:- Rudolf Mitterdorfer: *Robert Schuman - Architekt des neuen Europa* (Hildesheim 1983). Robert Rochefort: *Robert Schuman* (Paris 1968), 44, 55, 57. Raymond Poidevin: *Robert Schuman* (Paris 1986). Jean Monnet et Robert Schuman: *Correspondance 1947-1953* (Lausanne 1986). Gilbert Ziebura: *Die deutsch-französischer Beziehungen seit 1945, Mythen und Realitäten* (Stuttgart 1970). Christian Pennera: *Robert Schuman: La Jeunesse et les débuts d'un grand Européen de 1886 à 1924* (Sarreguemines 1985). René Lejeune: *Une âme pour l'Europe* (Paris 1986). Robert Schuman: *Pour l'Europe* (Paris 1963), 56, 70, 77. Frank Buchman: *Refaire le Monde* (Paris 1950 - French edition of *Remaking the World* (op.cit.)). *André Philip par lui-meme* (Paris 1971). *France-Forum*, Nov. 1963 (quotation from André Philip).

Chapter 14 - Prospects for the Renewal of Civilisation
1. Morals and marriage: Emmanuel Le Roy Ladurie: *Montaillou, Cathars and Catholics in a French Village 1294-1324* (tr. B.Bray, Harmondsworth, 1980). C.S. Lewis: *The Allegory of Love* (Oxford 1936). Wilhelm Wühr: *Das abendländischen Bildungswesen im Mittelalter* (Munich 1950) - also English translation. James Bowen: *A History of Western Education* (London 1972). Nicholas Orme: *English Schools in the Middle Ages* (London 1973). *Paston Letters and Papers*, ed. Norman Davis (Oxford 1971). T.M. Lindsay: *Luther and the German Reformation* (Edinburgh 1913), 200 seq. St. Francis de Sales: *Introduction to the Devout Life* (op.cit.), 188, 190-2; *Selected Letters* (op.cit.): 26 (Intro.), 103, 63, 95, 119, 135, 136. Philippe Ariès: *L'Enfant et la vie familiale sous l'ancien régime* (Paris 1960). W.

Notestein in *Studies in Social History*, ed. J.H. Plumb (London 1955). D.J.A. Matthew: *The Medieval European Community* (London 1977). W.J. Goode: *World Evolution and Family Patterns* (New York 1963). Lawrence Stone: *The Family, Sex and Marriage in England 1500-1800* (London 1977). P. Goubert and E. Shorter in T.K. Rabb and R.I. Rotberg: *The Family in History* (New York 1973), 48 seq. Flora Thompson: *Lark Rise to Candleford* (Oxford 1954). Joseph Williamson: *Father Joe* (Oxford 1963). *Sunday Times*, 29/3/70 (report on sex and marriage: "The chaste majority"). *The Times*, 6/12/83, 8/12/83. *The Guardian*, 18/3/84. Mary Whitehouse: *Whatever happened to Sex?* (Hove 1977). Christopher Booker: *The Neophiliacs* (London 1969). *Executive Intelligence Review* (Wiesbaden, August 1989): "New Age und Satanismus". *The Times*, 13/3/90. Arnold Lunn and Garth Lean: *The New Morality* (London 1964) and *The Cult of Softness* (London 1965). Sydney Cook and Garth Lean: *The Black and White Book* (London 1972). St. Augustine: *De Mendacio*, xix (*A Library of the Fathers*, op.cit.), 421.

2. **Modern decadence:** A.J. Balfour (later Lord Balfour) speaking at the British Association on "The Nineteenth Century" (Cambridge 1900): quoted:- "the cumulative products of research ..." E.R. Dodds: *The Ancient Concept of Progress* (Oxford 1973), 13, 20. Bernard Bosanquet: *Some Reflections on the Idea of Decadence* (op.cit.), 15, 16. J. Carcopino: *Daily Life in Ancient Rome* (tr. E.O. Lorimer, Yale 1977), 73. Lord Acton: *Lectures on Modern History* (London 1907), 12. B.H. Streeter: *The God who Speaks* (London 1936), 4. Burckhardt and Kierkegaard references, see Chapter 1, sections 2 and 3. Albert Schweitzer: *The Decay and Restoration of Civilization* (tr. C.T. Campion, London 1932), vii, 84, 38. Sidney Pollard: *The Idea of Progress* (Harmondsworth 1971). M. Levey: *A History of Western Art* (London 1968). P. Descargues: *Goya* (tr. R. Bloom, Milan and New York, 1976). Sigmund Freud: *The Interpretation of Dreams* (tr. and ed. James Strachey, London 1954, first published Leipzig and Vienna 1900); *The Psychopathology of Everyday Life* (tr. A. Tyson, Harmondsworth 1975).

3. **The Gorbachev revolution:** Avo Tuominen: *The Bells of the Kremlin* (Hanover, NH, USA 1983). Mark Frankland: *The Sixth Continent* (London 1987), 76 (Andropov), 80 ("an all-embracing system ..."), 174 ("questions of moral order ... of our society"). Mikhail Gorbachev: *Perestroika* (London 1987), 30, 31, ("today our main job .. We must look at ourselves ... alien to us"), 55 ("We must begin ... courage, initiative ... socialism"), 216 (right of every nation "independently to choose ..."), 39 ("people's loyalty to the free choice"), 193 ("the European states made their choice"), 199 ("sabotage the accords"), 163 ("freedom to reign supreme"), 211 ("draw lessons from the past"). Leroy-Beaulieu (op.cit.): II, 69, 104. Paul Newman: "The Soviet Union today - a business and financial perspective" (Oxford University seminar, St. Antony's College, 1990 - "the USSR was having to export ..."). Martin Walker: *The Waking Giant* (London 1986), 180 (women in hospital), 59 (Gorbachev, "we have to achieve a breakthrough"), 123 ("an independent and ... integral world" - G.). Almedingen (op.cit.), 111, 114, 50, 71, 115. C. Schmidt-Hauer: *Gorbachev, the Path to Power* (London 1986), 183 ("profound transformations" - Gorbachev), 152 ("totally new situation" - G.). Geoffrey Hosking (*Listener*, 24/11/88: "elements of a civil society"), (Listener, 15/12/88 - "sullen egalitarianism"). Richard Cornwell (*Independent*, 10/6/89: Rhyzhkov). L. Kolakowski in Michael Charlton: *The Eagle and Small Birds* (London 1984), 133. A.A. Adams (ed.) *Imperial Russia after 1861* (Boston 1965), 63 (Lenin on Stolypin's reforms).

Nicholas Zernov: *The Russian Religious Renaissance of the Twentieth Century* (London 1963). Donald Morrison (ed.): *Mikhail S. Gorbachev* (New York 1988), 194.

Chapter 15 - Conditions for Renewal

1. Resolving conflicts: reintegration with nature: Max Nordau (op.cit.), 37, 39. Laurens van der Post: *A Walk with a White Bushman* (Harmondsworth 1987), 33. *The New Yorker*, 11 September 1989: Bill McKibben: "The end of nature", 79. Genesis, 4:5. Walt Whitman: *Complete Poetry and Collected Prose* (ed. J. Kaplan, New York 1982), "Song of Myself", 208, 211. Frank Buchman, (op.cit.), 163. Boris Pasternak: *Doctor Zhivago* (tr. M. Hayward and M. Harari, London 1958), 237. Alexander King: *The State of the Planet* (Oxford 1980).

2. The democratic alternative to Marxism-Leninism: L.B. Namier: *1848: the Revolution of the Intellectuals* (London 1956). David Thomson: *Europe since Napoleon* (London 1963). *The Independent Magazine*, 30/12/1989: Hugh Trevor-Roper: "On Europe's New Order". Thomas Hill Green: *Lectures on the Principles of Political Obligation* (London 1882, reprinted with Preface by Bernard Bosanquet and Introduction By A.D. Lindsay, London 1941), 34. Bernard Bosanquet: *The Philosophical Theory of the State* (1899, 2nd edition, London 1910), 68, 127, 193-4. Leroy-Beaulieu (op.cit.): II, 69. Lenin: *State and Revolution* (op.cit.). Mark Frankland: *The Sixth Continent* (London 1987). *Encounter*, March 1990, K. Minogue: "Societies collapse, faith lingers on", 10. Robert Schuman: *Pour l'Europe* (Paris 1963), 56. Sir Michael Howard: Valedictory Lecture as Regius Professor of History at the University of Oxford, 19/5/1989. A. Schweitzer (op.cit.); 60, 64,67. A.J. Toynbee: *A Study of History* (Oxford 1934), IV, 5-6 (for "creative minority").

3. The strategy of world change: Charles Piguet and Michel Sentis: *Ce Monde que Dieu nous confie* (Paris 1979). *Robert Carmichael par lui-même* (Caux 1975), 63-5, 70, 78, 79, 98. Carmichael Papers. G. Jacobson and J. Hillkirk: *Xerox American Samurai* (New York 1986), 115, 113, 201. Basil Entwistle: *Japan's Decisive Decade* (London 1985), 19, 78, 81, 108, 177-8. J.M. Roberts: *The Triumph of the West* (London 1985). N. Berdyaev: *The Origin of Russian Communism* (London 1937), 206. R. Lane Fox (op.cit.), 22. Frank Buchman (op.cit.), 351 (Streeter); 72 ("disciplined direction"). Proverbs 29:18. Micah 4:3. André Chouraqui: *Ce que je crois* (Paris 1979), 160, 146; 256, 308; *Lettre à un ami arabe* (Paris 1969), 66-7; *Lettre à un ami chrétien* (Paris 1971), 199; *Retour aux racines* (Paris 1981), 255; *Cantique pour Nathanaël* (Paris 1960), 280; *L'Amour fort comme la mort* (Paris 1990 - autobiography). Renée de Tryon-Montalembert: *André Chouraqui* (Paris 1979). Pierre Teilhard de Chardin: *The Phenomenon of Man* (London 1967), 236. Claude Lévi-Strauss: *The View from Afar* (Oxford 1985), 23. L. van der Post (op.cit.), 82, 140, 144. Henri Bergson: *The Two Sources of Morality and Religion* (Eng. tr. London 1935), 77. Boris Pasternak: *Doctor Zhivago* (op.cit.), 453. *For a Change*, April 1990, John Lester: "In my View". Alexander Solzhenitsyn: *Cancer Ward* (Harmondsworth 1971), 459-460. A. Gratry: *Les Sources* (op.cit.), ibid. John 14:30, Luke 17:21. Theophil Spoerri: *Dynamik aus der Stille* (Luzern 1971; Eng.tr. London 1976). Marshall Berman: *All that is Solid melts into Air* (New York 1982). Marilyn Ferguson: *The Aquarian Conspiracy* (London 1981).

INDEX

Münster, 169, 296
Galileo, Galilei, 116
Galla, daughter of Symmachus, 97
Galla Placidia, Empress, mausoleum at
Ravenna, 58; life, 281
Gasperi, Alcide De - *see* De Gasperi
Gatling gun, 6
GATT (General Agreement on Tariffs
and Trade) 199, 235
Gaul, 39, 48, industries, 50; 77;
Cassian's monasteries, 92; Ammianus
Marcellinus, 277
Gaulle, Charles de - *see* de Gaulle
Geneva, Calvin; St. Francis de Sales,
112; Rousseau, 117; Russian
revolutionaries, 134; World Council
of Churches meeting 1946, 196; Lake,
197; Vietnam settlement, 266; League
of Nations: C.W. Hambro, 307
Genseric, 85
Gerlach, Leopold von, 289
Gerlach, Ludwig von, Bismarck, 140-1,
289; 173
German-Christianity, German-
Christians, 169, 172, 186
German Workers National Socialist
Party (NSDAP), 165
German Democratic Republic, 186, 249
Germany, Germans, Teutonic, invaders
of Roman Empire, 4; inventions, 5;
Burckhardt's prediction, 12, 198; cf.
France, Macedon, Sparta, 15, 16, 265;
occupy Rome (410 AD), 46; war-
bands, 47, 51; Sidonius Apollinaris,
79; 84; Crusaders, 103; 104; Münster,
107; Pietism, 110, 141; German-
speaking colonists in America, 110;
"Benevolent Despotism", cf. Russia,
126; "German Quarter", Moscow, 127-
8, German-type civil service, Russia,
128; philosophy in Russia, 131;
opposition to disarmament and
arbitration, 140; Bismarck, 140-1;
Hitler, demonism, 154-5; nationalism;
Social Democratic Party (SPD), 156,
293; delegates at International
Socialist conference 1914; Navy
League, Wehrverein, 157; Haldane
Mission 1912; national anthem;
nationalism in schools, 158;
nationalism as religion, myth,
psychic disease; Empire proclaimed
1871, 160ff; Nazism, 162ff; Jews:
civilised element among Teutonic

peoples, 161; threatened by Russians
and Slavs; overrun by French, 162;
"German Order"; German Workers'
National Socialist Party, 165; "a Jew-
free Aryan Utopia", 167; Nazi
empire; Evangelical Church, 169; the
Confessing Church; "German-
Christians", 172ff; Church struggle,
cf. Norway, 177; ignorance of death-
camps, etc, 178; von Moltke's plans
for post-war, 178-9; German
Democratic Republic (GDR): Church
policy, 186; Sangnier's call for
economic agreement: anticipates
European Community, 191; French
zone of occupation: enlightened
officials, 192-3, 298; post World War
II boycotts, 193; Niemöller:
Declaration of Guilt, 194; Caux;
British Zone; Franco-German
reconciliation, 196-8, 236, 298;
Russian zone of occupation, 196;
Federal Republic - constitution, 197;
East - in Soviet Empire; West - plans
for union and reconstruction, 198;
economic aims of France and Britain,
199; Germany's economic future; the
Saar, 200; submarine offensive, 1917,
202; re-arming West Germany after
World War II; Lorraine, 204;
reintegration in Europe: Schuman,
206ff; industrial developments, 235;
Satanism, 214; conferences at The
Hague 1899 and 1907, 231; 1848
revolutions; GDR and Federal
Republic, 249; integration in
"Community", 252; US policy post-
war, 255ff; Moravians, 279, 285;
Bismarck, 289; mass bombing, 291;
hopes for religious awakening, 295;
Milward: *The Reconstruction of Europe*,
298; postwar idealism, 299; convents:
unmarried daughters, 301
Germersheim, 192
Georgia, religious persecution, church
closures, 183; nationalism, 249
Gestapo, 175, 178; von Moltke visits
HQ, 178; Fredrik Ramm, 196;
Schuman, 200, 205; report on Moral
Re-Armament (Oxford Group), 297
Gibbon, Edward, 3
Gibson, John, 217
Gipsies, 161, 169
Gladstone, William Ewart, Concert of

344

Malevich, Casimir, 136
Malta, 15; Quaker women missionaries, 284
Manchu Empire, China, 153
Manet, Edouard, 6
Mani, Manicheism, Manichees, Augustine, 64, 75; Diocletian's persecutions, 280
Maori, 158
Maquis (French Resistance movement), Chouraqui, 306
Marathon, 15, 71
Marcella, 82, 83
Marcellina, 83
Marcianopolis, Battle, 47, 279
Marcomanni, 50
Marcus Aurelius Antoninus, Roman Emperor, 21; Marcomanni, 50
Marguerite de Valois, Queen, 285
Marie-Antoinette, Queen, 272
marriage and family, women and men at Athens, 2; Athens: position of wives; polygamy in Macedonia, Sparta, 27ff; Theocritus, Homer, 27; relationships improve: hetairai, 30ff, 269-70; Menander, Theocritus, 30-1; dining together, 32, 33; Rome, 32ff; Musonius Rufus; discipline; relations with slave-girls; Plutarch, 34-5; Pliny and Calpurnia, 35-6; Ausonius and Sabina; Christianity strengthens, 36; Juvenal, 38-40; Christian ambiguities, 61ff: St. Paul, 62; St. Augustine, 62ff, 211, 281-2; hermits and monks: celibacy and virginity, 61ff; Palladius, St. Basil, 69; St. Jerome, 81ff; St. Gregory and his *familia*; care of families, 97; Wilberforce and friends, 114; anti-family ideas among Nazis (Rosenberg), 168; Bonhoeffer's views, 173; von Moltke on married partnership, 180; changing attitudes, 211ff; Montaillou, cf. early Greece or Rome, 209; girls' and boys' education in Middle Ages, 210; Martin and Katherine Luther, 211; St. Francis de Sales and Jeanne de Chantal, 212-3; Industrial Revolution; 19th century; permissiveness; William Blake, 213; spiritual/moral basis, 215; Soviet Union, 221; USA, 268; Rome, 272-3, 275-6; Augustus: laws, 273; Romans with Jews, Greeks, Egyptians prohibited, 277; Montaillou, 209, 301;

L. Stone: *The Family, Sex and Marriage*, 300, 302; Law of King Gondebaud; query about extended family, 301; L. Stone: "ideal of conjugal affection" replaces "medieval Catholic ideal of chastity"; the romantic novel; mistresses; France; Jefferson, 302; Paris, cf. ancient Rome, 303
Marseilles, 18, 197
Marshall, George C., Plan (aid for Europe), 199-200, 267; European Recovery Program, 204; increase of prosperity, 266; United States of Europe? 299
Martin, St., of Tours, 77
Marx, Karl - *see also* Marxism, xxiii, 3, 6, 119ff; *Capital*, The Communist Manifesto, 120-1, 240; Russian revolutionaries, 134-5; expectation of religion withering, 137; errors: embryonic social orders, 240; dependence of economy on culture, 251; Chernyshevsky, 287-8; the Internationals, 291
Marxism, Marxism-Leninism - *see also* Communism, xxii, 50, 53; analysis, 119ff; replacing Orthodox Christianity, 137-8; Tsarist Russia, 129, 134; Lenin's revolution, 136ff; Lenin's re-expression of Marxism, 137; atheist "orthodoxy" in Russia, 138; Sangnier's response, 151; main competitor with Christianity; German, French and British socialism, 156; German Social-Democratic Party (SPD), 161; loses meaning, 181; Central Europe: religion, 184ff; Andropov: believer in the ideology: its power, 223-4; class struggle as basis of morality, 229; discrediting; waning of regimes, exc. China, 234; class co-operation, not conflict as embryo of new social orders, 240; Gorbachev's attempt to make system work, 250; false antithesis Communism/capitalism; restricting spontaneity, 251; religious element: "History"; a Christian heresy, 287; overturning the moral order, 292; Raisa Gorbachev, 303
Maurice, East Roman Emperor, 96; Gregory I, 99; 284
Mary, sister of Pachomius, 69